The Best of History Web Sites

Thomas Daccord

D1307624

Neal-Schuman Publishers, Inc.

New York

London

Published by Neal-Schuman Publishers, Inc.
100 William St., Suite 2004
New York, NY 10038

Printed and bound in the United States of America.

The paper used in this publication meets the minimum requirements of American National Standard for Information Sciences - Permanence of Paper for Printed Library Materials, ANSI Z39.48-1992.

Library of Congress Cataloging-in-Publication Data

Daccord, Thomas.
   The best of history web sites / Thomas Daccord.
        p. cm.
   ISBN 978-1-55570-611-1 (alk. paper)
   1. World history—Computer network resources—Directories. 2. History—Study and teaching—Computer network resources—Directories. 3. Scholarly Web sites—Directories. I. Title.
   D16.255.C65D33 2007
   025.06'9—dc23

                                                              2007024102

Contents

List of Figures

Foreword

The Internet has the potential to dramatically alter the way we teach and learn history. Instead of listening passively to lectures or reading the pre-digested conclusions found in secondary sources, new technologies allow students to actually do history.

Until very recently, technology has been used in rather mundane ways in history teaching; not surprisingly, its impact has been limited. E-mail has certainly enhanced student-faculty communication. Databases like JSTOR have made scholarly articles readily available. Meanwhile, products like Turnitin.com monitor plagiarism.

But now we are reaching a point where new technologies can genuinely transform student learning. *The Best of History Web Sites* shows how this transformation can happen. Using new technologies is as easy as ABC. A stands for active learning. The Internet allows teachers to devise assignments that emphasize hands-on exploration and inquiry. By exploring authentic historical questions and tapping primary sources, students can acquire the skills characteristic of history as a discipline: Locating and evaluating sources, constructing and substantiating historical arguments, and presenting conclusions in a clear and compelling manner.

B stands for the Internet's boundless resources. Right now, the World Wide Web is a bit like a vast used bookstore, with a vast array of resources of wildly divergent quality. Gradually, scholars, libraries and archives, historical societies, and commercial vendors are placing high-quality primary and secondary sources online. Already, as this book demonstrates, students and teachers have access to kinds of materials—from census registers to election returns, maps, recorded speeches, and a wealth of letters and diaries—that were previously accessible only to scholars.

C stands for collaboration. In the past, historical research was largely a solitary pursuit. Today, exciting new models for collaborative research are opening up. Especially exciting is the opportunity for students to create online encyclopedias, virtual tours, and historical documentaries and digital stories.

There is little doubt that the World Wide Web's wealth of resources will transform the way we research and read. Keyword searches are certain to become more common. At the same time, the sheer quantity of online materials encourages readers to skim, scan, and sample rather than to read in detail. What this means is that it is essential for students to acquire new skills and competencies. Students must develop a sophisticated facility in conducting online searches and evaluating Web sites. Students also need to learn how to use new tools to gather, annotate, organize, cross-reference, and cite online materials, such as Zotero and MediaMatrix.

Given the immense quantity and highly variable quality of resources on the World Wide Web, it is extraordinarily helpful to have an expert guide to shepherd us as we traverse the digital frontier. It is advantageous to have practical advice of someone who has thought deeply about such topics as locating and evaluating Web sites and integrating them into classes. In this regard, Thomas Daccord is the ideal guide. With his wealth of knowledge about history, the Internet, and teaching, I can think of no better escort as one taps the riches available online.

An experienced international history teacher who has taught in Canada, France, and Switzerland, as well as in the United States, and who has been featured in the *Boston Globe* for his contributions to teaching with technology, Thomas Daccord has given many presentations on educational technology topics across the nation. *The Best of History Web Sites* offers a highly accessible introduction to engaging educational content and stimulating multimedia technologies. Its wide-ranging and unique classification system can help readers find historical topics of interest easily and quickly. The recommended Web sites can help enhance instruction by providing creative and flexible ways for teachers to teach and students to learn.

But the volume also does more. Teacher-oriented resources, such as Lesson Plans and Activities, are all conveniently classified by type and grade level. The book's introductory chapters and listings of recommended sites help K–12 history and social studies teachers incorporate technology effectively into their courses. Even more importantly, it includes many of Tom Daccord's classroom-tested strategies for creating engaging and effective Internet-infused lessons.

There is no better entryway into the exciting new world of history teaching in the twenty-first century than the book you are holding in your hands.

Steven Mintz, the John and Rebecca Moores Professor of History at the University of Houston, is past president of H-Net: Humanities and Social Sciences Online, and the incoming chair of the Organization of American Historians' Teaching Committee.

Preface

The Web provides access to a remarkable range of valuable historical and cultural information from around the world, all at the click of a mouse. It also offers educators tremendous opportunities to involve students in stimulating and interactive research and activities. For librarians, the Web is an invaluable resource for getting researchers started on specific subjects, helping students complete assignments, and answering history-related reference questions. But as the volume of online historical resources continues to grow, so does the challenge of sifting through and evaluating these materials. *The Best of History Web Sites* is designed to help librarians, educators, and students identify credible and appropriate Web sites for use in teaching and research.

The Best of History Web Sites book is based on the award-winning Web portal, "Best of History Web Sites," at www.besthistorysites.net. The site, seven years old at this writing, receives more than 125,000 visitors per month and has been named as a "Best of Reference" Web site by the New York Public Library, "Site of the Week" by *School Library Journal*, and an "Education Best Bet" by *USA Today*. This book adaptation of "Best of History Web Sites," through its organization and multiple indexes, enables users to easily find a specific site by title, to find titles on narrow topics, or to find all sites that apply to a particular grade level or type of resource (such as tests or quizzes). The indexes also make it easy to browse widely in topics that are covered in more than one chapter (for example, to find sites covering World War II from both European and American perspectives). Favorite sites can be easily marked or highlighted for ongoing reference. And, of course, the portability of a book means that Web-based lessons can be planned even when you're not in front of your computer.

The Best of History Web Sites offers a number of innovations that are not found on the Web site. First, because in workshops and presentations over the last few years, teachers have consistently said that they would like to see suggestions of appropriate grade levels added to annotated lesson plans and activities, these have been added to the book. Second, new sites have been added in almost every category, and most of the annotations have been enhanced over what is on the Web. And finally, *The Best of History Web Sites* contains technology tips and advice on integrating the sites into the curriculum, which are not available on the Web site.

The following chapters contain recommendations of over 1,000 sites on more than 50 broad history topics. Each site has been carefully reviewed for quality, accuracy, and usefulness. The annotations denote those sites that feature especially engaging educational content or use innovative multimedia. There is a particular focus on pages created by outstanding educational and news organizations, such as the Library of Congress, the Smithsonian Institution, the Public Broadcasting Service, the British Broadcasting Corporation, and the Center for History and New Media.

The Best of History Web Sites reflects an international perspective, because I have taught and worked in not only the United States but also in Canada, France, and Switzerland. As a historian and an educator, I have been astonished by the range of materials produced around the world. The Internet has created a revolution in the breadth of information that is available to the average person. Every chapter includes sites offering international viewpoints on a wide range of topics.

Throughout the book, the reader will find links to hundreds of sites that feature quality K–12 history lesson plans, teacher guides, activities, course models, teaching units, games, tests, and quizzes. At the end of most topics, a subsection headed "Lesson Plans, Activities, Teaching Guides, and More" lists the bulk of teacher-oriented resources, all classified by type and grade level.

Organization

The Best of History Web Sites is divided into 12 chapters organized around broad historical concepts. Each chapter is further divided into subtopics to help readers find topics of interest easily and locate appropriate resources quickly. For instance, Chapter 7, "Prehistory and Ancient World History," includes sections on prehistory, general ancient history resources, ancient Mesopotamia, ancient Egypt, ancient Greece, Rome, China, India, Africa, and Mesoamerica.

Two introductory chapters provide advice and information for the reader. Chapter 1, "Locating and Evaluating History Web Sites," outlines proactive and active search strategies. Chapter 2, "Integrating History Web Sites in the Classroom," lists practical ideas for technology integration and seven ways to use *The Best of History Web Sites* in the classroom.

Chapters 3 through 6 offer American history resources covering the age of European discovery through 9/11. Chapter 3 presents an overview of the rich world of American history resources through sites from a wide range of reputable sources. Chapters 4, 5, and 6 discuss specific American history topics in chronological order.

Chapter 7, "Prehistory and Ancient World History," reviews sites on ancient civilizations in places as different as Mesoamerica, Africa, and China. Chapter 8, "The Origins of World Religions," covers the early histories of Judaism, Christianity, Islam, Hinduism, and Buddhism.

Chapter 9, "Medieval and Early Modern Europe," lists sites on medieval history, the Renaissance, the Reformation, the Scientific Revolution, the Enlightenment, the French Revolution, and early modern Britain. Chapter 10, "Twentieth Century," picks up where chapter 9 leaves off, focusing on the last hundred years of European and Asian history.

Two chapters on special topics conclude the book. Chapter 11, "History through a Different Lens," explores art history and oral history resources. Chapter 12, "Focus on History Topics," includes information on maps and geography, research, the best general history sites, and general history lesson plans and activities.

Sample Annotation

****Library of Congress
www.loc.gov/index.html

The Library of Congress is an outstanding site for American history and general studies. The Library of Congress Learning Page provides a "teacher's eye view" of over seven million historical documents, photographs, maps, films, and audio recordings. Lesson plans can be searched by theme, topic, discipline, or era. The American Memory collection, a must-see, contains the bulk of digitalized materials: historic maps, images, documents, audio, and video. The Thomas collection (named for Thomas Jefferson) contains both current and historical national legislative information, while Exhibitions offers dozens of presentations drawn from Library of Congress collections.

Resource Type: General Reference; Primary Source Collection

All listings (except those under "Lesson Plans" headings) are given a rating of 5 stars (excellent), 4 stars (very good), or 3 stars (good).

Each site is given one or more of the following *"Resource Type"* designations so that readers can easily identify the type of resource they are looking for.

- *Art History*
- *Course Model* (a resource that includes a wide range of instructional materials)
- *Game*
- *General Reference*
- *Image Collection* (a site that includes a significant number of images)
- *Lesson or Activity*
- *Links Collection*
- *Map*
- *Multimedia Presentation*
- *Primary Source Collection*
- *Test or Quiz*
- *Virtual Tour* (a site that uses images to lead visitors on a "guided tour" of a subject)

Resources under the "Lesson Plan" heading are categorized by grade level: LS, MS, HS, and College. "LS" is short for Lower School and refers to grades K–4. "MS" is short for Middle School, grades 5–8, and HS is short for High School, grades 9–12. "College" represents undergraduate college or university courses.

Readers may notice that some entries appear more than once. Some excellent Web sites cover a wide range of topics and so merit mention in several sections.

It is easy to get bogged down in the mechanics of Internet research and forget to remember why you are doing research in the first place. The materials that historians once had to spend long hours in archives to find are now at our fingertips. These are the stories and sources that helped many of us fall in love with history in the first place, and it has never been easier for students to access these same pieces of history. The Web sites highlighted in the following pages let students not just learn history, but be historians. I hope that *The Best of History Web Sites* will prove to be an invaluable resource for librarians, history educators, and their students.

Acknowledgments

I would like to recognize a few individuals who helped me put this publication together. I would like to thank Justin Reich, my colleague at Noble & Greenough School, and a terrific history teacher, who contributed greatly to the "Integrating History Web Sites in the Classroom" chapter and helped format and edit several sections of the book. (I am thrilled that Justin has joined me as coeditor of the online "Best of History Web Sites" and "The Center for Teaching History With Technology," at www.thwt.org.) I would also like to thank Henry Foote, a wonderful student and advisee, who did yeoman's work formatting hundreds of pages for this publication. I also owe thanks to numerous colleagues and students at Noble & Greenough who have helped recommend and review online content for "Best of History Web Sites" over the years. Last, but not least, I would like to thank my incredible wife Debbie for her advice, encouragement, and support throughout the duration of this project.

CHAPTER 1

Locating and Evaluating History Web Sites

The roots of this book are in my Web site, "Best of History Web Sites," which was originally created in the summer of 2000. It began as a three-week project to assemble a collection of Web sites useful in teaching three high school courses: World History to 1500, United States History, and Twentieth Century History. The Noble & Greenough School, where I teach, had just purchased fifteen wireless Apple iBook computers, and I was approached about the possibility of using laptop computers in my World History classroom. I readily agreed and was eager to find useful Web resources to incorporate into my "experimental" laptop-based class.

At the time, I relied heavily on "active" Google searches and a few Internet history directories to create the foundation of my site. Since then, I have incorporated "proactive" search strategies and have expanded the base of my Internet history directories considerably.

Here are some techniques and resources for locating and evaluating the best history Web sites.

ACTIVE AND PROACTIVE SEARCH STRATEGIES

"Active" Google Searches

Google's basic search box is rarely useful when searching for history Web sites. In many cases it leads to a considerable waste of time, making you wade through site after site trying to find the information you really want.

For any serious Internet search you need to use Google's Advanced Search. It helps refine a search by defining key parameters and also helps eliminate unwanted "hits." And it doesn't take much time. To get to Advanced Search, click on the Advanced Search link to the right of the text box at www.google.com.

Before you proceed, outline a simple **search strategy**. I mention this because too often students come to me and say they can't find anything on the Web, or they can't find anything "good." Often it is because they do not have an effective search strategy. For instance, a student was researching the importance of art in church history entered "church art" in a basic Google search and was directed to sites offering Christian T-shirts and clip-art images. If the student had undertaken a **presearch** by reading an encyclopedic entry or textbook chapter on the topic she would have come up with more specific keyword terms in proper historical context. Then she could have come up with related terms such as "early Christian

Figure 1.1: Google Advanced Search

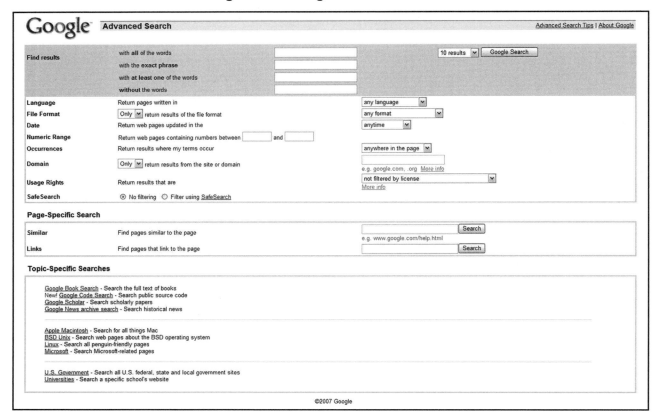

Source: www.google.com/advanced_search?hl=en

art" or "medieval cathedral art," and she would have had much better initial success. It is important to constantly brainstorm related, broader, and narrower search terms to improve search results.

If searching for sites on, say, Jackie Robinson, start by typing "Jackie Robinson" in the "with the exact phrase" box. Next, determine the keywords you want to search in connection with Jackie Robinson and list these in order of priority (since Google prioritizes keywords as per the order of their placement). If you are looking for teaching resources on Jackie Robinson, then you can likely include "lesson activity exercise teaching unit assignment project discussion" in the "with at least one of the words" text box (commas not necessary). In other words, you are telling Google to search for these specific types of resources in connection with Jackie Robinson. You can also often refine a search by going to the "Domain" line and telling Google to search only .edu and .org Web sites. Taking advantage of the features of Google's Advanced Search can save significant time in searching for the best material online.

"Proactive" Google Searches

In "proactive" Google searches, resources are delivered to you as a result of your registering specific keywords. In other words, you direct Google to send you news and information on keywords that you enter in advance. Instead of going out looking for information, the information comes to you.

Google News
www.google.com/news

Google News gathers news stories from 4,500 sources and organizes them into eight categories: Top Stories, World, U.S. Business, Sci/Tech, Sports, Entertainment, and Health. But what sets Google News apart from other online news sources is that you can customize Google News and create your own categories. To do so, select the "Customize this page" option (upper right of Google News page) and then click on "Add a Custom Section." You can edit/delete categories and physically change their placement on the screen. So, for instance, you can create categories entitled Vietnam War, French Revolution, etc.—whatever you like.

Google Alerts
www.google.com/alerts

You can also have Google e-mail you news and Web updates, called **News Alerts**. With News Alerts, Google will search the Web and its news sources for new information on the keywords you choose. News Alerts will notify you—daily or less frequently—when information matching your keywords is found. With Google News and News Alerts the trick is to select your keywords carefully so that they are neither too broad nor two narrow in scope. Other good news options include Yahoo Daily News, topix.net, and daypop.com (for blogs).

Newsletters

There are various organizations that provide or evaluate academic content on the Internet. Many of these offer free newsletters that are emailed directly to you. Many are subject specific (history, math, art, etc.).

Here are a few you may find useful:

PBS Teacher Source
www.pbs.org/teachersource/

Library of Congress Learning Page
lcweb2.loc.gov/ammem/ndlpedu/

SCORE—Schools of California Online Resources for Educators
www.score.k12.ca.us/

New York Daily Lesson Plans & Archive
www.nytimes.com/learning/teachers/lessons/index.html

Blue Web'n Weekly Updates
www.kn.pacbell.com/wired/bluewebn/updates.cfm

CNN Student News
www.cnn.com/EDUCATION/

Education World
www.education-world.com/index.shtml

C-Span in the Classroom
www.c-spanclassroom.org/

Listervs

Listservs enable a large group of people to communicate with one another without requiring each person to maintain a mailing list of all the other participants. Any member of the list may take part in a conversation or begin a new topic. Hence, listservs are great for getting information, ideas, and opinions on a topic of common interest. Often listservs archive their postings in a searchable online database, send indexed digests to participants instead of individual messages, and make sets of files publicly accessible by e-mail. You can subscribe to as many listservs as you like. Note that some listservs get plenty of traffic and hence you may get many e-mails daily. Others get little traffic. You can unsubscribe to any listserv at any time.

A comprehensive and up-to-date list of all mailing lists does not exist, so you should search in several places:

> **Teaching and Educational Related LISTSERV Listings**
> www.mste.uiuc.edu/listservs/listserv.html
>
> **Education listservs**
> www.greece.k12.ny.us/taylor/suny/listservs.htm
>
> **H-Net: Humanities and Social Sciences Online** (Discussion Networks).
> www.h-net.org/lists/

H-Net is extremely useful; it offers over a hundred e-mail lists to choose from.

RSS Feeds

Recently, many have come to use RSS, commonly known as Really Simple Syndication. Through RSS, information can come to you without you actively searching for it. This is accomplished through an **RSS feed**, a source of information that is regularly updated and to which you subscribe. You select the type of information you would like to receive and the updated information is sent to you by what's called an **RSS aggregator**. There are Web-based aggregators and downloadable aggregator software, which enables users to subscribe to select RSS feeds.

Here is a simple and easy way to select and receive RSS feeds: Bloglines (at www. bloglines.com) is a personal Web aggregator that enables you to make your own personalized news page tailored to your interests. It draws from millions of live Internet content feeds, including articles, blogs, images, and audio. It's free and you don't need aggregate software to use it. After you join Bloglines, you search for the content you are interested in and identify the feeds you want to track. Bloglines will constantly check those feeds for changes or additions and send new information to your Bloglines personal page.

Two excellent feeds are from the History News Network Blogs and from the BBC. Add these feeds to Bloglines or your favorite aggregator to keep up to date:

> **History News Network Blogs**
> hnn.us/blogs/2.html
>
> **BBC News**
> newsrss.bbc.co.uk/rss/newsonline_world_edition/front_page/rss.xml#

INTERNET HISTORY DIRECTORIES

Although keyword searching is the most popular Internet search strategy, it may actually be more effective for you to search with a **subject directory** rather than with a search engine. Search engines don't evaluate the sites they retrieve, and since they may retrieve hundreds, thousands, or even millions of sites in a search, you might have a lot of work to do sifting through them! They can also retrieve some pretty irrelevant information—way off your topic—if you do not carefully strategize your keywords and search parameters.

Subject directories are built by humans, not by computers, and are organized into subject categories. Some are academic or professional directories (for example, Academic Info at www.academicinfo.net/hist.html) and others are commercial directories (for example, Yahoo! Directories at http://dir.yahoo.com/). Web sites recommended by a search directory are often carefully evaluated and annotated, and this is a big advantage over search engines. Fortunately there is a wide assortment of educational, commercial, nonprofit, governmental, and individual directories to help you find quality Web sites quickly.

"Best of History Web Sites" portal has a page called **General Resources** that contains many search directories related to history and social studies, and this page can be a great place to start your search. The **Research** page on the site is another good place to find search directories.

Using Best of History Web Sites

"Best of History Web Sites" at www.besthistorysites.net/ is an award-winning portal created for history teachers, students, and general history enthusiasts. Throughout its pages, it contains annotated links to over 1,000 history Web sites and links to hundreds of quality history lesson plans, teacher guides, activities, games, quizzes, and more. "Best of History Web Sites" is ranked #1 by Google for "history Web sites" and receives upwards of 125,000 visitors per month.

In the left navigation column of the homepage are 12 major categories, and three special sections. The broadest and most popular category is **American History**. Click on this link and you will notice in the left column that the American History sites are clustered around six topics and 19 periods. Click on any of the topics or periods, for instance "Civil War," to discover an annotated list of relevant Web sites rated on the basis of historical content, multimedia interactivity, and educational effectiveness. Sites are ranked from one to five stars; the most highly rated sites are closest to the top of the page. The Civil War page alone has 22 annotated sites and 60 different links.

> TIP: You can quickly perform a keyword search of any page by using the **Find** function on your PC or Mac. If yu are on a PC, press the control button and F key simultaneously. If you are on a Mac, press the Command button and F key simultaneously. A dialogue box will appear in which you can type the keyword or words you are searching for on the page. If that word appears on the page, it will be highlighted each time it appears on the page. If you want to search all of Best of History Web Sites, go back to the homepage and use the search engine. Just make sure that the radio button for Best of History Web Sites is selected.

Scroll down to the bottom of the Civil War page, or any other "Best of History Web Sites" page, and you will come across **Lesson Plans, Teacher Guides, Activities and more**. Under this subcategory you will find sites offering lesson plans, classroom activities, course projects,

Figure 1.2: Best of History Web Sites Homepage

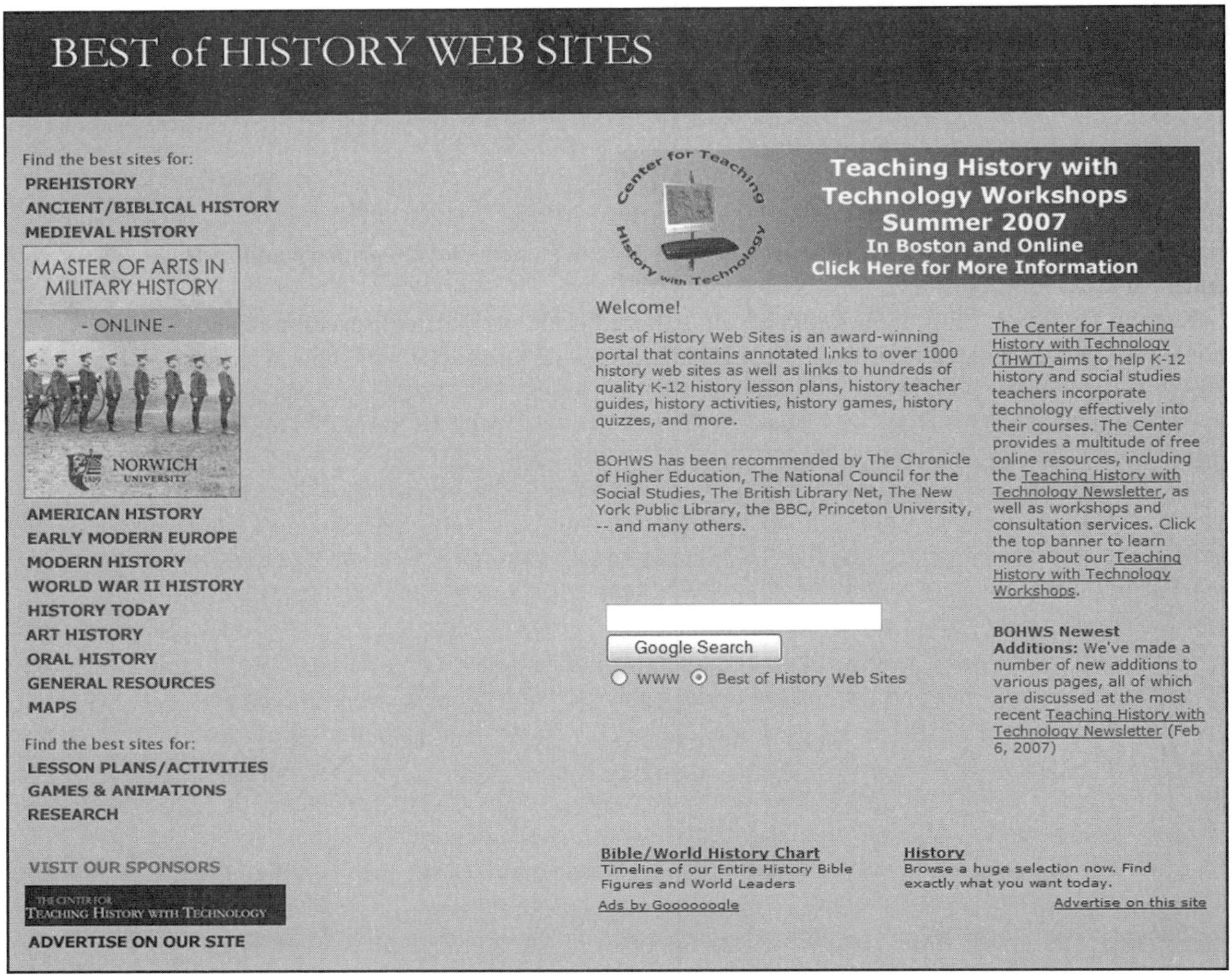

online quizzes, PowerPoint presentations, and more. Most of these sites offer educational lessons and activities appropriate for grades 5 through 12.

While the American History section is the site's broadest category, there is plenty for the student of world history to discover. If you browse the **Ancient/Biblical History** section, you will find sites clustered around famous ancient civilizations such as Mesopotamia, Egypt, Greece, Rome, and China. There is also coverage of Ancient religions such as Hinduism, Buddhism, Judaism, Christianity, and Islam. You will also find excellent Web sites for learning about Medieval times, especially Medieval Europe, in the **Medieval History** category.

The **Early Modern Europe** page is one of the site's most popular categories and contains terrific resources on the Reformation and Discovery, Scientific Revolution, Enlightenment, French Revolution, and Modern Britain.

Those interested in twentieth-century history should go the **Modern History** section. There are excellent sites on World War I, Russian Revolution, Hitler, Stalin, China and Tibet, Cold War, Middle East History, Lebanon, Terrorism and 9/11, and the Post-Cold War Era.

World War II History is its own category in "Best of History Web Sites" and is the most visited page on the site. In this popular section you will find general World War II Web sites and much information on special topics, such as famous battles and the Holocaust.

A special category popular with teachers is **Lesson Plans/Activities**. While almost every page has a section on lesson plans particular to the page's topic, this section provides an annotated list of excellent Web sites that provide quality lesson plans and classroom activities for history and social studies subjects. These comprise a foundation of Web sites that were frequented to create annotated lists for individual "Best of History Web Site" pages. "Best of History Web Sites" also offers a **Research** section to help students locate primary and secondary sources for projects.

Keep in mind that "Best of History Web Sites" portal is always updated; several new sections were being unveiled at time of publication. **Games & Animations** includes a list of great history games and animations organized around broad historical periods. **History Today** features varied perspectives on current historical topics of interest from liberal, conservative, and international perspectives. Finally, the **Oral History** category features general resources on Oral History as well as select projects and lesson plan resources.

The "Best of History Web Sites" site is constantly being updated and expanded; the newest material is described on the homepage. You can visit it regularly to learn more about its offerings.

HELPING YOU (AND YOUR STUDENTS) EVALUATE WEB SITES

Two great sources for evaluating Web sites come from Kathy Schrock, who is the Administrator for Technology for the Nauset Public Schools in Massachusetts, but is better known as the creator of "Kathy Schrock's Guide for Educators" Web site. She is a highly acclaimed educational technology guru and her articles, Web sites, and books have helped countless teachers, students, and educators. Here are two Web sites where you can find her work:

Evaluating Web Sites: Criteria for the Classroom
www.lesley.edu/library/guides/research/evaluating_web.html

Kathy Schrock's Guide for Educators: Critical Evaluation Surveys
http://school.discovery.com/schrockguide/eval.html

CHAPTER 2

Integrating History Web Sites in the Classroom

by Tom Daccord and Justin Reich

- *What am I doing now that I'd like to do better?*
- *What pedagogical problems would I like to solve?*
- *What do I wish my students did more often or differently?*

Before you explore specific ways to integrate *The Best of History Web Sites* resources in an educational setting, you should first think carefully about your curriculum objectives. Don't use history Web sites just for the sake of incorporating technology. Technology should serve to enhance your instruction and provide creative and flexible ways for teachers to teach and students to learn. The more clearly you are able to answer the questions above, the more effective your educational technology integration will be.

Our hope is that your primary objective is to enhance learning and understanding—and not necessarily to enhance standardized test scores. Indeed, that's what hundreds of history teachers across the United States told the Department of Education in a survey: "[Teachers] say they want their students more engaged with learning; they want students to construct new and better relationships to knowledge, not just represent it on tests; and they want students to acquire deeper, more lasting understanding of essential concepts." (Department of Education, 1999)

If you would like your students more engaged with learning, and better able to construct new and creative relationships to knowledge, then technology in general—and the Web sites in this book in particular—can be of great service to you. The National Council for the Social Studies identified several advantages of using technology in the classroom:

- Technology is a powerful way to introduce authentic primary-source research and problem-solving activities in a student-centered environment. *The Best of History Web Sites* is full of primary source activities and projects.
- Technology can bring traditional classrooms otherwise inaccessible resources—information, people, media, and events. *The Best of History Web Sites* provides access to

documents and multimedia resources that would be difficult or time-consuming to find somewhere else.

- Technology provides teachers with resources and flexibility to develop and tailor instructional materials to better meet individual student needs. *The Best of History Web Sites* is full of challenging and creative activities that address multiple intelligences. (National Council for the Social Studies, 2005)

"DIGITAL NATIVES" AND THE "LIVING WEB"

Another reason to incorporate technology in the classroom is that it plays such a pervasive role in the lives of the children we teach. Today's elementary grades and middle schools are filled with "Digital Natives," kids who have grown up entirely in the age of the Internet. Digital Natives, as well as many children now in high school, expect a high degree of online interactivity and are helping change the nature of Internet usage. Not content to be merely passive recipients of Internet information, children and young adults are looking to publish, edit, and shape Web content. The growth of online social communities over the last few years is but one example of how "screenagers" and others are using the "Living Web" to publish and share information and to establish and sustain relationships with others. The anticipated dramatic growth of the Digital Native population in the years to come, coupled with the ubiquitous nature of the Web, is changing the way our students retrieve, process, and use information. As a result, schools may be forced to rethink their pedagogical strategies, since students may increasingly reject passive modes of instruction (lectures, PowerPoint presentations, etc.) and advocate for challenging, inquiry-based activities that put independent student learning in the forefront.

CATEGORIES OF TECHNOLOGY INTEGRATION STRATEGIES

Now that we have considered in broad terms how technology can positively impact your teaching and student learning, let's consider possible technology integration frameworks and strategies for your classroom. Following is a list of a few general frameworks and strategies for effective teaching with technology, as well as ways *The Best of History Web Sites* can help you achieve them. As you read them, consider how each might fit your curriculum objectives:

- **Authentic Skills and Resources**
  "Authentic" learning means that students should be using real-life skills, such as critical analysis, reflection, discussion, debate, and presentation. From an historian's perspective, authentic history involves discovering, analyzing, and presenting primary sources. Primary sources are the building blocks of historical analysis and writing, and they should be central in history activities. *The Best of History Web Sites* is an excellent vehicle for finding primary sources and activities that involve primary sources. It can also be used to help students learn how to find primary sources on their own.
- **Inquiry-Based Critical Thinking**
  One of the most exciting and effective uses of technology is inquiry or problem-based learning. In inquiry-based learning, students are presented with a task that typically

involves strategic decisions and careful analysis of source material. Technology can aid in the construction of problem-based projects and activities, and *The Best of History Web Sites* contains many excellent examples available on the Internet.

- **Interactive Learning**

  The Internet provides several tools to enhance interactive learning. For instance, animated maps guide students through historic military campaigns. Historical games and simulations provide opportunities for cooperative-learning skills. "Best of History Web Sites" and its sister site, "The Center for Teaching History with Technology," can lead you to excellent sites that incorporate interactive learning activities.

- **Public Presentation and Accountability**

  Studies demonstrate that when students are asked to present their work in a public forum they are more motivated to perform at a higher level. The Internet provides plenty of resources and tools to help students create public projects, and "Best of History Web Sites" includes numerous examples of classroom project and student-directed presentation technology tools, such as a Web site, blog, or PowerPoint presentation. Learn how to provide tremendous opportunities for creative, engaging, and effective presentations of student work.

Mind you, there is no single "right way" to integrate technology in history education. Indeed, technology integration means different things to different teachers. For some it may simply mean finding a lesson plan on the Web. For others it may mean creating a virtual tour or building a Web site. Some teachers are keenly interested in new and emerging technologies, while others are not. There are innumerable ways of integrating technology into the curriculum.

Our hope is that you will use technology to create inquiry-oriented activities that help deepen understanding of subject matter and promote critical thinking and technology skills. In order to help you create a well-structured and engaging inquiry-based activity, the following section provides some technology integration models and templates to assist you.

TEMPLATES FOR TECHNOLOGY INTEGRATION

The WebQuest Page
http://webquest.sdsu.edu/

WebQuests are inquiry-oriented educational activities produced by various educators. Web Quests all follow the same format: Introduction, Task, Process, Resources, Evaluation, Conclusion, and Teacher Directions. These tend to be extended activities that can take a few classes or a few weeks to complete.

Teachers provide links to various Web sites that their students have to consult and use in order to complete the task at hand. WebQuests are popular because the format is clear and easy to understand.

To search for examples of WebQuests, click on "Portal" on the homepage or go to www.webquests.org.

We also suggest you visit **Best WebQuests** at http://bestwebquests.com.

The WebQuests were selected by Tom March, a former colleague of Bernie Dodge with whom he was one of the earliest WebQuest developers.

> TIP: WebQuests are probably the best known and most popular format for educational technology integration of Internet materials. Some WebQuests are very impressive—others less so.
>
> Whenever you visit a WebQuest, make sure to check that the links are active. If a link or two is broken you can probably still use the activity. If most or all of the links are broken it may be difficult to complete the task.

To learn more about WebQuests, go to the WebQuest page (http://webquest.sdsu.edu/) and click on Training Materials. You can even follow a WebQuest about WebQuests to really know and understand the process:

- **Weaving the Web into Your K-12 Curriculum:**
  www.pitt.edu/~edindex/WebQuests/frames.htm
  A WebQuest designed for use with pre-service and in-service teachers:

When you are finally ready to create your own WebQuest, it is time to visit the Quest Garden, at http://webquest.org/questgarden/author/. This tool will help you design a Web Quest even if you don't know how to create a Web site or work with HTML, the language of the World Wide Web.

ThinkQuest
www.thinkquest.org/

A ThinkQuest is an Internet project by students who work in teams to create the best educational Web sites and compete for prizes. We suggest you select the "Library" and review the ThinkQuests in the History and Government section. We make it a point to show at least one ThinkQuest to students so that they see what great projects kids their age are creating.

The History Lab
http://hlab.tielab.org

The History Lab is both an inquiry-based pedagogy and a learning tool designed to make learning about history more an act of interpretation and less of memorization. John Raymond, the creator of History Lab, is a former high school history and philosophy teacher and is now an education-technology expert in Connecticut. Rooted in constructivist thinking, it is a tool that enables teachers to build student inquiry activities and lessons around resources they find on the Internet. Teachers use the free and ready-made template to insert instructions for students, provide external links to primary and secondary sources, and attach documents as needed. Projects are stored in the database and are available online.

TrackStar
http://trackstar.4teachers.org/trackstar/index.jsp

TrackStar is a starting point for online lessons and activities for multiple disciplines. Simply collect Web sites, enter them into TrackStar, add annotations for your students, and you have an interactive online lesson called a "Track." Create your own Track or use one of the thousands already made by other educators. For a quick and easy activity, search the database by subject, grade, or theme and standard. The instructions are clear and well illustrated, and by all accounts the system is stable, well designed, and easy to use. You can search or create Tracks by subject, grade level, standards, etc., and the template is flexible.

ESSAYS ON TECHNOLOGY INTEGRATION IN HISTORY AND SOCIAL STUDIES

Most of the following essays were written by history and social studies teachers, and they describe their technology integration activities and experiences.

Technology in the History Classroom: Lessons Learned After Four Years of Technology-Aided Instruction and Research
www.thwt.org/laptoparticle.htm

I wrote this article for The Center for Teaching History with Technology about his early experiences as a "laptop teacher." Explains early technology integration successes and setbacks, and what he learned from them.

Rewiring the History and Social Studies Classroom: Needs, Frameworks, Dangers, and Proposals
www.air.org/forum/abBass.htm

Randy Bass and Roy Rosenzweig. "White Paper for Department of Education, Forum on Technology in K–12 Education: Envisioning a New Future, December 1999." Read this thoughtful overview of technology use in K–12 history and social studies with brief examples from classrooms around the country.

TechLearning at www.techlearning.com publishes several online newsletters with great advice for teachers about integrating technology in the classroom. Here are some of my favorite articles on history and social studies.

Making History Matter
www.techlearning.com/db_area/archives/WCE/archives/shantate.htm

Shannon Tate and her colleagues integrated community service and historical preservation for both English and social studies classes and created a Virtual Museum of Unionville History.

A Digital Journey Through the Past
www.techlearning.com/db_area/archives/WCE/archives/huschak2.htm

Altoona, Pennsylvania high school students researched and wrote about local sites of interest, matched old photos with text, and posted the results on the Internet so elementary students could read about their city's rich past. Irene Huschak, author.

Investigating The Civil War: A Multimedia Approach
www.techlearning.com/db_area/archives/WCE/archives/civwarmh.html

Michael Hutchison, an award-winning technology integration specialist, shows how a teacher can make use of the electronic revolution and bring both his teaching and his students' learning into the modern age.

Collaborative Internet Learning: Strategies and Success Stories
www.techlearning.com/db_area/archives/WCE/archives/tate.htm

Joanne Tate describes an assortment of cross-cultural, technology based, globally collaborative "ventures," including discussions with students in Japan about both the Holocaust and Hiroshima, as well as a National Identity Project in which students in rural Australia and in Moscow exchanged thoughts on their respective cultures.

SELECT TECHNOLOGY INTEGRATION ACTIVITIES AND PROJECTS FROM OUR CLASSROOMS

Here are a few examples of projects that we have done in class to incorporate technology. Details on most of the activities listed below are available via the "The Center for Teaching History with Technology" at http://thwt.org/tomslessons.html.

Life of a Hobo: Interdisciplinary Project
This creative writing/historical simulation activity calls on students to research the plight of homeless teenagers during the Great Depression and then create their own fictionalized account of a day in the life of a hobo. Students post their story on their blog and read each other's work. Students comment by stating what they liked about the story they read—and what made it seem authentic. The blogs provide a public form to present and share student work. Students are also interviewed in character and their audio becomes part of a "1930s Radio Show" podcast.

Interdisciplinary Project: American History/American Literature
Students create a multimedia magazine that covers aspects of culture, politics, arts, music, and lifestyles from the 1920s. Working in small groups, students analyze a magazine to develop an understanding of how a magazine's contents provide clues to the socioeconomic class, education level, gender, age group, and political views of its audience.

Student choose a magazine format to imitate, and after analyzing the current magazine's format, style, publishers, and readers, students create one of their one that mimics a chosen format. In the course of the project, students post their editorials on their blogs, and other students read and critique them.

Governor of Alabama Press Release
Students are the press secretary for the Governor of Alabama and must write a press release to be sent to each newspaper, radio station, and television station in Alabama to explain what happened in Birmingham during the 1963 civil rights campaign there. Students consider a variety of primary source documents found on the Web and then advise the Governor on how to respond.

Sarajevo Times Project
Students studying the Bosnian civil war work in teams to produce a newspaper published on March 1, 1993, in the midst of the conflict and as the failed Vance-Owen peace plan was being debated at the United Nations. Student use the Internet to research newspaper articles and personal accounts of the war in Bosnia, and then create a special section of a newspaper

focusing on the history of the conflict, the terms of the Vance-Owen peace plan and the prospects for peace.

Origins of Man WebQuest

In this Web-based activity, students play the role of an esteemed paleoanthropologist who is to give the keynote address at the annual conference of the American Paleoanthropologists Association: "Are We Any Closer To Discovering Our True Ancestor?" Students use both articles and images of important hominid skeletal discoveries to make their case. In their written speech to the association and invited guests, students must state clearly whether they feel that the discoveries of the last few years have furthered or negated progress toward the discovery of a "missing link" between apes and humans.

Special Report: The Fate of Jerusalem

Students adopt the role of a foreign policy advisor to the U.S. Secretary of State, Condoleeza Rice. They are instructed to prepare a three- to five-page report that explains why both Israelis and Palestinians lay claim to Jerusalem. At the end of the brief, they must make a recommendation for a resolution of the competing claims.

Beacon Hill Photo Scavenger Hunt

Students in a class on the history of Boston spent several days studying the Federalist and Neoclassical styles of architecture that were popular in nineteenth-century Boston. On a field trip to Boston's famous Beacon Hill neighborhood, students had to photograph particular architectural design elements from those two important schools of design.

HHC (History of the Human Community/World History)
Visual Evidence Project

The HHC project is designed for several purposes: (1) To provide students with a culminating opportunity to research, select, interpret, and present historical and visual evidence in areas related to their coursework. (2) To teach skills of information literacy, iMovie, and presentation. (3) To provide a group learning experience that asks students to collaborate on research projects and then to be responsible for each other's work. (4) To provide a body of evidence that helps students review for the final exam.

Each HHC section will be divided into four or five groups of three or four students. Each group will be assigned to one of the following subject areas: (1) Mesopotamia and Egypt (2) Greece (3) Rome (4) Renaissance/ Reformation Europe.

Vietnam Editorial Project

Students assume the role of an important individual who is living in the United States during the Vietnam War. They use a combination of Internet resources to research the biographical elements that would inform their leader's perspective on the war. They then write an editorial from that leader's point of view.

Origins of the Cold War

In this example, blogging is the culminating activity of a one-night assignment that mixes traditional textbook reading with Web page reading. The specific purpose of this assignment is to have students provide a clear opinion on Churchill's Iron Curtain speech. These statements then can be used in class the next day as a foundation for a broader discussion on the origins of the Cold War.

USING *THE BEST OF HISTORY WEB SITES* EVERY DAY IN CLASS

While technology projects are among the most exciting ways to integrate technology into your classroom, there are many other simple ways as well. Here are seven easy ways to use *The Best of History Web Sites* in your classroom:

1. **Start class with a primary source**.
   The site's annotations can point you to many Web sites that provide primary source documents giving students a fascinating glimpse into the past. Start class with a little piece of history, and give students a chance to explain the source.

2. **Project an image**.
   Visual evidence is another great way to draw students into history. Find Web sites with images of art and architecture, and then use a projector to show a few of those images to class. Ask students to find specific details in the images that connect to the larger themes of the unit.

3. **Create a Web site treasure hunt**.
   If you find a great Web site and want students to read several different pages from the site, make it a treasure hunt by giving them 10 to 15 questions that they need to answer in groups. Make it a race to have a little competition excite the classroom.

4. **Play a song or speech recording**.
   For topics in modern history, many sites will have not only images and text, but audio as well. Reading a Dr. Martin Luther King, Jr. speech is one experience, but hearing it draws students into history in a much deeper way. Some streaming video of important speeches or events can be found through the site as well.

5. **Have a mini-research class**.
   Short-term research projects are feasible and fun if you require students to find sites only through *The Best of History Web Sites*. Since we have prescreened the sites, you can be confident that students will not spend the class period wandering through the junk on the Internet and will be able to focus on history gems.

6. **Play a game or take a quiz**.
   The site has a whole page dedicated to games and animations, and many of the annotated sites include games as well. Games about history can provide a great break from the usual rhythm of the classroom, and well-designed simulations help students understand the challenges and choices faced by historical actors. Many online sites have quizzes where students can test their knowledge of a given subject.

7. **Go on a virtual field trip**.
   Many museum and archeological Web sites that can be found on *The Best of History Web Sites* allow you to go on virtual tours of important artwork and historically significant places. It might be too expensive to fly to Egypt to visit the pyramids, but that doesn't mean you can't explore them from your own room.

TECHNOLOGY INTEGRATION AND MULTIPLE INTELLIGENCES

Whether you believe that there are seven, eight (or 21!) different fundamental learning styles, integrating technology can help you vary your teaching to address different learning needs. While no one activity can target all learning styles, the templates and examples described in this chapter can help you reach out to a variety of types of learners. For instance, a project involving the creation of a mock ancient Greek newspaper might involve logical skills such as the analysis of historical data, verbal skills such as the critique of a draft editorial, and visual skills such as the layout and design of a newspaper page. Students who struggle with tests or essays might have skills that let them shine with this type of project. As you sift through the pages ahead, I hope you will be inspired to use these resources to enliven and diversify your teaching.

REFERENCES

National Council for the Social Studies. 2005. "Powering Social Studies with Technology," *Social Education*, Vol. 69, no. 3: 136–171.

"Rewiring the History and Social Studies Classroom: Needs, Frameworks, Dangers, and Proposals" White Paper for Department of Education, Forum on Technology in K–12 Education: Envisioning a New Future (December 1, 1999). Available: www.air.org/forum/abBass.htm

CHAPTER 3

General American History Resources

****Library of Congress
www.loc.gov/index.html

The Library of Congress is an outstanding site for American history and general studies. The Library of Congress Learning Page provides a "teacher's eye view" of over 7 million historical documents, photographs, maps, films, and audio recordings. Lesson plans can be searched by theme, topic, discipline, or era. The American Memory collection, a must-see, contains the bulk of digitalized materials: historic maps, images, documents, audio, and video. The Thomas collection (named for Thomas Jefferson) contains both current and historical national legislative information, while Exhibitions offers dozens of presentations drawn from Library of Congress collections.
Resource Type: General Reference; Primary Source Collection

Focus on Library of Congress

Take stock of the impressive breadth and diversity of primary documents. The Library of Congress is simply a great resource for any research project in American history and culture. Note that while many Library of Congress exhibitions are primarily text-based, some include audio and video clips that could played in class or assigned for homework. The "Churchill and the Republic" addition is a great example of just such a multimedia exhibition.

I would encourage American history teachers to start with **American Memory**. The bulk of the Library of Congress collections are to be found here. You can browse by topic or search by keyword. All of these exhibitions include guides as to how to understand and work with the collections. Even so, it is easy to get lost in the exhibitions because they are so darn big! I typically scour around to see if there is a "Special Presentation" within the collection. These are often great teaching tools that highlight the most significant documents in the collection.

If you teach civics and/or constitutional history you should definitely explore Thomas. You'll find a multitude of documents on current and past national legislation, a guide entitled "How Congress Makes Laws," official Web sites of the three branches of federal government, congressional records and committees, a guide to law online, and much more. In the **Exhibitions** section you will find dozens of large online exhibitions. Some topics are hardly surprising ("The Gettysburg Address"), while others are refreshingly quirky ("Blondie Gets Married!"). The Exhibitions generally provide historical overviews and the teaching resources are typically chock-full of primary sources.

(cont'd.)

****Digital History
www.digitalhistory.uh.edu

This impressive site from Steven Mintz at the University of Houston includes an up-to-date U.S. history textbook; annotated primary sources; and succinct essays on the history of ethnicity and immigration, film, private life, and science and technology. Visual histories of Lincoln's America and America's Reconstruction contain text by Eric Foner and Olivia Mahoney. The Doing History feature lets users reconstruct the past through the voices of children, gravestones, advertising, and other primary sources. Reference resources include classroom handouts, chronologies, encyclopedia articles, glossaries, and an audiovisual archive including speeches, book talks, and e-lectures by historians, and historical maps, music, newspaper articles, and images. The site's Ask the HyperHistorian feature allows users to pose questions to professional historians.
Resource Type: General Reference; Course Model

****PBS Online
www.pbs.org/

PBS is a great source for information on a myriad of historical events and personalities. PBS's assorted and diverse Web exhibits supplement specific individual television series and generally include a résumé of each episode, interviews (often with audio excerpts), a timeline , a glossary, photos, and links to relevant sites. Go to the PBS Teacher Source for lessons and activities—arranged by topic and grade level—and sign up for their newsletter. Categories include American History, World History, History on Television, and Biographies. Some lesson plans require viewing PBS video, but many do not. Categories in American History include American Experience and People's Century.
Resource Type: General Reference; Lesson or Activity

****National Archives and Records Administration
www.nara.gov/

The NARA offers federal archives, exhibits, classroom resources, census records, Hot Topics, and more. The NARA is another great resource for American history research, especially government records and constitutional history. The Constitution of the United States of America, the Declaration of Independence, and the Bill of Rights are all preserved by NARA and available here online as well as many other original documents. Most of the scanned images of these documents are high resolution, and you can zoom in and examine them in great detail. Visit the Exhibit Center and Digital Classroom sections for some excellent exhibitions and lesson plans that incorporate NARA holdings. In the Digital Classroom, visit Teaching With Documents to find reproducible copies of primary documents, standards-based teaching, and cross-curricular ideas. The Resources section houses the Documents Analysis Worksheets, which help students analyze primary sources. The Our Documents feature contains 100 milestone documents of American history.

Resource Type: General Reference; Primary Source Collection

Focus on National Archives and Records Administration

The NARA is another great resource for American history research, especially as it relates to government records and constitutional history. The **Constitution of the United States of America**, the **Declaration of Independence**, and the **Bill of Rights** are all preserved by NARA and available here online as well as many other original documents. Most of the scanned images of these documents are high resolution and you can zoom in and examine them in great detail. (Hence, a great opportunity for "authentic" research.) I would suggest you go to the **Exhibit Center** and the **Digital Classroom** sections for some excellent exhibitions and lesson plans that incorporate NARA holdings. In the Digital Classroom click on **Teaching With Documents** (upper left) to download reproducible copies of primary documents, standards-based teaching, and cross-curricular ideas. There are eight topical collections to explore. Also, look at the **Resources** (on the left), especially the **Documents Analysis Worksheets**. (Many teachers across the country use these worksheets to help kids analyze primary sources.) Afterward, go to **Our Documents** for special features on 100 milestone documents of American history. Impressive stuff everywhere!

****The Gilder Lehrman Institute of American History

www.gilderlehrman.org/

The Gilder Lehrman Institute of American History promotes the study and love of American history and targets students, scholars, and the general public. Its Web site provides a portal to American history sites and offers quality educational materials. The Institute provides online exhibitions and an online magazine, modules on major topics in American history, recommended scholarly resources, and more.

Resource Type: General Reference; Course Model

****The Avalon Project*

www.yale.edu/lawweb/avalon/chrono.htm

"The Avalon Project" is a great research site from Yale University, rich with primary source documents relating to American and world history. The searchable database is organized into centuries. For American history, visit "A Documentary Record 1492–Present." There is an extensive list of documents pertaining to Law, History, Economics, Politics, Diplomacy, and Government.

Resource Type: Primary Source Collection

****American Rhetoric

www.americanrhetoric.com

This is a massive multimedia site that contains an Online Speech Bank, Rhetorical Figures in Sound, and American Top 100 Speeches. The Online Speech Bank contains 291 active links to 5,000+ full text, audio, and video (streaming) versions of public speeches, sermons, legal

proceedings, lectures, debates, interviews, other recorded media events, and a declaration or two. Figures in Sound has 200+ short audio clips from well-known speeches, movies, sermons, popular songs, and sensational media events by famous (and infamous) politicians, actors, preachers, athletes, singers, and other noteworthy personalities. You'll also find significant American political speeches of the twentieth century and even Hollywood speeches. Links are arranged alphabetically by first name and checked for errors.
Resource Type: Primary Source Collection; Multimedia

****Smithsonian National Museum of American History
http://americanhistory.si.edu/

The Smithsonian Museum houses more than three million objects and you can view many of them online. Visit the online Treasures of American History Exhibition and see historical objects from various periods in American history. Or try the History Explorer, an interactive timeline of museum exhibits, collections, and programs. Our Story In History is aimed at a young audience and includes the online You Be the Historian activity, where students examine clues about life in the past. Tools for Educators includes online activities organized by grade level. History Wired provides a glimpse into the documents held at the Smithsonian and Hunt for History is a self-guided tour for grades 6–9.
Resource Type: Virtual Tour; Primary Source Collection

****The Price of Freedom: Americans at War
http://americanhistory.si.edu/militaryhistory/

This Smithsonian Web site skillfully integrates Flash video and text to examine armed conflicts involving the United States, from the Revolutionary War to the war in Iraq. Each conflict contains a brief video clip, statistical information, and a set of artifacts. There is also a Civil War mystery, an exhibition self-guide, and a teacher's guide. The World War I section contains a short essay on the conflict as well as historic images and artifacts.
Resource Type: Multimedia Presentation

****Images of American Political History
http://teachpol.tcnj.edu/amer_pol_hist/

"Images of American Political History" is a collection of over 500 public domain images of American Political History that can be browsed, searched, and downloaded. The intent of this collection "is to support the teaching of American political history by providing quick access to uncopyrighted images for inclusion in teaching materials." Links to images contain brief captions and are listed in chronological order. No attempt is made to provide the historical context or interpretation of the relevance of these images, since it is assumed that the user is already familiar with their importance to U.S. political history.
Resource Type: Image Collection

****Famous American Trials
http://www.law.umkc.edu/faculty/projects/ftrials/salem/salem.htm

A professor of law at the University of Missouri-Kansas City Law School has created a Web site on famous trials that include: the Salem Witchcraft Trials (1692), Amistad Trials (1839–40), Andrew Johnson Impeachment Trial (1868), Susan B. Anthony Trial (1873), Sacco-Vanzetti

Trial (1921), Scopes Monkey Trial (1925), Scottsboro Trials (1931–37), Nuremberg Trials (1945–49), Rosenberg Trial (1951), Mississippi Burning Trial (1967), Chicago Seven Conspiracy Trial (1969–70) and the My Lai-Court Martial (1970). Most of these include background information on the case, biographies and photographs of trial participants, trial transcript excerpts and articles from newspapers that covered the trial.
Resource Type: General Reference; Primary Source Collection

****History News Network
www.hnn.us/

"The History News Network" (HNN) was created in June 2001 and features articles, blogs, and podcasts by historians on both the left and the right who provide historical perspective on current events. HNN provides historians and other experts a national forum in which to educate Americans about important and timely issues; it is the only Web site on the Internet wholly devoted to this task. HNN is a nonprofit publication run by George Mason University.
Resource Type: General Reference

****History Channel
www.history.com/

A companion to the popular television channel, this commercial site contains a myriad of features and highlights for educators and students alike. You can watch history video, listen to podcasts, browse articles, and visit four special features. Key educational offerings include: study guides and activities, ideas from teachers, special exhibits, speech archives, discussions, and This Day in History.
Resource Type: Multimedia Presentation; Lesson or Activity

****Great Debates in American History
www.peterpappas.com/journals/greatdebates.htm'

Part of the award-winning "Teaching With Documents" site, "Great Debates in American History"—a supplement to *A History of the United States* by Daniel Boorstin—consists of 12 debates, one for every unit of the text. Units feature the conflicting viewpoints of two or more historical figures or organizations and a worksheet that helps students analyze the debate through a series of comprehension and critical thinking questions.
Resource Type: General Reference

**** History/Social Studies Web Site for K–12 Teachers
http://k-12historysocialstudies.com//amer.html

A retired high school history teacher has produced a well-organized and super-stocked resource of links to history and education-related sites. The categories are so full of links it can feel overwhelming at times. Check out Research and Critical Thinking for teaching ideas.
Resource Type: Links Collection

****The American Presidency: A Glorious Burden
http://americanhistory.si.edu/presidency/

This Smithsonian site explores the history and operation of the American presidency. The exhibit displays more than 375 images of documents, paintings, photographs, buttons, posters,

paraphernalia, and objects along with short texts explaining their significance.
Resource Type: Multimedia Presentation

****Women and Social Movements in the United States, 1775–2000
http://womhist.binghamton.edu/about.htm

This Web site is a project of the Center for the Historical Study of Women and Gender at the State University of New York at Binghamton and includes roughly 900 documents, 400 images, and 350 links to other Web sites. There are twenty comprehensive lesson plans with over a hundred lesson ideas mounted in the Teacher's Corner.
Resource Type: General Reference; Course Model

****America's Library
www.americaslibrary.gov/

"America's Library" is presented by the Library of Congress and is aimed at young people. It is filled with interesting information about American people and historical events.
Resource Type: General Reference; Lesson or Activity

****United States Historical Census Data Browser
http://fisher.lib.virginia.edu/census

The Census Bureau provides data from census records and other government sources for 1790–1970. Users can view extensive population- and economics-oriented statistical information at state and county levels, arranged according to a variety of categories. Also includes an essay on the history of the census.
Resource Type: General Reference; statistical data

Lesson Plans, Teacher Guides, Activities, and More

History Matters
http://historymatters.gmu.edu

"History Matters" is a wonderful online resource for history teachers and students. Among the many digital resources are lesson plans, syllabi, links, and exhibits. Resources include a list of "best" web sites, links to syllabi and lesson plans, essays on history and new media, a link to the Center for History and New Media, and more. Resources are designed to benefit professional historians, high school teachers, and students of history. "History Matters" is a production of the American Social History Project/Center of Media and Learning at the City of University New York, and the Center for History and New Media at George Mason University.
Resource Type: Course Model
Grade Level: HS, College

Digital History: Resource Guides
www.digitalhistory.uh.edu/resource_guides/default.cfm

"Digital History" features resource guides by topic and period. Reference resources include classroom handouts, chronologies, encyclopedia articles, glossaries, and an audiovisual archive including speeches, book talks and e-lectures by historians, and historical maps,

music, newspaper articles, and images. The site's Ask the HyperHistorian feature allows users to pose questions to professional historians.
Resource Type: Course Model
Grade Level: HS, College

Focus on Digital History

"Digital History" was designed and developed to support the teaching of American history in K–12 schools and colleges and is supported by the Department of History and the College of Education at the University of Houston. The site was created by a team led by Steven Mintz, the John and Rebecca Moores Professor of History and Director of American Cultures Program at the University of Houston. It is a must-see for teachers and professors of American History courses.

The materials on this Web site include a U.S. history textbook; over 400 annotated documents from the Gilder Lehrman Collection on deposit at the Pierpont Morgan Library, supplemented by primary sources on slavery, Mexican American and Native American history, and U.S. political, social, and legal history; succinct essays on the history of film, ethnicity, private life, and technology; multimedia exhibitions; and reference resources that include a searchable database of 1,500 annotated links, classroom handouts, chronologies, glossaries, an audio archive including speeches and book talks by historians, and a visual archive with hundreds of historical maps and images. The site's **Ask the HyperHistorian** feature allows users to pose questions to professional historians.

"Digital History" has introduced a host of new resources that allow students to "do history." These include:

- **Annotated documents in Asian American history.**
  Asian American Voices includes a timeline of Asian American history, biographies of key individuals, and a guide to Asian American history resources on the Web.

- **Historical music.**
  Collection of pre-1923 copyright-free music plus links to other historical music that is available on the Web.

- **eXplorations.** These are inquiry-based, interactive modules designed to give students the opportunity to do history: to conduct research, analyze primary sources, and draw their own conclusions. There are units on such subjects as: Zheng He, Timbuctu, Cahokia, Columbus and the Columbian exchange, fugitive slave and indentured servant advertisements, Pocahontas, Squanto, music and the American Revolution, the Alamo, Indian removal, children and the westward movement, children and the Civil War, the late nineteenth-century West, turn of the century, photography as history, lynching, Worlds Fairs and history, and children of the Great Depression, and many other topics.

- **User-Created Online American History Exhibitions.**
  Students and teachers can create multimedia presentations featuring historical images from an extensive database. These presentations can be e-mailed, downloaded, or saved on servers.

- **Trailers of Historically Significant Films.**
  This database contains trailers of films for educational use.

PBS Teacher Source
www.pbs.org/teachersource/

PBS's assorted and diverse American history Web sites supplement specific individual television series and generally include a resume of each episode, interviews (often with sound bites), a timeline, a glossary, photos, and links to relevant sites. Go to the PBS Teacher Source for lessons and activities, arranged by topic.
Resource Type: Lesson or Activity
Grade Level: LS, MS, HS

Library of Congress Learning Page
http://lcweb2.loc.gov/ammem/ndlpedu/

"Library of Congress Learning Page" provides activities, tools, ideas, and features for educators and students. Sections include: Thanksgiving, Presidents, Immigrants, Women, Elections, and Inaugurations.
Resource Type: Lesson or Activity; Primary Source Collection
Grade Level: LS, MS, HS

The Gilder Lehrman Institute of American History:
Modules on Major Topics in American History
www.gilderlehrman.org/

The Gilder Lehrman Institute offers quality educational materials, including teaching modules on major topics in American history. Each module includes: A succinct historical overview; learning tools including lesson plans, quizzes, and activities; recommended documents, films, and historic images. These modules were prepared by Steven Mintz, the John and Rebecca Moores Professor of History and the Director of the American Cultures Program at the University of Houston. Other helpful Institute online sources include include American History Quizzes, Letters from America's Wars Featured Documents for your Classroom, and Primary Source Documents from the Collection.
Resource Type: Course Model
Grade Level: HS

EDSITEment: Humanities
http://edsitement.neh.gov/

EDSITEment is a partnership among the National Endowment for the Humanities, the Council of the Great City Schools, MarcoPolo Foundation, and the National Trust for the Humanities. All Web sites linked to EDSITEment have been reviewed for content, design, and educational impact in the classroom. This impressive site features reviewed links to top sites, professionally developed lesson plans, classroom activities, materials to help with daily classroom planning, and search engines. You can search lesson plans by subcategory and grade level; middle school lessons are the most numerous.
Resource Type: Course Model
Grade Level: MS, HS

TeachingAmericanHistory.org
http://teachingamericanhistory.org/

"TeachingAmericanHistory.org" is a project of the Ashbrook Center for Public Affairs at Ashland University. At their Web site are special exhibits on the Constitution and other topics as well as dozens of audio lectures on key themes and events in American history. Browse their online Library to find documents in the following categories: Founding Era; Progressive Era; Expansion Era; Post World War II Era; Civil War Era; General Resources. Also, the Teaching American History podcast provides subscribers with a weekly seminar from a leading historian.
Resource Type: General Reference; Course Model
Grade Level: HS, College

Schools of California Online Resources for Educators (SCORE): History
http://score.rims.k12.ca.us/

The Schools of California Online Resources for Educators (SCORE) project is a terrific resource for teachers and students alike. Here you'll find reviews of education and history-related Web sites, lesson plans, maps, and much more, all arranged by grade level and content area. There are over 5,000 Web sites aligned to California's History/Social Science Curriculum and ten special features.
Resource Type: Lesson or Activity
Grade Level: LS, MS, HS

Discoveryschool.com Lesson Plan Library: U.S. History
http://school.discovery.com/lessonplans/ushis.html

"Discoveryschool.com Lesson Plan Library" offers history and government lesson plans for Ancient History, U.S History, and World History. Lesson plans are organized as per Grades K–5, Grades 6–8, Grades 9–12 and provide: Objectives, Materials, Procedures, Adaptations, Discussion Questions, Evaluation, Extensions, Suggested Readings, Links, Vocabulary, Academic Standards, and Credit.
Resource Type: Lesson or Activity
Grade Level: LS, MS, HS

Awesome Stories
www.awesomestories.com/history/index2.htm

"AwesomeStories.com" is a free, noncommercial educational Web site for educators and students. Stories link to organized primary and secondary source materials found principally at U.S. and other worldwide national archives, museums, libraries, universities, news organizations and government Web sites. The purpose of the site is to take visitors on a virtual guided tour of relevant online source materials. Be sure to check out "Click2History."
Resource Type: Primary Source Collection; Lesson or Activity
Grade Level: LS, MS, HS

C-Span Classroom
www.c-spanclassroom.org/

Access C-SPAN's complete program archives. "C-SPAN Classroom" is a free membership service that offers information and resources to assist educators in their use of primary source, public affairs video from C-SPAN television. You do not have to be a member to use C-SPAN online resources in your classroom, but membership includes access to teaching ideas, activities and classroom tools.
Resource Type: Multimedia Presentation; Lesson or Activity
Grade Level: LS, MS, HS

The WebQuest Page
http://webquest.sdsu.edu/webquest.html

A WebQuest is a form of project-based and problem-based learning in which the resources are located on the Web. These inquiry-oriented educational sites are produced by educators for use by students and are modeled on a template developed by Professor Bernie Dodge. Some

WebQuests are very impressive—others are less so. I would suggest consulting the Portal, which contains an updated matrix of preselected WebQuests, and then looking for WebQuests in the "top" category. WebQuest links should be checked to make sure they are active.
Resource Type: Lesson or Activity
Grade Level: LS, MS, HS

Education World: History Center
www.education-world.com/history/

"Education World" provides practical resources for history educators. You'll find lesson plans, articles about what other teachers are doing, professional development resources and more. Education World offers timelines, activities, work sheets, games, homework help, clip art, images, and articles.
Resource Type: Course Model
Grade Level: LS, MS, HS

HistoryTeacher.net
www.historyteacher.net/

An impressive, award-winning site from a high school teacher in upstate New York. Features many research links and curriculum resources for U.S. Advanced Placement History and for American History and Government. Also has many DBQs, PowerPoints, quizzes, news links, and more.
Resource Type: Course Model
Grade Level: HS

Mr. Donn's Pages: Free Lesson Plans, Activities, and Resources
http://members.aol.com/donnandlee/SiteIndex.html

Teacher Don Donn of the Corkran (Maryland) Middle School provides complete units on various historical topics with daily lesson plans and resources. Units include U.S. History & U.S. Government and most lessons are aimed at students in grades 5–9. The numerous lesson plans and resources available at this popular site have been developed by Mr. Donn and his wife, Lin, and other contributors.
Resource Type: Course Model
Grade Level: LS, MS, HS

The Educator's Reference Desk: U.S. History Lesson Plans
www.eduref.org/cgi-bin/lessons.cgi/Social_Studies/US_History

Formerly AskEric, "The Educator's Reference Desk" is a project of the Information Institute of Syracuse. The Lesson Plan section contains unique social studies and history lesson plans written and submitted by teachers for various grade levels. There are only fifteen history lesson plans but dozens of social studies lesson plans.
Resource Type: Lesson or Activity
Grade Level: LS, MS, HS

Out of Many: A History of the American People
www.phschool.com/advanced/lesson_plans/hist_faragher_2000/index.cfm

Focus Lessons for the *Out of Many* textbook highlights important ideas and concepts in each chapter as well as the relevant sections in the program's ancillaries. The Focus Lessons, written

by an experienced AP teacher, suggest strategies for assessing how well your students under-stand the important points in each chapter and also provide test-taking tips that will help your students prepare for and take the AP U.S. History test successfully.
Resource Type: Course Model
Grade Level: HS

The American Nation: A History of the United States
www.phschool.com/advanced/lesson_plans/hist_garraty_2000/index.cfm

Focus Lessons for "The American Nation" highlights important ideas and concepts in each chapter as well as the relevant sections in the program's ancillaries. The Focus Lessons, writ-ten by an experienced curriculum developer, suggest strategies for assessing how well your students understand the important points in each chapter and also provide test-taking tips that will help your students prepare for and take the AP U.S. History test successfully.
Resource Type: Course Model
Grade Level: HS

American History Lesson Plans from the New York Times
www.nytimes.com/learning/teachers/lessons/americanhistory.html

This informative site offers detailed lesson plans and quizzes built around *New York Times* articles. Check out the Lesson Plan Archive and search by keyword, subject, or grade level. Social studies lesson plans are objective and standard-based and are well supported by charts, graphs, and images.
Resource Type: Lesson or Activity
Grade Level: LS, MS, HS

The History Lab
http://hlab.tielab.org

"The History Lab" is both an inquiry-based pedagogy and a learning tool designed to make learning about history more an act of interpretation and less of memorization. Rooted in con-structivist thinking, it is a tool that enables teachers to build student inquiry activities and lessons around resources they find on the Internet. Teachers use the free ready-made template to insert instructions for students, provide external links to primary and secondary sources, and attach documents as needed. Projects are stored in the database and are available online.
Resource Type: Lesson or Activity
Grade Level: MS, HS

Focus on The History Lab

John Raymond, the creator of "The History Lab," is a former high school history and philosophy teacher and now an ed-tech expert based in Connecticut. When I show teachers his *History Lab* during workshops they are invariable impressed with its clear and easy-to-use template. Several have gone on to to create their own history lab or use existing ones. If you do decide to create one I would recommend you copy and save all the content you add to the template in a Word file. If you have a technical malfunction with the Lab at least you will have a copy of the activity.

(cont'd.)

Focus on The History Lab *(Continued)*

To see some "History Labs," select Search (in logo) and then Select All. John Raymond created the first one in the list, and teachers I show it to are usually impressed. The activity layout is clear and concise. John has included links to primary source documents in pdf format, but you could just add the URL for a Web page that has a relevant source.

Try it out for yourself by going to the homepage and filling out the "signup" section. Then follow the steps. Find appropriate primary sources (you now know some great online collections!), copy and paste URLs into the link, and then give the links titles. Try to link to a primary source that sits by itself on the page, and not to a Web page where the primary source is explained and analyzed in detail. You can save your work and come back and edit it later (see bottom of template), without having to make it part of the *History Lab* database. When you are done, add it to the database and tell the class about it!

Please note that when you logout and return you need to go to the Resources section to login. You can't login from "The History Lab" homepage (oddly enough).

The American President
www.americanpresident.org/home6.htm'

This Web site is geared toward teaching the history of the American presidency, primarily to high school students, and contains detailed biographies of each president.
Resource Type: Lesson or Activity
Grade Level: HS

Primary Source Materials and Document-Based Questions
www.kn.pacbell.com/wired/fil/pages/listdocumentpa.html

An Internet hotlist on document-based questions. Many useful links here.
Resource Type: Lesson or Activity; Primary Source Collection
Grade Level: HS

Economics Resources for K–12 Teachers
http://ecedweb.unomaha.edu/teach.htm

EcEdWeb is a helpful resource for teaching resources for K–12 or pre-college economics. If you need a lesson or information on a particular concept (e.g., scarcity), start with Concepts.
Resource Type: General Reference; Lesson or Activity
Grade Level: LS, MS, HS

CHAPTER 4

The Age of European Discovery—
The South and Slavery (1492–1860s)

PRE-COLONIAL/AGE OF DISCOVERY

*****The Sport of Life and Death: The Mesoamerican Ballgame
www.ballgame.org/

"The Sport of Life and Death" was voted Best Overall Site for 2002 by Museums and the Web and has won a slew of other Web awards. The site is based on a traveling exhibition and bills itself as "an online journey into the ancient spectacle of athletes and gods." "The Sport of Life and Death" features dazzling special effects courtesy of Macromedia Flash technology and its overall layout and organization are superb. Not just stylish, the site's content is excellent and engaging as well. For instance, there are helpful interactive maps, timelines, and samples of artwork in the Explore the Mesoamerican World section. The focus of the site, however, is the Mesoamerican ballgame, the oldest organized sport in history. The sport is explained through a beautiful and engaging combination of images, text, expert commentary, and video.
Resource Type: General Reference; Multimedia Presentation

****Columbus and the Age of Discovery
www.millersville.edu/~columbus/

Created by Millersville University, this award-winning site is part of text retrieval system that contains over 1,100 text articles from magazines, journals, newspapers, speeches, official calendars, and other sources relating to various encounter themes. There is an index of articles and categories, links to Discovery Literature and related sites, and you can email the webmaster Dr. Tirado. A great site for research on Columbus and European contact with native americans.
Resource Type: General Reference; Primary Source Collection

****1492 Exhibit
www.ibiblio.org/expo/1492.exhibit/Intro.html

This Library of Congress exhibit examines the 1492 expedition and its consequences with sections on What Came to be Called America, the Mediterranean World, Inventing America, Christopher Columbus, Europe Claims America, and an Epilogue. There are primary sources, artifacts, drawings, maps, and more.
Resource Type: General Reference; Primary Source Collection

****Vikings: The North Atlantic Saga
www.mnh.si.edu/vikings/

This Smithsonian Institution National Museum of Natural History site was created around an exhibit commemorating the 1000th anniversary of the Viking landing in the New World. Besides a cool Flash-generated introduction, the site contains extensive documentation on the contents of the exhibit, as well as a Virtual Viking Voyage, a multimedia feature including 3-D animations of ship building, runes and sagas, video interviews with leading experts in the field, and detailed histories of Viking settlements and journeys from Scandinavia to Newfoundland.
Resource Type: General Reference; Multimedia Presentation

****Passages: A Treasure Trove of North American Exploration
www.collectionscanada.ca/passages/index-e.html

As this site points out, North America was discovered "one step at a time and it took more than four centuries of exploration, to discover and traverse the famous Northwest Passage." This site is a historical account of the voyages of exploration to the North American continent based on the Rare Book Collection of the National Library of Canada.
Resource Type: General Reference; Primary Source Collection

****World Cultures to 1500: Cultures in America
www.wsu.edu/~dee/CULAMRCA/CULAMRCA.HTM

This online course by Professor Thomas Hooker, based at Washington State University, offers a terrific overview of world cultures, including America. It offers clear and informative lecture notes, maps, a photo gallery, timelines, links to relevant sites, and more. Topics include Beginnings, The Land, Social Life, Languages, Civilizations in America, Native American Culture, Native American Creation Stories, and The Iroquois League. Resources include The Native American Anthology, Glossary of Native American Culture, Gallery of Native American Cultures, and Internet Resources on Native Americans. In all, it is an excellent introduction to Native Americans. Click Contents to begin.
Resource Type: General Reference; Course Model

****World Cultures to 1500: Civilizations in America
www.wsu.edu/~dee/CIVAMRCA/CIVAMRCA.HTM

More from "World Cultures," this time with a focus on Mesoamerican civilizations. Topics include Olmecs, Teotihuacan, Toltecs, Mexicas/Aztecs, Mayas, Chav'n, Tiahuanaco, Incas, and Native American Languages. Resources include a Gallery of American Cultures, American Cultures Timeline, The Native American Anthology, Atlas of American Cultures, A Glossary of Native American Terms and Concepts, and Internet Resources on Native Americans. Click Contents.
Resource Type: General Reference; Course Model

****American Indians and the Natural World
www.carnegiemnh.org/exhibits/north-south-east-west/index.html

Through exploration of four different visions of living in and with the natural world, those of the Tlingit of the Northwest Coast, the Hopi of the Southwest, the Iroquois of the Northeast, and the Lakota of the Plains. North, South, East, West: American Indians and the Natural

World from the Carnegie Museum of Natural History examines the belief systems, philosophies, and practical knowledge that guide Indian peoples' interactions with the natural world. Concise essays with beautiful images.
Resource Type: General Reference; Image Collection

****NativeWeb
www.nativeweb.org/

"NativeWeb" is an international, nonprofit, educational organization dedicated to using technology and the Internet to disseminate information from and about indigenous nations, peoples, and organizations around the world. It is also a comprehensive gateway for Native American studies. The Resource Database contains many, many subcategories; the U.S. subcategories include 1400s through 1600s, 1700s through 1800s, 20th Century, Biographies, Living History/Reenacting, and Tribal Histories. Explore and you'll find abundant annotated links. You may also want to explore the Nations Index and Geographic Region Index. It is also a great site for Native American news, current events, books and music, and legal issues. Note: Links are not actively maintained.
Resource Type: General Reference; Links Collection

****Internet Modern History Sourcebook
www.fordham.edu/halsall/mod/modsbook.html

"Internet Modern History Sourcebook" is a wonderful collection of public domain and copy-permitted historical texts for educational use by Paul Halsall at Fordham University. The site and its documents are well organized, and the breadth of materials is impressive. "Internet Modern History Sourcebook" contains two sections of special interest. Early Modern World has documents pertaining to the European "Age of Discovery," Rivals of European Powers, Mercantile Capitalism, and Reflections on the Trade and the New Economy, while the Colonial North America section includes documents on Early Conquest and Exploitation, Political Forms, Virginia, New England, Middle Atlantic, and American Society.
Resource Type: Primary Source Collection

****The Columbus Navigation Homepage
www.columbusnavigation.com/

"Examining the History, Navigation, and Landfall of Christopher Columbus," this site explores Columbus and "dead reckoning" navigation, Columbus and "celestial" navigation, Columbus's "league," Columbus and longitude, Columbus's ships, and Columbus's crew. The creator of the site is is a computer systems consultant and historian who has authored two scholarly papers on Columbus's navigation.
Resource Type: General Reference

****Index of Native American Resources on the Web
www.hanksville.org/NAresources/

Part of the World Wide Web Virtual Library, the information at this Index is organized to be useful to the Native American community and the education community. There are many categories of links pertaining to American Indians, and the site is updated regularly. Maintained by Karen Strom.
Resource Type: Links Collection

****The Earliest Americans
www.cr.nps.gov/archeology/

The National Parks Service asked the Society for American Archaeology to lead an initiative to nominate archeological sites as National Historic Landmarks. This Web site highlights historic contexts related to Early American archeological sites for regions east of the Mississippi.
Resource Type: General Reference

**** First Nations Histories
www.tolatsga.org/Compacts.html

Provides a geographic overview of First Nation (Indian) histories as well as a location list of native tribes in the United States and Canada. Has a search function as well.
Resource Type: General Reference

****Native American Documents Project
www.csusm.edu/nadp/

This project was begun in 1992 by Prof. E.A. Schwartz at California State University to develop methods for making documents of federal Indian policy history accessible by computer. This site includes a number of indexes and explanatory articles as well as a search engine.
Resource Type: Primary Source Collection

****Conquistadors
www.pbs.org/opb/conquistadors/home.htm

The "Conquistadors" online learning adventure resource is geared toward middle and high school classrooms to help students learn about the Spanish Conquistadors in the New World and the legacy of their contact with Native Americans. There are lesson plans for teachers and in-depth online content for students available in both English and Spanish.
Resource Type: General Reference; Lesson or Activity

****Ancient Mesoamerican Civilization
www.angelfire.com/ca/humanorigins/index.html

This is a broad site by the University of Minnesota Department of Anthropology, which supplies information regarding Mesoamerican civilizations. The primary groups addressed are the Maya, Mixtec, Zapotec, and Aztec. Major topics include Writing Systems, Government, Religion, Mayan Calendar, and more.
Resource Type: General Reference

**** GB's Online Mesoamerica
http://pages.prodigy.com/GBonline/mesowelc.html

A popular Web site for students of Native American languages and culture, "GB's Online Mesoamerica" is linked to by over 500 related sites and has over 9,000 visitors per month. Major features include Ancient Writing, Archeological Sites, Native Issues, Pre-Columbian Art, and Mesoamerican Calendar.
Resource Type: General Reference

**** Maya Adventure
www.sci.mus.mn.us/sln/ma/top.html

The Science Museum of Minnesota presents "Maya Adventure," a Web site that highlights science activities and information related to ancient and modern Maya culture. "Maya Adventure" includes images from the Science Museum's anthropological collections and activities developed by the Science Museum's education division. Featured in the project is information from two exhibits about the Maya developed by the Science Museum of Minnesota: Cenote of Sacrifice and Flowers, Saints, and Toads.
Resource Type: General Reference; Multimedia Presentation

****Native Tech
www.nativetech.org/

"NativeTech" is an educational Web site that covers topics of Native American technology and emphasizes the Eastern Woodlands region. It focuses on revising use of the term "primitive" with respect to Native American technology and art. Its topics include Beadwork, Birds & Feathers, Clay & Pottery, Leather & Clothes, Metalwork, Plants & Trees, Porcupine Quills, Stonework & Tools, and Weaving & Cordage. The site also provides background on the history of Native American technologies. Maintained by Tara Prindle at the University of Connecticut.
Resource Type: General Reference

****Conquest of America by Hernando de Soto, Coronado and Cabeza de Vaca
www.floridahistory.com/inset11.html

Drs. Larry Clayton, Jim Knight, and Ed Moore's two-book set, *The DeSoto Chronicles*, was used for this study. The book departs from the long-standing contention that Spain came to North America mainly to explore for gold. The Web site focuses on Hernando de Soto's exploration of America for a seaway to China in order to trade Spain's New World gold and Vaca's effort to describe the continent. Teachers may use any material on these Internet pages—including all graphics, maps, illustrations, and text—free of charge.
Resource Type: General Reference; Lesson or Activity

****Native American Sites and Home of the American Indian Library Association Web Page
www.nativeculturelinks.com/indians.html

The goal of this site is to facilitate communication among Native peoples and between Indians and non-Indians by providing access to homepages of Native American nations and organizations, and to other sites that provide solid information about American Indians. It is actively maintained by a mixed-blood Mohawk urban Indian, formerly a librarian for 14 years at the University of Pittsburgh, and social sciences subject editor for anthropology, history, and sociology for *CHOICE* magazine.
Resource Type: General Reference; Links Collection

****Why Do Civilizations Collapse?
www.learner.org/exhibits/collapse/

Part of the Annenberg/CPB exhibits, this site focuses on the fall of ancient civilizations in four areas: Maya, Mesopotamia, Chaco Canyon (southwest United States), and Mali and Songhai. Nice images and interesting presentation.
Resource Type: General Reference; Lesson or Activity

****Sir Francis Drake
www.mcn.org/2/oseeler/drake.htm

These pages are focused on Sir Francis Drake, and in particular on his "Famous Voyage"—the circumnavigation of the world in the sixteenth century, during the reign of Queen Elizabeth.
Resource Type: General Reference

****Mystery of the Maya
www.civilization.ca/civil/maya/mminteng.html

Based on the IMAX film of the same name, this kid-oriented site from the Canadian Museum of Civilization features slide shows, info, links, and more. There is a synopsis of the film, a feature on the People of the Jaguar, and much information on Maya civilization.
Resource Type: Multimedia Presentation; Lesson or Activity

Pre-colonial Lesson Plans, Teacher Guides, Activities, and More

Why Did Slavery Emerge in Virginia?
www.dhr.history.vt.edu/us/mod02_slavery/index.html

"Why Did Slavery Emerge in Virginia?" is an exemplary tech-integration activity. The activity involves issue-centered analysis and decision making and the sources the students use are appropriate, varied, and engaging. In the Economics resources, students use a Profit/Cost of Labor calculator and should come to realize that slaves became more profitable than servants after 1660. The documents help students understand the context in which Virginia's wealth white settlers made the critical decision to enslave Africans.
Resource Type: Lesson Plan or Activity
Grade Level: HS, College

Focus on The Digital History Reader

"The Digital History Reader" is an evolving technology-based teaching project involving historians, educators, and technology specialists at Virginia Tech and provides content-rich, inquiry-based, and instructionally-proven resources for teaching European and U.S. history. Modern Europe in a Global Context provides materials exploring links between European and world history in the late nineteenth and twentieth centuries.

The modules follow a similar organization: a statement of the module's "objectives" and the historical questions students will be asked to consider; the "story" or context for the question with historical background; an "archive" of documents—text, visual, and multimedia—with questions to guide students' use of the documents; and a student assessment section that evaluates what students have learned.

NOTE: At the moment there are several American history and European history modules that do not require any password. The remaining modules are restricted while DHR completes their different components. Though incomplete, these modules offer many valuable resources.

Conquistadors Teaching Guide: Different Views of the World
www.pbs.org/opb/conquistadors/teachers/teachers.htm

Was the fall of the Aztec Empire inevitable? Was Cortes a hero or a villain? What would the world be like today if the Aztecs had been the "conquistadors" and conquered Europe? Contains complete PBS lesson plans.

Resource Type: Lesson or Activity
Grade Level: MS

Conquistadors Teaching Guide: The What Ifs of History
www.pbs.org/opb/conquistadors/teachers/teachers.htm

Why do you think that such a well-governed and peaceful empire, which stretched 2,500 miles from Ecuador south to Chile, could have been conquered by only 200 Spanish Conquistadors? What is the legacy of the Incas? Contains complete PBS lesson plans.
Resource Type: Lesson or Activity
Grade Level: MS

Two Worlds Meet: The Spanish Conquest of America
www.pbs.org/foodancestors/hsplan1.html

Through primary sources, learn about early interactions between the Aztecs and Spaniards. PBS Grades 9–12.
Resource Type: Lesson or Activity
Grade Level: HS

Mr. Donn's Ancient History Page
http://members.aol.com/donnandlee/index.html#ROME

Don Donn of the Corkran (Maryland) Middle School provides a complete unit with 17 daily lesson plans and unit test for sixth-graders on Incas, Mayans, and Aztecs. There are also links to multiple K–12 lesson plans and activities.
Resource Type: Lesson or Activity
Grade Level: MS

A Critical Bibliography of North American Indians, for K–12
www.nmnh.si.edu/anthro/outreach/Indbibl/

This bibliography was compiled by P. Ann Kaupp, head of the Department of Anthropology's Outreach Office at the Smithsonian Institution's National Museum of Natural History (NMNH); Fiona Burnett, an intern in the Museum Studies Program at George Washington University; Maureen Malloy, now Coordinator of Public Programs at the National Museum of Health and Medicine; and Cheryl Wilson, presently editor in the publications office of the Smithsonian's National Museum of the American Indian (NMAI).
Resource Type: General Reference
Grade Level: LS, MS, HS

Digital History Resource Guides
www.digitalhistory.uh.edu/resource_guides/

"Digital History Resource Guides" provide links to American history Web sites by period and present historical overviews, readings (online textbook chapter, Reader's Companion), primary source documents (documents, maps, cartoons), teaching resources (chronologies, maps, quizzes), audiovisual resources, and additional resources. The Guides provide an excellent and comprehensive teaching resource.
Resource Type: Course Model
Grade Level: HS, College

Course Models: The Land and People Before Columbus
www.history.ctaponline.org/center/hsscm/index.cfm?Page_Key=1309

Part of the California History-Social Science content standards and annotated course, this site includes background information, focus questions, pupil activities and handouts, an assessment, and references to books, articles, web sites, literature, audio-video programs, and a historic site. Grade 5.
Resource Type: Course Model
Grade Level: MS

Course Models: The Age of Exploration
www.history.ctaponline.org/center/hsscm/index.cfm?Page_Key=1318

Part of the California History-Social Science content standards and annotated course, this site includes background information, focus questions, pupil activities and handouts, an assessment, and references to books, articles, Web sites, literature, audiovisual programs, and a historic site. Grade 5.
Resource Type: Course Model
Grade Level: MS

Native North Americans: What was early contact like between Europeans and the Natives?
www.learningcurve.gov.uk/snapshots/snapshot37/snapshot37.htm

Using primary source evidence students investigate what the early contact was like. Were the Native Americans savage and vicious hosts? Were the Europeans unreasonable and unfair? Or did they all just get along fine? From Learning Curve of the (U.K.) National Archives.
Resource Type: Lesson or Activity
Grade Level: MS

Vikings in America
www.pbs.org/wgbh/nova/teachers/activities/2202_vikings.html

Discover through an activity how researchers are re-creating the Viking voyages and searching for archaeological clues along the North American coastline. PBS Nova.
Resource Type: Lesson or Activity
Grade Level: HS

The World's History: Demography and Migration, 1500–1750
http://cwx.prenhall.com/bookbind/pubbooks/spodek2/chapter14/deluxe.html

The online guide to Howard Spodek's *The World's History* features quizzes (multiple-choice questions, true/false questions, interactive review questions), primary sources, maps, a bulletin board, a live chat, Web links, and faculty resources for each chapter/topic.
Resource Type: Course Model
Grade Level: HS

Western Civilization: Europe Reaches Out
http://wps.prenhall.com/hss_king_westernciv_2/0,6774,208328-,00.html

The online study companion to Margaret King's *Western Civilization: A Social and Cultural History* has many features: chapter learning objectives, online quizzes, writing activities,

essay questions, Web links, built-in search engines, and faculty modules that include Power-Point outlines, presentation graphics, and lecture hints and activities.
Resource Type: Course Model
Grade Level: HS

The American People: Ancient America and Africa
http://wps.ablongman.com/long_nash_ap_6/0,7361,592970-,00.html

PowerPoint presentation as part of the online companion to *The American People*. Click PowerPoint Presentations and then Chapter 1.
Resource Type: Multimedia Presentation
Grade Level: HS

The American People: Europeans and Africans Reach the Americas
http://wps.ablongman.com/long_nash_ap_6/0,7361,592970-,00.html

PowerPoint presentation as part of the online companion to *The American People*. Click PowerPoint Presentations and then Chapter 2.
Resource Type: Multimedia Presentation
Grade Level: HS

Native Americans—Searching for Knowledge and Understanding
www.thirteen.org/edonline/lessons/native_americans/index.html

In this middle school lesson, students study Native Americans in order to become familiar with the contributions to and influences on American society particularly, but not exclusively, in the Western region of the United States. This lesson focuses on some of the cultural history, writings, and symbols of the southwestern tribes. After researching, studying, and comparing the differences among the various tribes in small groups, students produce individual reports about a specific Native American perspective.
Resource Type: Lesson or Activity
Grade Level: MS

Europe Discovers America: Multiple Choice Quiz, Fill-in-the-Blank, Flashcards, American History Glossary, and an American History Appendix
http://wps.ablongman.com/long_carnes_an_11/0,7137,250689-,00.html

The Student Resources section of *The American Nation* companion Web site features introductions to chapters, interactive quizzes, flashcards, Web links, an American History Glossary, and an American History Appendix.
Resource Type: Course Model
Grade Level: HS

Interpreting Primary Sources: European Discovery of the New World
www.digitalhistory.uh.edu/historyonline/us1.cfm

"Digital History" provides brief excerpts from primary sources and statistics on European Discovery and questions to think about.
Resource Type: Lesson or Activity; Primary Source Collection
Grade Level: HS, College

HistoryTeacher.net: AP United States History Quizzes
www.historyteacher.net/USQuizMainPage.htm

A teacher at the Horace Greeley High School in Chappaqua, New York, has produced a great general site for history teachers that offers AP-level U.S. history quizzes on many different periods and topics.
Resource Type: Test or Quiz
Grade Level: HS

The American Nation: Internet Activities
www.phschool.com/atschool/TAN/Survey/Teacher_Area/TAN1_T_BK_index.html

Prentice Hall's phschool.com offers Internet activities based on their *The American Nation* textbook chapters. Middle school grades.
Resource Type: Lesson or Activity
Grade Level: MS

A History of the United States: Internet Activities and Student Self-Test Questions
www.phschool.com/atschool/history_us/Student_Area/HUS_S_BK_index.html

Prentice Hall's phschool.com offers Internet activities and interactive quizzes based on *A History of the United States* textbook chapters. Middle school level.
Resource Type: Lesson or Activity; Test or Quiz
Grade Level: MS

Africa-America Migration: Blank Map
http://wps.ablongman.com/long_nash_ap_6/0,7361,592970-,00.html

The companion Web site to *The American People* offers blank maps related to various topics in American history. The maps can be printed or placed in a PowerPoint presentation.
Resource Type: Map
Grade Level: MS

COLONIAL

***** DoHistory: Martha Ballard
http://dohistory.org/

"DoHistory" invites you to explore the process of piecing together the lives of ordinary people in the past (see Figure 4.1). It is an experimental, interactive case study based on the research that went into the book and PBS film *A Midwife's Tale*, which were both based upon the remarkable 200-year-old diary of midwife/healer Martha Ballard. There are thousands of downloadable pages from original documents: Diaries, letters, maps, court records, town records, and more as well as a searchable copy of the 27-year diary of Martha Ballard. "DoHistory" engages users interactively with historical documents and artifacts from the past and introduces visitors to the pivotal questions and issues raised when "doing" history. "DoHistory" was developed and maintained by the Film Study Center at Harvard University and is hosted and maintained by the Center for History and New Media, George Mason University.
Resource Type: Primary Source Collection; Multimedia Presentation; Lesson or Activity

Figure 4.1: DoHistory Homepage

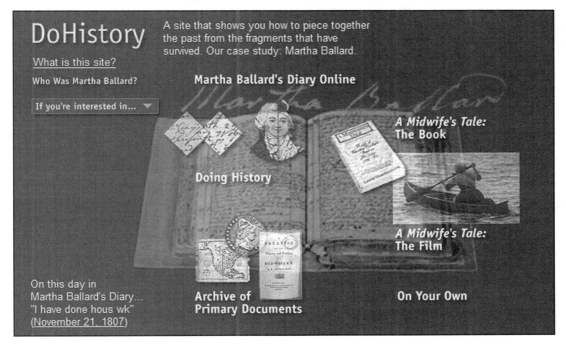

Focus on DoHistory: Martha Ballard

"DoHistory": Martha Ballard is a great example of an online interactive history Web site. You could easily create a research-oriented project or student-centered activity with this site. Click the If You're Interested In button and select **Teaching with this Web Site** for some excellent teaching ideas. There are several suggested activities worth considering and you could easily create your own grade-appropriate project. The documents at this Web site are authentic; you see the actual handwritten notes of midwife Martha Ballard and others living during this period.

**** Raid on Deerfield: The Many Stories of 1704
www.1704.deerfield.history.museum/

The Pocumtuck Valley Memorial Association/Memorial Hall Museum in Deerfield, Massachusetts, has launched a rich and impressive Web site that focuses on the 1704 raid on Deerfield, with the goal of commemorating and reinterpreting the event from the perspectives of all the cultural groups who were present—Mohawk, Abenaki, Huron, French, and English (see Figure 4.2). The Web site brings together many resources—historical scenes, stories of people's lives, historical artifacts and documents, essays, voices and songs, historical maps, and a timeline—to illuminate broad and competing perspectives on this dramatic event. *Resource Type: Multimedia Presentation; Primary Source Collection*

**** The Plymouth Colony Archive Web Site
http://etext.virginia.edu/users/deetz/

This site focuses on Plymouth from 1620 to 1691 and has been selected as one of the best humanities sites on the Web by the National Endowment for the Humanities. Includes fully

Figure 4.2: Raid on Deerfield: The Many Stories of 1704

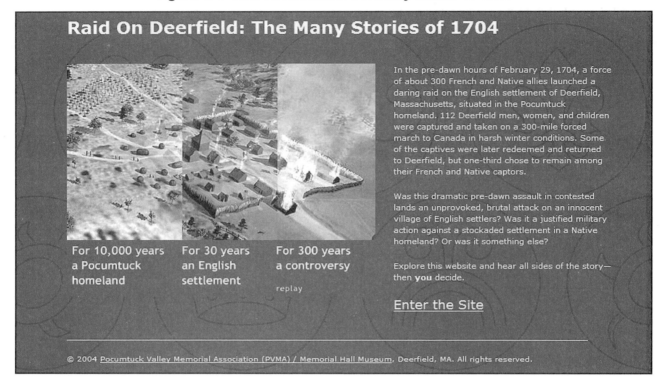

Raid On Deerfield: The Many Stories of 1704

In the pre-dawn hours of February 29, 1704, a force of about 300 French and Native allies launched a daring raid on the English settlement of Deerfield, Massachusetts, situated in the Pocumtuck homeland. 112 Deerfield men, women, and children were captured and taken on a 300-mile forced march to Canada in harsh winter conditions. Some of the captives were later redeemed and returned to Deerfield, but one-third chose to remain among their French and Native captors.

Was this dramatic pre-dawn assault in contested lands an unprovoked, brutal attack on an innocent village of English settlers? Was it a justified military action against a stockaded settlement in a Native homeland? Or was it something else?

Explore this website and hear all sides of the story—then **you** decide.

Enter the Site

For 10,000 years   For 30 years   For 300 years
a Pocumtuck   an English   a controversy
homeland   settlement
                                  replay

searchable texts of early laws, court records, wills, and probates; analyses of the colony legal structure, domestic relations, early settlement, criminal records, and interactions of the Wampanoag people and the colonists; biographical and social network profiles of members of the colony; a study of social and legal relationships between indentured servants and masters; and archaeological analyses of house plans and material culture.
Resource Type: Primary Source Collection

**** Archiving Early America
www.earlyamerica.com/

A worthwhile commercial site for links to historical documents, biographies, and even online books on eighteenth-century America. These archival materials are displayed in their original formats so they can be read and examined close-up and in detail. Of special interest is the *Maryland Gazette* containing George Washington's Journal of his historic trip to the Ohio Valley. It is the only original copy privately held. Materials are free for personal use.
Resource Type: Primary Source Collection

****Divining America: Religion and the National Culture—17th and 18th Centuries
www.nhc.rtp.nc.us/tserve/divam.htm

TeacherServe® is an interactive curriculum enrichment service offering teachers practical help in planning courses and presenting rigorous subject matter to students. "Divining America: Religion and the National Culture—17th and 18th Centuries" is designed to help teachers of American history bring their students to a greater understanding of the role religion has played in the development of the United States. In The First Great Awakening section, Historian Christine Leigh Heryman of the University of Delaware offers a concise explanation of the scope and impact of the First Great Awakening. In Puritanism and Predestination she offers a clear explanation of Puritan beliefs. Other topics include Witchcraft in Salem Village; Religion, Women, and the Family in Early America; The Church of England in Early America; Religious Pluralism in the Middle Colonies; Native American Religion in Early America; and Religion and the American Revolution.

One of the links, "America's Story: Colonial America (1492–1763)," is a site for children from the Library of Congress and is designed to be both entertaining and fun to use. The Colonial America (1492–1763) section contains "stories" (concise essays with images), including "Give Me Liberty or Give Me Death!" "Jamestown Was Established," "Salem Witch Trials," "Christopher Columbus Saw Land!" and "George Washington Was Born."
Resource Type: General Reference; Lesson or Activity

****Early America's Digital Archives
www.mith2.umd.edu/eada

The Maryland Institute for Technology in the Humanities has produced a searchable collection of electronic texts written in or about the Americas from 1492 to approximately 1820. The Archive also features a collection of links to early American texts on the Internet. Open to the public for research and teaching purposes.
Resource Type: Primary Source Collection; Image Collection

****Religion and the Founding of American Republic
www.loc.gov/exhibits/religion/overview.html

Part of a special exhibit by the Library of Congress, this site provides an interesting mix of images, primary text, and background information on the role of religion in the European settlement of America. America as a Religious Refuge: The 17th Century looks at religious persecution in Europe that drove so many to British North America, where settlers often established colonies centered on passionate religious convictions. Religion in 18th-Century America concentrates on the nation's first major religious revival, the Great Awakening, which took place from 1740 to 1745.
Resource Type: Primary Source Collection

****The American Colonist's Library
www.freerepublic.com/forum/a3a6605427caf.htm

A massive collection of historical works which contributed to the formation of American politics, culture, and ideals. Arranged in chronological sequence (500 BC–1800 AD). A very helpful scholarly resource.
Resource Type: Primary Source Collection

**** American Centuries: View from New England
www.americancenturies.mass.edu/

Explore American history with this digital collection of approximately 2000 objects and transcribed document pages. An image of each of these items appears on an Item Page accompanied by interpretive text available on age-appropriate levels. Museum staff authored the text

content, with review by teachers, school librarians, and nationally recognized scholars. This site is essentially a large library of primary resources, curricula, and interactive student activities, mostly presented in age-appropriate, user-friendly formats.
Resource Type: Primary Source Collection; Lesson or Activity

****Virtual Jamestown
www.virtualjamestown.org/

The Virtual Jamestown Archive is an ongoing digital research, teaching, and learning project that explores the legacies of the Jamestown settlement and "the Virginia experiment." There are first-hand accounts and letters, interpretive essays, and more.
Resource Type: Primary Source Collection; General Reference

****Jamestown Rediscovery
www.apva.org/

The Association for the Preservation of Virginia Antiquities' Jamestown Rediscovery archaeological project provides a history of Jamestown and resources. There is a timeline of events and references leading up to and through the establishment of Jamestown and lists of early settlers with occupations. There are also online exhibits that provide a "behind the scenes" look at the way archaeologists find out about objects excavated on Jamestown Island.
Resource Type: General Reference; Primary Source Collection

****Secrets of the Dead: Death at Jamestown
www.pbs.org/wnet/secrets/case_jamestown/index.html

This PBS site puts forth the theory that residents died of arsenic poisoning and the plague. Among the multimedia features are an interactive tour of Jamestown, as well as videos of a rebuilt church in Jamestown, an archaeological dig, and views of the city.
Resource Type: Multimedia Presentation

****Africans in America: The Terrible Transformation, 1450–1750
www.pbs.org/wgbh/aia/part1/narrative.html

Part of PBS's "African American Journey" site, here you'll find part one of a rich collection of resources—images, documents, stories, biographies, commentaries—on the experience of slavery in America. There is also a useful teacher's guide and activities for students. There are three other parts to explore: Revolution: 1750–1805, Brotherly Love:1791–1831, and Judgment Day: 1831–1865.
Resource Type: General Reference; Lesson or Activity

****Slaves and the Courts, 1740–1860
http://lcweb2.loc.gov/ammem/sthtml/

"Slaves and the Courts, 1740–1860" is part of the American Memory Historical Collections of the Library of Congress and features pamphlets and books documenting the experiences of African and African American slaves in the American colonies and the United States. There are cases; reports; examinations of cases; and works concerning slaves, fugitive slaves, slave revolts, the African slave trade, and more. A great site for research.
Resource Type: Primary Source Collection

****MayflowerHistory.com
www.mayflowerhistory.com/

A worthwhile site for researching the history of the *Mayflower*. Contains important primary source documents related to the ship's voyage, a history of the *Mayflower*, representations of the ship, and more.
Resource Type: General Reference; Primary Source Collection

****Plimoth Plantation
www.plimoth.org/

This "Plimoth Plantation" site tells of Wampanoags and Pilgrims at Plymouth Colony from 1620 to 1692. In the Historical Background section you can browse articles site historians have written on a broad range of topics. There is also a comprehensive interactive activity that builds students' understanding about the harvest celebration of 1621, which is often erroneously referred to as "The First Thanksgiving." It is supported by an online teacher's guide, "Becoming a Historian," which has lessons that correspond to each activity on the site along with additional resources and information. There are also details about how "Plimoth Plantation" fulfills the Massachusetts Curriculum Frameworks.
Resource Type: General Reference; Lesson or Activity

****The Pilgrims and Plymouth Colony, 1620
www.rootsweb.com/~mosmd/index.htm#part1

This is a detailed study guide for use by teachers, students, and enthusiasts. You can use the "Search this Site" field that will look for any topic within the 75 options. Also, clicking on the "Site Map" will produce an interactive map that allows for selection of any of the individual Web pages. Duane Cline, the creator of the site, has written two books—*Navigation in the Age of Discovery: an Introduction* and *Centennial History: General Society of Mayflower Descendants*—and has twice been invited to serve as a Guest Curator at Pilgrim Hall in Plymouth, Massachusetts.
Resource Type: General Reference; Lesson or Activity

****U.S. History.org
www.ushistory.org/

The Independence Hall Association in Philadelphia has produced this fun and engaging site where you can enjoy a virtual tour of Philadelphia and visit Betsy Ross's House. You can also learn why Pennsylvania is misspelled on the Liberty Bell and the story of its crack. The Electric Franklin provides resources for you to explore the diversity of Benjamin Franklin's pursuits, and there are several section that deal with the Revolutionary war.
Resource Type: General Reference; Lesson or Activity

****Pilgrim Hall Museum
www.pilgrimhall.org/

Through its exhibition of Pilgrim possessions and Native American artifacts, Pilgrim Hall tells the stories of America's founding and traditions. The museum features an online tour of artifacts owned by Pilgrims. "The Pilgrim Story" combines artifacts with historical information to illuminate the Pilgrim and Native American story to 1692, when Plymouth Colony as

an independent entity came to an end. "Beyond the Pilgrim Story" gives additional information about particular aspects of the Pilgrim story of interest to visitors.
Resource Type: Virtual Tour; Image Collection

****Colonial Williamsburg Foundation
www.history.org/

A tourist-oriented site, but one with useful links to resources for students and teachers. Sections include Teacher Resources, Electronic Field Trips, History Explorer, Clothing, Gardens, Archaeology, and more. There are lesson plans, pictures, and information about daily life. Check out the "Almanack."
Resource Type: General Reference; Lesson or Activity

****Salem Witch Trials
http://etext.lib.virginia.edu/salem/witchcraft/

This site is a documentary archive of the Salem witch trials and features court records, personal letters, maps of the area, and more. The Archive contains educational information, such as biographical profiles, a collection of images containing portraits of notable people involved in the trials, pictures of important historic sites, historical paintings, and published illustrations taken from nineteenth- and early-twentieth-century literary and historical works. The Documentary Archive is created under the supervision of Professor Benjamin C. Ray, University of Virginia.
Resource Type: Primary Source Collection

****Famous American Trials: Salem Witch Trials
www.law.umkc.edu/faculty/projects/ftrials/salem/salem.htm

This site include transcripts of trial records and examinations of six accused witches and other relevant primary source documents. There is a chronology, selected images, a map of Salem, Petitions of Accused Witches, an interactive game, and much more. The materials included in the Famous Trials Web site are original works of authorship, government records, works for which copyright protection has expired, works reprinted with permission, or works the Webmaster believes are within the fair use protection of the copyright laws.
Resource Type: General Reference; Primary Source Collection

****Scientific American Frontiers: Unearthing Secret America
www.pbs.org/saf/1301/features/lives.htm

In this episode, archaeologists shed new light on life in Colonial America and the lives of slaves. Archaeologists Marley Brown and Fraser Neiman uncover evidence that reveals much about the lives of slaves in America during the Colonial period up through the nineteenth century. Nice mix of concise texts and historic images.
Resource Type: General Reference

****Internet Modern History Sourcebook
www.fordham.edu/halsall/mod/modsbook.html

"Internet Modern History Sourcebook" is a wonderful collection of public domain and copy-permitted historical texts for educational use by Paul Halsall at Fordham University. The site and its documents are well organized and the breadth of materials is impressive.

Under the heading of The Early Modern World is Colonial North America, which includes documents on Early Conquest and Exploitation, Political Forms, Virginia, New England, Middle Atlantic, American Society. Some external links are broken as the site does not appear to be actively maintained.
Resource Type: Primary Source Collection

****Smithsonian: Within These Walls
http://americanhistory.si.edu/house/default.asp

The National Museum of American History presents the history of a 250-year-old house built in the mid-1760s, in Ipswich, Massachusetts, and five of the families that occupied it. The site helps understand the great events of the nation's past through these families.
Resource Type: Virtual Tour

****Omohundro Institute of Early American History and Culture (OIEAHC)
www.wm.edu/oieahc/

The College of William and Mary and The Colonial Williamsburg Foundation founded the Institute of Early American History and Culture in 1943 and still jointly sponsor its work. The Institute's full-time professional and support staff is responsible for a variety of valuable research and publication programs for scholars. Most services are fee-based, but *Uncommon Sense* is a free online journal on early American history to which you can subscribe. Important site for serious scholars.
Resource Type: Primary Source Collection

****Virginia Colonial Records Project
www.lva.lib.va.us/whatwehave/gov/vcrpabout.htm

The Library of Virginia provides a fully searchable index to nearly 15,000 reports which are housed in repositories in Great Britain and other European countries and that survey and describe documents relating to colonial Virginia history that. The survey report images are available online, and there are references to microfilm reels for the original documents.
Resource Type: Primary Source Collection

****The American Thanksgiving Tradition
www.plimoth.org/visit/what/exhibits/thanksgiving.asp

This site on Thanksgiving, prepared by Plimoth Plantation museum staff, responds to the most frequently asked questions about the First Thanksgiving and attempts to re-create the original seventeenth-century event.
Resource Type: General Reference; Lesson or Activity

****Ben Franklin: Glimpses of the Man
http://sln.fi.edu/franklin/

This site explores Franklin's roles as a scientist, an inventor, a statesman, a printer, a philosopher, a musician, and an economist. It is meant to help you learn about Ben Franklin and to let you see how Ben's ideas are still alive in our world today. You might begin by looking at the family tree. There are recommended resource materials, enrichment activities, and a brief glossary.
Resource Type: General Reference

****Salem
www.nationalgeographic.com/features/97/salem/

A flashy interactive introduction to the Salem Witch trials by National Geographic where the visitor "experiences" the trials. Engaging site for students.
Resource Type: Multimedia Presentation

****The Leslie Brock Center for the Study of Colonial Currency
http://etext.lib.virginia.edu/users/brock/

A well-organized and informative project developed at Notre Dame University. Read the introductory article "Colonial Currency, Prices, and Exchange Rates." Explore contemporary pamphlets, dealing primarily with Massachusetts and New England, or references that are less well known, such as unpublished dissertations and manuscripts. Interesting and useful page for professional historians, as well as casual visitors.
Resource Type: General Reference

****Builders of America: The Jewish Heritage
www.borisamericanjews.org/

This site is part of an exhibit that celebrates the many peoples who built America in partnership. Most of the material comes from the American Jewish Archives, Cincinnati; the American Jewish Historical Society, Waltham, Massachusetts; and the B'nai B'rith Klutznick Museum, Washington, D.C. Go to Browse the Exhibit to see panels From America's Beginnings to the American Revolution and The American Revolution and the Birth of the Nation.
Resource Type: General Reference

*** The Atlantic Slave Trade and Slave Life in the Americas: A Visual Record
http://hitchcock.itc.virginia.edu/Slavery/

This searchable collection of a thousand images is useful to teachers, researchers, students, and the general public. The collection provides a glimpse into pre-Colonial Africa and the experiences of enslaved Africans who were transported to the Americas. Compiled by Jerome Handler (Virginia Foundation for the Humanities) and Michael Tuite (Digital Media Laboratory, University of Virginia).
Resource Type: Primary Source Collection

***13 Originals: Founding the American Colonies
www.timepage.org/spl/13colony.html

This site offers concise essays on various aspects of the original 13 colonies. Also provides access to several different maps of the colonies, and Colonial charters, grants, and related documents.
Resource Type: General Reference; Map

***Classics of American Colonial History
www.dinsdoc.com/colonial-3.htm

This collection of historical documents from Dinsmore Documentation contains select scholarly books and articles on American colonial history. Their goal is to add four documents

(articles or book chapters) per week, and readers are invited to suggest further public domain documents for digitalization. The directory of documents by subject includes African Americans and Slavery, British Colonial Policy, Economics and Trade, Immigration from Europe, Religion, Wars and more. You can also browse by author. Very helpful resource for scholars.
Resource Type: Primary Source Collection

***History Buff.com: Colonial Newspapers
www.historybuff.com/library/refseventeen.html

A series of concise essays from "HistoryBuff.com" about Colonial newspapers: "The First Ten Newspapers in America," "America's First Papermill: The Rittenhouse Mill," "The Beginnings of Illustrated Journalism," "Roger E'LeStrange Aristocratic Publisher," "The Defeat of the Spanish Armada," "The Acquittal of John Peter Zenger," and "The Revolutionary War in the West." See also: "Producing Newspapers 1692–1792."
Resource Type: General Reference

***Colonial America 1600–1775: K–12 Resources
http://falcon.jmu.edu/~ramseyil/colonial.htm

You'll find annotated links to maps, lesson plans, bibliographies, and curriculum content materials here. Links are not actively maintained.
Resource Type: Course Model

***Early American and Colonial Literature to 1700
http://falcon.jmu.edu/~ramseyil/amlitcol.htm

The Internet School Library Media Center offers the "Early American and Colonial Literature to 1700" page for librarians, teachers, parents, and schools. You can search this site, use an index, or site map. Note: Links are not maintained.
Resource Type: General Reference

***The Hall of Church History: The Puritans
www.spurgeon.org/~phil/puritans.htm

Billed as "Theology from a Bunch of Dead Guys," this section of the "Hall of Church History" is basically a gateway to links about Puritans.
Resource Type: Links Collection

***Fire and Ice: History & Biography
www.puritansermons.com/hist.htm

Part of "Fire and Ice: Puritan and Reformed Writings," this section has materials written by various authors about the Puritans or other Reformed subjects. There are separate listings for the sermons and extracts in the Table of Contents.
Resource Type: General Reference

***The Real Pocahontas
http://pocahontas.morenus.org/

Compares and contrasts the real Pocahontas with her portrayal in the Disney movie.
Resource Type: General Reference; Lesson or Activity

***1755: French and Indian War Homepage
http://web.syr.edu/~laroux/

Plenty of information and links on soldiers, battles, documents, and references.
Resource Type: General Reference

***Chronicling Black Lives in Colonial America
www.csmonitor.com/durable/1997/10/29/feat/feat.1.html

Concise *Christian Science Monitor* feature from the October 29, 1997 edition.
Resource Type: General Reference

Colonial Lesson Plans, Teacher Guides, Activities, and More

Life in Early America
www.libsci.sc.edu/miller/Colony.htm

This grades 3–5 lesson plan was written by Kimberly Cox Burkett and Brenda Morton. The lessons are primarily "hands on." For instance, among the included activities are map making and the construction of an Indian humming toy.
Resource Type: Lesson or Activity
Grade Level: LS

CEC: Colonial Government
www.col-ed.org/cur/sst/sst169.txt

This brief mini-lesson for grades 10–12 introduces students to Colonial government. Students research and compare three types of Colonial governments.
Resource Type: Lesson or Activity
Grade Level: HS

State of Affairs Between the Native Americans and the European Settlers
www.vcdh.virginia.edu/teaching/jamestown/affairs.html

Students will be able to analyze multiple resources to explain the contacts between the American Indians and the European settlers in early Colonial Virginia during the Age of Discovery.
Resource Type: Lesson or Activity
Grade Level: HS

A Colonial Family and Community
www.hfmgv.org/education/smartfun/colonial/intro/

Be a history detective. Go back in time and investigate the daily lives of the Daggetts, a Colonial family from northeastern Connecticut. Collect clues to uncover answers to seven questions about colonial life in the 1700s. Then prove your skills as a history detective by discovering "What's wrong with this picture?"
Resource Type: Lesson or Activity
Grade Level: MS

George Washington
http://memory.loc.gov/learn/lessons/gw/gwintro.html

Using letters from the Library of Congress collection "George Washington Papers, 1741–1799," three units are designed to allow students to examine Washington's leadership during pivotal events in early American history: the French and Indian War, the Federal Convention, and Washington's presidency. A main goal is to understand both Washington's role in early America and the reasons for his rise to prominence. Featuring preselected letters from Library of Congress collections and focus questions to evaluate each document, the lesson promotes careful explication of the meaning and implications of primary sources. Designed for grades 8–12.
Resource Type: Lesson or Activity
Grade Level: MS, HS

Tinker, Tailor, Farmer, Sailor
http://memory.loc.gov/learn/lessons/01/tinker/index.html

To understand how geographic factors affected where European settlers established colonies, students compare primary sources from the Library of Congress' American Memory collections for three distinct regions: New England, the mid-Atlantic, and the South. By comparing and contrasting the experiences of settlers, students understand the importance of regional differences and how settlers adapted to new environments. A wide range of sources including drawings, business proposals and government documents are used to address the role of region in settlement. The lesson plan includes specific activities and guides on how to use class time and also identifies specific American Memory items to be used. Designed for grades 4–8.
Resource Type: Lesson or Activity
Grade Level: LS, MS

The Scarlet Letter: Resources and Lesson Plans
http://thwt.org/NewsletterE1-Scarlet.htm

Nathaniel Hawthorne's classic tale, set in a New England Puritan community, addresses moral and spiritual issues and remains one of the most widely taught books in American high schools. Follow this link to the *Teaching Literature and Writing Newsletter* and to a blend of historical, biographical, literary, and teaching resources on Hawthorne and *The Scarlet Letter*.
Resource Type: Lesson or Activity
Grade Level: HS

The American People: Colonizing a Continent in the Seventeenth Century
http://wps.ablongman.com/long_nash_ap_6/0,7361,592970-,00.html

PowerPoint presentation on Colonial America as part of the online companion to *The American People*. Click on PowerPoint Presentations and then Chapter 3.
Resource Type: Multimedia Presentation
Grade Level: HS

Interpreting Primary Sources
www.digitalhistory.uh.edu/historyonline/handouts.cfm

"Digital History" provides brief excerpts from primary sources and statistics and questions to think about Motivations for English Colonization, Peopling of America, The Puritan Mind, and Witchcraft in Salem.
Resource Type: Lesson or Activity: Primary Source Collection
Grade Level: HS, College

The American People: The Maturing of Colonial Society
http://wps.ablongman.com/long_nash_ap_6/0,7361,592970-,00.html

PowerPoint presentation on Colonial America as part of the online companion to *The American People*. Click on PowerPoint Presentations and then Chapter 4.
Resource Type: Multimedia Presentation
Grade Level: HS

American Society in the Making: Multiple Choice Quiz, Fill-in-the-Blank, Flashcards, American History Glossary, American History Appendix
http://wps.ablongman.com/long_carnes_an_11/0,7137,250745-,00.html

The Student Resources section of *The American Nation* companion Web site features introductions to chapters, interactive quizzes, flashcards, Web links, an American History Glossary, and an American History Appendix.
Resource Type: Course Model
Grade Level: HS

Digital History Lesson Plan: Salem Witch Trials
www.digitalhistory.uh.edu/historyonline/lesson_plans_display.cfm?lessonID=23

Students gather research about the Salem witchcraft trials and participate in a mock trial. High school level.
Resource Type: Lesson or Activity
Grade Level: HS

Death at Jamestown
www.thirteen.org/edonline/lessons/jamestown/index.html

Acting as historians and scientists, students read primary and secondary source materials, evaluate data, and analyze artifacts to learn about the mystery surrounding the Jamestown deaths. Based on a PBS video. Students are prompted to take a critical look at information and evaluate the motives, interests and biases expressed in primary and secondary sources.
Resource Type: Lesson or Activity
Grade Level: HS

American Religious History
http://exchanges.state.gov/education/amstudy/currents.htm

The *Currents in American Scholarship* series offers updates on the status of theory and practice in disciplines relevant to the study of the society, culture, and institutions of the United States. "American Religious History," an essay by Catherine L. Albanese of the University of

California Santa Barbara, is available free of charge on the site.
Resource Type: General Reference
Grade Level: HS

Digital History Resource Guides
www.digitalhistory.uh.edu/resource_guides/

"Digital History Resource Guides" provide links to American history Web sites by period and provide historical overviews, readings (online textbook chapter, Reader's Companion), primary source documents (documents, maps, cartoons), teaching resources (chronologies, maps, quizzes), audiovisual resources, and additional resources. The Web site is an excellent and comprehensive teaching resource.
Resource Type: Course Model
Grade Level: HS, College

HistoryTeacher.net: AP United States History Quizzes
www.historyteacher.net/USQuizMainPage.htm

A New York teacher has produced a great general site for history teachers that offers AP-level U.S. history quizzes on many different periods and topics.
Resource Type: Test or Quiz
Grade Level: HS

The American People: The Strains of Empire
http://wps.ablongman.com/long_nash_ap_6/0,7361,592970-,00.html

PowerPoint presentation on the road to the War of Independence as part of the online companion to *The American People*. Click PowerPoint Presentations and then Chapter 5.
Resource Type: Multimedia Presentation
Grade Level: HS

The Colonial Challenge
www.quia.com/rr/4049.html

Answer a range of easy-to-difficult questions and test your knowledge of early U.S. history.
Resource Type: Test or Quiz
Grade Level: HS

Thanksgiving
http://lcweb2.loc.gov/ammem/ndlpedu/features/thanks/thanks.html

Through this Library of Congress Learning Page activity students investigate the American tradition of celebrating Thanksgiving, which began in Colonial times.
Resource Type: Lesson or Activity
Grade Level: MS

Will the Real Ben Franklin Please Stand Up?
www.thirteen.org/edonline/lessons/ben_franklin/index.html

In this middle school or high school lesson plan, students will research and debate Benjamin Franklin's most significant role and contribution to the history of the United States.

Which was most important to American history—Benjamin Franklin's work as a printer, a writer, a statesman, or an inventor? After completing their research, students will have to prepare ten-minute oral and visual presentations to support their position. After presenting their work, they will also be expected to answer questions and ask them of the other groups.
Resource Type: Lesson or Activity
Grade Level: MS, HS

Thirteen Colonies: Blank Map
http://wps.ablongman.com/long_nash_ap_6/0,7361,592970-,00.html

The companion Web site to *The American People* offers blank maps related to various topics in American history. The maps can be printed or placed in a PowerPoint presentation. Go to Blank Maps for Quizzes.
Resource Type: Map
Grade Level: HS

English Colonies in 1700: Blank Map
http://wps.ablongman.com/long_nash_ap_6/0,7361,592970-,00.html

The companion Web site to *The American People* offers blank maps related to various topics in American history. The maps can be printed or placed in a PowerPoint presentation. Go to Blank Maps for Quizzes.
Resource Type: Map
Grade Level: HS

Jamestown Historic Briefs
www.nps.gov/colo/Jthanout/JtvsPly.html

Concise handouts on Jamestown history are made available by the National Parks Service.
Resource Type: Lesson or Activity
Grade Level: MS

The American Nation: Internet Activities
www.phschool.com/atschool/TAN/Survey/Teacher_Area/TAN1_T_BK_index.html

Prentice Hall's phschool.com offers Internet activities based on their *The American Nation* textbook chapters. Middle school grades.
Resource Type: Lesson or Activity
Grade Level: MS

A History of the United States: Internet Activities and Student Self Test Questions
www.phschool.com/atschool/history_us/Student_Area/HUS_S_BK_index.html

Prentice Hall's phschool.com offers Internet activities and interactive quizzes based on *A History of the United States* textbook chapters. High School level.
Resource Type: Lesson or Activity; Test or Quiz
Grade Level: HS

Rare Map Collection—Colonial America
http://scarlett.libs.uga.edu/darchive/hargrett/maps/colamer.html

The University of Georgia Libraries provides dozens of historic maps of America from the seventeenth and eighteenth centuries.
Resource Type: Map
Grade Level: HS

AMERICAN REVOLUTION AND INDEPENDENCE

****LIBERTY! The American Revolution
www.pbs.org/ktca/liberty/

PBS's assorted and diverse Web exhibits supplement specific individual television series and generally include a summary of each episode, interviews (often with sound bites), a timeline, a glossary, photos, and links to relevant sites. Liberty explores the impact of the Revolutionary era on the lives of African Americans and is an engaging introduction geared to a young audience.
Resource Type: General Reference; Lesson or Activity

****Religion and the American Revolution
www.loc.gov/exhibits/religion/rel03.html

Religion played a major role in the American Revolution by offering a moral sanction for opposition to the British—an assurance to the average American that revolution was justified in the sight of God. This informative Library of Congress page uses primary source documents to illustrate this role.
Resource Type: Primary Source Collection; General Reference

****Africans in America: Revolution, 1750–1805
www.pbs.org/wgbh/aia/part2/title.html

Part of PBS's excellent African American Journey site, here you'll find part one of a rich collection of resources—images, documents, stories, biographies, commentaries—on the experience of slavery in America. There is also a useful teacher's guide and activities for students. There are three other parts to explore: The Terrible Transformation: 1450–1750, Brotherly Love: 1791–1831, and Judgment Day: 1831–1865.
Resource Type: General Reference; Lesson or Activity

****Spy Letters of the American Revolution
www.clements.umich.edu/spies/index.html

The interesting exhibit is based on spy letters from the William L. Clements Library, University of Michigan, Ann Arbor, Michigan. The Gallery of Letters provides a brief description of each letter and links to more information about the stories of the spies in the letter or the secret methods used to make the letter.
Resource Type: Primary Source Collection

***The History Place: American Revolution
www.historyplace.com/unitedstates/revolution/index.html

This three-part exhibit contains two detailed timelines, a picture gallery of George Washington, and an audio reading of the Declaration of Independence.
Resource Type: General Reference

***Modern History—A Soviet Viewpoint
www.mcps.k12.md.us/curriculum/socialstd/MH/Contents.html

The War of Independence from a 1965 Soviet viewpoint.
Resource Type: General Reference

American Revolution Lesson Plans, Teacher Guides, Activities, and More

The American War for Independence
http://edsitement.neh.gov/view_lesson_plan.asp?id=682

In this impressive three-lesson NEH EDSITEment curriculum unit, students learn about the diplomatic and military aspects of the American War for Independence. Students study military campaigns and documents, as well as American diplomacy with Great Britain and France. Central to the unit is an interactive map that walks students through the major campaigns in the North and the South.
Resource Type: Course Model
Grade Level: HS

Women in the American Revolution
http://score.rims.k12.ca.us/score_lessons/women_american_revolution/

Women contributed to the American Revolution in a variety of ways. Enter this Virtual Museum to learn more.
Resource Type: Lesson or Activity; Virtual Tour
Grade Level: MS

Midnight Ride—A Paul Revere Virtual Museum
www.cvesd.k12.ca.us/finney/paulvm/_welcomepv.html

Students explore North Boston on an interactive map, visit Paul Revere's House, and travel with Paul across Boston Harbor to Medford and Concord.
Resource Type: Lesson or Activity; Multimedia Presentation
Grade Level: MS

American Revolutionary War PowerPoint Project
www.lessonplanspage.com/SSLACIRevolutionaryWarPowerPointPres58.htm

Students will explore the American Revolutionary War by choosing main ideas from various sources (textbook, Internet, etc.) and then will demonstrate their knowledge of the war by creating a PowerPoint slide show.
Resource Type: Multimedia Presentation
Grade Level: MS

George Washington as a Military Leader: Lesson Plan
www.pbs.org/georgewashington/classroom/military_leader.html

A high school level lesson plan presented by PBS, this classroom outline focuses on George Washington's strategies and victories. In the end, students are asked to evaluate Washington as a military leader. The Web page has a strong narrative voice and most of the necessary information is directly on the page. A bibliography is included.
Resource Type: Lesson or Activity
Grade Level: HS

Lesson Plan: Voices of the American Revolution
http://edsitement.neh.gov/view_lesson_plan.asp?id=423

In this EDSITEment lesson plan, students focus on the issues and sentiments of the Colonial population immediately prior to the Revolution. The lesson plan is quite comprehensive, listing many activities and essay projects. Recommended for high school students.
Resource Type: Lesson or Activity
Grade Level: HS

"I Cannot Tell a Lie"—Examining Myths in American History
www.nytimes.com/learning/teachers/lessons/20030630monday.html

In this *New York Times* lesson, students examine and debunk historical myths, using the American Revolution as a starting point. They then create and play a game of "American History: Fact or Fiction?"
Resource Type: Lesson or Activity
Grade Level: MS

All Fired Up: Explaining Fourth of July Related Themes and Images
www.nytimes.com/learning/teachers/lessons/20020704thursday.html

In this *New York Times* lesson, students brainstorm images and themes associated with the American Fourth of July holiday. They then create illustrated posters to explain the processes or history behind these themes.
Resource Type: Lesson or Activity
Grade Level: MS

American Revolutionaries
http://projects.edtech.sandi.net/hoover/amrevolt/

In this WebQuest, students explore the uses and abuses of propaganda in the Revolution, as well as today.
Resource Type: Lesson or Activity
Grade Level: HS

Lesson Plan: George Washington
http://edsitement.neh.gov/view_lesson_plan.asp?id=315

EDSITEment designed this George Washington lesson plan. The plan draws from a wide array of sources, including the NARA, PBS, and many others. Students are asked to compare

the real George Washington with the heroic, patriotic legend he has become. Recommended for high school students.
Resource Type: Lesson or Activity
Grade Level: HS

Lesson Plan: Background on the Patriot Attitude Toward the Monarchy
http://edsitement.neh.gov/view_lesson_plan.asp?id=462

Created by EDSITEment, this lesson plan is meant to provide students with a basic knowledge of how the American patriots felt toward the English government. Ample resources and printable worksheets included. Intended for grades 6–8.
Resource Type: Lesson or Activity
Grade Level: MS

Lesson Plan: Colonial Broadsides and the American Revolution
http://edsitement.neh.gov/view_lesson_plan.asp?id=390

"Broadsides" address virtually every aspect of the American Revolution, providing a wide range of suitable classroom topics. In this lesson (by ESDITEment), students will use the resources of the Library of Congress's Printed Ephemera Collection to experience the news as the colonists heard it. Grades 6–8.
Resource Type: Lesson or Activity
Grade Level: MS

The Gilder Lehrman Institute Modules in American History: The Revolutionary War
www.gilderlehrman.org/teachers/module1/index.html

The Gilder Lehrman Institute offers quality educational materials, including teaching modules on major topics in American history. Each module includes: a succinct historical overview; learning tools including lesson plans, quizzes, and activities; recommended documents, films, and historic images . These modules were prepared by Steven Mintz, the John and Rebecca Moores Professor of History and the Director of the American Cultures Program at the University of Houston. Other helpful Institute online sources include include "American History Quizzes," "Letters from America's Wars Featured Documents for your Classroom," and "Primary Source Documents from the Collection."
Resource Type: Course Model
Grade Level: HS

Interpreting Primary Sources
www.digitalhistory.uh.edu/historyonline/handouts.cfm

This site provides brief excerpts from primary sources and statistics and questions to think about. Try the Toward the Revolution and Impact of the Revolution lessons.
Resource Type: Lesson or Activity; Primary Source Collection
Grade Level: HS

America in the British Empire: Multiple Choice Quiz, Fill-in-the-Blank, Flashcards, American History Glossary, and an American History Appendix
http://wps.ablongman.com/long_carnes_an_11/0,7137,250799-,00.html

The Student Resources section of *The American Nation* companion Web site features

introductions to chapters, interactive quizzes, flashcards, Web links, an American History Glossary, and an American History Appendix.
Resource Type: Course Model
Grade Level: HS

The World's History: Political Revolutions in Europe and the Americas, 1688–1850
http://cwx.prenhall.com/bookbind/pubbooks/spodek2/chapter15/deluxe.html

The online guide to Howard Spodek's *The World's History* features quizzes (multiple-choice questions, true/false questions, interactive review questions), primary sources, maps, a bulletin board, a live chat, Web links, and faculty resources for each chapter/topic.
Resource Type: Course Model
Grade Level: HS

Western Civilization: Inalienable Rights
http://wps.prenhall.com/hss_king_westernciv_2/0,6774,208527-,00.html

The online study companion to Margaret King's *Western Civilization: A Social and Cultural History* has many features: Chapter learning objectives, online quizzes, writing activities, essay questions, Web links, built-in search engines, and faculty modules that include PowerPoint outlines, presentation graphics, and lecture hints and activities.
Resource Type: Course Model
Grade Level: HS

HistoryTeacher.net: AP United States History Quizzes
www.historyteacher.net/USQuizMainPage.htm

A teacher at the Horace Greeley High School in Chappaqua, New York, has produced a great general site for history teachers that offers AP-level U.S. history quizzes on many different periods and topics.
Resource Type: Test or Quiz
Grade Level: HS

Causes of the American Revolution: Lesson Plan
http://school.discovery.com/lessonplans/programs/revwar1

In this lesson plan, students will understand that taxation of the American colonists by the British led to the revolution. Grades 6–8.
Resource Type: Lesson or Activity
Grade Level: MS

The American People: A People in Revolution
http://wps.ablongman.com/long_nash_ap_6/0,7361,592970-,00.html

A PowerPoint presentation on the American Revolution as part of the online companion to *The American People*. Click PowerPoint Presentations and then Chapter 6.
Resource Type: Multimedia Presentation
Grade Level: HS

AP United States History DBQs: 1775–1825
www.historyteacher.net/1998DBQsMainPage.htm

These student-created Documents-Based Questions are part of this excellent site.
Resource Type: Lesson or Activity; Primary Source Collection
Grade Level: HS

Yorktown Historic Briefs
www.nps.gov/colo/Ythanout/ytbriefs.html

Handouts for teachers on the siege of Yorktown, created by the National Parks Service.
Resource Type: Lesson or Activity
Grade Level: HS

Celebrating Independence Day
http:usinfo.state.gov/scv/life_and_culture/holidays/july_4.html

The U.S. Department of State International Information Programs provides essays and photographs that illustrate diverse aspects of the American Fourth of July experience.
Resource Type: Lesson or Activity
Grade Level: HS

Paul Revere's True Account of the Midnight Ride
www.historynet.com/historical_conflicts/3032316.html

In a letter written in 1798 to Massachusetts Historical Society founder Dr. Jeremy Belknap, Paul Revere described his actual adventures during his "Midnight Ride" of April 18–19, 1775.
Resource Type: Primary Source Collection
Grade Level: MS

Places of the American Revolution Game
www.quia.com/jg/66325.html

This Quia.com game prompts the player to match important places during the American Revolution with their historical significance.
Resource Type: Game
Grade Level: MS

Kid's Page at Valley Forge
www.ushistory.org/valleyforge/kids/index.html

Includes a game and other "fun stuff."
Resource Type: Game
Grade Level: LS

Who Wants to Marry a Founding Father?
www.law.umkc.edu/faculty/projects/ftrials/conlaw/marry.htm

Kids can test their knowledge of the Founding Fathers via an engaging game modeled on *Who Wants to Marry a Millionaire?*
Resource Type: Game
Grade Level: LS

American Revolution Quiz 1
www.digitalhistory.uh.edu/modules/revwar/quiz1.html

From a series of quizzes at the University of Houston's "Digital History" Web site.
Resource Type: Test or Quiz
Grade Level: MS, HS

American Revolution Quiz 2
www.digitalhistory.uh.edu/modules/revwar/quiz2.html

From a series of quizzes at the University of Houston's "Digital History" Web site.
Resource Type: Test or Quiz
Grade Level: MS, HS

Digital History Resource Guides
www.digitalhistory.uh.edu/resource_guides/

"Digital History Resource Guides" present links to American history Web sites by period and provide historical overviews, readings (online textbook chapter, Reader's Companion), primary source documents (documents, maps, cartoons), teaching resources (chronologies, maps, quizzes), audiovisual resources, and additional resources. The guides provide an excellent and comprehensive teaching resource.
Resource Type: Course Model
Grade Level: HS, College

The American Nation: Internet Activities
www.phschool.com/atschool/TAN/Survey/Teacher_Area/TAN1_T_BK_index.html

Prentice Hall's phschool.com offers Internet activities based on their *The American Nation* textbook chapters. Middle school grades.
Resource Type: Lesson or Activity
Grade Level: MS

A History of the United States: Internet Activities and Student Self-Test Questions
www.phschool.com/atschool/history_us/Student_Area/HUS_S_BK_index.html

Prentice Hall's phschool.com offers Internet activities and interactive quizzes based on *A History of the United States* textbook chapters. Middle school.
Resource Type: Lesson or Activity
Grade Level: MS

CONSTITUTION

**** Documents from the Continental Congress and the Constitutional Convention
http://memory.loc.gov/ammem/collections/continental/

The impressive Library of Congress Continental Congress Broadside Collection (256 titles) and the Constitutional Convention Broadside Collection (21 titles) contain documents relating to the work of Congress and the drafting and ratification of the Constitution. Items include extracts of the journals of Congress, resolutions, proclamations, committee reports, treaties,

and early printed versions of the U.S. Constitution and the Declaration of Independence. There are two special presentations: "To Form a More Perfect Union" and "The Work of the Continental Congress and the Constitutional Convention."
Resource Type: Primary Source Collection; General Reference

****NARA Exhibit Hall: The Charters of Freedom

www.archives.gov/national-archives-experience/charters/charters.html

The National Archives and Records Administration offers a copy of the U.S. Constitution and biographies of the document's 55 framers (see Figure 4.3). The article "A More Perfect Union" is an in-depth look at the Constitutional Convention and the ratification process. "Questions and Answers Pertaining to the Constitution" presents dozens of fascinating facts about the Constitution.
Resource Type: Primary Source Collection; General Reference

Figure 4.3: The Charters of Freedom

****The Avalon Project: The American Constitution—A Documentary Record
www.yale.edu/lawweb/avalon/constpap.htm

The Yale Law School offers primary source documents on The Roots of the Constitution, Revolution and Independence, Credentials of the Members of the Federal Convention, The Constitutional Convention, and Ratification and Formation of the Government.
Resource Type: Primary Source Collection

****U.S. Constitution Resource Center
http://tcnbp.tripod.com/

The TCNbP guide to the U.S. Constitution offers three types of resources to aid in your online and offline study of the U.S. Constitution. Constitution Notebook Program (offline study guide) is available for free download. There are also links to other sites on the Web with information related to the Constitution and links to Amazon.com for book listings related to the Constitution.
Resource Type: General Reference; Lesson or Activity

****Election Central
www.crf-usa.org/Foundation_docs/Foundation_home.html

"Election Central" is an online resource that helps teachers and students explore the electoral process past and present, in the United States and around the world. There are lessons, readings, and activities in U.S. history, world history, and government. There is also an online lesson titled "Political Parties, Platforms, and Planks." These lessons are designed to help students explore documents that serve as the foundation for American democracy. Each lesson in Foundations of Our Constitution consists of three components: (1) a reading with discussion questions, (2) an interactive activity, and (3) the complete text of the document that the lesson explores.
Resource Type: General Reference; Lesson or Activity

****James Madison Center
www.jmu.edu/madison/center/home.htm

"James Madison Center" serves as a repository for information on Madison's life and times (1751–1836), as well as on the Federalist Era. Go to the Madison Archives for contextual information and primary sources on Confederation and Constitution and other topics related to Madison's life. Additional materials include audio files of the Bill of Rights and pictures and descriptions of materials from the James Madison Collection. The Center's online newsletter, *Liberty & Learning*, contains current articles, factual information, and primary source materials. Teacher's Resources include lesson plans on American history and a book-length history of the United States organized by learning objectives.
Resource Type: General Reference; Primary Source Collection

****Internet Modern History Sourcebook
www.fordham.edu/halsall/mod/modsbook.html

"Internet History Sourcebooks Project" is a wonderful collection of public domain and copy-permitted historical texts for educational use by Paul Halsall at Fordham University. The site

and its documents are well organized, and the breadth of materials is impressive. "Internet Modern History Sourcebook" contains documents of special interest in the American Independence section on The Establishment of the American State, Commentators on America, Native Americans, and Slavery.
Resource Type: Primary Source Collection

****The Federalist: A Collection of Essays
www.law.emory.edu/FEDERAL/federalist/federser.html

The electronic desk of Emory Law School has put the *Federalist Papers* online and offers a keyword search function and an index.
Resource Type: Primary Source Collection

****Alexander Hamilton on the Web
www.isidore-of-seville.com/hamilton/

On this site you will find biographies, Hamilton's writing—including the complete *Federalist Papers*—images of Hamilton, reviews and excerpts from some of the recent books about Hamilton, essays on the Hamilton/Burr duel, and more.
Resource Type: General Reference; Primary Source Collection

****The American Presidency: A Glorious Burden
http://americanhistory.si.edu/presidency/home.html

This Smithsonian site explores the history and operation of the American presidency. The exhibit displays more than 375 images of documents, paintings, photographs, buttons, posters, paraphernalia, and objects along with short texts explaining their significance.
Resource Type: General Reference; Multimedia Presentation

****Ben's Guide to U.S. Government for Kids
http://bensguide.gpo.gov/

This educational site by the U.S. Government Printing Office teaches K–12 students how the U.S. government works. There are resources for teachers and parents as well.
Resource Type: General Reference; Lesson or Activity

****American President.org
www.americanpresident.org/

This Web site is geared toward teaching the history of the American presidency, primarily to high school students. The Presidency in History contains detailed biographies of each of the 43 past and present Presidents and First Ladies. The site also contains biographies of Cabinet members, staff, and advisers; timelines detailing significant events during each administration; and multimedia galleries to explore. The Presidency in Action delves into the function and responsibilities of the modern presidency. Here you will find detailed descriptions of the areas of presidential responsibility, updated organization charts, staff listings, and biographies of past and present staff and advisers. Brought to you by the University of Virginia's Miller Center of Public Affairs.
Resource Type: General Reference; Lesson or Activity

****Africans in America: The Terrible Transformation, 1750–1805
www.pbs.org/wgbh/aia/part2/narrative.html

Part of PBS's excellent "African American Journey" site, here you'll find part one of a rich collection of resources—images, documents, stories, biographies, commentaries—on the experience of slavery in America. There is also a useful teacher's guide and activities for students. See Part 2, Revolution: 1750–1805.
Resource Type: General Reference; Lesson or Activity

****Archiving Early America
www.earlyamerica.com/

A worthwhile commercial site for links to historical documents, biographies, and even online books on eighteenth-century America. These archival materials are displayed in their original formats so they can be read and examined close-up and in detail. Of special interest is the *Maryland Gazette* containing George Washington's journal of his historic trip to the Ohio Valley. It is the only original copy privately held. Materials are free for personal use.
Resource Type: Primary Source Collection

****Early America's Digital Archives
www.mith2.umd.edu:8080/eada/index.jsp

The Maryland Institute for Technology in the Humanities has produced a searchable collection of electronic texts written in or about the Americas from 1492 to approximately 1820. The Archive also features a collection of links to early American texts on the Internet. Open to the public for research and teaching purposes.
Resource Type: Primary Source Collection

****The American Colonist's Library
www.freerepublic.com/forum/a3a6605427caf.htm

A massive collection of the historical works that contributed to the formation of American politics, culture, and ideals. Arranged in chronological sequence (500 BC–1800 AD). Go to Eighteenth Century Sources Which Profoundly Impacted American History. Very helpful collection of primary sources.
Resource Type: Primary Source Collection

****George Washington Resources
http://etext.virginia.edu/washington/fitzpatrick/

This electronic collection of papers by and to George Washington contains a staggering 17,400 letters and documents. Search keyword "Constitution" and you'll find letters Washington wrote to James Madison about the Constitution.
Resource Type: Primary Source Collection

****Omohundro Institute of Early American History and Culture (OIEAHC)
www.wm.edu/oieahc/

The College of William and Mary and The Colonial Williamsburg Foundation founded the Institute of Early American History and Culture in 1943 and still jointly sponsor its work. The Institute's full-time professional and support staff is responsible for a variety of valuable

research and publication programs for scholars. Most services are fee-based, but *Uncommon Sense* is a free online journal on early American history. Important site for serious scholars.
Resource Type: Primary Source Collection

****The Thomas Jefferson Digital Archive
http://etext.lib.virginia.edu/jefferson/

Though not present at the Constitutional Convention, Jefferson followed the proceedings closely. "Thomas Jefferson Digital Archive" provides more than 1,700 texts written by or to Thomas Jefferson. The site also includes a biography of Jefferson and The Jeffersonian Cyclopedia, which organizes more than 9,000 quotes according to theme and other categories. An impressive source for research.
Resource Type: Primary Source Collection

***James Madison and the Great Events of His Era
www.jmu.edu/madison/gpos225-madison2/adopt.htm

Part of a James Madison University presentation on James Madison, this site offers a concise overview of the Constitutional Convention. Highlights include Madison's "Notes on the Confederacy," as well as his reflections on division of powers and the constitutionality of a national bank.
Resource Type: General Reference; Primary Source Collection

***The Constitution Society
www.constitution.org/

The Constitution Society is a private nonprofit organization dedicated to research and public education on the principles of constitutional republican government. It publishes documentation, engages in litigation, and organizes local citizen groups to work for reform. It offers a Liberty Library of Constitutional Classics, a Constitutional Weblog, and a Constitutional Examination.
Resource Type: General Reference; Primary Source Collection

***Biographies of the Founding Fathers
www.colonialhall.com/biography.php

Colonial Hall provides bios of the signers of the Declaration of Independence. The sketches of America's Founding Fathers are taken from the 1829 book *Lives of the Signers to the Declaration of Independence* by the Rev. Charles A. Goodrich.
Resource Type: General Reference

***ushistory.org
www.ushistory.org/

The Independence Hall Association in Philadelphia has produced this fun and engaging site where you can enjoy a virtual tour of Philadelphia and visit Betsy Ross's House. You can also learn why Pennsylvania is misspelled on the Liberty Bell and the story of the crack. There are several section that deal with the Revolutionary War, and you can learn about The President's House in Philadelphia, Executive Mansion of the United States from 1790 to 1800 during Philadelphia's tenure as the national capital.
Resource Type: Virtual Tour; General Reference

Constitution Lesson Plans, Teacher Guides, Activities, and More

Lesson Plans: Constitution
www.civiced.org/lesson-plans.html

Provided by the Civic Center of Education, these excellent lesson plans use probing questions to analyze the framing of the Constitution. They offer guidelines for both teachers and students, as well as supplemental lessons regarding James Madison and George Washington.
Resource Type: Lesson or Activity
Grade Level: LS, MS, HS

C-Span's U.S. Constitution
www.c-spanclassroom.org/VideoDetail.aspx?category=C

"C-Span's U.S. Constitution" page provides access to video clips, related activities, and links. All content is copyright cleared for classroom use. An excellent resource for Civics teachers.
Resource Type: Lesson or Activity; Multimedia Presentation
Grade Level: HS

The Gilder Lehrman Institute Modules in American History: The Constitution
www.gilderlehrman.org/teachers/module2/index.html

The Gilder Lehrman Institute offers quality educational materials, including teaching modules on major topics in American history. Each module includes: a succinct historical overview; learning tools including lesson plans, quizzes, and activities; recommended documents, films, and historic images. These modules were prepared by Steven Mintz, the John and Rebecca Moores Professor of History and the Director of the American Cultures Program at the University of Houston. Other helpful Institute online sources include include American History Quizzes, Letters from America's Wars Featured Documents for Your Classroom, and Primary Source Documents from the Collection.
Resource Type: Course Model
Grade Level: HS

Bill of Rights Institute
http://billofrightsinstitute.networkats.com/

If you haven't discovered the Bill of Rights Institute, this should be an early stop on your lesson planning journey. They have a curriculum book with videos that is very useful, as well as a new book of lesson plans (*Media and American Democracy*), and an abundance of great stuff on their Web site.
Resource Type: Lesson or Activity
Grade Level: HS

Bill of Rights in Action
www.crf-usa.org/lessons.html#BRIA

This is the online archive of *Bill of Rights in Action*, the Constitutional Rights Foundation's curricular newsletter. The Constitutional Rights Foundation seeks to instill in American youth a deeper understanding of citizenship through values expressed in the Constitution and its Bill of Rights, and to educate them to become active and responsible participants in American

society. Each edition has a lesson (reading, discussion questions, and interactive activity) on U.S. history, world history, and a current issue. Lessons are balanced to present various viewpoints. *Bill of Rights in Action* has been published for more than 30 years, and the Constitutional Rights Foundation has archived about 10 years of the newsletter. An impressive resource.
Resource Type: Lesson or Activity
Grade Level: HS

CQ Press: U.S. Constitution
http://cqpress.com/incontext/

"CQ Press in Context" is a great free Web site for information on pivotal events shaping today's world of politics. In honor of National Constitution Day, *CQ Press* devoted a section of the "CQ Press in Context" Web site to documents and analytical content related to the U.S. Constitution located here. This includes a ready-to-teach, downloadable lesson plan written by *CQ Press* author Maryam Ahranjani and designed specially for teachers who want to take advantage of Constitution Day as a classroom learning tool. The lesson plan, titled "The First Amendment and Protection of Students' Rights," is designed for instruction of grades 9–12 and focuses on the history of the Pledge of Allegiance and the groundbreaking Supreme Court case *Tinker vs. Des Moines Independent School District*, which addressed the issue of teacher and student First Amendment rights in schools. Teachers can use these tools to engage students in lively discussions of how the First Amendment relates to their own lives and their rights as students and citizens.
Resource Type: Lesson or Activity
Grade Level: HS

National Endowment for the Humanities: Constitution Day
http://edsitement.neh.gov/ConstitutionDay/

The National Endowment for the Humanities invites you to take a few moments to read the U.S. Constitution carefully, to engage with its history, its content, its authors' aspirations, and its lasting legacy. NEH has assembled a helpful collection of documents, background essays, and a bibliography to help you celebrate and deepen your understanding of the U.S. Constitution.
Resource Type: Lesson or Activity
Grade Level: LS, MS, HS

The Constitution: Our Plan for Government
www.col-ed.org/cur/sst/sst172.txt

Submitted by a middle school teacher Willie Jefferson of Wichita, Kansas, this constitution lesson plan is intended for grades 8–9.
Resource Type: Lesson or Activity
Grade Level: MS, HS

Constitution and the Idea of Compromise: Lesson Plan
www.pbs.org/georgewashington/classroom/index.html

In this PBS lesson plan, students analyze the various changes and compromises that went into the framing of the constitution. Written for high school students, the lesson plan also asks several follow-up questions at the end.

Resource Type: Lesson or Activity
Grade Level: HS

You and the U.S. Constitution
www.ofcn.org/cyber.serv/academy/ace/soc/cecsst/cecsst091.html

Written by teacher Kim-Scott Miller of the Columbia Education Center in Portland, Oregon, this grade 4 lesson plan is very "activity oriented" and attempts to explain the rules and laws of the United States.
Resource Type: Lesson or Activity
Grade Level: LS

Teacher Lesson Plan: Created Equal?
http://memory.loc.gov/ammem/ndlpedu/lessons/01/equal/overview.html

This Library of Congress lesson focuses on a few key concepts of the Declaration of Independence, beginning with the phrase "All men are created equal." Students gain an appreciation of Thomas Jefferson's efforts to deal with the complex issues of equality and slavery in the Declaration of Independence. Recommended for high school students.
Resource Type: Lesson or Activity
Grade Level: HS

Digital History: Legal History
www.digitalhistory.uh.edu/resource_guides/content.cfm?tpc=38

"Digital History" features resource guides by topic and period. Reference resources include classroom handouts, chronologies, encyclopedia articles, glossaries, and an audiovisual archive including speeches, book talks and e-lectures by historians, and historical maps, music, newspaper articles, and images. The site's "Ask the HyperHistorian" feature allows users to pose questions to professional historians.
Resource Type: Course Model
Grade Level: HS, College

The Federalist Era: Multiple Choice Quiz, Fill-in-the-Blank, Flashcards, American History Glossary, and an American History Appendix
http://wps.ablongman.com/long_carnes_an_11/0,7137,250911-,00.html

The Student Resources section of *The American Nation*'s companion Web site features introductions to chapters, interactive quizzes, flashcards, Web links, an American History Glossary, and an American History Appendix.
Resource Type: Course Model
Grade Level: HS

Constitutional Convention Lesson Plan
www.uen.org/Lessonplan/preview?LPid=661

Supplied by the Utah Education Network, this is a three-day lesson plan to help students understand the structure and function of the United States government established by the Constitution.
Resource Type: Lesson or Activity
Grade Level: HS

The Constitution: Counter Revolution or National Salvation?
http://lcweb2.loc.gov/ammem/ndlpedu/lessons/broad/intro.html

This lesson plan encourages students to make critical observations on the nature of the U.S. Constitution. It is presented by the Library of Congress and includes multiple online resources for students. Intended for grade 11.
Resource Type: Lesson or Activity
Grade Level: HS

Constitutional Issues: Separation of Powers
www.archives.gov/education/lessons/separation-powers/

Presented by the National Archives and Records Administration, this lesson plan examines FDR's attempt to add a Justice to the Supreme Court.
Resource Type: Lesson or Activity
Grade Level: HS

Teaching With Documents: Observing Constitution Day
www.archives.gov/education/lessons/constitution-day/

The National Archives and Records Administration celebrates the signing of the Constitution by presenting activities, lesson plans, and information.
Resource Type: Lesson or Activity
Grade Level: HS

Bill of Rights Institute: Lesson Ideas
www.billofrightsinstitute.org/Instructional/showPage.htm

Activities and lesson plans are free for use in the classroom.
Resource Type: Lesson or Activity
Grade Level: HS

Bill of Rights WebQuest
www.bellmore-merrick.k12.ny.us/webquest/social/billofrights.html

In this study of the Bill of Rights, students create a television news program about controversial issues today that relate to the Bill of Rights.
Resource Type: Lesson or Activity
Grade Level: MS

U.S. Constitution WebQuest
http://projects.edtech.sandi.net/marston/constitution/

Designed by a middle school teacher, the mission for this project is to become a member of one of the three branches of government and to investigate information about that branch of government.
Resource Type: Lesson or Activity
Grade Level: MS

U.S. Constitution WebQuest
www.maxwell.syr.edu/plegal/tips/t2prod/gonzalezwq.html

"You are a journalist for a school newspaper. In your research you have discovered that many of your peers do not know anything about the U.S. Constitution." This WebQuest helps students

understand the U.S. Constitution and to be able to teach their classmates about its origins, significance, and relevance to our society.
Resource Type: Lesson or Activity
Grade Level: MS

The Constitution WebQuest
www.greece.k12.ny.us/oly/techprep/webquest/constitution.html

"The year is 1787 and you have been elected to represent your state at the Constitutional Convention in Philadelphia. You will be 'rubbing shoulders' with the likes of James Madison, Patrick Henry, George Washington, Benjamin Franklin, and Alexander Hamilton." In this WebQuest, students may be a supporter (Federalist) or an opponent (Anti-Federalist) of the Constitution.
Resource Type: Lesson or Activity
Grade Level: MS

The Constitutional Convention WebQuest
www.people.virginia.edu/~llb7e/345/finalproject/taskpage.html

In this WebQuest, students in groups act as reporters in 1787. It is their responsibility to let the people know about the Constitution.
Resource Type: Lesson or Activity
Grade Level: MS

CEC: Separation of Powers between the Three Branches of Government
www.col-ed.org/cur/sst/sst102.txt

Recommended for grades 10–12, this mini-lesson uses a class activity to teach students about checks and balances.
Resource Type: Lesson or Activity
Grade Level: HS

Interview with Signers of the Constitution
www.education-world.com/a_lesson/00-2/lp2047.shtml

This Education World lesson plan is for grades 6–8. Students work in small groups to develop three questions that a newspaper reporter assigned to cover the signing of the Constitution might have asked each of the following signers of the Constitution: George Washington, Benjamin Franklin, James Madison, and Alexander Hamilton.
Resource Type: Lesson or Activity
Grade Level: MS

What Conflicting Opinions Did the Framers Have about the Completed Constitution?
www.civiced.org/index.php?page=high_school

This lesson describes some conflicting points of view of the leading Framers of the Constitution. The position of one of these, George Mason, is explored in detail. You also will examine Benjamin Franklin's statement in defense of the Constitution. High school level.
Resource Type: Lesson or Activity
Grade Level: HS

First Amendment Lesson Plans

www.freedomforum.org/templates/document.asp?documentID=13588

Education for Freedom is offered by The Freedom Forum's First Amendment Center, a non-partisan center dedicated to the understanding and appreciation of the values of the First Amendment. These lessons (beginning and advanced levels) address constitutional principles and contemporary issues involving the First Amendment.
Resource Type: Lesson or Activity
Grade Level: LS, MS, HS

Create a New Amendment

www.education-world.com/a_lesson/00-2/lp2052.shtml

This Education World lesson plan is for grades 6–12. Students demonstrate critical and creative thinking skills in developing a new amendment.
Resource Type: Lesson or Activity
Grade Level: MS, HS

The Constitution: The Foundation of American Society Practice Test

www.phschool.com/curriculum_support/brief_review/us_history/

High school level quiz on the U.S. Constitution from Prentice Hall.
Resource Type: Test or Quiz
Grade Level: HS

The Constitution Tested: Nationalism and Sectionalism Practice Test

www.phschool.com/curriculum_support/brief_review/us_history/

High school level quiz on Constitutional issues in American history from Prentice Hall.
Resource Type: Test or Quiz
Grade Level: HS

The Constitution Tested: Document Based Essay Question

www.phschool.com/curriculum_support/brief_review/us_history/essay_questions/unit2.cfm

This Prentice Hall activity is designed to test your ability to work with historical documents and is based on the accompanying documents (1–6).
Resource Type: Lesson or Activity; Primary Source Collection
Grade Level: HS

CEC: Articles of Confederation Game

www.col-ed.org/cur/sst/sst192.txt

By playing this simple game, students will learn firsthand why the Articles of Confederation failed. Grades 10–12.
Resource Type: Game
Grade Level: HS

Constitutional Examination

www.constitution.org/exam/hp/index.htm

The Constitutional Society offers multiple-choice questions on constitutional government, history, and law. There are some browser requirements in order to view the exams.

Resource Type: Test or Quiz
Grade Level: MS

Is Everyone Protected by the Bill of Rights?
www.thirteen.org/edonline/lessons/billofrights/index.html

In this high school lesson plan, students explore whether gays should be entitled to serve in the military. To understand this issue, students take a look at the civil rights afforded to every U.S. citizen. All this is used to gather information for a final debate about the issue using skills and research found in the lesson.
Resource Type: Lesson or Activity
Grade Level: HS

On the Edge and Under the Gun
www.thirteen.org/edonline/lessons/under_gun/index.html

This middle school lesson will expose students to the issues of gun control, the right to bear arms, and the overwhelming seriousness of gun-related violence. After exploring the complexities of this problem, students will then examine what can be done and what has been done to redress the situation, using the Million Mom March as a reference point. Students will be required to synthesize Web information on the topic in the form of a research paper.
Resource Type: Lesson or Activity
Grade Level: MS

Mixed Blessings: Exploring the Separation of Church and State in Patriotic Poetry
www.nytimes.com/learning/teachers/lessons/20020628friday.html

In this *New York Times* lesson, students will learn about the federal appeals court decision finding the Pledge of Allegiance unconstitutional. They then further investigate the notions of constitutionality and separation between church and state by researching and analyzing another patriotic American poem or song.
Resource Type: Lesson or Activity
Grade Level: MS, HS

Burning Hatred: Discussing the Constitutional Conflict Over Cross Burning
www.nytimes.com/learning/teachers/lessons/20021213friday.html

In this *New York Times* lesson, students examine the constitutionality of various forms of expression; they then take part in a mock trial on the issue of cross burning.
Resource Type: Lesson or Activity
Grade Level: MS, HS

Interpreting Primary Sources
www.digitalhistory.uh.edu/historyonline/us8.cfm

"Digital History" provides brief excerpts from primary sources and statistics and questions regarding the conflict over the ratifying of the Constitution.
Resource Type: Lesson or Activity; Primary Source Collection
Grade Level: HS

Digital History Resource Guides
www.digitalhistory.uh.edu/resource_guides/

"Digital History Resource Guides" provide links to American history Web sites by period and provide historical overviews, readings (online textbook chapter, Reader's Companion), primary source documents (documents, maps, cartoons), teaching resources (chronologies, maps, quizzes), audiovisual resources, and additional resources. They are an excellent and comprehensive teaching resource.
Resource Type: Course Model
Grade Level: HS, College

HistoryTeacher.net: AP United States History Quizzes
www.historyteacher.net/USQuizMainPage.htm

A teacher at the Horace Greeley High School in Chappaqua, New York, has produced a great general site for history teachers that offers AP-level U.S. history quizzes on many different periods and topics.
Resource Type: Test or Quiz
Grade Level: HS

AP United States History DBQs: 1775–1825
www.historyteacher.net/1998DBQsMainPage.htm

These student-created Documents-Based Questions are part of this excellent site.
Resource Type: Lesson or Activity; Primary Source Collection
Grade Level: HS

The American Nation: Internet Activities
www.phschool.com/atschool/TAN/Survey/Teacher_Area/TAN1_T_BK_index.html

Prentice Hall's phschool.com offers Internet activities based on their *The American Nation* textbook chapters. Middle school grades.
Resource Type: Course Model
Grade Level: MS

A History of the United States: Internet Activities and Student Self Test Questions
www.phschool.com/atschool/history_us/Student_Area/HUS_S_BK_index.html

Prentice Hall's phschool.com offers Internet activities and interactive quizzes based on *A History of the United States* textbook chapters. High school level.
Resource Type: Lesson or Activity; Primary Source Collection
Grade Level: HS

EARLY REPUBLIC

*****Lewis and Clark: The National Bicentennial Exhibition
www.lewisandclarkexhibit.org/

The Missouri Historical Society has developed an extensive, award-winning Web site and Web-based curriculum to complement their "Lewis and Clark: The National Bicentennial Exhibition" (see Figure 4.4). Written for grades 4–12, the units focus on nine major themes of

Figure 4.4: Lewis and Clark: The National Bicentennial Exhibition

the exhibit and feature hundreds of primary sources from the exhibit. The curriculum uses the Lewis and Clark expedition as a case study for larger themes, such as Diplomacy, Mapping, Animals, Language, and Trade and Property. It presents both the Euro-American perspective and a particular Native American perspective. The online exhibit has two sections. One is a thematic approach that highlights the content from the main galleries of the exhibit. The other is a map-based journey that follows the expedition and introduces primary sources along the way, including interviews with present-day Native Americans.
Resource Type: Course Model; Multimedia Presentation

****Lewis and Clark
www.pbs.org/lewisandclark

A companion to Ken Burns' PBS film, this site provides background on the world of Lewis and Clark, an archive of their expedition, audio excerpts by historians, a discussion of Native American tribes they encountered, classroom resources, and an interactive story where you lead the expedition.
Resource Type: General Reference; Lesson or Activity

****Lewis and Clark and the Revealing of America
www.loc.gov/exhibits/lewisandclark/lewisandclark.html

This Library of Congress exhibition features the trek of the Corps of Discovery as a culmination in the quest to connect the East and the West by means of a waterway passage. The exhibition's epilogue focuses on the transcontinental railroad, which replaced the search for a direct water route with a "river of steel." The site also features a virtual tour and animations of the cross-country exploration.
Resource Type: General Reference; Multimedia Presentation

****Discovering Lewis and Clark
www.lewis-clark.org

This site has more than 1,400 pages and revolves around a 19-part analysis of the Lewis and Clark expedition by historian Harry Fritz.
Resource Type: General Reference

****The Price of Freedom: Americans at War
http://americanhistory.si.edu/militaryhistory/

This Smithsonian Web site skillfully integrates Flash video and text to examine armed conflicts involving the United States, from the Revolutionary War to the war in Iraq. Each conflict contains a brief video clip, statistical information, and a set of artifacts. There is also a Civil War mystery, an exhibition self-guide, and a teacher's guide. The War of 1812 and Eastern Indian Wars sections contain an introductory movie and short essay on each conflict, as well as historic images and artifacts.
Resource Type: Multimedia Presentation

****They Made America
www.pbs.org/wgbh/theymadeamerica

This engaging American Experience Web site complements a PBS four-part television series and focuses on the lives and accomplishments of twelve American inventors throughout the nation's history. "Who Made America?" is a Flash-generated feature to learn about each inventor and one can view each profile by category, chronologically, geographically. The Web site also contains primary documents, firsthand reports, and a discussion area in the About the Series section. The Revolutionaries section is about four early American innovators "who got the new nation up and going."
Resource Type: Multimedia Presentation

****Tales of the Early Republic
www.earlyrepublic.net

This is an organized collection of essays, original sources, and reference material about the early American Republic. Nearly all of it is about the years 1815–1850.
Resource Type: General Reference

****Alexander Hamilton on the Web
www.isidore-of-seville.com/hamilton

On this site you will find biographies, Hamilton's writings—including the complete *Federalist Papers*—images of Hamilton, reviews and excerpts from some of the recent books about

Hamilton, essays on the Hamilton/Burr duel, and more.
Resource Type: General Reference; Primary Source Collection

****James Madison: His Legacy
www.jmu.edu/madison/center/index.htm

Part of the James Madison Center at James Madison University, this site covers the public life of James Madison through a presentation of primary sources.
Resource Type: Primary Source Collection

****The Triumph of Nationalism: The House Dividing
www.nhc.rtp.nc.us/pds/triumphnationalism/triumphnationalism.htm

The National Humanities Center has produced this site on nationalism and sectionalism in the United States from 1815 to 1850. It features primary sources and the contributions of a dozen high school history teachers.
Resource Type: General Reference; Lesson or Activity

****George Washington Resources
http://etext.virginia.edu/washington/fitzpatrick

This electronic collection of papers by and to George Washington contains a staggering 17,400 letters and documents.
Resource Type: Primary Source Collection

****Thomas Jefferson
www.pbs.org/jefferson

This site accompanies Ken Burn's PBS film on Jefferson. It explores the Enlightenment spirit in Jefferson's words and provides an archive of his most important and controversial writings.
Resource Type: General Reference; Primary Source Collection

****The Thomas Jefferson Digital Archive
http://etext.lib.virginia.edu/jefferson

Provides more than 1,700 texts written by or to Thomas Jefferson. The site also includes a biography of Jefferson and The Jeffersonian Cyclopedia, which organizes more than 9,000 quotes according to theme and other categories.
Resource Type: Primary Source Collection

****Thomas Jefferson Papers
http://memory.loc.gov/ammem/collections/jefferson_papers

From the Library of Congress. The largest collection of its kind, with 27,000 documents.
Resource Type: Primary Source Collection

****Jefferson's Blood
www.pbs.org/wgbh/pages/frontline/shows/jefferson/

This interesting companion site to the PBS *Frontline* program deals with the controversy regarding Thomas Jefferson and his relationship with Sally Hemings, his slave. It contains video clips and historical evidence surrounding the controversy.
Resource Type: General Reference

****Religion in 18th-Century America

www.loc.gov/exhibits/religion/rel02.html

This Library of Congress exhibition contains access to over 200 primary source documents. Provides brief overviews and some pictures.
Resource Type: Primary Source Collection

****Divining America: Religion and the National Culture—17th and 18th Centuries

www.nhc.rtp.nc.us/tserve/divam.htm

TeacherServe is an interactive curriculum enrichment service offering teachers practical help in planning courses and presenting rigorous subject matter to students. "Divining America: Religion and the National Culture—17th and 18th Centuries" features concise essays by scholars designed to help teachers of American history bring their students to a greater understanding of the role religion has played in the development of the United States.
Resource Type: Course Model

****Sullivan-Clinton Campaign of 1779

http://sullivanclinton.com

The Sullivan-Clinton Campaign was the largest expedition ever mounted against the Indians of North America and led to the development of the East Coast, the Erie Canal, and eventual expansion of the United States. This informative Web site is a culmination of recent and historical photographs, texts written by Generals and Native Americans, and contemporary artists responding to this historical event.
Resource Type: General Reference; Primary Source Collection

****America's West—Development & History

www.americanwest.com

Covers westward expansion, Native Americans, Cowboys, Pioneers, Gunslingers, etc. Has images, maps, music, small "research" areas, and even a 3-D tour.
Resource Type: General Reference

****Daniel Webster: Dartmouth's Favorite Son

www.dartmouth.edu/~dwebster/exhibit.html

Features Webster's writings and speeches and contains an image gallery, a short exhibit, and a timeline.
Resource Type: General Reference; Primary Source Collection

***Andrew Jackson Links

http://americanhistory.about.com/od/ageofjackson

About.com has a helpful set of links to Age of Jackson sites.
Resource Type: Links Collection

****The Alexis de Tocqueville Tour: Exploring Democracy in America

www.tocqueville.org

This C-Span site contains biographical information on de Tocqueville, modern references to Tocqueville and his writings, information on Tocqueville's visit to America, famous passages

from *Democracy in America*, writings by Tocqueville and Beaumont from each stop along their journey, and more.
Resource Type: General Reference; Primary Source Collection

****American Studies
http://xroads.virginia.edu

Features a museum for American Studies, cultural maps, ongoing hypertext projects, an electronic classroom, and special features. Check out the section on Tocqueville's America.
Resource Type: General Reference

****History of the Cherokee
http://cherokeehistory.com

A tribal member of the Cherokee Nation of Oklahoma produced this well-organized and informative site. Topics headings: Before the Europeans, First Contacts with Europeans, The New United States, The Removal, and Between Two Fires.
Resource Type: General Reference

****Women and Social Movements in the United States, 1600–2000
http://womhist.binghamton.edu/about.htm

This excellent Web site is a project of the Center for the Historical Study of Women and Gender at the State University of New York at Binghamton. About a fourth of the projects on Women and Social Movements remain freely available; the other projects, in addition to 25,000 pages of primary documents and enhanced searching tools, are available through Alexander Street Press. In the Teacher's Corner, there are 20 comprehensive lesson plans with over 100 lesson ideas and six DBQ units, although some of these materials require a subscription.
Resource Type: Primary Source Collection; Lesson or Activity

****Feature Presentation on Immigration in America
http://lcweb2.loc.gov/ammem/ndlpedu/features/immig/immigration_set1.html

This impressive Library of Congress feature provides an introduction to the study of immigration to the United States. It focuses only on the immigrant groups that arrived in greatest numbers during the nineteenth and early twentieth centuries. The presentation was shaped by the primary sources available in the Library's online collections and several guiding questions.
Resource Type: General Reference; Primary Source Collection

***African-American Mosaic: Abolition
www.loc.gov/exhibits/african/afam005.html

Part of a Library of Congress exhibit, this section includes antislavery petitions and other original sources documenting the struggle to abolish slavery.
Resource Type: General Reference; Primary Source Collection

***Stanton and Anthony Papers Project Online
http://ecssba.rutgers.edu/project.html

The mission of this project is to find and copy all of the Elizabeth Cady Stanton and Susan B. Anthony papers that still survive—manuscripts and printed texts—and make these primary

sources available for research.
Resource Type: Primary Source Collection

***Museum of Women's History: Political Culture and Imagery of American Women Suffrage

www.nmwh.org/exhibits/exhibit_frames.html

Provides a succinct overview of the suffrage movement in words and pictures.
Resource Type: General Reference; Image Collection

Early Republic Lesson Plans, Teacher Guides, Activities, and More

Activity: The Alien and Sedition Acts

http://hti.osu.edu/content/lessonplans/The%20Alien%20and%20Sedition%20Acts.cfm

Students will study the Alien and Sedition Acts in this SCORE lesson plan. Students are encouraged to make connections to present-day politics as well. Recommended for grade 11.
Resource Type: Lesson or Activity
Grade Level: HS

War of 1812 in the News

www.eduref.org/cgi-bin/printlessons.cgi/Virtual/Lessons/Social_Studies/US_History/USH0032.html

A good class or individual exercise for grades 7–9. Students will act as reporters in 1812 and create a newspaper that details the war. The lesson plan only provides one resource link (which sometimes doesn't work), so students must conduct research on their own.
Resource Type: Lesson or Activity
Grade Level: MS, HS

Mount Vernon Educational Resources

www.mountvernon.org

Go to the Learn section and you'll find an online tour of Mount Vernon, lesson plans about George Washington's life and times, an online exhibit about George Washington and slavery, a Reading List, and an Essay and Discussion section.
Resource Type: Lesson or Activity; Virtual Tour
Grade Level: MS, HS

Tribal Truths—Exploring the American-Indian Perspectives Toward the Bicentennial of the Lewis and Clark Expedition

www.nytimes.com/learning/teachers/lessons/20030616monday.html

In this *New York Times* lesson, students research and analyze the interactions of American Indian tribes with Meriwether Lewis and William Clark. Then they stage displays to inform the public about their findings.
Resource Type: Lesson or Activity
Grade Level: MS, HS

Lewis and Clark and the Revealing of America: Lesson Plans
http://memory.loc.gov/ammem/ndlpedu/community/cc_lewisandclark.php

This Library of Congress page provides many helpful online resources, including "Fill Up the Canvas—Rivers of Words: Exploring with Lewis and Clark," a Learning Page Activity in which students experience Lewis and Clark's journey westward through words, images, maps and other documents. In "American Treasures: Lewis and Clark," visitors examine maps and manuscripts documenting the Lewis and Clark expedition. There are also lesson plans, which debate the controversies inherent in conservation programs and the historical perspectives of nature and the environment.
Resource Type: Lesson or Activity
Grade Level: HS

Lewis and Clark: Classroom Resources
www.pbs.org/lewisandclark/class/idx_les.html

The 17 Lewis and Clark lesson plans on this page offer a wide array of classroom activities. Created by PBS, the activities address all parts of the famous expedition.
Resource Type: Lesson or Activity
Grade Level: MS

Lewis and Clark: Lesson Plan
http://school.discovery.com/lessonplans/programs/lewisclark

In this lesson plan, students answer the questions and compare their ideas to archaeological work.
Resource Type: Lesson or Activity
Grade Level: MS

Lewis and Clark: A Legacy to Remember
www.nationalgeographic.com/xpeditions/lessons/04/g68/remember.html

In this National Geographic lesson plan, students design a memorial that illustrates the legacy of the expedition from a geographic perspective.
Resource Type: Lesson or Activity
Grade Level: MS

The Gilder Lehrman Institute Modules in American History: The New Nation, Jeffersonian Era, Jacksonian Era
www.gilderlehrman.org/teachers/module3/index.html

The Gilder Lehrman Institute offers quality educational materials, including teaching modules on major topics in American history. Each module includes: a succinct historical overview; learning tools including lesson plans, quizzes, and activities; recommended documents, films, and historic images . These modules were prepared by Steven Mintz, the John and Rebecca Moores Professor of History and the Director of the American Cultures Program at the University of Houston. Other helpful Institute online sources include include American History Quizzes, Letters from America's Wars, Featured Documents for your Classroom, and Primary Source Documents from the Collection.

Resource Type: Course Model
Grade Level: HS

Jeffersonian Democracy: Multiple Choice Quiz, Fill-in-the-Blank, Flashcards, American History Glossary, and an American History Appendix

http://wps.ablongman.com/long_carnes_an_11/0,7137,250964-,00.html

The Student Resources section of *The American Nation* companion Web site features introductions to chapters, interactive quizzes, flashcards, Web links, an American History Glossary, and an American History Appendix.
Resource Type: Course Model
Grade Level: HS

Thomas Jefferson: Lesson Plan

http://school.discovery.com/lessonplans/programs/realthomasjefferson

In this lesson plan, students will learn that Thomas Jefferson was accomplished in many spheres of human activity. Grades 6–8.
Resource Type: Lesson or Activity
Grade Level: MS

HistoryTeacher.net: AP United States History Quizzes

www.historyteacher.net/USQuizMainPage.htm

A teacher at the Horace Greeley High School in Chappaqua, New York, has produced a great general site for history teachers that offers AP-level U.S. history quizzes on many different periods and topics.
Resource Type: Test or Quiz
Grade Level: HS

Toward a National Republic: Multiple Choice Quiz, Fill-in-the-Blank, Flashcards, American History Glossary, American History Appendix

http://wps.ablongman.com/long_carnes_an_11/0,7137,251077-,00.html

The Student Resources section of *The American Nation* companion Web site features introductions to chapters, interactive quizzes, flashcards, Web links, an American History Glossary, and an American History Appendix.
Resource Type: Course Model
Grade Level: HS

Interpreting Primary Sources

www.digitalhistory.uh.edu/historyonline/handouts.cfm

"Digital History" provides brief excerpts from primary sources and statistics and questions to think about. Check out Federalists and Jeffersonians; War of 1812; Jacksonian Democracy; Indian Removal; Political Battles of the Jacksonian Era; An Industrializing Nation; and Religion and Social Reform.
Resource Type: Lesson or Activity; Primary Source Collection
Grade Level: HS

The American People: Consolidating the Revolution
http://wps.ablongman.com/long_nash_ap_6/0,7361,592970-,00.html

PowerPoint presentation on the early American republic as part of the online companion to *The American People*. Click PowerPoint Presentations and then Chapter 7.
Resource Type: Multimedia Presentation
Grade Level: HS

The American People: Creating a Nation
http://wps.ablongman.com/long_nash_ap_6/0,7361,592970-,00.html

PowerPoint presentation on the young American nation as part of the online companion to *The American People*. Click PowerPoint Presentations and then Chapter 8.
Resource Type: Multimedia Presentation
Grade Level: HS

The American People: Society and Politics in the Early Republic
http://wps.ablongman.com/long_nash_ap_6/0,7361,592970-,00.html

PowerPoint presentation as part of the online companion to *The American People*. Click PowerPoint Presentations and then Chapter 9.
Resource Type: Multimedia Presentation
Grade Level: HS

The American People: Economic Transformations in the Northeast and the old Northwest
http://wps.ablongman.com/long_nash_ap_6/0,7361,592970-,00.html

PowerPoint presentation on economic growth in the early American republic as part of the online companion to The American People. Click PowerPoint Presentations and then Chapter 10.
Resource Type: Multimedia Presentation
Grade Level: HS

Slavery: How Did the [British] Abolition Acts of 1807 and 1833 Affect Slavery?
www.learningcurve.gov.uk/snapshots/snapshot27/snapshot27.htm

In 1807, the British trade in slaves from Africa was abolished. Students use primary source photos and documents at the British National Archive site to examine this event and its impact on the United States, the Americas, and Africa.
Resource Type: Lesson or Activity
Grade Level: HS

Old Sturbridge Village: Teacher Resources
www.osv.org

This site provides information about everyday life in New England during the early nineteenth century. Old Sturbridge Visitor Articles is a searchable archive of articles from the Village's quarterly magazine. Look under Education and Curriculum Plans.
Resource Type: Course Model
Grade Level: LS, MS, HS

Digital History Resource Guides
www.digitalhistory.uh.edu/resource_guides

"Digital History Resource Guides" provides links to American history Web sites by period and provide historical overviews, readings (online textbook chapter, Reader's Companion), primary source documents (documents, maps, cartoons), teaching resources (chronologies, maps, quizzes), audiovisual resources, and additional resources. The Guides are an excellent and comprehensive teaching resource.
Resource Type: Course Model
Grade Level: HS, College

AP United States History DBQs: 1775–1825
www.historyteacher.net/1998DBQsMainPage.htm

These student-created Documents-Based Questions are part of this excellent site.
Resource Type: Lesson or Activity; Primary Source Collection
Grade Level: HS

AP United States History DBQs: 1810–1860
www.historyteacher.net/2002DBQsMainPage.htm

These student-created Documents-Based Questions are part of this excellent site.
Resource Type: Lesson or Activity; Primary Source Collection
Grade Level: HS

Missouri Compromise: Blank Map
http://wps.ablongman.com/long_nash_ap_6/0,7361,592970-,00.html

This companion Web site to *The American People* offers blank maps related to various topics in American history. The maps can be printed or placed in a PowerPoint presentation.
Resource Type: Map
Grade Level: HS

U.S. in the 1810s: Blank Map
http://wps.ablongman.com/long_nash_ap_6/0,7361,592970-,00.html

This companion Web site to *The American People* offers blank maps related to various topics in American history. The maps can be printed or placed in a PowerPoint presentation.
Resource Type: Map
Grade Level: HS

Jacksonian Democracy: Multiple Choice Quiz, Fill-in-the-Blank, Flashcards, American History Glossary, and an American History Appendix
http://wps.ablongman.com/long_carnes_an_11/0,7137,251134-,00.html

The Student Resources section of *The American Nation* companion Web site features introductions to chapters, interactive quizzes, flashcards, Web links, an American History Glossary, and an American History Appendix
Resource Type: Course Model
Grade Level: HS

Democracy in America Teaching Modules
www.c-span.org/classroom/tocqueville

C-Span.org offers NCSS strands for teaching about de Tocqueville.
Resource Type: Course Model
Grade Level: HS

Digital History Lesson Plan: Indian Removal
www.digitalhistory.uh.edu/historyonline/us12.cfm

Students act as journalists reporting on the Indian Removal Act. They visit designated Web sites and write factual articles about the developments.
Resource Type: Lesson or Activity
Grade Level: HS

Course Models: Reform Movements of the 1830s
www.history.ctaponline.org/center/hsscm/index.cfm?Page_Key=1766

Part of the California History-Social Science content standards and annotated course, this site includes excellent background information, focus questions, pupil activities and handouts, an assessment, and references to books, articles, Web sites, literature, audiovisual programs, and a historic site.
Resource Type: Course Model
Grade Level: MS

The Making of Middle Class America: Multiple Choice Quiz, Fill-in-the-Blank, Flashcards, American History Glossary, and an American History Appendix
http://wps.ablongman.com/long_carnes_an_11/0,7137,251191-,00.html

The Student Resources section of *The American Nation* companion Web site features introductions to chapters, interactive quizzes, flashcards, Web links, an American History Glossary, and an American History Appendix.
Resource Type: Course Model
Grade Level: HS

A Democratic Culture: Multiple Choice Quiz, Fill-in-the-Blank, Flashcards, American History Glossary, and an American History Appendix
http://wps.ablongman.com/long_carnes_an_11/0,7137,251245-,00.html

The Student Resources section of *The American Nation* companion Web site features introductions to chapters, interactive quizzes, flashcards, Web links, an American History Glossary, and an American History Appendix.
Resource Type: Course Model
Grade Level: HS

U.S. Women's History: Lesson Ideas and Document Based Questions
http://womhist.binghamton.edu/teacher/women.htm

The Center for the Historical Study of Women and Gender at the State University of New York at Binghamton offers lesson plans, Documents-Based Questions, links, and more on American women's history.

Resource Type: Lesson or Activity;
Grade Level: HS

National Growing Pains: Multiple Choice Quiz, Fill-in-the-Blank, Flashcards, American History Glossary, and an American History Appendix
http://wps.ablongman.com/long_carnes_an_11/0,7137,251022-,00.html

The Student Resources section of *The American Nation* companion Web site features introductions to chapters, interactive quizzes, flashcards, Web links, an American History Glossary, and an American History Appendix
Resource Type: Course Model
Grade Level: HS

The American People: Shaping America in the Antebellum Age
http://wps.ablongman.com/long_nash_ap_6/0,7361,592970-,00.html

PowerPoint presentation on Religion and Reform as part of the online companion to *The American People*. Click PowerPoint Presentations and then Chapter 12.
Resource Type: Multimedia Presentation
Grade Level: HS

Pre-Civil War Reform Quiz
www.digitalhistory.uh.edu/modules/precivilwar/quiz.cfm

Multiple choice questions from "Digital History."
Resource Type: Test or Quiz
Grade Level: MS

Early Reformers of the 1800s Game
www.quia.com/jg/66217.html

Four Quia-based activities with a list of terms.
Resource Type: Game
Grade Level: MS

Early National Era Maps
www.digitalhistory.uh.edu/maps/maps.cfm

Links from "Digital History."
Resource Type: Map
Grade Level: HS

The American Nation: Internet Activities
www.phschool.com/atschool/TAN/Survey/Teacher_Area/TAN1_T_BK_index.html

Prentice Hall's phschool.com offers Internet activities based on their *The American Nation* textbook chapters. Middle school grades.
Resource Type: Lesson or Activity
Grade Level: MS

Animated Map of U.S. Expansion

www.ac.wwu.edu/%7Estephan/48states.html

This animated map provides a quick and easy visual illustration of westward expansion.

Resource Type: Map
Grade Level: MS

THE SOUTH AND SLAVERY

****Documenting the American South

http://docsouth.unc.edu/

"Documenting the American South" (DAS) is an impressive collection of sources by the University of North Carolina on Southern history, literature and culture from the Colonial period through the first decades of the twentieth century (see Figure 4.5). DAS supplies teachers,

Figure 4.5: Documenting the American South

PRIMARY RESOURCES FOR THE STUDY OF SOUTHERN HISTORY, LITERATURE, AND CULTURE

Documenting the American South (DocSouth) is a digital publishing initiative that provides Internet access to texts, images, and audio files related to southern history, literature, and culture. Currently DocSouth includes ten thematic collections of books, diaries, posters, artifacts, letters, oral history interviews, and songs.

The University Library of the University of North Carolina at Chapel Hill sponsors *Documenting the American South*, and the texts and materials come primarily from its southern holdings. The UNC University Library is committed to the long-term availability of these collections and their online records. An editorial board guides development of this digital library.

Contact Us | FAQ | Home | UNC University Library | University of North Carolina at Chapel Hill

© Copyright 2004 by the University Library, The University of North Carolina at Chapel Hill, all rights reserved
Copyright / Usage Statement
URL: http://docsouth.unc.edu/index.html
Last updated March 09, 2007

students, and researchers with a wide range of titles they can use for reference, studying, teaching, and research. Currently, DAS includes 10 thematic collections of primary sources for the study of Southern history, literature, and culture including Oral Histories of the American South, True and Candid Compositions: Antebellum Writings, First-Person Narratives of the American South, and North American Slave Narratives.

Resource Type: Primary Source Collection

****The Valley of the Shadow

http://valley.vcdh.virginia.edu/

"The Valley of the Shadow" depicts two communities—one Northern and one Southern—through the experience of the American Civil War (see Figure 4.6). The project focuses on Augusta County, Virginia, and Franklin County, Pennsylvania, presenting a hypermedia archive of thousands of sources that creates a social history of the coming, fighting, and aftermath of the Civil War. Those sources include newspapers, letters, diaries, photographs, maps, church records, population census, agricultural census, and military records. Students can explore the conflict and write their own histories or reconstruct the life stories of women, African Americans, farmers, politicians, soldiers, and families. The project is intended for secondary schools, community colleges, libraries, and universities. A must-see.

Resource Type: Primary Source Collection; Lesson or Activity

Figure 4.6: The Valley of the Shadow

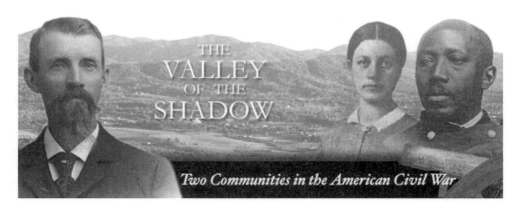

The Valley Project details life in two American communities, one Northern and one Southern, from the time of John Brown's Raid through the era of Reconstruction. In this digital archive you may explore thousands of original letters and diaries, newspapers and speeches, census and church records, left by men and women in Augusta County, Virginia, and Franklin County, Pennsylvania. Giving voice to hundreds of individual people, the Valley Project tells forgotten stories of life during the era of the Civil War.

Enter the Valley Archive

Copyright 1993-2007, All Rights Reserved Edward L. Ayers

****Africans in America: Judgment Day, 1831–1865
www.pbs.org/wgbh/aia/part4/title.html

Part of PBS's "African American Journey" site, here you'll find part one of a rich collection of resources—images, documents, stories, biographies, and commentaries—on the experience of slavery in America. There is also a useful teacher's guide and activities for students. There are three other parts to explore: The Terrible Transformation: 1450–1750, Revolution: 1750–1805, and Brotherly Love: 1791–1831.
Resource Type: General Reference; Lesson or Activity

****The African-American Mosaic Exhibition
http://lcweb.loc.gov/exhibits/african/intro.html

A Library of Congress resource guide for the study of Black History and Culture, the Mosaic explores colonization, abolition, migration, and the WPA. Included are maps, charts, primary sources, and background information.
Resource Type: Primary Source Collection; General Reference

****The Frederick Douglass Papers at the Library of Congress
http://memory.loc.gov/ammem/doughtml/doughome.html

The Frederick Douglass Papers at the Library of Congress, available on the "American Memory" Web site, contain approximately 7,400 items (38,000 images) relating to Douglass's life as an escaped slave, abolitionist, editor, orator, and public servant. The impressive collection of papers consist of correspondence, speeches and articles by Douglass and his contemporaries, a draft of his autobiography, financial and legal papers, scrapbooks, and miscellaneous items. Topics include politics, emancipation, racial prejudice, women's suffrage, and prison reform. Included are correspondences with Susan B. Anthony, William Lloyd Garrison, Horace Greeley, Grover Cleveland, Benjamin Harrison, and others.
Resource Type: Primary Source Collection

****American Slave Narratives
http://xroads.virginia.edu/%7EHYPER/wpa/wpahome.html

Over 2,000 former slaves, most born in the last years of the slave regime or during the Civil War, provide firsthand accounts of their experiences on plantations, in cities, and on small farms. At this Web site you can read a sample of these narratives and see some photographs taken at the time of the interviews. There is an annotated list of narratives, sound files, and related resources. Part of the American Hypertext Workshop at the University of Virginia.
Resource Type: Primary Source Collection

****John Brown's Holy War
www.pbs.org/wgbh/amex/brown/index.html

Special features of this PBS companion site include a QuickTime VR tour of the farmhouse where John Brown's army gathered before the raid on Harpers Ferry. There are also extended interviews with program participants and excerpts from letters and speeches, as well as an editorial list of books, articles, and Web sites relating to the program topic.
Resource Type: General Reference; Primary Source Collection

****The Underground Railroad
www.nationalgeographic.com/features/99/railroad/

An informative and engaging presentation on the Underground Railroad by National Geographic.
Resource Type: Multimedia Presentation

****The Abolition Movement
www.loc.gov/exhibits/african/afam005.html

This Library of Congress site has a plentiful amount of primary source documents and an introduction to the abolitionist movement in America.
Resource Type: Primary Source Collection; General Reference

****Exploring Amistad
http://academic.sun.ac.za/forlang/bergman/real/amistad/history/msp/main_wel.htm

This site explores the famous slave ship revolt and offers a detailed narrative, time lines, teaching guides, a resource collection, and more.
Resource Type: General Reference

****Frederick Law Olmsted: A Journey in the Seaboard States
http://odur.let.rug.nl/%7Eusa/D/1851-1875/olmsted/jourxx.htm

Beginning in 1856, Olmstead traveled for 14 months in the South as a journalist examining plantation life. Many modern historians consider his work one of the best contemporary descriptions of plantation slavery.
Resource Type: Primary Source Collection

***Slave Voices
http://scriptorium.lib.duke.edu/slavery/

Duke University Collections offers this useful source for documents on slave life from the late eighteenth century through the nineteenth century.
Resource Type: Primary Source Collection

*** African-American Mosaic: Abolition
http://lcweb.loc.gov/exhibits/african/afam005.html

Part of an interesting Library of Congress exhibit, this section includes antislavery petitions and other original sources documenting the struggle to abolish slavery.
Resource Type: Primary Source Collection

The South and Slavery Lesson Plans, Teacher Guides, Activities, and More

Africans in America: Teachers Guide
www.pbs.org/wgbh/aia/tguide/

A four-part PBS lesson plan that covers slavery throughout American history. Lessons make good use of primary sources.
Resource Type: Lesson or Activity
Grade Level: HS

John Brown's Holy War: A Teachers Guide
www.pbs.org/wgbh/aia/tguide/

Presented by PBS, this lesson plan puts emphasis on class discussion and debate. There are several debate questions, as well as an activities section of the guide. Activities include research projects and putting John Brown on trial.
Resource Type: Lesson or Activity
Grade Level: HS

Lesson Plan: Families in Bondage
http://edsitement.neh.gov/view_lesson_plan.asp?id=280

This two-part EDSITEment lesson plan draws on letters written by African Americans in slavery and by free blacks to loved ones still in bondage, singling out a few among the many slave experiences to offer students a glimpse into slavery and its effects on African American family life. Grades 9–12.
Resource Type: Lesson or Activity
Grade Level: HS

Lesson Plan: Attitudes Toward Emancipation
http://edsitement.neh.gov/view_lesson_plan.asp?id=290

This lesson plan, provided by EDSITEment, examines the Emancipation Proclamation and the factors that inspired its creation. Special attention is also paid to newspaper opinion articles of the time. Please note: The material in this lesson plan may contain offensive language and racial stereotypes. EDSITEment asks teachers to weigh the benefits and drawbacks of presenting this to students. Grades 9–12.
Resource Type: Lesson or Activity
Grade Level: HS

Southern Defense of Slavery
www.vcdh.virginia.edu/teaching/vclassroom/proslaveinst.html

This lesson plan uses resources from the outstanding "The Valley of the Shadow" Web site. Students can examine documents—newspaper articles in particular—in order to understand why many Southerners supported slavery. Recommended for grades 9–12.
Resource Type: Lesson or Activity
Grade Level: HS

Attitudes about Slavery in Franklin County, Pennsylvania
www.vcdh.virginia.edu/teaching/vclassroom/Northernatt.html

Students can read transcriptions of articles from two Franklin County, Pennsylvania, newspapers in order to compare the county's Republican and Democratic Parties' positions on slavery. Lesson plan provided by "The Valley of the Shadow."
Resource Type: Lesson or Activity
Grade Level: HS

Teaching with Documents Lesson Plan: The Amistad Case
www.archives.gov/digital_classroom/lessons/amistad_case/amistad_case.html

Part of the NARA site, this lesson plan focuses on the *Amistad*. The lesson plan contains five online documents and a teacher guideline.
Resource Type: Lesson or Activity
Grade Level: HS

Stateside Slavery: Addressing Slavery's Past on This Side of the Atlantic
www.nytimes.com/learning/teachers/lessons/20030714monday.html

In this lesson, students learn about President Bush's July 8, 2003 speech about slavery on Gorée Island, Senegal. They then research and conduct a teach-in on slavery issues in U.S. history.
Resource Type: Lesson or Activity
Grade Level: MS, HS

"Been Here So Long" Lesson Plans
www.newdeal.feri.org/asn/lesson00.htm

Created by the New Deal Network, these three lessons teach students about slavery through the use of authentic first-person narratives. Students are asked to read, analyze, and compare the different narratives and resources provided.
Resource Type: Lesson or Activity
Grade Level: MS

OUSD Lesson Plan: Frederick Douglas
http://urbandreams.ousd.k12.ca.us/lessonplans/frederickdouglass/index.html

This Oakland Unified School District lesson plan is designed for grade 9 students. You'll be impressed with the array of teaching ideas, lesson templates, handouts, worksheets, and tech integration. The goal of the lesson is to encourage students to read purposefully, learn reading strategies, and develop expository writing strategies for improving critical thinking skills. The themes of Social Justice, Social Reconciliation, and Social Transformation play a central role in the lessons.
Resource Type: Lesson or Activity
Grade Level: HS

The Gilder Lehrman Institute Modules in American History: Slavery
http://www.gilderlehrman.org/teachers/module7/index.html

The Gilder Lehrman Institute offers quality educational materials, including teaching modules on major topics in American history. Each module includes: a succinct historical overview; learning tools, including lesson plans, quizzes, and activities; and recommended documents, films, and historic images . These modules were prepared by Steven Mintz, the John and Rebecca Moores Professor of History and the Director of the American Cultures Program at the University of Houston. Other helpful Institute online sources include include American History Quizzes, Letters from America's Wars, Featured Documents for your Classroom, and Primary Source Documents from the Collection.
Resource Type: Course Model
Grade Level: HS

Interpreting Primary Sources: Slavery
www.digitalhistory.uh.edu/historyonline/us16.cfm

"Digital History" provides brief excerpts from primary sources and statistics on slavery, as well as questions to think about.
Resource Type: Lesson or Activity; Primary Source Collection
Grade Level: HS

The Atlantic Slave Trade and Slave Life in the Americas
http://hitchcock.itc.virginia.edu/Slavery/

This site, by the Virginia Foundation for the Humanities and the Digital Media Lab at the University of Virginia Library, provides hundreds of images from a wide range of sources, most of them dating from the period of slavery. This collection is envisioned as a tool and a resource that can be used by teachers, researchers, students, and the general public.
Resource Type: Image Collection
Grade Level: HS

Expansion and Slavery: Multiple Choice Quiz, Fill-in-the-Blank, Flashcards, American History Glossary, American History Appendix
http://wps.ablongman.com/long_carnes_an_11/0,7137,251303-,00.html

The Student Resources section of *The American Nation* companion Web site features introductions to chapters, interactive quizzes, flashcards, Web links, an American History Glossary, and an American History Appendix.
Resource Type: Course Model
Grade Level: HS

Digital History Resource Guides
www.digitalhistory.uh.edu/resource_guides/

"Digital History Resource Guides" provide links to American history Web sites by period and provide historical overviews, readings (online textbook chapter, Reader's Companion), primary source documents (documents, maps, cartoons), teaching resources (chronologies, maps, quizzes), audiovisual resources, and additional resources. The Guides are an excellent and comprehensive teaching resource.
Resource Type: Course Model
Grade Level: HS, College

HistoryTeacher.net: AP United States History Quizzes
www.historyteacher.net/USQuizMainPage.htm

A teacher at the Horace Greeley High School in Chappaqua, New York, has produced a great general site for history teachers that offers AP-level U.S. history quizzes on many different periods and topics.
Resource Type: Test or Quiz
Grade Level: HS

AP United States History DBQs: 1810–1860
www.historyteacher.net/2002DBQsMainPage.htm

These student-created Documents-Based Questions are part of the excellent historyteacher.net site.

Resource Type: Lesson or Activity; Primary Source Collection
Grade Level: HS

The American People: Slavery and the Old South
http://wps.ablongman.com/long_nash_ap_6/0,7361,592970-,00.html

PowerPoint presentation on the South and Slavery as part of the online companion to *The American People*. Click PowerPoint Presentations and then Chapter 11.
Resource Type: Multimedia Presentation
Grade Level: HS

Slavery Fact Sheets
www.digitalhistory.uh.edu/historyonline/slav_fact.cfm

"Digital History" offers a concise but informative overview of slavery in America. Also myths versus facts.
Resource Type: Lesson or Activity
Grade Level: HS

Burning Hatred: Discussing the Constitutional Conflict Over Cross Burning
www.nytimes.com/learning/teachers/lessons/20021213friday.html

In this *New York Times* lesson, students examine the constitutionality of various forms of expression; they then take part in a mock trial on the issue of cross burning.
Resource Type: Lesson or Activity
Grade Level: MS, HS

The South: Blank Map
http://wps.ablongman.com/long_nash_ap_6/0,7361,592970-,00.html

This companion Web site to *The American People* offers blank maps related to various topics in American history. The maps can be printed or placed in a PowerPoint presentation. Go to Blank Maps for Quizzes.
Resource Type: Map
Grade Level: HS

The American Nation: Internet Activities
www.phschool.com/atschool/TAN/Survey/Teacher_Area/TAN1_T_BK_index.html

Prentice Hall's phschool.com offers Internet activities based on their *The American Nation* textbook chapters. Middle school grades.
Resource Type: Lesson or Activity; Test or Quiz
Grade Level: MS

A History of the United States: Internet Activities and Student Self Test Questions
www.phschool.com/atschool/history_us/Student_Area/HUS_S_BK_index.html

Prentice Hall's phschool.com offers Internet activities and interactive quizzes based on *A History of the United States* textbook chapters. High school level.
Resource Type: Lesson or Activity; Test or Quiz
Grade Level: HS

CHAPTER 5

The Civil War—The Great Depression (1860s–1939)

CIVIL WAR

*****The Valley of the Shadow
http://valley.vcdh.virginia.edu/

"The Valley of the Shadow" depicts two communities, one Northern and one Southern, through the experience of the American Civil War. The project focuses on Augusta County, Virginia and Franklin County, Pennsylvania, and creates a social history of the coming, fighting, and aftermath of the Civil War. The project is a hypermedia archive of thousands of sources for the period before, during, and after the Civil War for Augusta County, Virginia, and Franklin County, Pennsylvania. Those sources include newspapers, letters, diaries, photographs, maps, church records, population census, agricultural census, and military records. Students can explore the conflict and write their own histories, or reconstruct the life stories of women, African Americans, farmers, politicians, soldiers, and families. The project is intended for secondary schools, community colleges, libraries, and universities. A must-see.
Resource Type: Primary Source Collection; Course Model

****The Price of Freedom: Americans at War
http://americanhistory.si.edu/militaryhistory/

This Smithsonian Web site skillfully integrates Flash video and text to examine armed conflicts involving the United States from the Revolutionary War to the war in Iraq. Each conflict contains a brief video clip, statistical information, and a set of artifacts. There is also a Civil War mystery, an exhibition self-guide, and a teacher's guide. The World War I section contains a short essay on the conflict as well as historic images and artifacts.
Resource Type: Multimedia Presentation

****U.S. Civil War Center
www.cwc.lsu.edu/

Produced by Louisiana State University, the site is not a museum or library but serves to locate, index, and make available Civil War data on the Internet. A great place to begin Web

research; start with the Civil War Index.
Resource Type: General Reference; Links Collection

****The American Civil War Homepage
http://sunsite.utk.edu/civil-war/

This site is maintained by Dr. George H. Hoemann at the University of Tennessee. It has useful information including timelines, descriptions of battles (state by state), letters, documents, and links.
Resource Type: General Reference

****Civil War and Reconstruction, 1861–1877
http://lcweb2.loc.gov/ammem/ndlpedu/features/timeline/civilwar/civilwar.html

This Library of Congress exhibition contains succinct overviews of several aspects of the Civil War and Reconstruction and features primary sources, maps, and images.
Resource Type: General Reference; Primary Source Collection

****Selected Civil War Photographs
http://memory.loc.gov/ammem/cwphtml/cwphome.html

There are over a thousand Civil War photographs for you to explore at this Library of Congress site. Most are scenes of military personnel, preparations for battle, and battle aftereffects.
Resource Type: Primary Source Collection; Image Collection

****Civil War Resources from the VMI Archives
www.vmi.edu/archives/cwsource.html

This site highlights collections of the Virginia Military Institute, including manuscripts and battle resource guides. Special topics include VMI's Civil War generals, Stonewall Jackson's resources, a war chronology, Robert E. Lee's funeral, and more (see Figure 5.1).
Resource Type: General Reference; Primary Source Collection

****Great American History
http://members.tripod.com/~greatamericanhistory/index.html

This is a diverse site on the Civil War that provides educational materials and research services. Some of the unconventional topics covered are religious revivalism in the armies, unsung heroes, and Lincoln's belief in God.
Resource Type: General Reference

****Civil War Interactive
www.civilwarinteractive.com/

"Civil War Interactive" is a daily news source for Civil War related news, events, reviews, etc. and is free. The News Archives can be browsed by date, by state, or by keyword. LinkCentral features Web sites rated as "5-Star" or "Editors Choice." The new Book Nook focuses on books that are published within the last 6 months. An all-new section allows you to play Civil War–related games and puzzles online and one of the most requested features is the Trivia Archives.
Resource Type: General Reference

Figure 5.1: Civil War Resources from the VMI Archives

Virginia Military Institute Archives

Home   Civil War & Jackson   Genealogy & Alumni   Manuscripts   Photos   Oral History   VMI Records   Exhibits   FAQs   Contact Us   Search

Civil War Resources

Featuring Full-Text Online

Popular Research Topics

Stonewall Jackson Resources

VMI's Civil War Generals

Battle of New Market & the "Ghost Cadet"

VMI's Civil War Alumni

Wartime Cadet Life

Gen. David Hunter in the Shenandoah Valley

Execution of John Brown

Funeral of Gen. Robert E. Lee

VMI's Civil War Chronology

Books about VMI History

VMI Archives

Letters & Diaries

Civil War Manuscripts Full Text Online

Battles & Units Guide

Photographs

Online Photos Database

VMI Official Records

Superintendent's Letters

Cadet Orders

Board of Visitors Minutes

Reports

Other Useful Resources

Civil War & Genealogy on the Web

© VMI Archives Lexington, VA 24450

****Abraham Lincoln Papers

http://memory.loc.gov/ammem/alhtml/malhome.html

The complete "Abraham Lincoln Papers" at the Library of Congress consists of approximately 20,000 documents. The impressive collection is organized into three "General Correspondence" series which include incoming and outgoing correspondence and enclosures, drafts of speeches, and notes and printed material. Most of the 20,000 items are from the 1850s through Lincoln's presidential years. Excellent site for a research project. There are two special presentations: Emancipation Proclamation provides an introduction to the Emancipation Proclamation as well as a timeline and four related primary sources. Assassination of President Lincoln provides an introduction, timeline, and photo gallery that documents the assassination of the nation's 16th President (1860–1865).

Resource Type: Primary Source Collection

****Abraham Lincoln Online

http://showcase.netins.net/web/creative/lincoln.html

"Abraham Lincoln Online" brings you news about Lincoln books, speeches and writings, historic places, and events. Sections include This Week in History, Today in Lincoln's Life, Lincoln News Highlights, and Photo Tours of Lincoln Places. Find out about Lincoln events, new books about Lincoln, and more.

Resource Type: General Reference

****Lincoln/Net
http://lincoln.lib.niu.edu/

"Lincoln/Net" provides historical materials from Abraham Lincoln's Illinois years, including Lincoln's writings and speeches, as well as other materials illuminating antebellum Illinois. This site includes helpful interpretive materials, featuring a brief Lincoln biography and discussions of eight major historical themes. "Lincoln/Net" provides over 15 million words of primary source materials, over 1,500 images, video commentary on various aspects of Lincoln's life by historians and, and even a sound archive. "Lincoln/Net" also offers lesson plans that utilize the primary source documents found in the "Lincoln/Net" database.
Resource Type: Primary Source Collection

****Assassination of President Lincoln
http://memory.loc.gov/ammem/alhtml/alrintr.html

This Library of Congress site provides an introduction, timeline, and photo gallery to document the assassination of the nation's 16th President.
Resource Type: General Reference; Image Collection

****Mr. Lincoln's White House (and affiliated sites)
http://mrlincolnswhitehouse.org/

This Lincoln Institute site describes the White House and nearby Washington, and profiles Lincoln family members, Cabinet officers and Vice Presidents, members of Congress, generals, and others. "Mr. Lincoln and Freedom," a related site, details the progress of Mr. Lincoln's opposition to slavery from his years in the Illinois State Legislature to the passage of the 13th Amendment abolishing slavery. Other related sites include: "Mr. Lincoln and Friends," which reviews the many men and a few women whose friendships helped determine Mr. Lincoln's political progress and success in the state capital in Springfield, Illinois and the nation's capital in Washington, D.C.; "Mr. Lincoln and the Founders," which examines the impact of the Founders, the Declaration of Independence, and the Constitution on Mr. Lincoln's life, political thinking and political actions in the 1850s and 1860s; and "Mr. Lincoln and New York," which appraises how the center of political, media, and economic power in 19th century America interacted with, supported, and tormented Mr. Lincoln both before and during his Presidency.
Resource Type: General Reference

****Abraham Lincoln Presidential Library & Museum
www.alplm-library.com/home.html

The official Web site of the Abraham Lincoln Presidential Library and Museum, this site offers an interactive timeline of Abraham Lincoln's life, a Civil War soldier's database, and various articles related to Lincoln.
Resource Type: General Reference

****Abraham Lincoln Research Center
http://members.aol.com/RVSNorton/Lincoln2.html

This teacher-produced site has three main sections: Abraham Lincoln Research Site, Abraham Lincoln's Assassination, and the Mary Todd Lincoln Research Site. Offers a clear and

engaging mix of text, images, and primary sources.
Resource Type: Lesson or Activity

****Harper's Weekly Reports, 1857–1874
http://blackhistory.harpweek.com/

For over a quarter of a century, *Harper's Weekly* had an extensive national newspaper audience. Materials from this important historical source are presented in order to give a true historical picture of the leading nineteenth-century newspaper's view of black Americans.
Resource Type: Primary Source Collection

****Racial Satire and the Civil War
http://xroads.virginia.edu/~cap/scartoons/cartoons.html

Presented by the University of Virginia, this site is a case study that explores racial caricature in editorial cartoons at the time of Lincoln.
Resource Type: Primary Source Collection

****The Battle of Antietam
www.npr.org/templates/story/story.php?storyId=1150149

This NPR audio clip features the views of renowned historian James McPherson, who argues that Antietam was a turning point in the war.
Resource Type: Multimedia

****The History Place—U.S. Civil War 1861–1865
www.historyplace.com/civilwar/

"The History Place" adopts a "fact-based, common sense approach" to the presentation of the history and is owned and published by author Philip Gavin. Here you'll find a Lincoln timeline, biographies, resumes of famous battles and events, photos, and a chronology.
Resource Type: General Reference

****Civil War Women
http://scriptorium.lib.duke.edu/collections/civil-war-women.html

Duke University uses diaries and papers to profile three Civil War-era women.
Resource Type: Primary Source Collection

Civil War Lesson Plans, Teacher Guides, Activities, and More

The Crisis at Fort Sumter
www.tulane.edu/~sumter/

"Crisis at Fort Sumter" is an interactive historical simulation and decision-making program. Using text, images, and sound, it reconstructs the dilemmas of policy formation and decision-making in the period between Abraham Lincoln's election in November 1860 and the battle of Fort Sumter in April 1861.
Resource Type: Lesson or Activity
Grade Level: HS

Teaching with Documents: Civil War and Reconstruction
www.archives.gov/education/lessons/index.html

The NARA has compiled many Civil War primary sources, including several sound files of interviews with the last surviving confederate veteran. Lesson plans and activity worksheets are at the bottom of the page and can be applied to any visual document.
Resource Type: Lesson or Activity; Primary Source Collection
Grade Level: HS

The Mathew Brady Bunch: Civil War Newspapers
http://memory.loc.gov/learn/lessons/98/brady/home.html

Designed for use toward the end of a unit on the Civil War, this lesson allows students to analyze photographs and evaluate how they can influence understanding of and attitudes about the war. Much of the lesson is spent discussing how to use photographic primary sources; students learn that photographers often manipulated the scenes they were capturing and discuss how these sources should therefore be utilized. Materials are from the Library of Congress American Memory collections. Designed for grade 7, but adaptable to high school.
Resource Type: Lesson or Activity; Image Collection
Grade Level: MS, HS

Photojournalism
http://memory.loc.gov/learn/lessons/97/photo/home.html

By close analysis of photographs from several wars, including the Civil War, students consider how and why photographers covered war and how pictures can reflect their biases. Students also learn to differentiate between observations and conclusions. The lesson includes a thorough procedure with instructional tips for teachers to follow, preselected photographs from the Library of Congress American Memory collections and worksheets for students. Designed for grades 5–8.
Resource Type: Lesson or Activity; Image Collection
Grade Level: MS

Civil War Battle Fields—Virtual Field Trip
www.lessonplanspage.com/SSCICivilWarVirtualFieldTripPlusHyperStudioPres59.htm

Using the provided Web sites, students will follow Kelly Fortner's lesson plan to understand the significance of each Civil War battle. Activities include writing battle outlines and reading eyewitness accounts of the fighting.
Resource Type: Lesson or Activity
Grade Level: MS

Lesson Plan: The Civil War
www.smplanet.com/civilwar/civilwar.html

This Civil War lesson plan includes many topics of discussion. It also encourages students to build their background knowledge of the Civil War through research and a suggested reading list.
Resource Type: Lesson or Activity
Grade Level: HS

The Time of the Lincolns: A Teacher's Guide
www.pbs.org/wgbh/amex/lincolns/tguide/index.html

The PBS film *Abraham and Mary Lincoln: A House Divided* and this companion Web site, "The Time of the Lincolns," offer excellent insights into topics in American history including women's rights, slavery, abolition, politics and partisanship, the growth of the industrial economy, and the Civil War. You can use part or all of the film, or delve into the rich resources available on this Web site to learn more, either in a classroom or on your own. PBS provides a lesson plan that encourages debate and discussion among students.
Resource Type: Lesson or Activity
Grade Level: MS, HS

The Civil War Through a Child's Eye
http://memory.loc.gov/learn/lessons/99/civilwar/index.html

This lesson uses primary sources such as photos and daguerreotypes, as well as historical fiction, to encourage students to view the Civil War from a different perspective, that of a child. The plan culminates in each student using Readers Theater and writing a literary first-person account of one of the photographed children. Preselected photos and daguerreotypes from the Library of Congress American Memory collections are provided, as well as instructional material on use of the primary sources and links to a variety of other Civil War Web sites. Designed for grades 6–8.
Resource Type: Lesson or Activity; Image Collection
Grade Level: MS

Ladies, Contraband, and Spies: Women in the Civil War
http://memory.loc.gov/learn/lessons/01/spies/index.html

In this concise lesson, students use primary sources from the Library of Congress American Memory collections to research and understand the impact of the Civil War on women. By studying women who had different roles in and perspectives on the war, ranging from plantation mistresses to slave women and spies, students have to consider how the war affected women based on their position in society. In addition to advancing skills in using primary sources, the lesson also has students present their results visually with PowerPoint and in writing with a short textbook entry. Designed for grades 10–11.
Resource Type: Lesson or Activity; Primary Source Collection
Grade Level: HS

Lesson Plan: Lee and Grant at Appomattox Court House
www.pbs.org/civilwar/classroom/lesson_appomattox.html

In this PBS lesson plan, students are asked to examine the terms and conditions of Lee's surrender. The lesson plan provides ample material for research and discussion regarding the end of the Civil War. PBS recommends that this lesson plan be used in conjunction with the film *The Civil War*, directed by Ken Burns.
Resource Type: Lesson or Activity
Grade Level: MS, HS

Teacher Lesson Plan: What Do You See?
http://memory.loc.gov/ammem/ndlpedu/lessons/97/civilwar/hinesday.html

In this Library of Congress lesson plan, students will examine one Civil War photograph from the selected catalog in extreme detail. This lesson plan includes all the necessary hand-outs and class materials for convenience. Suitable for grades 5–12.
Resource Type: Lesson or Activity
Grade Level: MS, HS

Lesson Plan: Lincoln Goes to War
http://edsitement.neh.gov/view_lesson_plan.asp?id=263

In this EDSITEment lesson plan, students examine Abraham Lincoln's decision to mobilize the Union Army against the South. Particular attention is paid to external factors that influenced the President's decision. Recommended for grades 9–12.
Resource Type: General Reference
Grade Level: HS

Lesson Plan—We Must Not be Enemies: Lincolns First Inaugural Address
http://edsitement.neh.gov/view_lesson_plan.asp?id=246

Students will gain a greater knowledge of Lincoln's presidency in this EDSITEment lesson plan. A copy of the first inaugural address is included, along with many other documents and six complete lesson plans. Written for students in grades 6–8.
Resource Type: Lesson or Activity
Grade Level: MS

Lesson Plan—Eve of the Civil War: People and Places of the North and South
http://edsitement.neh.gov/view_lesson_plan.asp?id=358

This EDSITEment lesson plan is intended to provide students with a knowledge of the social climate immediately before the Civil War. It comes with six different lessons and a good selection of online resources. Recommended for grades 6–8.
Resource Type: Lesson or Activity
Grade Level: MS

Teaching with Documents Lesson Plan: The Fight for Equal Rights: Black Soldiers on the Battlefield
http://edsitement.neh.gov/view_lesson_plan.asp?id=358

This NARA lesson plan contains a lot of good background information and many online resources, as well as teacher activities and student assignments.
Resource Type: Lesson or Activity
Grade Level: MS

American Civil War Ethnography
http://oswego.org/staff/tcaswell/cw/index.html

This Web site has been designed in order to assist students in the creation of an ethnography of the United States during the Civil War Era.

Resource Type: Lesson or Activity
Grade Level: MS

September 11 & The Gettysburg Address

www.pbs.org/newshour/extra/teachers/lessonplans/terrorism/sept11_gettysburg.html

Abraham Lincoln's Gettysburg Address was read at the September 11 anniversary ceremony. Students are to read the Gettysburg Address and discuss with their partner(s) its main themes. "Why do you think the Gettysburg Address is appropriate now?"
Resource Type: Lesson or Activity
Grade Level: MS, HS

The Meaning of Memorials

www.thirteen.org/edonline/lessons/memorials/memorialsov.html

Inspired by the "American Visions" online content, middle school students will explore the historical and cultural meaning of memorials, our country's "organs of social memory," with a focus on works and structures eulogizing the American Civil War. Using a variety of online, multimedia, and community resources, students will also investigate how the Civil War impacted their community and how the War and its veterans are remembered locally. This lesson is especially appropriate as part of a unit on the Civil War, or as an excellent way to honor and give meaning to the Memorial Day holiday in May. Doing field research, students will learn about the lives of local Civil War soldiers firsthand and will gain confidence in their ability to discover the past for themselves.
Resource Type: Lesson or Activity
Grade Level: MS

The Coming of the Civil War: Multiple Choice Quiz, Fill-in-the-Blank, Flashcards, American History Glossary, American History Appendix

http://wps.ablongman.com/long_carnes_an_11/0,7137,251415-,00.html

"Abraham Lincoln made many hard decisions during the Civil War. What would you have done?" The objective of this activity is to give students (of various levels) an understanding of the Civil War by identifying the results of the decisions Abraham Lincoln made during the Civil War.
Resource Type: Lesson or Activity
Grade Level: LS, MS, HS

The War to Save the Union: Multiple Choice Quiz, Fill-in-the-Blank, Flashcards, American History Glossary, American History Appendix

http://wps.ablongman.com/long_carnes_an_11/0,7137,251471-,00.html

The Student Resources section of *The American Nation* companion Web site features introductions to chapters, interactive quizzes, flashcards, Web links, an American History Glossary, and an American History Appendix.
Resource Type: Course Model
Grade Level: MS

Interpreting Primary Sources
www.digitalhistory.uh.edu/historyonline/us16.cfm

"Digital History" provides brief excerpts from primary sources and statistics, as well as questions to think about the topics of: Sectional Conflict, Secession and the Civil War, and Civil War.
Resource Type: Lesson or Activity; Primary Source Collection
Grade Level: HS

Digital History Resource Guides
http://www.digitalhistory.uh.edu/resource_guides/

"Digital History Resource Guides" provide links to American history Web sites by period, historical overviews, readings (online textbook chapter, Reader's Companion), primary source documents (documents, maps, cartoons), teaching resources (chronologies, maps, quizzes), audiovisual resources, and additional resources. They are an excellent and comprehensive teaching resource.
Resource Type: Course Model
Grade Level: HS, College

HistoryTeacher.net: AP United States History Quizzes
www.historyteacher.net/USQuizMainPage.htm

A teacher at the Horace Greeley High School in Chappaqua, New York, has produced a great general site for history teachers that offers AP-level U.S. history quizzes on many different periods and topics.
Resource Type: Test or Quiz
Grade Level: HS

AP United States History DBQs: 1810–1860
www.historyteacher.net/1998DBQsMainPage.htm

These student-created DBQs are part of the excellent Historyteacher.net site.
Resource Type: Lesson or Activity; Primary Source Collection
Grade Level: HS

The American People: The Union in Peril
http://wps.ablongman.com/long_nash_ap_6/0,7361,592970-,00.html

PowerPoint presentation on the causes of the American Civil War as part of the online companion to *The American People*. Go to PowerPoint Presentations and click Chapter 14.
Resource Type: Multimedia Presentation
Grade Level: HS

The American People: The Union Severed
http://wps.ablongman.com/long_nash_ap_6/0,7361,592970-,00.html

PowerPoint presentation on the American Civil War as part of the online companion to *The American People*. Go to PowerPoint Presentations and click Chapter 15.
Resource Type: Multimedia Presentation
Grade Level: HS

Role of Women in the Civil War

www.digitalhistory.uh.edu/historyonline/lesson_plans_display.cfm?lessonID=3

Working in collaborative teams, students use a variety of sources to prepare multimedia presentations about the different roles that women played in the Civil War. High school level.

Resource Type: Lesson or Activity
Grade Level: HS

Women in the American Civil War

http://score.rims.k12.ca.us/activity/manswar/

Students learn about military battles and the lives of women during the American Civil War, 1861–1865, using both the Internet and other resources. In groups, students write letters from a woman who may have lived during the Civil War and letters from the woman's relative.

Resource Type: Lesson or Activity
Grade Level: MS, HS

The Civil War: Quizzes and Activities

www.mce.k12tn.net/civil_war/civil_war.htm

A series of quizzes and activities from Mountain City Elementary School, Tennessee.

Resource Type: Test or Quiz
Grade Level: LS

Civil War: Blank Map

http://score.rims.k12.ca.us/activity/manswar/

The companion Web site to *The American People* offers blank maps related to various topics in American history. The maps can be printed or placed in a PowerPoint presentation. Go to Blank Maps.

Resource Type: Map
Grade Level: MS, HS

A History of the United States: Internet Activities and Student Self Test Questions

www.phschool.com/atschool/history_us/Student_Area/HUS_S_BK_index.html

Prentice Hall's phschool.com offers internet activities and interactive quizzes based on *A History of the United States* textbook chapters. High school level.

Resource Type:
Grade Level: HS

The American Nation: Internet Activities

www.phschool.com/atschool/TAN/Survey/Teacher_Area/TAN1_T_BK_index.html

Prentice Hall's phschool.com offers internet activities based on their *The American Nation* textbook chapters. Middle school grades.

Resource Type: Course Model
Grade Level: MS

Timeline of the Civil War

http://memory.loc.gov/ammem/cwphtml/tl1861.html

From the Library of Congress.
Resource Type: Timeline
Grade Level: MS, HS, College

RECONSTRUCTION

****America's Reconstruction: People and Politics After the Civil War
www.digitalhistory.uh.edu/reconstruction/index.html

This exhibition is part of the excellent "Digital History" site that contains an up-to-date U.S. history textbook; annotated primary sources on slavery, United States, Mexican American, and Native American history; and succinct essays on the history of ethnicity and immigration, film, private life, and science and technology. The text is by Eric Foner, DeWitt Clinton Professor of History at Columbia University and a renowned expert on Reconstruction, and Olivia Mahoney, Director of Historical Documentation at the Chicago Historical Society.
Resource Type: General Reference

****Civil War and Reconstruction, 1861–1877
http://lcweb2.loc.gov/ammem/ndlpedu/features/timeline/civilwar/civilwar.html

This Library of Congress exhibition contains succinct overviews of several aspects of the Civil War and Reconstruction and features primary sources, maps, and images.
Resource Type: General Reference; Primary Source Collection

****Harper's Weekly Reports, 1857–1874
http://blackhistory.harpweek.com/

For over a quarter of a century, *Harper's Weekly* captured the lion's share of the national newspaper audience. Materials from the magazine are presented in order to give a true historical picture of the leading nineteenth-century newspaper's view of black Americans.
Resource Type: General Reference; Primary Source Collection

****Freedmen's Bureau Online
www.freedmensbureau.com/

The Freedmen's Bureau supervised all relief and educational activities relating to refugees and freedmen, including issuing rations, clothing, and medicine. This site contains the records of the Bureau and is a great site for research.
Resource Type: General Reference; Primary Source Collection

****Emma Spaulding Bryant Papers
http://odyssey.lib.duke.edu/bryant/

Emma Bryant's letters to her husband John, who worked for the Freedmen's Bureau in 1873, provide excellent insights into the problems of Reconstruction.
Resource Type: General Reference; Primary Source Collection

****The Impeachment of Andrew Jackson
www.impeach-andrewjohnson.com/

Harper's Weekly portrayed in everyday detail to its readers of 1865–1869 the current events, issues and personalities that were central to Reconstruction and the impeachment of Andrew Johnson. Among the *Harper's Weekly* materials on this Web site are 27 political cartoons, as well as 47 news articles, briefs, and explanations of some of the 34 illustrations. There are also 90 editorials and an index.
Resource Type: General Reference; Primary Source Collection

****American History 102: 1865–Present
http://us.history.wisc.edu/hist102/

Part of a university course, this set has excellent lecture notes on major topical areas in American history from 1865.
Resource Type: General Reference; Lesson or Activity

****Roanoke Island Freedmen's Colony
www.roanokefreedmenscolony.com

This new Web site presents an introduction to the Roanoke Island freedmen's colony and the colonial experiment that was conducted there from 1862 to 1867.
Resource Type: General Reference

****Through the Lens of Time: Images of African Americans
http://dig.library.vcu.edu/cdm4/index_cook.php?CISOROOT=/cook

This Web site is a joint project between VCU Libraries and the Valentine Richmond History Center and provides nearly 300 photographs of African American life in turn-of-the-century Central Virginia from the 1860s to the 1930s.
Resource Type: Images; Image Collection

Reconstruction Lesson Plans, Teacher Guides, Activities, and More

After Reconstruction: Problems of African Americans in the South
http://memory.loc.gov/ammem/ndlpedu/lessons/rec/rhome.html

Designed by The Learning Page of the Library of Congress, this lesson plan focuses on the problems that went unsolved throughout Reconstruction. Students are encouraged to conduct research using primary sources. Recommended for high school–aged students.
Resource Type: Lesson or Activity
Grade Level: HS

The Gilder Lehrman Institute Modules in American History: Reconstruction
www.gilderlehrman.org/teachers/module11/index.html

The Gilder Lehrman Institute offers quality educational materials, including teaching modules on major topics in American history. Each module includes: a succinct historical overview; learning tools including lesson plans, quizzes, and activities; recommended documents, films, and historic images. These modules were prepared by Steven Mintz, the John

and Rebecca Moores Professor of History and the Director of the American Cultures Program at the University of Houston. Other helpful Institute online sources include include American History Quizzes, Letters from America's Wars, Featured Documents for your Classroom, and Primary Source Documents from the Collection.
Resource Type: Course Model
Grade Level: HS

Reconstruction Learning Module
www.digitalhistory.uh.edu/modules/reconstruction/index.cfm

The learning module on Reconstruction presented by "Digital History" features learning tools, and recommended books, films, and Web sites.
Resource Type: Course Model
Grade Level: HS

Reconstruction in the South: Multiple Choice Quiz, Fill-in-the-Blank, Flashcards, American History Glossary, and an American History Appendix
http://wps.ablongman.com/long_carnes_an_11/0,7137,251530-,00.html

The Student Resources section of *The American Nation* companion Web site features introductions to chapters, interactive quizzes, flashcards, Web links, an American History Glossary, and an American History Appendix.
Resource Type: Course Model
Grade Level: HS

The American People: The Union Reconstructed
http://wps.ablongman.com/long_nash_ap_6/0,7361,592970-,00.html

PowerPoint presentation on Reconstruction in the South as part of the online companion to The American People. Click PowerPoint Presentations and then Chapter 16.
Resource Type: Multimedia Presentation
Grade Level: HS

Interpreting Primary Sources
www.digitalhistory.uh.edu/historyonline/handouts.cfm

"Digital History" provides brief excerpts from primary sources and statistics and also questions to think about. Check out Reconstruction and African Americans After Slavery.
Resource Type: Lesson or Activity; Primary Source Collection
Grade Level: HS

HistoryTeacher.net: AP United States History Quizzes
www.historyteacher.net/USQuizMainPage.htm

A New York teacher has produced a great general site for history teachers that offers AP-level U.S. history quizzes on many different periods and topics.
Resource Type: Test or Quiz
Grade Level: HS

Gilder Lehrman Institute of American History
www.gilderlehrman.org/

The Gilder Lehrman Institute of American History offers lessons, quizzes, activities and primary source documents on a variety of topics including the reconstruction era.
Resource Type: Course Model
Grade Level: HS

The American Nation: Internet Activities
www.phschool.com/atschool/TAN/Survey/Teacher_Area/TAN1_T_BK_index.html

Prentice Hall's phschool.com offers Internet activities based on their *The American Nation* textbook chapters. Middle school grades.
Resource Type: Lesson or Activity
Grade Level: MS

A History of the United States: Internet Activities and Student Self-Test Questions
www.phschool.com/atschool/history_us/Student_Area/HUS_S_BK_index.html

Prentice Hall's phschool.com offers Internet activities and interactive quizzes based on *A History of the United States* textbook chapters. High school grades.
Resource Type: Lesson or Activity; Test or Quiz
Grade Level: HS

GILDED AGE

*****Illinois During the Gilded Age
http://dig.lib.niu.edu/gildedage/labor.html

"Illinois During the Gilded Age" is not only useful to Illinoisans learning about their state's history, as it also illuminates larger themes in the history of the United States during the Gilded Age as well. "Illinois During the Gilded Age" is a great site for Gilded Age issues, especially labor and politics. Produced by the Northern Illinois University Libraries' Digitization Unit, the site offers background articles, analytical essays, lesson plans, and interactive maps. It also features video lectures by experts on Gilded Age topics. A must-see.
Resource Type: General Reference; Lesson or Activity

*****The Great Chicago Fire and the Web of Memory
www.chicagohs.org/fire/index.html

A first-rate exhibition created by the Chicago Historical Society and Northwestern University. There are two major parts: The history of Chicago in the nineteenth century, and how the Chicago Fire has been remembered over time. Included are essays, galleries, and sources.
Resource Type: General Reference; Image Collection

****America in the 1890s
www.bgsu.edu/departments/acs/1890s/america.html

A detailed look at the issues and personalities that dominated American society in the 1890s via Bowling Green University. Many primary source excerpts.
Resource Type: General Reference

****Mark Twain in his Times

http://etext.lib.virginia.edu/railton/index2.html

Contained here are dozens of texts and manuscripts, scores of contemporary reviews and articles, hundreds of images, and many different kinds of interactive exhibits. Produced by the Electronic Text Center, University of Virginia.

Resource Type: Primary Source Collection

****Election of 1896

http://jefferson.village.virginia.edu/seminar/unit8/home.htm

A detailed look at the issues and personalities that dominated the election. Contains historical cartoons and documents on William Jennings Bryan and William McKinley.

Resource Type: General Reference

****Richest Man in the World: Andrew Carnegie

www.pbs.org/wgbh/amex/carnegie/

A companion to the *American Experience* video series, this site includes an introduction to the era, a timeline, a teacher's guide, photos and cartoons, a bibliography, a look at the Homestead strike, and links to relevant sites.

Resource Type: General Reference; Lesson or Activity

****Jim Crow Online

www.pbs.org/wnet/jimcrow/

"Jim Crow Online" is the official companion Web site to the PBS documentary, *The Rise and Fall of Jim Crow*. The Web site explores segregation from the end of the Civil War to the onset of the civil rights movement and uses excellent interactive features that enable visitors to learn more about the history of Jim Crow in the United States and the real-life crusaders of the period who fought against it. There are firsthand narratives and interactive maps and in the Tools and Activities section students can analyze images, post their comments online, and explore the legacy of Jim Crow.

Resource Type: General Reference; Lesson or Activity

****The Centennial Exhibition: Philadelphia 1876

http://libwww.library.phila.gov/CenCol/index.htm

The Philadelphia Library has excellent digitized artifacts from the Centennial Exhibition in Philadelphia, which featured the wonders of the Industrial Age and exhibits from 37 countries. The most lasting accomplishment of the Exhibition was to introduce America as a new industrial world power, soon to eclipse the might and production of every other industrialized nation, and to showcase the city of Philadelphia as a center of American culture and industry.

Resource Type: General Reference; Primary Source Collection

****Digital History: Labor History

www.digitalhistory.uh.edu/modules/gilded_age/index.cfm

"Digital History" features resource guides by topic and period. Reference resources include classroom handouts, chronologies, encyclopedia articles, glossaries, and an audiovisual archive including speeches, book talks and e-lectures by historians, and historical maps,

music, newspaper articles, and images. The site's Ask the HyperHistorian feature allows users to pose questions to professional historians.
Resource Type: Course Model

****A History of American Sweatshops
http://americanhistory.si.edu/sweatshops/

This exhibition is divided into three sections: 1820–1880, 1880–1940, and 1940–1997. There are plenty of images and historical background.
Resource Type: General Reference

****American History 102: 1865–Present
http://us.history.wisc.edu/hist102/

Part of a university course, this site has excellent lecture notes on major topical areas in American history from 1865. Check out lecture number four, "The Gilded Age and the Politics of Corruption."
Resource Type: General Reference; Course Model

****Inventing Entertainment
http://memory.loc.gov/ammem/edhtml/edhome.html

The impressive collections in the Library of Congress Motion Picture, Broadcasting and Recorded Sound Division contain an extraordinary range of the surviving products of Edison's entertainment inventions and industries. This site features 341 motion pictures, 81 disk sound recordings, and other related materials, such as photographs and original magazine articles.
Resource Type: Primary Source Collection

****American Variety Stage: Vaudeville and Popular Entertainment, 1870–1920
http://memory.loc.gov/ammem/vshtml/vshome.html

"American Variety Stage" is a multimedia anthology selected from various Library of Congress holdings. This engaging collection illustrates the vibrant and rich forms of popular entertainment, especially vaudeville, that thrived from 1870 to 1920.
Resource Type: Primary Source Collection; Multimedia Presentation

****Technology in America—The Telephone
www.pbs.org/wgbh/amex/telephone/index.html

This PBS companion site focuses not only on the telephone but on other important inventions in American history as well.
Resource Type: General Reference; Timeline

***The Industrial Revolution
www.schoolshistory.org.uk/IndustrialRevolution/index.htm

The U.K. education site examines what factors led to industrial growth, how this affected the lives of ordinary people and find out how working conditions were changed forever by the quick succession of inventions and pieces of legislation.
Resource Type: General Reference; Lesson or Activity

***Edisonian Museum

www.edisonian.com/edisonian001.htm

Provides images and histories of inventions.
Resource Type: Image Collection; emuseum

Gilded Age Lesson Plans, Teacher Guides, Activities, and More

Child Labor in America

http://memory.loc.gov/ammem/ndlpedu/lessons/98/labor/plan.html

Using historic photographs and primary sources, students will research and learn about child labor in America with this Library of Congress lesson plan. The plan provides its own printable handouts and discussion questions. Recommended for grades 7–12.
Resource Type: Lesson or Activity
Grade Level: MS, HS

Lesson Plan: Child Labor in the United States

http://historymatters.gmu.edu/d/6967/

This lesson plan (from the American Social History Project) asks students to examine photographs of child factory laborers at an online exhibit about southern factory mill towns from the early twentieth century.
Resource Type: Lesson or Activity
Grade Level: HS

After Reconstruction: Problems of African Americans in the South

http://memory.loc.gov/ammem/ndlpedu/lessons/rec/rhome.html

Designed by The Learning Page of the Library of Congress, this lesson plan focuses on the problems that went unsolved throughout Reconstruction. Students are encouraged to conduct research using primary sources. Recommended for high school–aged students.
Resource Type: Lesson or Activity
Grade Level: HS

The Gilder Lehrman Institute Modules in American History: Gilded Age

www.gilderlehrman.org/teachers/module12/index.html

The Gilder Lehrman Institute offers quality educational materials, including teaching modules on major topics in American history. Each module includes: a succinct historical overview; learning tools including lesson plans, quizzes, and activities; recommended documents, films, and historic images. These modules were prepared by Steven Mintz, the John and Rebecca Moores Professor of History and the Director of the American Cultures Program at the University of Houston. Other helpful Institute online sources include include American History Quizzes, Letters from America's Wars, Featured Documents for your Classroom, and Primary Source Documents from the Collection.
Resource Type: Course Model
Grade Level: HS

Teaching US History with Primary Sources: Gilded Age Era Lesson Plans from the Illinois Historical Digitization Projects
http://dig.lib.niu.edu/teachers/gilded.html

This resourceful site offers nine different lesson plans including "The WCTU and the Lynching Controversy," "Death to King Alcohol! Temperance in the 19th Century," and "Is there such a thing as too much profit?: The Interstate Commerce Act of 1887."
Resource Type: Lesson or Activity
Grade Level: HS

Social Darwinism: Reason or Rationalization?
www.smplanet.com/imperialism/activity.html

Presented by Small Planet Communications, this lesson plan encourages debate over the theory of Social Darwinism. Students are also asked to write a short follow-up essay on their position. Includes necessary material. Intended for grade 11.
Resource Type: Lesson or Activity
Grade Level: HS

The Great Migration: Lesson Plan
http://school.discovery.com/lessonplans/programs/tpl-sweethomechicago/

In this lesson plan, students will understand that, in addition to being, except for Native Americans, a country of immigrants, the United States is also now remarkable for the frequency with which people move around the country, from region to region. Grades 6–8.
Resource Type: Lesson or Activity
Grade Level: HS

Course Models: Social Reformers—Women's Voices
http://history.ctaponline.org/center/hsscm/index.cfm?Page_Key=1684

Part of the California History-Social Science content standards and annotated course, this site includes background information, focus questions, pupil activities and handouts, an assessment, and references to books, articles, web sites, literature, audio-video programs, and a historic site. Grade 11.
Resource Type: Course Model
Grade Level: HS

Striking a Deal: Learning the History of American Labor Strikes
www.nytimes.com/learning/teachers/lessons/20020830friday.html

In this *New York Times* lesson, students explore the economic repercussions of a potential Major League Baseball strike. Then, through researching other labor strikes in American history, students will consider the importance and impact of labor unions in U.S. history.
Resource Type: Lesson or Activity
Grade Level: MS, HS

The Immigrant Experience in America
www.thirteen.org/edonline/lessons/immigration/immigrationov.html

Students in grades 5–8 will learn about immigration, Ellis Island, and tenement life from 1890 to 1924. Each student will create an identity of an immigrant and write an essay in the first person. Essays will describe the fictitious immigrants in terms of who they are, where they came from, and what they found when they arrived in New York City.
Resource Type: Lesson or Activity
Grade Level: MS

Digital History Resource Guides
www.digitalhistory.uh.edu/resource_guides/

"Digital History Resource Guides" provide links to American history Web sites by period and provide historical overviews, readings (online textbook chapter, Reader's Companion), primary source documents (documents, maps, cartoons), teaching resources (chronologies, maps, quizzes), audiovisual resources, and additional resources. The Guides are an excellent and comprehensive teaching resource.
Resource Type: Course Model
Grade Level: HS, College

Industrialization of the United States: Document-Based Essay
www.phschool.com/curriculum_support/brief_review/us_history/essay_questions/unit3.cfm

This Prentice Hall DBQ is designed to test students' ability to work with historical documents and is based on the accompanying documents (1–6). It asks whether or not the changes that occurred after the Civil War created a more democratic America with greater opportunities for all.
Resource Type: Lesson or Activity; Primary Source Collection
Grade Level: HS

Work, Culture, and Society in Industrial America—DBQs
www.peterpappas.com/journals/industry.htm

Part of the "Teaching With Documents" site, questions feature a selection of primary and secondary documents, graphics, cartoons, tables, and graphs. The titles of the topics are Rural Americans Move to the Cities, Progress and Poverty in Industrial America, and Re-Defining the Role of Women in Industrial America.
Resource Type: Lesson or Activity; Primary Source Collection
Grade Level: HS

In the Wake of War: Multiple Choice Quiz, Fill-in-the-Blank, Flashcards, American History Glossary, and an American History Appendix
http://wps.ablongman.com/long_carnes_an_11/0,7137,251587-,00.html

The Student Resources section of *The American Nation* companion Web site features introductions to chapters, interactive quizzes, flashcards, Web links, an American History Glossary, and an American History Appendix.
Resource Type: Lesson or Activity; Test or Quiz
Grade Level: HS

An Industrial Giant: Multiple Choice Quiz, Fill-in-the-Blank, Flashcards, American History Glossary, and an American History Appendix
http://wps.ablongman.com/long_carnes_an_11/0,7137,251641-,00.html

The Student Resources section of *The American Nation* companion Web site features introductions to chapters, interactive quizzes, flashcards, Web links, an American History Glossary, and an American History Appendix.
Resource Type: Course Model
Grade Level: HS

The Gilded Age Industry
http://oswego.org/staff/tcaswell/wq/gildedage/student.htm

This WebQuest asks the students to produce a multimedia PowerPoint presentation centered on technology, big business, immigration and its reaction, and urban issues. Some broken links.
Resource Type: Lesson or Activity
Grade Level: HS

Child Labor in America
www.historyplace.com/unitedstates/childlabor/

These "History Place" photos of children in an adult work environment could be the core of a moving multimedia presentation on child labor.
Resource Type: Image Collection
Grade Level: MS, HS

American Society in the Industrial Era: Multiple Choice Quiz, Fill-in-the-Blank, Flashcards, American History Glossary, and an American History Appendix
http://wps.ablongman.com/long_carnes_an_11/0,7137,251699-,00.html

The Student Resources section of *The American Nation* companion Web site features introductions to chapters, interactive quizzes, flashcards, Web links, an American History Glossary, and an American History Appendix.
Resource Type: Course Model
Grade Level: HS

Politics—Local, State, and National: Multiple Choice Quiz, Fill-in-the-Blank, Flashcards, American History Glossary, and an American History Appendix
http://wps.ablongman.com/long_carnes_an_11/0,7137,251813-,00.html

The Student Resources section of *The American Nation* companion Web site features introductions to chapters, interactive quizzes, flashcards, Web links, an American History Glossary, and an American History Appendix.
Resource Type: Course Model
Grade Level: HS

Interpreting Primary Sources
www.gilderlehrman.org/teachers/module12/mod_tools.html

The Gilder Lehrman Institute of American History offers lessons, quizzes, activities and primary source documents for a variety of topics including The Farmer's Revolt, and Responses

to Industrialization.
Resource Type: Lesson or Activity; Primary Source Collection
Grade Level: MS, HS

Workers and Work in America, 1600–Present
www.albany.edu/history/history316/

A multimedia course with many useful links.
Resource Type: Lesson or Activity; Multimedia Presentation
Grade Level: HS, College

Industrialization of the United States Practice Test
www.phschool.com/curriculum_support/brief_review/us_history/tests.html?unit=3&
number=35

High school level quiz on Industrial American history from Prentice Hall.
Resource Type: Test or Quiz
Grade Level: HS

HistoryTeacher.net: AP United States History Quizzes
www.historyteacher.net/USQuizMainPage.htm

A teacher at the Horace Greeley High School in Chappaqua, New York, has produced a great
general site for history teachers that offers AP-level U.S. history quizzes on many different
periods and topics.
Resource Type: Test or Quiz
Grade Level: HS

A People and a Nation, 7th edition
http://college.hmco.com/history/us/norton/people_nation/7e/instructors/hc_overview.html

The Instructor Companion presentation program for "A People and a Nation" displays approximately 520 images, 200 maps, and several dozen audio and video assets, organized by
book chapter. Launch the free program and select the appropriate chapter.
Resource Type: Course Model; Multimedia Presentation
Grade Level: HS

AP United States History DBQs:1875–1925
www.historyteacher.net/AHAP/AHAP-DBQMainPage.htm

These student-created Documents-Based Questions are part of the excellent Historyteacher.net site.
Resource Type: Test or Quiz
Grade Level: HS

Business and Strikes Game
http://www.quia.com/rr/6528.html

Answer a series of easy-to-difficult questions about businesses and labor strikes during the
late 1800s.
Resource Type: Game
Grade Level: HS

The American People: The Rise of Smokestack America
http://wps.ablongman.com/long_nash_ap_6/0,7361,592970-,00.html

PowerPoint presentation on Industrial America as part of the online companion to *The American People*. Click PowerPoint Presentations and then Chapter 18.
Resource Type: Multimedia Presentation
Grade Level: HS

The American People: Politics and Reform
http://wps.ablongman.com/long_nash_ap_6/0,7361,592970-,00.html

PowerPoint presentation on Gilded Age politics as part of the online companion to *The American People*. Click PowerPoint Presentations and then Chapter 19.
Resource Type: Multimedia Presentation
Grade Level: HS

1890s American Politics: Blank Map
http://wps.ablongman.com/long_nash_ap_6/0,7361,592970-,00.html

The companion Web site to *The American People* offers blank maps related to various topics in American history. The maps can be printed or placed in a PowerPoint presentation.
Resource Type: Maps
Grade Level: HS

Railroads: Blank Map
http://wps.ablongman.com/long_nash_ap_6/0,7361,592970-,00.html

The companion Web site to *The American People* offers blank maps related to various topics in American history. The maps can be printed or placed in a PowerPoint presentation.
Resource Type: Maps
Grade Level: HS

The American Nation: Internet Activities
www.phschool.com/atschool/TAN/Survey/Teacher_Area/TAN1_T_BK_index.html

Prentice Hall's phschool.com offers Internet activities based on their *The American Nation* textbook chapters. Middle school grades.
Resource Type: Lesson or Activity
Grade Level: MS

A History of the United States: Internet Activities and Student Self-Test Questions
www.phschool.com/atschool/history_us/Student_Area/HUS_S_BK_index.html

Prentice Hall's phschool.com offers Internet activities and interactive quizzes based on *A History of the United States* textbook chapters. High school grades.
Resource Type: Lesson or Activity; Test or Quiz
Grade Level: HS

Technology in America (PBS)—Timeline
www.pbs.org/wgbh/amex/telephone/timeline/index.html

From Benjamin Franklin's lightning rod to the Hubble Space Telescope, this timeline covers some of America's technological innovations and inventions.

Resource Type: Multimedia Presentation
Grade Level: MS, HS

WESTWARD EXPANSION

*****The West
www.pbs.org/weta/thewest/

"The West" is a worthwhile supplement to Ken Burn's PBS documentary. It offers a timeline, glossary, biographies, a photo gallery, maps, documents, and more. A great introductory site.
Resource Type: General Reference; Multimedia Presentation

****NativeWeb
www.nativeweb.org/

"Native Web" is a comprehensive site for Native American studies and contains news, and information on books, music, events and other sources.
Resource Type: General Reference

****American West
www.americanwest.com

Covers westward expansion, Native Americans, Cowboys, Pioneers, Gunslingers, etc. Has images, maps, music, small "research" areas and even a 3-D tour.
Resource Type: General Reference

Figure 5.2: American West

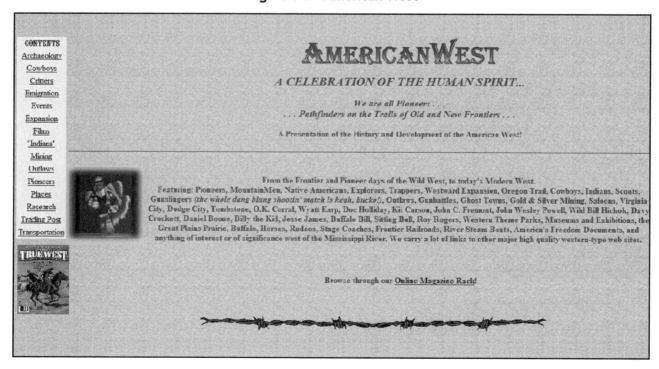

****WestWeb: Western History
www.library.csi.cuny.edu/westweb/

"West Web" is a topically organized site that offers an introduction to the era, primary and secondary sources, teaching guides, images, links to related sites, biographies, and bibliographical resources.
Resource Type: General Reference

****First Nations Histories
www.tolatsga.org/Compacts.html

Provides a geographic overview of First Nation (Indian) histories as well as a location list of native tribes in the United States and Canada. Also has a search function.
Resource Type: General Reference

****Lewis and Clark
www.pbs.org/lewisandclark/

A companion to Ken Burns' PBS film, this engaging site provides background on the world of Lewis and Clark, an archive of their expedition, audio excerpts by historians, a discussion of Native American tribes encountered, classroom resources, and an interactive story where you lead the expedition.
Resource Type: General Reference; Lesson or Activity

****Discovering Lewis and Clark
www.lewis-clark.org/

This site has more than 1,400 pages and revolves around a 19-part analysis of the Lewis and Clark expedition by historian Harry Fritz.
Resource Type: Primary Source Collection

****End of the Oregon Trail
www.endoftheoregontrail.org/joomlaeoctic/

This Web site is from the Oregon Trail Foundation, a nonprofit organization that exists to manage and develop the End of the Oregon Trail Interpretive Center in Oregon City, Oregon. The site contains a library of historical resources on the Oregon Trail and the early period of settlement in the Pacific Northwest.
Resource Type: General Reference; Primary Source Collection

****The Donner Party
www.pbs.org/wgbh/amex/donner/

Part of PBS's *American Experience* series, this site tells the story of an ill-fated immigrant group who set out for California in 1846. Included are a teacher's guide, background on Western migration, a map of the route, and recommended readings.
Resource Type: General Reference; Lesson or Activity

****The U.S.-Mexican War
www.pbs.org/kera/usmexicanwar/

Part of PBS Online, this bilingual (Spanish-English) site examines the Mexican-American War and includes a timeline, dialogues (essays), teaching resources, and more.
Resource Type: General Reference; Lesson or Activity

****Peopling North America
www.ucalgary.ca/applied_history/tutor/migrations/Fhome.html

The University of Calgary History Department provides an informative historical overview of migratory movements to and within Canada, the United States, Mexico, and the Caribbean from Europe, Asia, and Africa.
Resource Type: General Reference

****Mountain Men and the Fur Trade
www.xmission.com/~drudy/amm.html

This homepage is an online Research Center devoted to the history, traditions, tools, and mode of living of the trappers, explorers, and traders known as the Mountain Men. Features an archive, a gallery, a museum, a discussion group, and more.
Resource Type: General Reference

****Index of Native American Resources on the Web
www.hanksville.org/NAresources/

This large portal contains many categories of links from WWW Virtual Library—American Indians.
Resource Type: Links Collection

***The Iron Road
www.pbs.org/wgbh/amex/iron/

Part of PBS's *American Experience* series, this site is the story of the building of the first east-west railroad link. There is a teacher's guide, a bibliography, photos, and recommended readings.
Resource Type: General Reference; Lesson or Activity

***The Northern Great Plains, 1880–1920
http://memory.loc.gov/ammem/award97/ndfahtml/ngphome.html

This Library of Congress site has over 900 images of rural and small town life in the Northwest.
Resource Type: Image Collection

***Old Wild West
www.oldwildwest.com/history.html

This site features stories of the Old West from the *Abilene Reporter-News* archives and other resources. There is information on the Alamo, Sam Houston, Texas Rangers, Billy the Kid, Pancho Villa, Davy Crockett, and others.
Resource Type: General Reference

Westward Expansion Lesson Plans, Teacher Guides, Activities, and More

Lewis and Clark: Classroom Resources
www.pbs.org/lewisandclark/class/idx_les.html

The 17 Lewis and Clark lesson plans on this page offer a wide array of classroom activities. Created by PBS, the activities address all parts of the famous expedition.
Resource Type: Lesson or Activity
Grade Level: MS

The Gilder Lehrman Institute Modules in American History: Westward Expansion
www.gilderlehrman.org/teachers/module8/index.html

The Gilder Lehrman Institute offers quality educational materials, including teaching modules on major topics in American history. Each module includes: a succinct historical overview; learning tools including lesson plans, quizzes, and activities; recommended documents, films, and historic images. These modules were prepared by Steven Mintz, the John and Rebecca Moores Professor of History and the Director of the American Cultures Program at the University of Houston. Other helpful Institute online sources include include American History Quizzes, Letters from America's Wars, Featured Documents for your Classroom, and Primary Source Documents from the Collection.
Resource Type: Course Model
Grade Level: HS

The Iron Road: Teacher's Guide
www.pbs.org/wgbh/amex/iron/teachers.html

In this PBS teachers guide, students will examine the planning, funding and building of the transcontinental railroad; demonstrate map reading skills; compare and analyze sources of information; and discuss how the decision to build the railroad affected different ethnic communities.
Resource Type: Lesson or Activity
Grade Level: HS

Teacher Lesson Plan: Explorations in American Environmental History
http://lcweb2.loc.gov/ammem/ndlpedu/lessons/98/environ/intro.html

Part of the Library of Congress Learning Page, these two lesson plans make use of visual resources. Emphasis is put on understanding the environmental issues that arose with Westward expansion. Grades 8–12.
Resource Type: Lesson or Activity
Grade Level: MS, HS

Teacher Lesson Plan: Links to the Past
http://lcweb2.loc.gov/ammem/ndlpedu/lessons/99/links/intro.html

Students use documents to create a script depicting the "motivations, expectations, fears, and realizations" of immigrants who settled California between 1849 and 1900. The finished product will be a hyperscript, an online written dialogue containing links to illustrative written materials, images, and sound files from American Memory collections. Presented by the Library of Congress for grades 6–12.
Resource Type: Lesson or Activity
Grade Level: MS, HS

Lesson Plan: Life on the Great Plains
http://edsitement.neh.gov/view_lesson_plan.asp?id=265

In this four-part EDSITEment lesson plan, students will study the Great Plains. Plan includes a mapping activity and PBS resources. Recommended for grades 9–12.
Resource Type: Lesson or Activity
Grade Level: HS

Lesson Plan: On the Oregon Trail

http://edsitement.neh.gov/view_lesson_plan.asp?id=323

In this lesson, students work with primary documents and latter-day photographs to recapture the experience of traveling on the Oregon Trail. The lesson plan was created by EDSITEment and boasts a vast collection of resources.

Resource Type: Lesson or Activity
Grade Level: MS

Simulation: Oregon Trail

www.eduref.org/cgi-bin/printlessons.cgi/Virtual/Lessons/Social_Studies/US_History/USH0025.html

Written by Louise C. Murphy (an Arizona teacher), this AskERIC simulation lets students experience the Oregon Trail for themselves. Activities include reading maps, writing letters, and conducting research. Purchase of The Oregon Trail Computer simulation is required. Grades 5–8.

Resource Type: Lesson or Activity
Grade Level: LS, MS

CEC: Negotiating Treaties

www.col-ed.org/cur/sst/sst190.txt

A fun mini-lesson that addresses the treaties signed by the U.S. government during the Westward Expansion movement. Students choose a role (Settler, Native American, etc.) and then debate the Treaties. Grade 11.

Resource Type: Lesson or Activity
Grade Level: HS

CEC: Gunfighters of the Old West

www.col-ed.org/cur/sst/sst255.txt

In this mini-lesson, students learn what is fact and fiction in the Old West. Suitable for grades 7–12.

Resource Type: Lesson or Activity
Grade Level: MS, HS

Cowboys

http://school.discovery.com/lessonplans/programs/rediscoveringamerica-therealamericancowboy/

In this lesson plan, middle school students will learn that Old West cowboys produced a category of literature.

Resource Type: Lesson or Activity
Grade Level: MS

Interpreting Primary Sources: Indian Policy

www.digitalhistory.uh.edu/historyonline/us23.cfm

"Digital History" provides brief excerpts from primary sources and statistics and also questions to think about.

Resource Type: Lesson or Activity; Primary Source Collection
Grade Level: HS

Digital History Resource Guides
www.digitalhistory.uh.edu/resource_guides/

"Digital History Resource Guides" provide links to American history Web sites by period and provide historical overviews, readings (online textbook chapter, Reader's Companion), primary source documents (documents, maps, cartoons), teaching resources (chronologies, maps, quizzes), audiovisual resources, and additional resources. The Guides are an excellent and comprehensive teaching resource.
Resource Type: Course Model
Grade Level: HS, College

Declarations of Independence: Exploring American Indian Rights to Self-Governance
www.nytimes.com/learning/teachers/lessons/20021125monday.html

In this *New York Times* lesson, students will examine what they know about American Indians past and present, then research key issues facing American Indian tribes today. To synthesize their learning, students will write letters taking the perspective of an American Indian examining questions of tribe recognition.
Resource Type: Lesson or Activity
Grade Level: MS, HS

HistoryTeacher.net: AP United States History Quizzes
www.historyteacher.net/USQuizMainPage.htm

A teacher at the Horace Greeley High School in Chappaqua, New York, has produced a great general site for history teachers that offers AP-level U.S. history quizzes on many different periods and topics.
Resource Type: Test or Quiz
Grade Level: HS

The American People: Rural America: The West and the New South
http://wps.ablongman.com/long_nash_ap_6/0,7361,592970-,00.html

PowerPoint presentation as part of the online companion to *The American People*. Click Chapter 17.
Resource Type: Multimedia Presentation
Grade Level: HS

The American People: Moving West
http://wps.ablongman.com/long_nash_ap_6/0,7361,592970-,00.html

PowerPoint presentation on westward expansion as part of the online companion to *The American People*. Click Chapter 13.
Resource Type: Multimedia Presentation
Grade Level: HS

Territorial Acquisitions: Blank Map
http://wps.ablongman.com/long_nash_ap_6/0,7361,592970-,00.html

The companion Web site to *The American People* offers blank maps related to various topics in American history. The maps can be printed or placed in a PowerPoint presentation.

Resource Type: Maps
Grade Level: HS

U.S. Southwest in the 1840s: Blank Map
http://wps.ablongman.com/long_nash_ap_6/0,7361,592970-,00.html

The companion Web site to *The American People* offers blank maps related to various topics in American history. The maps can be printed or placed in a PowerPoint presentation.
Resource Type: Maps
Grade Level: HS

The American Nation: Internet Activities
www.phschool.com/atschool/TAN/Survey/Teacher_Area/TAN1_T_BK_index.html

Prentice Hall's phschool.com offers Internet activities based on their *The American Nation* textbook chapters. Middle school grades.
Resource Type: Lesson or Activity
Grade Level: MS

A History of the United States: Internet Activities and Student Self-Test Questions
www.phschool.com/atschool/history_us/Student_Area/HUS_S_BK_index.html

Prentice Hall's phschool.com offers Internet activities and interactive quizzes based on *A History of the United States* textbook chapters. High school grades.
Resource Type: Lesson or Activity
Grade Level: HS

Western History: Photography Collection
http://history.denverlibrary.org/images/index.html

This site contains a selection of 65,000, historic photographs from the collections of the Denver Public Library Western History/Genealogy Department and the Colorado Historical Society, including images of Native Americans, pioneers, early railroads, and mining towns.
Resource Type: Image Collection
Grade Level: MS, HS

Images of Indian Peoples of the Northern Great Plains
www.lib.montana.edu/epubs/nadb/

The digital collection was created in consultation with Native Americans, educators, librarians, and historians. The overall organization of the database is by tribe, including: Crow, Cheyenne, Blackfeet, Salish (Flathead), Kutenai, Chippewa-Cree, Gros Ventres (Atsina), and Assiniboine.
Resource Type: Image Collection
Grade Level: MS, HS

EARLY IMPERIALISM

****Crucible of Empire: The Spanish-American War
www.pbs.org/crucible/

This rich and diverse site offers a timeline of the major events before, during, and after the war; original 1890s sheet music popular during the war; photographs of the major figures involved; newspaper articles and headlines from 1890s newspapers; classroom activities for teachers and students; historical resources, including recent scholarship concerning the war, bibliographies, and links to other web sites; and a quiz designed to test visitor knowledge about the war and this colorful moment in American history.

Resource type: General Reference; Lesson or Activity

****Puerto Rico at the Dawn of the Modern Age
http://memory.loc.gov/ammem/collections/puertorico/

Created by the American Memory Project of the Library of Congress, this site seeks to inform and educate about nineteenth- and early–twentieth-century Puerto Rico and how it became a modern nation. An article by Marisabel Brás, a Senior Analyst at the Department of Defense, provides an excellent and in-depth report on the struggles through which Puerto Rico went to find its national identity. There are also 18 Puerto Rican maps and 39 political pamphlets, 13 monographs, and a journal that were published between 1831 and 1929. For each item, the full text is provided as well as images of the authentic document.

Resource type: Maps, General Reference

****Spanish-American War in Motion Pictures
http://memory.loc.gov/ammem/sawhtml/sawhome.html

This engaging multimedia presentation features 68 motion pictures produced between 1898 and 1901 of the Spanish-American War and the subsequent Philippine Revolution. These films were made by the Edison Manufacturing Company and the American Mutoscope & Biograph Company and consist of actualities filmed in the United States, Cuba, and the Philippines, showing troops, ships, notable figures, and parades, as well as reenactments of battles and other war-time events. The Special Presentation presents the motion pictures in chronological order together with brief essays that provide a historical context for their filming.

Resource Type: Multimedia Presentation

****The Age of Imperialism
www.smplanet.com/imperialism/toc.html

Commercial site, but one that contains a good mix of text, photos, links, and video clips about American imperialism at the turn of the century.

Resource Type: General Reference, Lesson or Activity

***Hawaii's Last Queen
www.pbs.org/wgbh/pages/amex/hawaii/

This PBS video companion site relates the interesting story of Queen Lili'uokalani and her legacy.

Resource Type: General Reference; Lesson or Activity

***McKinley Assassination Ink
http://mckinleydeath.com/

This rich collection currently contains 140 documents, articles, essays, editorials and other pieces of work that are helpfully indexed by author, date, title, type, keyword, source, and the people referenced in the document. The MAI aims not only to provide a view into the

presidency and assassination of McKinley, but also to speak to the history and culture of America. Due to the sensationalist nature of journalism at the time, and the tragic nature of the event, as the site points out, some reports may be more useful as tools to interpret the emotions and themes of the time than as strict factual evidence.
Resource Type: Primary Source Collection

Early Imperialism Lesson Plans, Teacher Guides, Activities, and More

Spanish American War from the Organization of American Historians Magazine
www.oah.org/pubs/magazine/1898/martinez-lesson.pdf

These PDF files may be printed off for classroom use. There are lessons for 10th- and 11th-grade teachers. In "Birth of the American Empire as Seen Through Political Cartoons 1898–1905," students review and discuss six political cartoons.
Resource Type: Lesson or Activity
Grade Level: HS

Spanish American War Educational Activities
www.pbs.org/crucible/frames/_resources.html

The PBS "Crucible of Empire" site offers essay questions and a Spanish American War quiz under its Education Activities link.
Resource Type: Lesson or Activity
Grade Level: HS

Lesson Plan: The Age of Imperialism
www.smplanet.com/imperialism/teacher.html#Outline

From the site: "The Age of Imperialism represents one chapter of an On-Line History of the United States, a new program that combines an engaging narrative with the broad resources available to students on the Internet. You can use this chapter in place of a standard textbook treatment of nineteenth-century American expansionism, or you can use it to supplement your existing Social Studies materials. The following lesson plan helps you establish and extend historical and instructional contexts and integrate the material into your U.S. history curriculum."
Resource Type: Course Model
Grade Level: HS

Debate: Should the U.S. Annex the Philippines?
http://historymatters.gmu.edu/d/6613/

In this activity, students analyze primary documents from a variety of perspectives to gain an understanding of contemporary arguments for and against U.S. annexation of the Philippines. After reading the documents, students choose one document, prepare their arguments, and debate U.S. annexation of the Philippines from the perspective of the author of their document. Provided by the American Social History Project.
Resource Type: Lesson or Activity
Grade Level: HS, College

Poetry Analysis: "The White Man's Burden"
http://historymatters.gmu.edu/d/6609/

This activity asks students to consider Rudyard Kipling's "The White Man's Burden," which urged the United States to take up the "burden" of empire. Designed for high school students, this interdisciplinary activity will help students to examine differing perspectives on imperialism at the turn of the century. Provided by the American Social History Project.
Resource Type: Lesson or Activity
Grade Level: HS, College

Activity: A Soldier's Letter Home From the Philippines
http://historymatters.gmu.edu/d/6611/

This insightful activity asks students to read and analyze letters written by U.S. soldiers serving in the Philippine-American War. Designed for high school students, it uses primary documents from the perspective of frontline soldiers to explore questions of imperialism, racial difference, and war in the early twentieth century. Designed by the American Social History Project.
Resource Type: Lesson or Activity
Grade Level: HS, College

Around the World in 1896
http://memory.loc.gov/learn/lessons/97/world/home.html

In this lesson, groups of students use photographs and documents from the Library of Congress's American Memory collections to explore technology and American perceptions of the world at the turn of the century. Students explore technology during this time period by planning a hypothetical trip around the world, being sure to identify the complete means of transportations. They also learn about William Henry Jackson and the development of photography, ultimately using visual images to both document their trip and evaluate contemporary perspectives on foreign cultures. Designed for grades 6–8.
Resource Type: Lesson or Activity
Grade Level: MS

The Gilder Lehrman Institute Modules in American History: U.S. World Power
www.gilderlehrman.org/teachers/module13/index.html

The Gilder Lehrman Institute offers quality educational materials, including teaching modules on major topics in American history. Each module includes: A succinct historical overview; learning tools including lesson plans, quizzes, and activities; recommended documents, films, and historic images. These modules were prepared by Steven Mintz, the John and Rebecca Moores Professor of History and the Director of the American Cultures Program at the University of Houston. Other helpful Institute online sources include include American History Quizzes, Letters from America's Wars, Featured Documents for your Classroom, and Primary Source Documents from the Collection.
Resource Type: Course Model
Grade Level: HS

Doing the Decades
http://memory.loc.gov/learn/lessons/theme.html

This is a broad, 10-week project where students focus on the major trends and changes in the United States from 1890 to 1941 and how these changes affected groups and individuals. Students are broken into groups by decade and cover six primary themes (such as immigration, industrialization and the growth of capitalism) and a series of topics. Students identify and utilize primary sources to discuss these changes, using materials from the Library of Congress American Memory collections and other materials they gather. Designed for grades 6–12.
Resource Type: Lesson or Activity
Grade Level: MS, HS

From Isolation to Empire: Multiple Choice Quiz, Fill-in-the-Blank, Flashcards, American History Glossary, and an American History Appendix
http://wps.ablongman.com/long_carnes_an_11/0,7137,251929-,00.html

The Student Resources section of *The American Nation* companion Web site features introductions to chapters, interactive quizzes, flashcards, Web links, an American History Glossary, and an American History Appendix.
Resource Type: Course Model
Grade Level: MS

Playing by Different Rules: Examining American Imperialism Abroad
www.nytimes.com/learning/teachers/lessons/20020918wednesday.html

In this *New York Times* lesson, students learn about the concept of American imperialism by researching and analyzing historical examples of American imperialism. They then draft a set of laws that would govern the actions of powerful nations in other countries.
Resource Type: Lesson or Activity
Grade Level: MS, HS

Imperial Notions: Examining the Effects of Colonialism on Peoples Around the World
www.nytimes.com/learning/teachers/lessons/20030604wednesday.html

In this *New York Times* lesson, students research how and why different parts of the world were colonized, considering the pros and cons for both the rulers and the ruled.
Resource Type: Lesson or Activity
Grade Level: MS, HS

Interpreting Primary Sources
www.digitalhistory.uh.edu/historyonline/us27.cfm

"Digital History" provides brief excerpts from primary sources and statistics and questions to think about Imperialism and the Spanish American War.
Resource Type: Lesson or Activity
Grade Level: HS, College

Digital History Resource Guides
www.digitalhistory.uh.edu/resource_guides/

"Digital History Resource Guides" provide links to American history Web sites by period and provide historical overviews, readings (online textbook chapter, Reader's Companion),

primary source documents (documents, maps, cartoons), teaching resources (chronologies, maps, quizzes), audiovisual resources, and additional resources. The Guides are an excellent and comprehensive teaching resource.
Resource Type: Course Model
Grade Level: HS, College

HistoryTeacher.net: AP United States History Quizzes
www.historyteacher.net/USQuizMainPage.htm

A teacher at the Horace Greeley High School in Chappaqua, New York, has produced a great general site for history teachers that offers AP-level U.S. history quizzes on many different periods and topics.
Resource Type: Test or Quiz
Grade Level: HS

AP United States History DBQs: 1875–1925
www.historyteacher.net/2000DBQsMainPage.htm

These student-created Documents-Based Questions are part of the excellent Historyteacher.net site.
Resource Type: Lesson or Activity; Primary Source Collection
Grade Level: HS

The American People: Becoming a World Power
http://wps.ablongman.com/long_nash_ap_6/0,7361,592970-,00.html

PowerPoint presentation on American imperialism as part of the online companion to *The American People*. Click on PowerPoint Presentations and then Chapter 20.
Resource Type: Multimedia Presentation
Grade Level: HS

Hawaii Quiz
www.pbs.org/wgbh/amex/hawaii/quiz.html

From PBS *Hawaii's Last Queen*, this quiz features 15 questions on Hawaii's history and geography.
Resource Type: Test or Quiz
Grade Level: HS

The American Nation: Internet Activities
www.phschool.com/atschool/TAN/Survey/Teacher_Area/TAN1_T_BK_index.html

Prentice Hall's phschool.com offers Internet activities based on their *The American Nation* textbook chapters.
Resource Type: Course Model
Grade Level: MS

A History of the United States: Internet Activities and Student Self-Test Questions
www.phschool.com/atschool/history_us/Student_Area/HUS_S_BK_index.html

Prentice Hall's phschool.com offers Internet activities and interactive quizzes based on *A History of the United States* textbook chapters.
Resource Type: Lesson or Activity; Test or Quiz
Grade Level: HS

PROGRESSIVISM

****America 1900
www.pbs.org/wgbh/amex/1900/

Key features of this site include an interactive map that provides you with a list of events in the region of the world you select, a search function for locating people and events of the early part of the century, a genealogical "tree building" program to trace your family's roots, and a teacher's guide.
Resource Type: General Reference; Lesson or Activity

****Immigration...The Changing Face of America
http://lcweb2.loc.gov/ammem/ndlpedu/features/immig/immigration_set1.html

The Library of Congress feature provides an excellent introduction to the study of immigration to the United States. There are student activities, educator guides, photos and links to useful resources. The presentation was shaped by the primary sources available in the Library's online collections and probing questions such as "Why did each immigrant group come to the United States?" and "How did United States government policies and programs affect immigration patterns?"
Resource Type: Primary Source Collection; Lesson or Activity

Figure 5.3: Immigration...The Changing Face of America

****TR, The Story of Theodore Roosevelt
www.pbs.org/wgbh/amex/tr

A companion to the PBS *American Experience* video series, this site features real audio interviews, biographies, a timeline, a teacher's guide and a discussion of TR's legacy.
Resource Type: General Reference; Lesson or Activity

****Theodore Roosevelt: His Life and Times on Film
http://memory.loc.gov/ammem/collections/troosevelt_film/

This Library of Congress presentation features 104 films that record events in Roosevelt's life from the Spanish-American War in 1898 to his death in 1919.
Resource Type: Primary Source Collection; Multimedia Presentation

****The Evolution of the Conservation Movement, 1850–1920
http://memory.loc.gov/ammem/amrvhtml/conshome.html

This Library of Congress site documents the development of the conservation movement and offers a collection of books, pamphlets, federal statutes and resolutions, prints and photographs, a motion picture, and more.
Resource Type: Primary Source Collection; Multimedia Presentation

****Women and Social Movements in the United States, 1775–2000
http://womhist.binghamton.edu/about.htm

This Web site is a project of the Center for the Historical Study of Women and Gender at the State University of New York at Binghamton. About a fourth of the projects on Women and Social Movements remain freely available; the other projects, in addition to 25,000 pages of primary documents and enhanced searching tools, are available through Alexander Street Press. In the Teacher's Corner there are twenty comprehensive lesson plans with over a hundred lesson ideas and six DBQ units, although some of these materials require a subscription.
Resource Type: Primary Source Collection; Lesson or Activity

****The Triangle Factory Fire
www.ilr.cornell.edu/trianglefire

This Web site provides a detailed account of the fire at the Triangle Shirtwaist Company in New York City on March 25, 1911, that claimed the lives of 146 young immigrant workers and highlighted inhumane working conditions.
Resource Type: General Reference

****The Wright Stuff
www.pbs.org/wgbh/amex/wright

A companion to a PBS *American Experience* series, this site focuses on the story of the famous vacation brothers. There is a QuickTime movie that features a replica of Kitty Hawk in flight as well as audio interviews and a bibliography.
Resource Type: General Reference; Lesson or Activity

****Not for Ourselves Alone: The Story of Elizabeth Cady Stanton and Susan B. Anthony
http://pbs.org/stantonanthony

This PBS companion site to the Ken Burns documentary film features an interactive, virtual trip through the women's suffrage movement. It also provides biographical and primary source information about Stanton and Anthony, classroom resources, and more.
Resource Type: General Reference; Lesson or Activity

****Half the People: 1917–1996
www.pbs.org/wgbh/peoplescentury/episodes/halfthepeople

Part of PBS's *People's Century* television series, this site focuses on women's fight for equal rights. There are interviews, a timeline, and a teacher's guide.
Resource Type: General Reference; Lesson or Activity

****Living the Legacy: Women's Rights Movement, 1848–1998
www.Legacy98.org/index.html

Sponsored by the National Women's History Project, the site provides a history of the movement and a detailed timeline.
Resource Type: General Reference; Timeline

****Agents of Social Change
www.smith.edu/libraries/libs/ssc/agents/index.html

Smith College offers an excellent online exhibit and several lesson plans drawn from its collections. The lesson plans are directed at middle and high school students and make use of both the text-based documents and visual images that can be found at the curriculum portion of the Web site. They highlight women's part in struggles for social change in the twentieth century including labor, socialism, civil liberties, peace, racial justice, urban reform, welfare rights, and women's rights.
Resource Type: General Reference; Primary Source Collection

****Inside A Factory: Westinghouse Works, 1904
http://lcweb2.loc.gov/ammem/papr/west/westhome.html

This Library of Congress site has 21 films of the Westinghouse companies that were intended to showcase the company's operations. There is background information on the factories, a timeline, an index, a search function, and recommended sources.
Resource Type: Primary Source Collection; Multimedia Presentation

****Life of Henry Ford
www.thehenryford.org/exhibits/hf/default.asp

Details Henry Ford's Life and his Ford Motor Company. Contains a chronology, "quick facts," and more.
Resource Type: General Reference

***Museum of Women's History: Political Culture and Imagery of American Women Suffrage
www.nmwh.org/exhibits/exhibit_frames.html

Provides a succinct overview of the suffrage movement in words and pictures.
Resource Type: General Reference; Virtual Tour

***American Leaders Speak
http://memory.loc.gov/ammem/nfhtml

The Library of Congress Web site provides 59 sound recordings of speeches by American leaders from 1918–1920. The speeches focus on issues and events surrounding the First

World War and the subsequent presidential election of 1920. An excellent multimedia resource.
Resource Type: Primary Source Collection

***Titanic
www.nationalgeographic.com/society/ngo/explorer/titanic

In 1998 National Geographic headquarters hosted screenings of a short, 3-D film shot at the wreck of the *Titanic*. See selected pictures from the filming, and more.
Resource Type: Multimedia Presentation

Progressivism Lesson Plans, Teacher Guides, Activities, and More

Conservation at a Crossroads—Lesson Plan
http://memory.loc.gov/learn/lessons/97/conser1/xroads.html

This Library of Congress lesson plan presents two independent units that use the decision to dam the Hetch Hetchy Valley in Yosemite National Park as a means to explore the history of the conservation movement. The first unit focuses on major conservation thinkers such as Thoreau, Muir and Pinchot, and how the movement diversified over time; students also draw parallels to current environmental debates. The second unit focuses specifically on the debate over using the Hetch Hetchy to supply San Francisco with water; students engage in a mock debate to explore different sides and tease out differences between "preservationists" and "conservationists." Both units feature preselected materials from Library of Congress collections, including writings by conversation advocates and opponents and Congressional documents. Designed for grades 11–12, but adaptable to grades 7–10.
Resource Type: Lesson or Activity
Grade Level: HS

Teacher Lesson Plan: Music and Our Reform History
http://memory.loc.gov/ammem/ndlpedu/lessons/99/sing/intro.html

By exploring sheet music, students analyze issues related to industrialization and reform to answer the essential question, "How does society respond to change?" Students will have the opportunity to create original lyrics and song covers that reflect the Progressive Era. Provided by the Library of Congress, recommended for grades 7–12.
Resource Type: Lesson or Activity
Grade Level: MS, HS

Suffragists and Their Tactics
http://memory.loc.gov/learn/lessons/00/women/index.html

This Library of Congress lesson plan utilizes close analysis of three different primary sources (photos, broadsides and period articles) to explore the fight for women's suffrage in terms of how and why women advocated change. Designed activities focus on what inferences can be made from primary sources and how to evaluate the efficacy of suffragists' arguments in the time period they were made. For grades 10–12.
Resource Type: Lesson or Activity
Grade Level: HS

Women, Their Rights & Nothing Less
http://memory.loc.gov/learn/lessons/99/suffrage/intro.html

This relatively succinct lesson teaches students about both the different societal roles of women from 1840 to 1920 and the methods they used to achieve desired reforms. Using primary sources from the Library of Congress' American Memory collections, students learn how tactics in the early women's rights movement changed with the times, ultimately leading to women's suffrage. The lesson culminates in a student-made timeline, which uses primary sources to explain the movement's transformation over time. Designed for grades 9–12.
Resource Type: Lesson or Activity
Grade Level: HS

United We Stand
http://memory.loc.gov/learn/lessons/00/labor/index.html

To understand American working conditions at the end of the twentieth century, students explore primary materials from the Library of Congress' American Memory collections. Using photographs, music, newspaper articles and editorials, the lesson allows students to explore the poor conditions that precipitated the rise of unions and to determine how such primary sources can be used to justify arguments of those who claimed organizing labor was necessary. The lesson includes links to many specific, relevant documents from the American Memory collections. Designed for grades 8–10.
Grade Level: MS, HS
Resource Type: Lesson or Activity

The Gilder Lehrman Institute Modules in American History: Progressivism
www.gilderlehrman.org/teachers/module14/index.html

The Gilder Lehrman Institute offers quality educational materials, including teaching modules on major topics in American history. Each module includes: A succinct historical overview; learning tools including lesson plans, quizzes, and activities; recommended documents, films, and historic images. These modules were prepared by Steven Mintz, the John and Rebecca Moores Professor of History and the Director of the American Cultures Program at the University of Houston. Other helpful Institute online sources include include American History Quizzes, Letters from America's Wars, Featured Documents for your Classroom, and Primary Source Documents from the Collection.
Resource Type: Course Model
Grade Level: HS

The Age of Reform: Multiple Choice Quiz, Fill-in-the-Blank, Flashcards, American History Glossary, and an American History Appendix
http://wps.ablongman.com/long_carnes_an_11/0,7137,251872-,00.html

The Student Resources section of *The American Nation* companion Web site features introductions to chapters, interactive quizzes, flashcards, Web links, an American History Glossary, and an American History Appendix.
Resource Type: Course Model
Grade Level: MS, HS

The Progressive Movement: Practice Test

www.phschool.com/curriculum_support/brief_review/us_history/tests.html?unit=4&number=35

High school level multiple-choice quiz on Progressivism from Prentice Hall.
Resource Type: Test or Quiz
Grade Level: HS

Then and Now: Public Health from 1900 to Today

www.thirteen.org/edonline/lessons/1900house/index.html

Throughout the twentieth century, the world has become a healthier place, for example, life expectancy has increased by almost 30 years. These changes can be attributed to improvements in public health, disease control, sanitation, immunization, better maternal and child health, and healthier lifestyles. This lesson plan will examine the public health issues and diseases doctors faced during the 1900s.
Resource Type: Lesson or Activity
Grade Level: MS, HS

Doing the Decades

http://memory.loc.gov/learn/lessons/theme.html

This is a broad, 10-week project where students focus on the major trends and changes in the United States from 1890 to 1941 and how these changes affected groups and individuals. Students are broken into groups by decade and cover six primary themes (such as immigration, industrialization and the growth of capitalism) and a series of topics. Students identify and utilize primary sources to discuss these changes, using materials from the Library of Congress American Memory collections and other materials they gather. Designed for grades 6–12.
Resource Type: Lesson or Activity
Grade Level: MS, HS

The Progressive Movement: Document-Based Essay

www.phschool.com/curriculum_support/brief_review/us_history/essay_questions/unit4.cfm

This Prentice Hall DBQ is designed to test your ability to work with historical documents and is based on the accompanying documents (1–6).
Resource Type: Lesson or Activity; Primary Source Collection
Grade Level: HS

Interpreting Primary Sources

www.digitalhistory.uh.edu/historyonline/handouts.cfm

"Digital History" provides brief excerpts from primary sources and statistics and questions to think about. Check out Urban Political Machines, Immigration, Problems of Youth, and Progressive Reform and the Trusts.
Resource Type: Lesson or Activity; Primary Source Collection
Grade Level: HS

Digital History Resource Guides

www.digitalhistory.uh.edu/resource_guides

"Digital History Resource Guides" provide links to American history Web sites by period and provide historical overviews, readings (online textbook chapter, Reader's Companion),

primary source documents (documents, maps, cartoons), teaching resources (chronologies, maps, quizzes), audiovisual resources, and additional resources. The Guides are an excellent and comprehensive teaching resource.
Resource Type: Course Model
Grade Level: HS, College

HistoryTeacher.net: AP United States History Quizzes
www.historyteacher.net/USQuizMainPage.htm

A teacher at the Horace Greeley High School in Chappaqua, New York, has produced a great general site for history teachers that offers AP-level U.S. history quizzes on many different periods and topics.
Resource Type: Test or Quiz
Grade Level: HS

AP United States History DBQs: 1875–1925
www.historyteacher.net/AHAP/AHAP-DBQMainPage.htm

These student-created Documents-Based Questions are part of the excellent historyteacher.net site.
Resource Type: Lesson or Activity; Primary Source Collection
Grade Level: HS

The American People: The Progressives Confront Industrial Capitalism
http://wps.ablongman.com/long_nash_ap_6/0,7361,592970-,00.html

PowerPoint presentation on the Progressive movement as part of the online companion to *The American People*. Click PowerPoint Presentations and then Chapter 21.
Resource Type: Multimedia Presentation
Grade Level: HS

U.S. Women's History: Lesson Ideas and Document-Based Questions
http://womhist.binghamton.edu/teacher/women.htm

The Center for the Historical Study of Women and Gender at the State University of New York at Binghamton offers lesson plans, DBQs, links, and more on American women's history.
Resource Type: Lesson or Activity; Primary Source Collection
Grade Level: HS

Rounding the Bases
http://memory.loc.gov/learn/lessons/00/base/index.html

This lesson challenges students to investigate the roles that race and ethnicity have played in the United States by utilizing the lens of baseball. Covering the period from 1860 to 1959, students are divided into groups each investigating a 20-year segment of time and use primary sources from the Library of Congress's American Memory collection to develop and defend a unique historical hypothesis about race and ethnicity. Students draw parallels between the changing role of race and ethnicity in the history of baseball to the changing role these factors played in broader American society. Designed for grades 9–12.
Resource Type: Lesson or Activity
Grade Level: HS

Stand Up and Sing
http://memory.loc.gov/learn/lessons/99/sing/intro.html

After receiving background on industrialization and the Progressive Era, students explore sheet music to identify themes within songs and address the broader question, "How does society respond to change?" Students use four different Library of Congress American Memory collections documenting American music from the late nineteenth and early twentieth century to explore how reform issues were reflected on and editorialized in songs. The lesson facilitates a discussion of what role music played in reform and how it has been utilized as a means of free speech. Designed for grades 7–12.
Resource Type: Lesson or Activity
Grade Level: MS, HS

Turn-of-the-Century Child
www.noodletools.com/debbie/projects/20c/turn/teach/lp1.html

This lesson focuses on using close analysis of photographs to teach students the difference between observation and deduction. By using photographs from their personal lives and then photographs from the Library of Congress's American Memory collections, students understand how photographs help form a historical record and how they can be used to generate research questions. Designed for grades 6–8.
Resource Type: Lesson or Activity
Grade Level: MS

Nature's Fury
http://memory.loc.gov/learn/lessons/00/nature/index.html

Students draw from a vast collection of primary sources from the late nineteenth and early twentieth century, including poems, diaries, photographs, motion pictures, interviews and more, to investigate human experience with and reaction to natural disaster. Drawing from 16 of the Library of Congress American Memory collections, students learn enough about a single natural disaster's effect on the population to present a mock first-person account of the event as if they were a witness to it. Designed for grades 5–8.
Resource Type: Lesson or Activity
Grade Level: MS

American Immigration
www.bergen.org/AAST/Projects/Immigration

"American Immigration" homepage was started as a part of a school project for a 10th-grade American History class. The project was meant to give information on how immigrants were treated, as well as why they decided to come to America.
Resource Type: Lesson or Activity
Grade Level: HS

The American Nation: Internet Activities
www.phschool.com/atschool/TAN/Survey/Teacher_Area/TAN1_T_BK_index.html

Prentice Hall's phschool.com offers Internet activities based on their *The American Nation* textbook chapters. Middle school grades.

Resource Type: Lesson or Activity; Test or Quiz
Grade Level: MS

A History of the United States: Internet Activities and Student Self-Test Questions
www.phschool.com/atschool/history_us/Student_Area/HUS_S_BK_index.html

Prentice Hall's phschool.com offers Internet activities and interactive quizzes based on *A History of the United States* textbook chapters. High school grades.
Resource Type: Lesson or Activity; Test or Quiz
Grade Level: HS

Technology in America Timeline
www.pbs.org/wgbh/amex/telephone/timeline/index.html

From Benjamin Franklin's lightning rod to the Hubble Space Telescope, this PBS site timeline covers some of America's technological innovations and inventions.
Resource Type: Timeline
Grade Level: HS, MS

World's Transportation Commission Photograph Collection
http://lcweb2.loc.gov/ammem/wtc/wtchome.html

Contains nearly 900 images by American photographer William Henry Jackson. From the Library of Congress.
Resource Type: Primary Source Collection; Virtual Tour
Grade Level: LS, MS, HS

WORLD WAR I

****Newspaper Pictorials: World War I Rotogravures
http://memory.loc.gov/ammem/collections/rotogravures

The three titles digitized for "Newspaper Pictorials: World War I Rotogravures" by the Library of Congress represent diverse contrasting pictorials published in Sunday pictorial sections by two of the most prominent U.S. newspapers of the day: The *New York Times* and *New York Tribune*. The images in this collection track American sentiment about the war in Europe, week by week, before and after U.S. involvement. They document events of the war alongside society news and advertisements touting products of the day, creating a pictorial record of both the war effort and life at home. An excellent research site.
Resource Type: General Reference; Image Collection

****The Price of Freedom: Americans at War
http://americanhistory.si.edu/militaryhistory/

This Smithsonian Web site skillfully integrates Flash video and text to examine armed conflicts involving the United States from the Revolutionary War to the war in Iraq. Each conflict contains a brief video clip, statistical information, and a set of artifacts. There is also a Civil War mystery, an exhibition self-guide, and a teacher's guide. The World War I section contains a short essay on the conflict as well as historic images and artifacts.
Resource Type: Multimedia Presentation

****The World War I Document Archive
www.lib.byu.edu/~rdh/wwi/

The World War I Document Archive from Brigham Young University is an important source of links to WWI primary documents, such as treaties and personal recollections.
Resource Type: General Reference

****The Great War and the Shaping of the 20th Century
www.pbs.org/greatwar/

This PBS site includes interviews, maps, an interactive timeline, education resources, and brief summaries of the series episodes. Among the multimedia highlights are dramatized audio recordings of letters and poems written by combatants and noncombatants, and streaming video of archival footage taken during World War I. There is also a section where historians for comment on how the Great War is still having an affect upon the world.
Resource Type: Multimedia Presentation; Lesson or Activity

***Eyewitness on World War I
www.eyewitnesstohistory.com/w1frm.htm

Has firsthand accounts of the assassination of Archduke Franz Ferdinand, the death of an American pilot, and a German U-boat attack.
Resource Type: Primary Source Collection

***The Great War
www.pitt.edu/~pugachev/greatwar/ww1.html

Provides a detailed list of WWI-related Web sites.
Resource Type: Links Collection

***The Great War Society 1914–1918
www.worldwar1.com/tgws/

A site for students and researchers that features numerous links to WWI topics.
Resource Type: Links Collection

***Influenza 1918
www.pbs.org/wgbh/amex/influenza/

This PBS site focuses on influenza attacks in America and features an interactive map.
Resource Type: General Reference; Multimedia Presentation

***American Leaders Speak
http://memory.loc.gov/ammem/nfhtml/

This Library of Congress site has 59 brief sound recordings of speeches by American leaders from 1918 to 1920. The speeches focus on issues and events surrounding the First World War and the subsequent presidential election of 1920.
Resource Type: Primary Source Collection; Multimedia Presentation

World War I Lesson Plans, Teacher Guides, Activities, and More

Lesson Plan: U.S. Entry into WWI
http://edsitement.neh.gov/view_lesson_plan.asp?id=471

Presented by EDSITEment, this lesson plan is for high school students. Students will examine the events and factors that led to U.S. participation in the war. The lesson plan provides some resources and several guiding questions for students to follow.
Resource Type: Lesson or Activity
Grade Level: HS

Lesson Plan: The Debate in the United States Over the League of Nations
http://edsitement.neh.gov/view_lesson_plan.asp?id=475

In this EDSITEment lesson plan, students revive the League of Nations debate and examine all sides of the argument. Lesson plan comes with Adobe Acrobat printout and links to relevant resources. For grades 9–12.
Resource Type: Lesson or Activity
Grade Level: HS

The Great War: Evaluating the Treaty of Versailles
http://edsitement.neh.gov/view_lesson_plan.asp?id=424

Designed by EDSITEment, this lesson plan comes with an ample supply of resources and documents. Students are asked to analyze the terms of the Treaty of Versailles and then analyze the German response. The lesson plan includes a copy of the treaty and Hitler's 1923 response. This is a high school level lesson plan.
Resource Type: Lesson or Activity
Grade Level: HS

The Gilder Lehrman Institute Modules in American History: World War I
www.gilderlehrman.org/teachers/module16/index.html

The Gilder Lehrman Institute offers quality educational materials, including teaching modules on major topics in American history. Each module includes: A succinct historical overview; learning tools including lesson plans, quizzes, and activities; recommended documents, films, and historic images. These modules were prepared by Steven Mintz, the John and Rebecca Moores Professor of History and the Director of the American Cultures Program at the University of Houston. Other helpful Institute online sources include include American History Quizzes, Letters from America's Wars, Featured Documents for your Classroom, and Primary Source Documents from the Collection.
Resource Type: Course Model
Grade Level: HS

Teacher's Guide: Lost Peace
www.pbs.org/wgbh/peoplescentury/teachers/tglost.html

Investigate the intersection of isolationism, fascism, and the establishment of the League of Nations at the close of World War I. From PBS *People's Century*.
Resource Type: Lesson or Activity
Grade Level: HS

Woodrow Wilson and the Great War: Multiple Choice Quiz, Fill-in-the-Blank, Flashcards, American History Glossary, and an American History Appendix
http://wps.ablongman.com/long_carnes_an_11/0,7137,251988-,00.html

The Student Resources section of *The American Nation* companion Web site features introductions to chapters, interactive quizzes, flashcards, Web links, an American History Glossary, and an American History Appendix.
Resource Type: Course Model
Grade Level: HS

CEC: Group Newspaper Presentations
www.col-ed.org/cur/sst/sst220.txt

In this mini-lesson, students will create a newspaper about World War I. Students work in small groups to research and write. Lesson plan includes grading outline. Recommended for grades 9–12.
Resource Type: Lesson or Activity
Grade Level: HS

Drums of War: Exploring How Politics Shapes American War Policy
www.nytimes.com/learning/teachers/lessons/20020923monday.html

In this *New York Times* lesson, students will research the political climate prior to major American wars of the past, then reflect on the current call for power to confront Iraq.
Resource Type: Lesson or Activity
Grade Level: MS, HS

Interpreting Primary Sources: World War I
www.digitalhistory.uh.edu/historyonline/us32.cfm

"Digital History" provides brief excerpts from primary sources and statistics and questions to think about.
Resource Type: Lesson or Activity
Grade Level: HS

Digital History Resource Guides
www.digitalhistory.uh.edu/resource_guides/

"Digital History Resource Guides" provide links to American history Web sites by period and provide historical overviews, readings (online textbook chapter, Reader's Companion), primary source documents (documents, maps, cartoons), teaching resources (chronologies, maps, quizzes), audiovisual resources, and additional resources. The Guides are an excellent and comprehensive teaching resource.
Resource Type: Course Model
Grade Level: HS, College

HistoryTeacher.net: AP United States History Quizzes
www.historyteacher.net/USQuizMainPage.htm

A teacher at the Horace Greeley High School in Chappaqua, New York, has produced a great general site for history teachers that offers AP-level U.S. history quizzes on many different periods and topics.

Resource Type: Test or Quiz
Grade Level: HS

AP United States History DBQs: 1875–1925
www.historyteacher.net/AHAP/AHAP-DBQMainPage.htm

These student-created Documents-Based Questions are part of the excellent Historyteacher.net site.
Resource Type: Lesson or Activity; Primary Source Collection
Grade Level: HS

The American People: The Great War
http://wps.ablongman.com/long_nash_ap_6/0,7361,592970-,00.html

PowerPoint presentation on America and World War I as part of the online companion to *The American People*. Click Chapter 22.
Resource Type: Multimedia Presentation
Grade Level: HS

World War I: Blank Map
http://wps.ablongman.com/long_nash_ap_6/0,7361,592970-,00.html

The companion Web site to *The American People* offers blank maps related to various topics in American history. The maps can be printed or placed in a PowerPoint presentation
Resource Type: Map
Grade Level: MS, HS

The American Nation: Internet Activities
www.phschool.com/atschool/TAN/Survey/Teacher_Area/TAN1_T_BK_index.html

Prentice Hall's phschool.com offers Internet activities based on their *The American Nation* textbook chapters. Middle school grades.
Resource Type: Lesson or Activity
Grade Level: MS

A History of the United States: Internet Activities and Student Self-Test Questions
www.phschool.com/atschool/history_us/Student_Area/HUS_S_BK_index.html

Prentice Hall's phschool.com offers Internet activities and interactive quizzes based on *A History of the United States* textbook chapters. High school grades.
Resource Type: Lesson or Activity; Test or Quiz
Grade Level: HS

ROARING TWENTIES

****Clash of Cultures in the 1910s and 1920s
http://history.osu.edu/Projects/Clash/default.htm

An attractive and informative site on cultural tensions, including information on prohibition, immigration, the KKK, the New Woman, and the Scopes Trial. Produced by the Ohio State University History Department (see Figure 5.4).
Resource Type: General Reference; Primary Source Collection

Figure 5.4: Clash of Cultures in the 1910s and 1920s

****Temperance and Prohibition
http://prohibition.osu.edu/

This Ohio State University production explores prohibition. It analyzes the Anti-Saloon League and presents arguments for and against Prohibition, among other features.
Resource Type: General Reference

****Lindbergh
www.pbs.org/wgbh/amex/lindbergh/

A companion to the *American Experience* video series, this site has special features on the *Spirit of St. Louis*, the kidnapping of Lindbergh's son, a discussion of Lindbergh's hero status, a timeline, maps, and a teacher's guide.
Resource Type: General Reference; Multimedia Presentation; Lesson or Activity

****Prosperity and Thrift: The Coolidge Era and the Consumer Economy, 1921–1929
http://lcweb2.loc.gov/ammem/coolhtml/coolhome.html

This Library of Congress site features materials from the 1920s that illustrate the prosperity of the Coolidge era, the nation's transition to a mass consumer economy, and the role of government in this transition.
Resource Type: Primary Source Collection; General Reference

****Jazz Age Culture
http://faculty.pittstate.edu/~knichols/jazzage.html

A professor of English at Pittsburgh State University has produced several sites centering on the Jazz Age. This link will take you to Part I of her "Jazz Age Culture" site, which offers many well-organized links on the following topics: Langston Hughes and other Harlem Renaissance writers, artists, musicians, and notables; F. Scott Fitzgerald, Edna St. Vincent Millay, and other modernist writers; Picasso, Dali, de Lempicka, Kandinsky, and other artists; resources on Prohibition, flappers, racial violence, sports, automobiles, aviators, art deco, movie stars, the Crash of '29, the scandals/trials of the decade, and the new technologies; and World War I poetry.
Resource Type: General Reference; Links Collection

****The 1920s Experience
www.angelfire.com/co/pscst/index.html

Another broad introduction to the 1920s, this commercial site has a vast amount of information and images on people, art, events, literature, music, and technology.
Resource Type: General Reference

****The Lawless Decade
www.paulsann.org/thelawlessdecade/20_s.html

"The Lawless Decade" is a pictorial history of the "convulsive shocks" from WWI armistice and prohibition to the repeal of the 18th Amendment and the New Deal. The site is based on the book by the same name and is organized by year.
Resource Type: General Reference, Art History

****Scopes Trial Home Page
www.law.umkc.edu/faculty/projects/ftrials/scopes/scopes.htm

This site features one of the most famous trials in American history. In a Dayton, Tennessee courtroom in the summer of 1925, a jury was to decide the fate of John Scopes, a high school biology teacher charged with illegally teaching the theory of evolution. The meaning of the trial emerged through its interpretation as a conflict of social and intellectual values between "traditionalists" and "modernists." The site features an introduction to the case, biographies of Scopes, Darrow, Bryan and other key participants, a chronology, trial satire, and more on the evolution controversy.
Resource Type: General Reference; Primary Source Collection

***Comrades: 1917–1945
http://cnn.com/SPECIALS/cold.war/

This site is part of a CNN Perspectives series and explores U.S.–U.S.S.R. relations up to the

Cold War. Included are interactive maps, rare footage, declassified documents, biographies, picture galleries, timelines, book excerpts, an educator's guide, and more.
Resource Type: General Reference, Multimedia Presentation

***Harlem: Mecca of the New Negro
http://etext.lib.virginia.edu/harlem/

This hypertext article is a Hypermedia Edition of the March 1925 Survey Graphic Harlem Number. *The Survey* magazine was the premier journal of social work in America in the 1920s. In November of 1924, *The Survey*'s chief editor devoted a special issue to the African American "Renaissance" underway in Harlem.
Resource Type: Primary Source Collection

Roaring Twenties Lesson Plans, Activities, and More

The Gilder Lehrman Institute Modules in American History: The 1920s
www.gilderlehrman.org/teachers/module17/index.html

The Gilder Lehrman Institute offers quality educational materials, including teaching modules on major topics in American history. Each module includes: A succinct historical overview; learning tools including lesson plans, quizzes, and activities; recommended documents, films, and historic images. These modules were prepared by Steven Mintz, the John and Rebecca Moores Professor of History and the Director of the American Cultures Program at the University of Houston. Other helpful Institute online sources include include American History Quizzes, Letters from America's Wars Featured Documents for your Classroom, and Primary Source Documents from the Collection.
Resource Type: Course Model
Grade Level: HS

1920s Magazine Project
http://www.howhist.com/fraser/twenties.htm

This project, designed by high school teacher Jen Fraser, asks students to create a magazine in the style of the Roaring Twenties. The site comes with suggested resources and a grading rubric.
Resource Type: Lesson or Activity
Grade Level: HS

Pacifism vs. Patriotism in the 1920s
http://womhist.binghamton.edu/teacher/milit.htm

This activity asks students to consider the different political positions on war and disarmament of two women's activist organizations from this period: the Daughters of the American Revolution (DAR) and the Women's International League for Peace and Freedom (WILPF). Students read and discuss letters and complete a short writing assignment analyzing political cartoons reprinted in DAR Magazine. From the "Women and Social Movements in the United States, 1775–2000" Web site.
Resource Type: Lesson or Activity
Grade Level: HS, College

Course Models: Harlem Renaissance
www.history.ctaponline.org/center/hsscm/index.cfm?Page_Key=1691

Part of the California History-Social Science content standards and annotated course which includes: Background information, focus questions, pupil activities and handouts, an assessment, and references to books, articles, Web sites, literature, audiovisual programs, and a historic site.
Resource Type: Course Model
Grade Level: HS

Activity: The Development of Jazz
http://catalog.socialstudies.com/c/@WBnaxsPAxNl9l/Pages/article.html?article@jazz

Written by the Social Studies School Service, this activity plan emphasizes the importance of jazz in our history. Students will learn about Harlem, jazz, and what jazz is today. Recommended for grade 11.
Resource Type: Lesson or Activity
Grade Level: HS

Postwar Society and Culture: Multiple Choice Quiz, Fill-in-the-Blank, Flashcards, American History Glossary, and an American History Appendix
http://wps.ablongman.com/long_carnes_an_11/0,7137,252046-,00.html

The Student Resources section of *The American Nation* companion Web site features introductions to chapters, interactive quizzes, flashcards, Web links, an American History Glossary, and an American History Appendix.
Resource Type: Test or Quiz; General Reference
Grade Level: MS

The New Era, 1921–1933: Multiple Choice Quiz, Fill-in-the-Blank, Flashcards, American History Glossary, and an American History Appendix
http://wps.ablongman.com/long_carnes_an_11/0,7137,252104-,00.html

The Student Resources section of *The American Nation* companion Web site features introductions to chapters, interactive quizzes, flashcards, Web links, an American History Glossary, and an American History Appendix.
Resource Type: Test or Quiz; General Reference
Grade Level: MS

Jazz Talk: Lesson Plan
http://school.discovery.com/lessonplans/activities/jazztalk/

In this lesson plan, students will analyze work songs, spirituals, blues, and gospel songs in order to develop an appreciation for the origins of jazz music. They will also examine works of poetry from African American artists and create their own poems. After completing this activity, students should be able to describe the impact of African American songs and writings on American culture. Grades 6–12.
Resource Type: Lesson or Activity
Grade Level: MS, HS

Interpreting Primary Sources
www.digitalhistory.uh.edu/historyonline/us33.cfm

"Digital History" provides brief excerpts from primary sources and statistics and questions regarding controversies of the 1920s.
Resource Type: Primary Source Collection; Lesson or Activity
Grade Level: HS, College

Digital History Resource Guides
www.digitalhistory.uh.edu/resource_guides/

"Digital History Resource Guides" provide links to American history Web sites by period and provide historical overviews, readings (online textbook chapter, Reader's Companion), primary source documents (documents, maps, cartoons), teaching resources (chronologies, maps, quizzes), audiovisual resources, and additional resources. It is an excellent and comprehensive teaching resource.
Resource Type: General Reference; Lesson or Activity; Primary Source Collection
Grade Level: HS, College

At Home and Abroad: Prosperity and Depression, 1917–1940 Practice Test
www.phschool.com/curriculum_support/brief_review/us_history/tests.html?unit=5&number=35

High school level multiple-choice quiz on Jazz Age and Great Depression from Prentice Hall.
Resource Type: Test or Quiz
Grade Level: HS

At Home and Abroad: Prosperity and Depression, 1917–1940: Document-Based Essay
www.phschool.com/curriculum_support/brief_review/us_history/essay_questions/unit5.cfm

This Prentice Hall DBQ is designed to test your ability to work with historical documents and is based on the accompanying documents (1–6).
Resource Type: Lesson or Activity
Grade level: HS

Streamlines and Breadlines
www.thirteen.org/edonline/lessons/streamlines/streamlinesov.html

From the site: "High School students will learn about the growth and development of cities in America from 1920 through 1940. Immigration, the migration of African-Americans from the South to the urban centers of the North, industrialization, and the Great Depression all affected cities during this period. This lesson will culminate in a student essay that compares two contrasting images from this time period. Students will view two sets of images from Thirteen/WNET's 'American Visions' Web site. Students will choose one image from each group and compare and contrast the images in an essay."
Resource Type: Lesson or Activity
Grade Level: HS

HistoryTeacher.net: AP United States History Quizzes
www.historyteacher.net/USQuizMainPage.htm

A teacher at the Horace Greeley High School in Chappaqua, New York, has produced a great general site for history teachers that offers AP-level U.S. history quizzes on many different

periods and topics.
Resource Type: Test or Quiz
Grade Level: HS

AP United States History DBQs: 1875–1925
www.historyteacher.net/AHAP/AHAP-DBQMainPage.htm

These student-created Documents-Based Questions are part of the excellent Historyteacher.net site.
Resource Type: Lesson or Activity
Grade Level: HS

The American People: Affluence and Anxiety
http://wps.ablongman.com/long_nash_ap_6/0,7361,592970-,00.html

PowerPoint presentation on America during the 1920s as part of the online companion to *The American People*. Click PowerPoint Presentations and then Chapter 23.
Resource Type: Lesson or Activity
Grade Level: HS

The American Nation: Internet Activities
www.phschool.com/atschool/TAN/Survey/Teacher_Area/TAN1_T_BK_index.html

Prentice Hall's phschool.com offers Internet activities based on their *The American Nation* textbook chapters.
Resource Type: Lesson or Activity
Grade Level: MS

A History of the United States: Internet Activities and Student Self-Test Questions
www.phschool.com/atschool/history_us/Student_Area/HUS_S_BK_index.html

Prentice Hall's phschool.com offers Internet activities and interactive quizzes based on *A History of the United States* textbook chapters.
Resource Type: Test or Quiz
Grade Level: HS

THE GREAT DEPRESSION

****New Deal Network
http://newdeal.feri.org/index.htm

The Franklin and Eleanor Roosevelt Institute (FERI), in collaboration with the Franklin D. Roosevelt Presidential Library, Marist College, and IBM, launched the "New Deal Network" (NDN). The impressive site features 20,000 items: Photographs, speeches, letters, documents, and exercises from the New Deal era (see Figure 5.5).
Resource Type: Primary Source Collection; Lesson or Activity

****The Hoover Dam
www.pbs.org/wgbh/pages/amex/hoover/index.html

A companion to the PBS *American Experience* video series, the interesting site focuses on the Hoover Dam construction. There is a timeline of construction, Dam facts and environmental

Figure 5.5: New Deal Network

This Month in New Deal History
A calendar of some of the notable events and dates in the history of the United States during the Roosevelt Administration.

Friday, March 9, 2007

NEW DEAL NETWORK

HOME PAGE
CONTACT US
ABOUT US
FAQ

CLASSROOM ★ DOCUMENTS ★ FEATURES ★ LINKS ★ FORUMS ★ PHOTOGRAPHS ★ SEARCH >search help [GO]

Research and Study

New Deal Document Library
Over 900 articles, speeches, letters and other texts, organized by subject, date and author.

New Deal Photo Gallery
Over 5000 Great Depression era images from the National Archives, the FDR Library and many other sources.

New Deal Network Classroom
Lesson plans, web projects, and bibliographical materials on the Great Depression.

H-US1918-45
A moderated H-Net discussion list for teachers and historians.

The New Deal Network, an educational guide to the Great Depression of the 1930s, is sponsored by the Franklin and Eleanor

Features

Archives in the Attic
Documents from the Great Depression. Contributed from the family collections of New Deal Network visitors.

The Great Depression and the Arts
Four lesson plans developed by teachers and historians working with the National Center for History in the Schools and the Organization of American Historians.

A New Deal for Carbon Hill, Alabama
A photo-documentary of the impact of the Great Depression and New Deal on a small Southern town, by WPA photographer William C. Pryor.

The Magpie Sings the Great Depression
During the 1930s, students from the Bronx's DeWitt Clinton High School documented their life and times. This feature includes 193 poems, articles, and short stories and 295 graphics.

issues, maps of the Dam, stories of key characters and incidents and a teacher's guide
Resource Type: General Reference; Lesson or Activity

****Breadline: 1929–1939**
www.pbs.org/wgbh/peoplescentury/episodes/breadline/

Part of PBS's *People's Century* television series, this site explores the massive unemployment in America during the Depression and offers interviews, a timeline, and a teacher's guide.
Resource Type: Primary Source Collection; Lesson or Activity

****American Life Histories, 1936–1940**
http://memory.loc.gov/ammem/wpaintro/wpahome.html

These fascinating life histories were written by the staff of the Folklore Project of the Federal Writers' Project for the U.S. Works Progress (later Work Projects) Administration (WPA)

from 1936 to 1940. The Library of Congress collection includes 2,900 documents representing the work of over 300 writers from 24 states. Typically 2,000–15,000 words in length, the documents consist of drafts and revisions, varying in form from narrative to dialogue to report to case history. The histories describe the informant's family education, income, occupation, political views, religion and morals, medical needs, diet and miscellaneous observations.
Resource Type: Primary Source Collection

****Surviving the Dust Bowl
www.pbs.org/wgbh/pages/amex/dustbowl/

Part of PBS's *American Experience* television series, this site examines the region in the Southwest renamed the "Dust Bowl" because of a catastrophic eight-year drought. Included is a timeline, maps, eyewitness accounts, New Deal remedies, people and events from the era, and a teacher's guide.
Resource Type: General Reference; Primary Source Collection; Lesson or Activity

****Voices from the Dust Bowl
http://memory.loc.gov/ammem/afctshtml/tshome.html

This Library of Congress site documents the everyday life of residents in central California in 1940 and 1941. There are audio recordings, photographs, manuscript materials, publications, related sources, and more.
Resource Type: Primary Source Collection; General Reference

**** Riding the Rails
www.pbs.org/wgbh/pages/amex/rails/

Part of PBS's *American Experience* television series, this site focuses on the plight of more than a quarter million teenagers living on the road in America. There is a timeline, maps, "tales from the rails," Hobo songs, a teacher's guide, recommended resources, and more. Great site to introduce teenagers to the effects of the Great Depression.
Resource Type: General Reference; Primary Source Collection

****America in the 1930s
http://xroads.virginia.edu/~1930s/front.html

This University of Virginia production features a museum for American studies, cultural maps, ongoing hypertext projects, an electronic classroom, and special features.
Resource Type: Primary Source Collection; General Reference

****Franklin D. Roosevelt Presidential Library and Museum
www.fdrlibrary.marist.edu/index.html

The "Franklin D. Roosevelt Presidential Library and Museum" educational program Web site includes biographies of Franklin D. Roosevelt and Eleanor Roosevelt, a Roosevelt Timeline, Online Documents and Photographs, a Research Guide, and Puzzles and Activities.
Resource Type: General Reference; Lesson or Activity

****The Flint Sit-Down Strike, 1936–1937
www.historicalvoices.org/flint/index.php

An audio gallery of the famous union strike that features a slide show and timeline.
Resource Type: General Reference; Primary Source Collection

****Depression Papers of Herbert Hoover
www.geocities.com/mb_williams/hooverpapers/

A large collection with many sections: Tariffs and Agriculture, Economic Stability Program, Relief, Unemployment and Public Works, The Dust Bowl, Banks & Finance, The Federal Budget, Economic Recovery Measures, and the Bonus March.
Resource Type: Primary Source Collection

****Studs Terkel: Conversations
www.studsterkel.org/

Produced by the Chicago Historical Society, this site explores the life and work of Studs Terkel, an important American oral historian. Galleries focus on interviews that Mr. Terkel did for his books, including one on the Depression, and also contains a multimedia interview with him.
General Reference: Multimedia Presentation; Primary Source Collection

****The Depression News
www.sos.state.mi.us/history/museum/explore/museums/hismus/1900-75/depressn/index.html

From the Michigan Historical Museum, the site explores the depression in a newspaper format and provides teacher and student resources.
Resource Type: General Reference

***Debunking the Roosevelt Myth
www.rooseveltmyth.com/

The Web site provides links to online e-books critical of or hostile to Roosevelt including: *The Roosevelt Myth* (John T. Flynn), *Communism at Pearl Harbor* (Anthony Kubek), *Roosevelt's Road to Russia* (George N. Crocker,) and *The Yalta Betrayal* (Felix Wittmer).
Resource Type: General Reference

The Great Depression Lesson Plans, Teacher Guides, Activities, and More

The Gilder Lehrman Institute Modules in American History: The Great Depression
www.gilderlehrman.org/teachers/module18/index.html

The Gilder Lehrman Institute offers quality educational materials, including teaching modules on major topics in American history. Each module includes: A succinct historical overview; learning tools including lesson plans, quizzes, and activities; recommended documents, films, and historic images. These modules were prepared by Steven Mintz, the John and Rebecca Moores Professor of History and the Director of the American Cultures Program at the University of Houston. Other helpful Institute online sources include include American History Quizzes, Letters from America's Wars Featured Documents for your Classroom, and Primary Source Documents from the Collection.
Resource Type: Course Model
Grade Level: HS

Brother Can You Spare a Dime: The Effects of the New Deal & the Great Depression
http://memory.loc.gov/learn/lessons/98/dime/intro.html

Part of the Library of Congress's impressive collection of exhibits, this site brings the pain of the Great Depression era to life.
Resource Type: Lesson or Activity
Grade Level: HS

The Great Depression and the 1990s
http://memory.loc.gov/learn/lessons/97/depress/overview.html

By using the American Memory's American Life Histories, 1936–1940 documents, personal interviews, and the Library of Congress's online legislative information, students will be able to gain a better understanding of why the government takes care of its people and how this type of welfare state started. Armed with this knowledge, they can then evaluate the current need of government programs, such as welfare, Medicare and Social Security, on the federal and state level.
Resource Type: Lesson or Activity
Grade Level: HS

Documentary Photography and The Photographic Essay
http://newdeal.feri.org/classrm/partr2.htm

Students will examine and interpret photographs taken by Rondal Partridge, a documentary photographer who worked with Dorothea Lange during the Depression Era. A study of the photographs will enable students to to visualize the effects of the Depression on some of America's young people. Reading the captions will provide background information and an opportunity to learn about historical perspective. This lesson plan is provided by the New Deal Network.
Resource Type: Lesson or Activity; Primary Source Collection
Grade Level: MS, HS

Examining the Causes and Effects of the 1929 Stock Market Crash
www.nytimes.com/learning/teachers/lessons/19991018monday.html?searchpv=learning_lessons

In this lesson, students use *New York Times* articles covering the stock market collapse in 1929 to analyze the reported causes of this stock market collapse, reactions on many levels to the collapse, and speculated short-term and long-term effects of the collapse. This lesson plan is intended for grades 6–12.
Resource Type: Lesson or Activity; Primary Source Collection
Grade Level: MS, HS

Roosevelt's New Deal
www.teachers.net/lessons/posts/2606.html

Written by teacher Brian Davis of Southern Columbia High School in Catawissa, Pennsylvania, this lesson plan instructs students on conducting online research and examining the New Deal.
Resource Type: Lesson or Activity
Grade Level: HS

Riding the Rails: Teacher's Guide
www.pbs.org/wgbh/amex/rails/tguide/index.html

Students will learn about "teenage hobos" in this PBS Depression-era lesson plan. Emphasis is put on the causes of homelessness and what made these young men leave home. The lesson plan also outlines topics for discussion, as well as small group activities.
Resource Type: Lesson or Activity
Grade Level: MS, HS

Surviving the Dust Bowl
www.pbs.org/wgbh/amex/dustbowl/tguide/index.html

In this PBS lesson plan, students begin studying "The Dust Bowl" and the way in which farmers reacted to it. The Teacher's Guide includes 8 activities and discussion topics. PBS recommends purchase of the film *Surviving the Dust Bowl* in order to fully utilize this lesson plan.
Resource Type: Lesson or Activity
Grade Level: MS, HS

Living Without Technology
www.pbs.org/wnet/1900house/lessons/lesson2a.html

Presented by PBS, this lesson plan introduces a project that allows students to experience the difficulties of the Great Depression. Students are instructed to live 24 hours without many of today's modern comforts.
Resource Type: Lesson or Activity
Grade Level: MS, HS

The Great Depression and the 1990s
http://memory.loc.gov/ammem/ndlpedu/lessons/97/depress/overview.html

The Library of Congress has provided this Great Depression lesson plan that allows students to examine the origins of the welfare state. Great Depression legislature is examined and discussed, as well as the connection to our present-day welfare system.
Resource Type: Lesson or Activity
Grade Level: HS

Visions in the Dust
http://lcweb2.loc.gov/ammem/ndlpedu/lessons/99/dust/intro.html

For grades 6–8, this lesson plan uses photographic examination to teach students about the Dustbowl. This Library of Congress lesson plan also uses PBS resources.
Resource Type: Lesson or Activity
Grade Level: MS

Worth a Thousand Words: Depression-Era Photographs
http://edsitement.neh.gov/view_lesson_plan.asp?id=304

Using authentic photographs that were taken to introduce the New Deal, students will follow this EDSITEment lesson plan and learn about the depression. Recommended for grades 9–12.
Resource Type: Lesson or Activity; Primary Source Collection
Grade Level: HS

Constitutional Issues: Separation of Powers

www.archives.gov/education/lessons/separation-powers/

Presented by the National Archives, this lesson plan examines FDR's attempt to add a Justice to the Supreme Court.

Resource Type: Lesson or Activity
Grade Level: HS, College

Hard Times, Soft Sell

www.thirteen.org/edonline/lessons/hardtimes/hardtimesov.html

From the site: "Using online content from the *American Visions episode* entitled Streamlines and Breadlines as a jumping-off point, students then explore the social, political, and artistic climate of the 1930s Great Depression and identify themes that permeated the zeitgeist of that era. Using a diverse array of sources—online, software, video, and multimedia resources—students will investigate diverse people's experiences of the Depression, conduct surveys and interviews, and create and publish a variety of media. highlighting Depression-era motifs and resources."

Resource Type: Lesson or Activity
Grade Level: HS

Streamlines and Breadlines

www.thirteen.org/edonline/lessons/streamlines/streamlinesov.html

From the site: "Students will learn about the growth and development of cities in America from 1920 through 1940. Immigration, the migration of African-Americans from the South to the urban centers of the North, industrialization, and the Great Depression all affected cities during this period. This lesson will culminate in a student essay that compares two contrasting images from this time period. Students will view two sets of images from Thirteen/WNET's "American Visions" Web site. Students will choose one image from each group and compare and contrast the images in an essay."

Resource Type: Lesson or Activity
Grade Level: HS

Digital History Resource Guides

www.digitalhistory.uh.edu/resource_guides/

"Digital History Resource Guides" provide links to American history Web sites by period and provide historical overviews, readings (online textbook chapter, Reader's Companion), primary source documents (documents, maps, cartoons), teaching resources (chronologies, maps, quizzes), audiovisual resources, and additional resources. The Guides are an excellent and comprehensive teaching resource.

Resource Type: Course Model; Lesson or Activity
Grade Level: HS, College

Course Models: Great Depression

www.history.ctaponline.org/center/hsscm/index.cfm?Page_Key=1611

Part of the California History-Social Science content standards and annotated course, which includes: Background information, focus questions, pupil activities and handouts,

an assessment, and references to books, articles, web sites, literature, audio-video programs, and historic sites.
Resource Type: Course Model
Grade Level: HS

The New Deal: Multiple Choice Quiz, Fill-in-the-Blank, Flashcards, American History Glossary, American History Appendix

http://wps.ablongman.com/long_carnes_an_11/0,7137,252157-,00.html

The Student Resources section of *The American Nation* companion Web site features introductions to chapters, interactive quizzes, flashcards, Web links, an American History Glossary, and an American History Appendix.
Resource type: Test or Quiz
Grade Level: MS

At Home and Abroad: Prosperity and Depression, 1917-1940 Practice Test

www.planet-think.net/curriculum_support/brief_review/us_history/tests.html?unit=5&number=35

High school level quiz on Jazz Age and Great Depression from Prentice Hall.
Resource type: Test or Quiz
Grade Level: HS

Interpreting Primary Sources

www.digitalhistory.uh.edu/historyonline/us34.cfm

"Digital History" provides brief excerpts from primary sources and statistics and questions to think about the Great Depression and the New Deal.
Resource Type: Lesson or Activity; Primary Source Collection
Grade Level: HS, College

At Home and Abroad: Prosperity and Depression, 1917–1940: Document-Based Essay

www.phschool.com/curriculum_support/brief_review/us_history/essay_questions/unit5.cfm

This Prentice Hall DBQ is designed to test your ability to work with historical documents and is based on the accompanying documents (1–6).
Resource Type: Lesson or Activity
Grade Level: HS

HistoryTeacher.net: AP United States History Quizzes

www.historyteacher.net/USQuizMainPage.htm

A teacher at the Horace Greeley High School in Chappaqua, New York, has produced a great general site for history teachers that offers AP-level U.S. history quizzes on many different periods and topics.
Resource type: Test or Quiz
Grade Level: HS

AP United States History Documents-Based Questions: 1920–1970

www.historyteacher.net/2001DBQsMainPage.htm

These student-created Documents-Based Questions are part of the excellent Historyteacher.net site.

Resource Type: Lesson or Activity
Grade Level: HS

The American People: The Great Depression and the New Deal
http://wps.ablongman.com/long_nash_ap_6/0,7361,592970-,00.html

PowerPoint presentation on the Great Depression and the New Deal as part of the online companion to *The American People*. Click PowerPoint Presentations and then Chapter 24.
Resource Type: Lesson or Activity
Grade Level: HS

The American Nation: Internet Activities
www.phschool.com/atschool/TAN/Survey/Teacher_Area/TAN1_T_BK_index.html

Prentice Hall's phschool.com offers Internet activities based on their *The American Nation* textbook chapters.
Resource Type: Lesson or Activity
Grade Level: MS

A History of the United States: Internet Activities and Student Self-Test Questions
www.phschool.com/atschool/history_us/Student_Area/HUS_S_BK_index.html

Prentice Hall's phschool.com offers Internet activities and interactive quizzes based on *A History of the United States* textbook chapters.
Resource Type: Lesson or Activity
Grade Level: HS

Economics Resources for K–12 Teachers
http://ecedweb.unomaha.edu/K-12/home.cfm

EcEdWeb is your headquarters for teaching resources for K–12 or pre-college economics. The menus at the top are designed to work the way you work: if you need a lesson or information on a particular concept (e.g., scarcity), start with Concepts.
Resource Type: Lesson or Activity
Grade Level: MS, HS

CHAPTER 6

World War II—Today (1939–Present)

WORLD WAR II: GENERAL RESOURCES

****Encyclopedia of the Second World War
www.spartacus.schoolnet.co.uk/2WW.htm

"Encyclopedia of the Second World War" is a Spartacus Educational Web site and enables one to research individual people and events of the war in detail. The sources are "hyper-texted" so that the visitor can research the newspaper, organization, etc., that produced the source. There are several subsections including those on: Background to the War; Nazi Germany, Chronology of the War, Political Leaders, European Diplomacy, Major Offensives, British Military Leaders, USA Military Leaders, German Military Leaders, Japanese Military Leaders, The Armed Forces, The Air War, The Resistance, Scientists & Inventors, War at Sea, Resistance in Nazi Germany, The Holocaust, War Artists, Weapons and New Technology.
Resource Type: General Reference

****Hyper War: World War II
www.ibiblio.org/hyperwar/

"Hyper War" is a "hypertext" history of the second World War and features diplomatic and political documents. The content is made up, primarily, of "public domain" (noncopyright) materials in English: Official government histories (United States and British Commonwealth/Empire); Source documents (diplomatic messages, Action Reports, logs, diaries, etc.); and primary references (manuals, glossaries, etc.). Wherever possible, hyperlinks between these histories and documents have been included.
Resource Type: General Reference; Primary Source Collection

****World War II Sites
http://connections.smsd.org/veterans/wwii_sites.htm

This site serves as a gateway to World War II sites appropriate for students and teachers. Links revolve around the following topics: The Rise of Fascism-Germany, Italy and Japan, Holocaust, Pearl Harbor and America's Response, D-Day and the War in the Pacific, The Home Front, Plans for Peace and the Atomic Bomb, Personalities, Literature, Propaganda,

Women in the War, and Miscellaneous. Updated regularly, the site leads you to movie clips, virtual tours, stories of the war, biographies, films, photographs, a links, and even a test.
Resource Type: General Reference

****BBC Online: World War II
www.bbc.co.uk/history/worldwars/wwtwo/

Covers various topics of the war such as campaigns and battles, politics, home front, and the holocaust. Multimedia zone offers interactive maps, photographs and audio and video clips. One of the links, "WW2 People's War," is a new Web site from BBCi History, aspiring to create a new national archive of personal and family stories from World War II.
Resource Type: General Reference; Multimedia Presentation

****The Price of Freedom: Americans at War
http://americanhistory.si.edu/militaryhistory/

This Smithsonian Web site skillfully integrates Flash video and text to examine armed conflicts involving the United States from the Revolutionary War to the war in Iraq. Each conflict contains a brief video clip, statistical information, and a set of artifacts. The World War II section contains an introductory movie and short essay on the conflict as well as historic images and artifacts.
Resource Type: Multimedia Presentation

Figure 6.1: The Price of Freedom: Americans at War

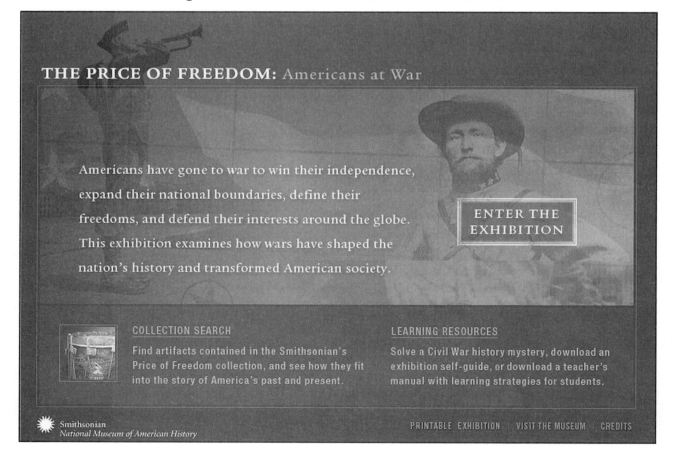

****Total War
www.pbs.org/wgbh/peoplescentury/episodes/totalwar/

Part of PBS's *People's Century* series, "Total War" discusses the contributions of civilians during WWII and their victimization. In "Total War," eyewitnesses from Britain, Germany, Russia, Korea, Japan, and the United States tell the story of how millions of civilians participated and came to be legitimate targets in the Second World War. There are eyewitness interviews, a teacher's guide, links to related sites, and chance to tell your own story.
Resource Type: General Reference; Primary Source Collection

****Open Directory Project: World War II
http://dmoz.org/Society/History/By_Time_Period/Twentieth_Century/Wars_and_Conflicts/World_War_II/

This comprehensive directory contains links to hundreds of Web sites on the Second World War: Air Forces, Arts and Literature, Atomic, Directories, Documents, Manuscripts and other Primary Sources, Education and Academic, Land Forces, Naval Forces, People, Regional, Theaters of Operations, War Crimes and Weapons and Equipment.
Resource Type: General Reference

****Armies of the Second World War
http://books.stonebooks.com/armies/

"Armies of the Second World War" is an impressive online database of day-by-day orders of battle and information about hundreds of division, brigade, and regiment-sized units in World War II. Information currently available in the database covers Commonwealth, Dominion, Colonial, Exile, and "Minor" Allied armies in Europe, Africa, and western Asia, from September 1, 1939, through May 7, 1945.
Resource Type: General Reference

****World War II Remembered
www.usd230.k12.ks.us/PICTT/index.html

Former Senator Bob Dole and historian Stephen Ambrose are among those who contribute to this site. It was created to preserve untold stories of those who lived during the World War II era.
Resource Type: Primary Source Collection

****The World at War, History of WW 1939–1945
www.euronet.nl/users/wilfried/ww2/ww2.htm

"The World at War, History of WW 1939–1945" is probably one of the best military history Web sites of WWII. Its goal is to be as complete as possible about the history of 1939–1945 and serve as a well-organized gateway to numerous sources. Information and links are organized around a timeline of events. The authors also provide a discussion forum, message board, and a mailing list and the site can be searched by keyword.
Resource Type: General Reference

***The Avalon Project at Yale Law School: World War II Documents
www.yale.edu/lawweb/avalon/wwii/wwii.htm

"The Avalon Project at Yale Law School: World War II Documents" offers a varied array of primary source documents on World War II as part of its major collections.
Resource Type: Primary Source Collection

***World War II Resources
www.ibiblio.org/pha/

Dedicated to combating "history by sound bites," the Pearl Harbor Working Group has produced this varied collection of original documents regarding all aspects of the war.
Resource Type: Primary Source Collection

***The World War II Sound and Image File
www.earthstation1.com/wwii.html

Part of the the Historical Sound & Image Archive, this WWII "Sounds and Pictures Page" features interesting graphics and radio excerpts. Topics include: Aircraft, Propaganda Posters, Warships, Sound Effects, and more. Has not been updated since 2001.
Resource Type: Multimedia Presentation; Primary Source Collection

****Paths of Memory
www.pathsofmemory.net/

This multilingual European museums site has well-organized sections on the First World War, Spanish Civil War, and the Second World War. In this developing project, a team of European historians has included, in addition to well-known places, lesser-known sites that nevertheless were the locations of events that influenced conflicts in one way or another.
Resource Type: General Reference

World War II General Resources, Lesson Plans, Activities, and More

Course Models: World War II
www.history.ctaponline.org/center/hsscm/index.cfm?Page_Key=1564

Part of the California History-Social Science content standards and annotated course, which includes: background information, focus questions, pupil activities and handouts, assessment, and references to books, articles, Web sites, literature, audiovisual programs, and historic sites. Recommended for Grade 11.
Resource Type: Course Model
Grade Level: MS, HS

Teacher's Guide: Total War
www.pbs.org/wgbh/peoplescentury/teachers/tgtotal.html

This PBS teacher's guide helps students explore the fire bombs, air raids, and the atomic bombs that killed millions of civilians and left many more injured. Students learn the effects of World War II on civilians.
Resource Type: Lesson or Activity
Grade Level: HS

Voices of the Past
http://oldsegundo.com/webquests/voices_from_past/student-home.htm

An oral history project for students in grades 6 through 12; students follow oral history processes to contact and interview a World War II veteran or person alive during the World War II era.
Resource Type: Lesson or Activity
Grade Level: MS, HS

Western Civilization: States in Conflict
http://wps.prenhall.com/hss_king_westernciv_2/0,6774,209073-,00.html

The online study companion to Margaret King's *Western Civilization: A Social and Cultural History* has many features: Chapter learning objectives, online quizzes, writing activities, essay questions, Web links, built-in search engines, and faculty modules that include Power-Point outlines, presentation graphics, and lecture hints and activities.
Resource Type: Course Model
Grade Level: HS

The American People: World War II
http://wps.ablongman.com/long_nash_ap_6/0,7361,592970-,00.html

PowerPoint presentation on America and World War II as part of the online companion to *The American People*. Click Chapter 25.
Resource Type: Multimedia Presentation
Grade Level: HS

World War II: The Home Front
http://library.thinkquest.org/15511/

This ThinkQuest site includes a timeline, an artifact museum and a simulation that allows students to follow the lives of five American families during the school year of September 1943–June 1944.
Resource Type: Lesson or Activity
Grade Level: MS, HS

HomeFront 1939–1945
www.learningcurve.gov.uk/homefront/bombing/default.htm

This interactive U.K. National Archives Learning Curve exhibition examines around life in Britain during World War II. Sections revolve around essential questions for students to answer and feature diaries, activities, worksheets, a timeline, and video. This page centers on the bombings of Britain.
Resource Type: Lesson or Activity
Grade Level: MS, HS

Interpreting Primary Sources
www.digitalhistory.uh.edu/historyonline/us35.cfm

"Digital History" provides brief excerpts from primary sources and statistics and questions to think about World War II.
Resource Type: Lesson or Activity; Primary Source Collection
Grade Level: HS

WORLD WAR II: BATTLES AND CAMPAIGNS

****D-Day
www.pbs.org/wgbh/amex/dday/

The special features of this excellent companion Web site include the Did You Know? section to learn about landing craft; battle reporting; the vast scale of the invasion, and what the "D"

stands for; Voices of D-Day, where the battle's fliers, the men who landed on Normandy's beaches, and German soldiers tell their stories; Hot Off the Presses, where you can read a newspaper account and Americans' reactions to news of the D-Day assault; Paratroopers, or soldiers who dropped behind enemy lines; and Letters from the Front, firsthand accounts of soldiers' experiences after D-Day.
Resource Type: General Reference; Primary Source Collection

****Normandy
www.britannica.com/dday

"Normandy" is part of an informative World War II study guide by Britannica online. Sections include: The Invasion, Leaders and Generals, and Veterans' Oral Histories. There are also combat videos, interactive charts and maps, a photo gallery, war documents, and learning activities guide.
Resource Type: General Reference; Lesson or Activity

****The Battle of Iwo Jima
www.iwojima.com/

This Web site includes much information about the battle of Iwo Jima, including strategy and the famous flag-raising photograph. There are numerous photographs at the site, as well as FAQs, information about books, movies, statues, and other related information.
Resource Type: General Reference

Figure 6.2: The Battle of Iwo Jima

****Battle of Midway
www.history.navy.mil/photos/events/wwii-pac/midway/midway.htm

This page is part of a special Naval Historical Center collection of online images of World War II in the Pacific. It features a historical overview and special image selection and links to other Center pages with more comprehensive coverage of the battle.
Resource Type: Image Collection; Primary Source Collection

****Battle of the Bulge
www.pbs.org/wgbh/amex/bulge/

This engaging PBS *American Experience* offering provides firsthand accounts from veterans of the fighting, a detailed timeline of events, as well as a gallery of photos taken during the winter of 1944–45. Other special features include dispatches from soldiers and nurses who were at the Bulge as well an interactive online poll, and a user forum.
Resource Type: General Reference; Primary Source Collection

****Battle of Stalingrad
http://users.pandora.be/stalingrad/

This Web site contains an impressive amount of information about the Battle of Stalingrad in the form of articles, essays, maps and statistics. It also includes primary sources from both Russian and German newspaper as well as a war diary and recommended links.
Resource Type: General Reference; Primary Source Collection

****Battle of Britain
www.raf.mod.uk/Bob1940/bobhome.html

This Battle of Britain history site is from the Royal Air Force. It offers official reports, background on the battle, historic photographs, strategy, and statistics. A special feature of the site are videos that show the Royal Air Force and Luftwaffe in action.
Resource Type: General Reference; Primary Source Collection

****Dunkirk Remembered
http://news.bbc.co.uk/2/hi/in_depth/uk/2000/dunkirk/default.stm

This interesting BBC News "In Depth" feature offers stories from veterans who were rescued at the beaches, as well as contemporary commentary, a user forum, and more. Multimedia features include a special BBC video report on Dunkirk as well as a slide show on the rescue.
Resource Type: General Reference; Primary Source Collection

****Enola Gay
www.nasm.si.edu/exhibitions/gal103/gal103_former.html

The Enola Gay exhibition at the National Air and Space Museum closed on May 18, 1998. This Web page provides a brief overview with images and highlights from that exhibition. The most luring feature of the site is a series of movie clips showing the interior cockpit and the exterior forward fuselage.
Resource Type: General Reference; Multimedia Presentation

****Pearl Harbor: Remembered
http://my.execpc.com/~dschaaf/mainmenu.html

This site is part of the USS *Arizona* Visitor Center located on the Pearl Harbor Naval Base adjacent to the sunken remains of the USS *Arizona*. The site provides an overview to the Pearl Harbor attack, a timeline of events, survivor remembrances, a map, audio files, and useful links.
Resource Type: General Reference

****Baatan Rescue
www.pbs.org/wgbh/amex/bataan/

This PBS *American Experience* site relates the story of an elite Ranger battalion that went 30 miles behind enemy lines in the Philippines in 1944 to rescue 500 survivors of the Bataan death march who were held captive by the Japanese. There are interviews with liberated POWs, a tour inside a Ranger training camp, a teacher's guide, and more.
Resource Type: General Reference; Primary Source Collection

****Maps of World War II
www.onwar.com/maps/wwii/

Maps of World War II provides an overview of WWII through a collection of maps that present the battles and campaigns fought in the various theaters of war. The material is organized by theater, in roughly chronological order. Most of these maps present operational level information.
Resource Type: Maps

***World War II in Europe Timeline
www.historyplace.com/worldwar2/timeline/ww2time.htm

A hyperlinked timeline with text and images by "The History Place."
Resource Type: Timeline

World War II: Battles and Campaigns, Lesson Plans, Activities, and More

History 20: Decision in Normandy
www.sasked.gov.sk.ca/docs/history20/summa.html

The Saskatchewan Social Studies Curriculum has developed a "resource hot sheet" dealing with topics identified in the History 20 (Modern World History) curriculum. Each page features images and often first-person accounts by individuals who were present during the event. There are also sound bites, mini-movies and Flash animations. Decision in Normandy is a simulation that provides students with the opportunity to recreate the events around the Normandy Invasion.
Resource Type: Course Model
Grade Level: HS

BBC History Games: Battle of the Atlantic
www.bbc.co.uk/history/worldwars/wwtwo/launch_gms_battle_atlantic.shtml

Play this engaging interactive game as Senior Officer Escort in charge of defending increasingly important convoys.
Resource Type: Multimedia Presentation
Grade Level: MS, HS, College

BBC History: The Fall of France Animation

www.bbc.co.uk/history/worldwars/wwtwo/launch_ani_fall_france_campaign.shtml

In this animation, one follows the progress of the German forces as they cross the border, occupy Belgium and the Netherlands, and trap the Allied forces at Dunkirk.
Resource Type: Multimedia Presentation
Grade Level: MS, HS, College

BBC History: The North Africa Campaign Animation

www.bbc.co.uk/history/worldwars/wwtwo/launch_ani_north_africa_campaign.shtml

In this animation, one follows the three years of battles in the North African desert, and see how Axis and Allied forces chased each other across this hostile terrain.
Resource Type: Multimedia Presentation
Grade Level: MS, HS, College

BBC History: Battle of El Alamein

www.bbc.co.uk/history/worldwars/wwtwo/launch_ani_el_alamein.shtml

In this BBC animation, the visitor follows the battle that signified "the end of the beginning" of World War II.
Resource Type: Multimedia Presentation
Grade Level: MS, HS, College

BBC History: Operation Overlord Animation

www.bbc.co.uk/history/worldwars/wwtwo/launch_ani_overlord_campaign.shtml

In this animation, one follows the Allies as they land on the Normandy coast on June 6, 1944, and then battle their way into Brittany and on to liberate Paris.
Resource Type: Multimedia Presentation
Grade Level: MS, HS, College

BBC History: The Italian Campaign Animation

www.bbc.co.uk/history/worldwars/wwtwo/launch_ani_italy_campaign.shtml

In this animation, one follows the Allied forces as they invade Sicily and battle their way into Italy.
Resource Type: Multimedia Presentation
Grade Level: MS, HS, College

MacArthur

www.pbs.org/wgbh/amex/macarthur/tguide/index.html

Use this site to explore the career of a controversial leader and understand events in the Pacific theater during WWII.
Resource Type: Lesson or Activity
Grade Level: HS

The Battle of the Bulge: Teacher's Guide

www.pbs.org/wgbh/amex/bulge/tguide/index.html

Presented by PBS, this teacher's guide is useful for WWII discussion. Many important issues

are addressed and offered for student debate. The guide also has several class activities and projects (map-making, research, etc.).
Resource Type: Lesson or Activity
Grade Level: HS

Prisoners of Another War
www.pbs.org/wnet/berga/teach/lp2.html

In this high school lesson plan, students are prompted to identify violations of the Geneva Convention in the treatment of American POWs at Berga and understand the role of international bodies in judging war crimes and crimes against humanity.
Resource Type: Lesson or Activity
Grade Level: HS

A-Bomb WWW Museum
www.csi.ad.jp/ABOMB/index.html

"A-Bomb WWW Museum" provides useful sources on the decision to drop atomic bombs on Hiroshima and Nagisaki.
Resource Type: Lesson or Activity
Grade Level: HS

HOLOCAUST AND SPECIAL WWII TOPICS

****Remember.org
www.remember.org/index.html

Remember.org is an educational forum that aims to bring together Holocaust survivors, and children of Holocaust survivors. This popular site is a great resource for classrooms, and has engaging resources, such as the Auschwitz Virtual tour.
Resource Type: General Reference; Virtual Tour

****The Holocaust—Crimes, Heroes and Villains
www.auschwitz.dk/

"The Holocaust—Crimes, Heroes and Villains" is today one of the largest Holocaust Web sites in the world. It is based on more than 30 years of research by the site's creator into the topics of World War II and the Holocaust. Most of these extensive articles have been published in newspapers and magazines.
Resource Type: General Reference

****Go for Broke
www.goforbroke.org/

The educational Web site GoForBroke.org is geared toward helping educators, students, researchers, and the general public to learn about Japanese American World War II veterans. It features lesson plans, student activities, streaming oral history videos, glossaries, timelines, photos, interactive maps and more.
Resource Type: General Reference; Lesson or Activity

****Women Who Came to the Front
www.loc.gov/exhibits/wcf/wcf0001.html

This Library of Congress exhibit tells the story of eight different women who participated as journalists, broadcasters, and photographers during World War II. The interesting women featured in this exhibit were chosen because of the strength and variety of their collections in the Library of Congress.
Resource Type: Primary Source Collection

****Bismarck: The Final Days
http://dsc.discovery.com/games/bismarck/attack/attack.html

This Discovery Channel interactive exhibit includes an interactive tour of the famous WWII battleship, a Flash presentation on "The Final Days," discussion of the findings and historical relevance by James Cameron, a quiz, and a "video peek" at the film.
Resource Type: Multimedia Presentation

****Oscar Schindler
www.oskarschindler.com/

Biography of the rescuer Oskar Schindler, who saved 1,200 Jews during the Holocaust and World War II. Stories of war crimes, survivors, and the entire Schindler's List.
Resource Type: General Reference

****World War II Poster Collection
www.library.northwestern.edu/govinfo/collections/wwii-posters/

The Government Publications Department at Northwestern University Library has a comprehensive collection of over 300 posters issued by U.S. federal agencies from the onset of war through 1945. Posters are searchable by Date, Topic, or Title.
Resource Type: Primary Source Collection

****Japanese American Internment
www.geocities.com/Athens/8420/main.html

This site offers many primary sources, maps, photos, links, and other resources regarding the internment of Japanese Americans during World War II. Topics include: Pre-War Intelligence, The Politics, An Exclusion Poster, The Camps, Memories, Shootings, Disillusionment, Timeline, Glossary, and Gallery. Content has not been updated since 2003, but site continues to be maintained.
Resource Type: General Reference

****World War II Posters: Powers of Persuasion
www.archives.gov/exhibits/powers_of_persuasion/powers_of_persuasion_home.html

An interesting National Archives exhibit that displays and explains American propaganda posters. It features 11 posters and one sound file from a more extensive exhibit that was presented in the National Archives Building in Washington, D.C., from May 1994 to February 1995. The exhibit is divided into two parts, which represent two psychological approaches used in rallying public support for the war.
Resource Type: Primary Source Collection

****A More Perfect Union: Japanese Americans and the U.S. Constitution**
http://americanhistory.si.edu/perfectunion/experience/index.html

An online exhibit from the Smithsonian, this site explores how a government balances human rights with a need for national security. Immigration, Removal, Internment, Loyalty, Service and Justice are the areas available for viewing, with a special user forum. Classroom Activities are found under the Resources link at the bottom of the page.
Resource Type: General Reference; Lesson or Activity

****Women and the Second World War**
www.spartacus.schoolnet.co.uk/2WWwomen.htm

This interesting Web site examines the important role played by women in the war and includes biographies of 20 secret agents, 20 women involved in the anti-Nazi resistance movement in Europe, and 12 women who risked their lives as war reporters.
Resource Type: General Reference

****The Winston Churchill Home Page**
www.winstonchurchill.org/i4a/pages/index.cfm?pageid=1

Produced by the Churchill Center, this site covers all aspects of Churchill's life. Of special interest are sound recordings of Churchill's speeches, a radio interview, and other primary source documents.
Resource Type: General Reference; Primary Source Collection

****Master Race: 1926–1945**
www.pbs.org/wgbh/peoplescentury/episodes/masterrace/

Part of the PBS's *People's Century* series, "Master Race: 1926–1945" probes the Nazi takeover in Germany. In it, Germans talk about the initial seduction of Nazism; Gypsies reminisce about life before Hitler; and Jews recall their persecution. There are eyewitness interviews, a teacher's guide, links to related sites, and a chance to tell your own story.
Resource Type: General Reference; Primary Source Collection

****Nuremberg—The Doctor's Trial**
www.ushmm.org/research/doctors/index.html

This informative presentation is part of a larger site—"The United States Holocaust Memorial Museum"—and contains the testimonies and evidence used during this trial against Nazi physicians who conducted scientific experiments on concentration camp prisoners. There are numerous primary source documents that describe the surgical atrocities.
Resource Type: General Reference; Primary Source Collection

****Nazi Persecution of Homosexuals**
www.ushmm.org/museum/exhibit/online/hsx/

This United States Holocaust Memorial Museum online exhibition examines the campaign of persecution and violence against homosexuals in Germany under the Third Reich. The Museum offers online resources, bibliographies, personal histories, video clips, curator comments, and public programs.
Resource Type: General Reference; Primary Source Collection

****Hitler's Bunker
http://dsc.discovery.com/guides/history/unsolvedhistory/hitler/photogallery/photogallery.html

This Discovery Channel photo gallery explores what happened in Hitler's bunker during the final months of the war. View the photo gallery of the people who lived in the bunker and find out their fate. Also offers a quiz on the "last gasp" of World War II.
Resource Type: General Reference; Virtual Tour

Holocaust and Special WWII Topics Lesson Plans, Activities, and More

South Carolina Voices: Lessons from the Holocaust
www.scetv.org/education/holocaust_forum/contents.cfm

A teacher's guide to teaching about the Holocaust and its aftermath. This page has several lesson plans as well as links to background information and printable handouts. Intended for grades 7–12.
Resource Type: Lesson or Activity
Grade Level: MS, HS

A Teachers Guide to the Holocaust: High School lesson plans
http://fcit.coedu.usf.edu/holocaust/activity/HighSchl.htm

This Florida Center for Instructional Technology page has multiple lesson plans. Lessons analyze all aspects of the Holocaust and urge students to take advantage of primary sources. The lessons come with their own worksheets. These are high school level assignments.
Resource Type: Lesson or Activity
Grade Level: HS

Anne Frank in the World: Teacher Book
www.uen.org/annefrank/

Produced by The Friends of Anne Frank in Utah and the Intermountain West Region, the workbook features lesson plans and activities for grades 5–8, lesson plans and activities for grades 7–12, readings and overviews, timelines, and a glossary.
Resource Type: Lesson or Activity
Grade Level: MS, HS

The Holocaust: A Tragic Legacy
http://library.thinkquest.org/12663/

An impressive student-produced ThinkQuest on the Holocaust.
Resource Type: Lesson or Activity
Grade Level: MS, HS

Learning Resources Open Hearts/Closed Doors: Teachers guide
www.virtualmuseum.ca/Exhibitions/orphans/english/themes/resources/page1.html

This 13-page guide contains lesson ideas, discussion questions, "extensions" and supporting resources that relate directly to the Jewish orphans' narratives and nine different themes. It provides opportunities for individual student and small group work. You must download the file to view it.
Resource Type: Lesson or Activity
Grade Level: MS, HS

Was Hitler a Passionate Lunatic?
www.learningcurve.gov.uk/snapshots/snapshot06/snapshot6.htm

This exercise is aimed at getting students to look at conflicting evidence and assessing their reliability. It can be used as an introduction to looking at the issue of appeasement and the decisions that were made in the run up to the outbreak of the war. From Learning Curve. Key Stage 3–4.
Resource Type: Lesson or Activity
Grade Level: HS

Assassinate Hitler: How Did the British Plan to Kill Hitler?
www.learningcurve.gov.uk/snapshots/snapshot17/snapshot17.htm

In 1944, the SOE (Special Operations Executive) drew up some plans to kill Hitler, and as Head of SOE it is your job to decide which of two ways of killing Hitler should be adopted. From the Learning Curve (UK National Archives). Key Stage 3–4.
Resource Type: Lesson or Activity
Grade Level: HS

Chamberlain and Hitler, 1938: What Was Chamberlain Trying to Do?
www.learningcurve.gov.uk/snapshots/snapshot31/snapshot31.htm

Chamberlain's account of his meeting with Hitler over the Sudetenland crisis of 1938 is the center of this activity. Is it unfair to criticize Chamberlain for misjudging Hitler? Students couuld try to make a case for Chamberlain. From the U.K. National Archives. Key Stage 3–4.
Resource Type: Lesson or Activity
Grade Level: HS

German Occupation of the Rhineland, 1936: What Should Britain Do about It?
www.learningcurve.gov.uk/snapshots/snapshot30/snapshot30.htm

Documents reveal the motives and attitudes of the British government as they discuss their options. The extracts from the Cabinet minutes also show how little room for maneuvering British politicians actually had. This provides a good case-study of British appeasement policy. From the Learning Curve (UK National Archives). Key Stage 3–4.
Resource Type: Lesson or Activity
Grade Level: MS, HS

Changing Perspectives on the Japanese Internment Experience
www.thirteen.org/edonline/lessons/internment/index.html

In this interactive and multidisciplinary lesson, students learn about the role that perspective plays in the writing of history by focusing on the changing views about Japanese-American internment camps during World War II. Along the way, students will be asked to identify the ways in which biases affect what gets retold as a "history."
Resource Type: Lesson or Activity
Grade Level: HS

Asylum Talk Show
www.pbs.org/pov/pov1999/wff/lesson1.html

Role play various real-life persons in the case of the SS *St. Louis*, a German ship containing

Jewish refugees seeking asylum from Nazi persecution in the late 1930s. PBS.
Resource Type: Lesson or Activity
Grade Level: HS

Teacher's Guide: Master Race
www.pbs.org/wgbh/peoplescentury/teachers/tgmaster.html

Study the racial philosophies and ethnic cleansing policies of Nazi Germany through this PBS *People's Century* teacher's guide.
Resource Type: Lesson or Activity
Grade Level: HS

Nazi Designers of Death
www.pbs.org/wgbh/nova/teachers/activities/2204_nazidesi.html

Students learn how a British historian gathered powerful evidence to show how Nazi death camps were planned and constructed. PBS activity for middle school students.
Resource Type: Lesson or Activity
Grade Level: MS

Drums of War: Exploring How Politics Shapes American War Policy
www.nytimes.com/learning/teachers/lessons/20020923monday.html

In this *New York Times* lesson, students will research the political climate prior to major American wars of the past, then reflect on the current call for power to confront Iraq.
Resource Type: Lesson or Activity
Grade Level: MS, HS

War and Peace: Multiple Choice Quiz, Fill-in-the-Blank, Flashcards, American History Glossary, American History Appendix
http://wps.ablongman.com/long_carnes_an_11/0,7137,252216-,00.html

The Student Resources section of *The American Nation* companion Web site features introductions to chapters, interactive quizzes, flashcards, Web links, an American History Glossary, and an American History Appendix.
Resource Type: Course Model
Grade Level: MS, HS

The United States in an Age of Global Crisis Practice Test
www.phschool.com/curriculum_support/brief_review/us_history/tests.html?unit=6&number=35

High school level quiz on America and World War II from Prentice Hall.
Resource Type: Test or Quiz
Grade Level: MS, HS

The United States in an Age of Global Crisis Document-Based Essay
www.phschool.com/curriculum_support/brief_review/us_history/essay_questions/unit6.cfm

This Prentice Hall DBQ is designed to test your ability to work with historical documents and is based on the accompanying documents (1–6).

Resource Type: Lesson or Activity
Grade Level: MS, HS

Between the Wars Review Game
www.quia.com/cb/12326.html

This exercise provides review for events, people, and terms associated with the period between World War I and World War II.
Resource Type: Lesson or Activity
Grade Level: MS, HS

World War II in Europe and the Pacific: Blank Maps
http://wps.ablongman.com/long_nash_ap_6/0,7361,592970-,00.html

The companion Web site to *The American People* offers blank maps related to various topics in American history. The maps can be printed or placed in a PowerPoint presentation. Click Blank Maps for Quizzes.
Resource Type: Maps; Test or Quiz
Grade Level: MS, HS

Chronology of World War II Game—Pacific
www.quia.com/rd/3777.html

Put WWII events in chronological order.
Resource Type: Lesson or Activity
Grade Level: MS, HS

Identify the World War II Leaders Game
www.quia.com/quiz/105597.html

Identify the World War II leaders through descriptions of their actions and decisions during the war.
Resource Type: Lesson or Activity
Grade Level: MS, HS

Simon Wiesenthal Center Museum of Tolerance: Teacher's Resources
http://motlc.wiesenthal.com/site/pp.asp?c=gvKVLcMVIuG&b=358201

Includes a Multimedia Learning Center, Virtual Exhibits, and a Teacher's Resources section that has a glossary, a timeline, bibliographies, 36 questions and answers about the Holocaust, and curricular resources for teachers.
Resource Type: Course Model
Grade Level: MS, HS

BBC History: Nazi Propaganda Gallery
www.bbc.co.uk/history/worldwars/wwtwo/nazi_propaganda_gallery.shtml

Professor David Welch uses six Nazi-era posters to explain how Hitler used propaganda as a vehicle of political salesmanship.
Resource Type: Lesson or Activity
Grade Level: MS, HS

EARLY COLD WAR ERA

*****Cold War: From Yalta to Malta
http://cnn.com/SPECIALS/cold.war/

This CNN Perspectives series, in the following 10 episodes, explores the Cold War experience. Included are interactive maps, rare video footage, declassified documents, biographies, picture galleries, timelines, interactive activities, a search function, book excerpts, an educator's guide and more.
Resource Type: General Reference; Multimedia Presentation

Figure 6.3: CNN Perspectives Homepage

****Episode One: Comrades 1917–1945
www.cnn.com/SPECIALS/cold.war/episodes/01

This presentation displays the United States and Russia as allies through video interview with George Kennan, a tour of a Cold War prison, historical documents, and more.

****Episode Two: The Iron Curtain 1945–1947
www.cnn.com/SPECIALS/cold.war/episodes/02/

This presentation examines the Iron Curtain through a Cold War military museum, a Brinkmanship interactive game, a video interview with George Kennan, a spotlight on the Oder-Niesse Line, a look at post Cold War U.S.-Russian relations, and more.

****Episode Three: The Marshall Plan 1947–1952
www.cnn.com/SPECIALS/cold.war/episodes/03/

Has a brinkmanship simulation, a feature on the birth of the CIA, an analysis of the IMF, discussion of the Czech coup in 1948, and more.

****Episode Four: Berlin 1948–1949
www.cnn.com/SPECIALS/cold.war/episodes/04/

Features a West German radio report, reflections of a Berlin mayor, a look at propaganda, a brinkmanship simulation, and more.

****Episode Five: Korea 1949–1953
www.cnn.com/SPECIALS/cold.war/episodes/05/

The special features of this site include spotlights on the Russian connection, the continuing divide between North and South Korea, a look at America's Korean War memorial, a brinkmanship game, interviews, and more.

****Episode Six: Reds 1948–1949
www.cnn.com/SPECIALS/cold.war/episodes/06

Based on the Intensification of the Cold War, this presentation features a look at the Red Scare then and now, the United States Communist Party, and totalitarianism, and it has an excerpt from Daniel Moynihan's "Secrecy."

****Episode Seven: After Stalin 1953–1956
www.cnn.com/SPECIALS/cold.war/episodes/07

This presentation features reflections by Krushchev's son and sections on Kremlin power struggles, NATO's importance, and a German radio report.

****Episode Eight: After Sputnik 1949–1961
www.cnn.com/SPECIALS/cold.war/episodes/08/

Explores the new arms race launched by the Soviet atomic bomb. There are features on espionage, Russia's space exploits, and an interactive timeline.

****Episode Nine: The Wall 1959–1963
www.cnn.com/SPECIALS/cold.war/episodes/09/

Explores shootings at the Berlin Wall, U.S. unpreparedness, and offers some reflections on the wall.

****Episode Ten: Cuba 1959–1968
www.cnn.com/SPECIALS/cold.war/episodes/10/

Features the ExComm files, the hotline between Kennedy and Khrushchev, contemporary Cuba, and an interview with Fidel Castro

****People's Century
www.pbs.org/wgbh/peoplescentury/

The "People's Century" site is based on the 26-episode PBS television series and features a teacher's guide, a timeline, a thematic overview, and RealAudio excerpts. The highlights of the Web site are the first-person narratives, often by ordinary people who lived through turbulent times. *Resource Type: Primary Source Collection; General Reference*

****Young Blood: 1950–1975
www.pbs.org/wgbh/peoplescentury/episodes/youngblood/

Focus is on youth movement in America in the 1960s.

****Skin Deep: 1945–1994**
www.pbs.org/wgbh/peoplescentury/episodes/skindeep/

Probes the challenge to racial oppression in the United States and South Africa.

****Fallout: 1945–1995**
www.pbs.org/wgbh/peoplescentury/episodes/fallout/

Examines the atomic age in the Cold War era.

****Picture Power: 1939–1997**
www.pbs.org/wgbh/peoplescentury/episodes/picturepower/

Probes how television transformed society, culture, and politics.

****Boomtime: 1945–1973**
www.pbs.org/wgbh/peoplescentury/episodes/boomtime/

Examines how postwar prosperity transformed lifestyles and cultural values in the United States and abroad.

****Race for the Super Bomb**
www.pbs.org/wgbh/pages/amex/bomb/

There are some quirky but interesting features at this site, including a panic quiz and a Nuclear Blast Map. You will also be treated to interviews, film footage of explosions, a map of target sites in the U.S., a weapons stockpile list for 1945 to 1997, a timeline, primary sources, transcripts, a teacher's guide, and a people and events section.
Resource Type: General Reference; Multimedia Presentation

****The Race to Build the Atomic Bomb—A Resource for Students and Teachers**
http://intergate.cccoe.k12.ca.us/abomb/

"The Race to Build the Atomic Bomb—A Resource for Teachers and Students" provides information on the men who built the Atomic Bomb and circumstances surrounding its construction. Categories include: Timeline, Competition, Exodus of Scientists, Physics, Those Responsible, Research, Lesson Plans, and Resources.
Resource Type: General Reference; Lesson or Activity

****The Marshall Plan**
http://lcweb.loc.gov/exhibits/marshall/mars0.html

The Library of Congress presents this special anniversary exhibit on the origins and effects of the Marshall Plan. It features a detailed chronology, photographs and cartoons from the Prints and Photographs Division, and items from the papers of Averell Harriman, the ERP special representative in Europe from 1948 to 1950.
Resource Type: Primary Source Collection; General Reference

****The Alger Hiss Story**
http://homepages.nyu.edu/~th15/

"The Alger Hiss Story" is an engaging and comprehensive site that recreates one of the most important legal cases in U.S. history. According to the site: "Dedicated to students, scholars, archivists, and teachers, and to a general audience.... The Alger Hiss Story acts as

an authoritative portal to primary information about Alger Hiss, the Hiss case, and the early Cold War years. . . . It also functions as the digitized and online counterpart to the Alger Hiss Papers at the Harvard Law School Library." Among the many interesting leads to explore through the site are exclusive new interviews from eyewitnesses and others, Freedom of Information Act releases of government documents, Grand Jury secret testimony, and HUAC files released in 2001.
Resource Type: Primary Source Collection; General Reference

****Space Race
www.nasm.si.edu/exhibitions/gal114/gal114.htm

Explores military origins of the space race and provides a gallery map and more. From the National Air and Space Museum.
Resource Type: Virtual Tour; General Reference

****The Kennedy Assassination
http://mcadams.posc.mu.edu/home.htm

This Web site by a political science professor is "dedicated to debunking the mass of misinformation and disinformation surrounding the murder of JFK." Provides a balanced look at John F. Kennedy's death.
Resource Type: General Reference

***Soviet Archives Exhibit
www.ibiblio.org/expo/soviet.exhibit/soviet.archive.html

This site, designed by the Library of Congress and hosted by www.ibiblio.org, contains declassified Soviet documents from 1917 to 1991, arranged as a museum exhibit of primary sources.
Resource Type: Primary Source Collection; Virtual Tour

Early Cold War Era Lesson Plans, Teacher Guides, Activities, and More

Cold War Lesson Plan
www.nancymatson.com/CLDWR1.HTM

Geared primarily for high school students, this lesson plan asks students to research America's fear of Communism. The lesson plan outlines three different research activities that revolve around HUAC and the Hollywood Blacklist. Somewhat opinionated lessons.
Resource Type: Lesson or Activity
Grade Level:HS

The Cold War: America During the 1950s
www.teachers.net/lessons/posts/1756.html

A midlevel lesson plan, this outline is for 7th- and 8th-graders. Through the creation of a "guide book," students learn about what America was like during the 1950s and the Cold War. Students work in small groups and conduct a WebQuest.
Resource Type: Lesson or Activity
Grade Level: MS

Follow the Marx: Learning About Communism
www.nytimes.com/learning/teachers/lessons/20020909monday.html

In this well-organized *New York Times* lesson, students explore communism from historical and theoretical perspectives to present to fellow classmates at a teach-in.
Resource Type: Lesson or Activity
Grade Level: MS, HS

Intervene or Interfere? Exploring Forty Years of United States Intervention in Foreign Affairs
www.nytimes.com/learning/teachers/lessons/20030407monday.html

In this well-organized lesson, students esearch the motives, actions, and results of U.S. intervention in foreign affairs between the 1961 Bay of Pigs invasion and the 2003 invasion of Iraq; they then present their research to class for comparative analysis.
Resource Type: Lesson or Activity
Grade Level: HS

Drums of War: Exploring How Politics Shapes American War Policy
www.nytimes.com/learning/teachers/lessons/20020923monday.html

In another *New York Times* lesson, students research the political climate prior to major American wars of the past, then reflect on the current call for power to confront Iraq.
Resource Type: Lesson or Activity
Grade Level: MS, HS

Course Models: War in Korea
www.history.ctaponline.org/center/hsscm/index.cfm?Page_Key=1746

Part of the California History-Social Science content standards and annotated course, which includes: Background information, focus questions, pupil activities and handouts, an assessment, and references to books, articles, Web sites, literature, audiovisual programs, and a historic site. Grade 11.
Resource Type: Course Model
Grade Level: HS

Student Information Guide: Communism and Containment
http://score.rims.k12.ca.us/activity/communism/

This SCORE guide provides some background information and student activities that teach about the Cold War. The main focus is on the Truman Doctrine and the U.S. containment of Communism. Lessons are included in the Teacher Guide section.
Resource Type: Lesson or Activity
Grade Level: HS

The U.S. Response to the Cuban Missile Crisis
http://score.rims.k12.ca.us/activity/tobeornot/

In this SCORE activity, students pretend to be members of EX-COMM and hold a "meeting" with President Kennedy about the Cuban Missile Crisis. The activity site comes with its own

information and handouts. Recommended for grade 11.
Resource Type: Lesson or Activity
Grade Level: HS

Digital History Resource Guides
www.digitalhistory.uh.edu/resource_guides/

"Digital History Resource Guides" provide links to American history Web sites by period and provide historical overviews, readings (online textbook chapter, Reader's Companion), primary source documents (documents, maps, cartoons), teaching resources (chronologies, maps, quizzes), audiovisual resources, and additional resources. It is an excellent and comprehensive teaching resource.
Resource Type: Course Model
Grade Level: HS, College

The American Century: Multiple Choice Quiz, Fill-in-the-Blank, Flashcards, American History Glossary, American History Appendix
http://wps.ablongman.com/long_carnes_an_11/0,7137,252269-,00.html

The Student Resources section of *The American Nation* companion Web site features introductions to chapters, interactive quizzes, flashcards, Web links, an American History Glossary, and an American History Appendix.
Resource Type: Test or Quiz; Lesson or Activity
Grade Level: MS

Society in Flux: Multiple Choice Quiz, Fill-in-the-Blank, Flashcards, American History Glossary, American History Appendix
http://wps.ablongman.com/long_carnes_an_11/0,7137,252372-,00.html

The Student Resources section of *The American Nation* companion Web site features introductions to chapters, interactive quizzes, flashcards, Web links, an American History Glossary, and an American History Appendix.
Resource Type: Test or Quiz; Lesson or Activity
Grade Level: MS

The American People: Postwar America at Home, 1945–1960
http://wps.ablongman.com/long_nash_ap_6/0,7361,592970-,00.html

PowerPoint presentation on America after World War II as part of the online companion to *The American People*. Click PowerPoint Presentations and then Chapter 26.
Resource Type: Lesson or Activity
Grade Level: HS

The American People: Chills and Fevers During the Cold War, 1945–1960
http://wps.ablongman.com/long_nash_ap_6/0,7361,592970-,00.html

PowerPoint presentation on Cold War America as part of the online companion to *The American People*. Click PowerPoint Presentations and then Chapter 27.
Resource Type: Lesson or Activity
Grade Level: HS

The World in Uncertain Times, 1950–Present Practice Test
www.phschool.com/curriculum_support/brief_review/us_history/tests.html?unit=7&number=35

High school level quiz on Cold War America from Prentice Hall.
Resource Type: Test or Quiz
Grade Level: HS

The World in Uncertain Times, 1950–Present Document-Based Essay
www.phschool.com/curriculum_support/brief_review/us_history/essay_questions/unit7.cfm

From the site: "This Prentice Hall DBQ is designed to test your ability to work with historical documents and is based on the accompanying documents (1–6)."
Resource Type: Lesson or Activity
Grade Level: HS

HistoryTeacher.net: AP United States History Quizzes 1920–1970
www.historyteacher.net/USQuizMainPage.htm

A teacher at the Horace Greeley High School in Chappaqua, New York, has produced a great general site for history teachers that offers AP-level U.S. history quizzes on many different periods and topics.
Resource Type: Test or Quiz
Grade Level: HS

The American Nation: Internet Activities
www.phschool.com/atschool/TAN/Survey/Teacher_Area/TAN1_T_BK_index.html

Prentice Hall's phschool.com offers Internet activities based on their *The American Nation* textbook chapters.
Resource Type: Lesson or Activity
Grade Level: MS

A History of the United States: Internet Activities and Student Self-Test Questions
www.phschool.com/atschool/history_us/Student_Area/HUS_S_BK_index.html

Prentice Hall's phschool.com offers Internet activities and interactive quizzes based on *A History of the United States* textbook chapters.
Resource Type: Test or Quiz
Grade Level: HS

THE CIVIL RIGHTS MOVEMENT

*****Civil Rights Special Collection
www.teachersdomain.org/special/civil/

The Teachers' Domain "Civil Rights Special Collection" is produced by WGBH Boston, in partnership with the Birmingham Civil Rights Institute and Washington University in St. Louis. Materials are free but you have to sign up. Features an impressive array of audio, video, and text sources from Frontline and American Experience shows, Eyes on the Prize, and other sources. Also offers an interactive civil rights movement timeline and four lesson plans: Campaigns for Economic Freedom/Re-Examining Brown/Taking a Stand/Understanding White Supremacy.
Resource Type: Multimedia Presentation; Primary Source Collection; Lesson or Activity

****Martin Luther King, Jr., Research and Education Institute
www.stanford.edu/group/King/

This project out of Stanford University provides historical information about Dr. King and the social movements in which he participated. There are papers, speeches, sermons, book chapters, scholarly articles, a biography and a chronology. Excellent research site.
Resource Type: Primary Source Collection; General Reference

Figure 6.4: Martin Luther King, Jr., Research and Education Institute

****Martin Luther King, Jr. and the Civil Rights Movement
http://seattletimes.nwsource.com/mlk/

This *Seattle Times* exhibit helps students learn about King as a civil rights leader and his sweeping influence on the civil rights movement and beyond. Included are a photo gallery, biography, study guide, quizzes, essays from students and others and a focus on black history.
Resource Type: General Reference; Primary Source Collection

****The National Civil Rights Museum
www.civilrightsmuseum.org/

The National Civil Rights Museum in downtown Memphis, Tennessee offers an overview of the civil rights movement in exhibit form. It is especially helpful in conveying the impact of

the civil rights movement. Go to Exhibits/Gallery and get a virtual tour of the civil rights movement and Martin Luther King's life and legacy.
Resource Type: Virtual Tour; General Reference

****The History of Jim Crow
www.jimcrowhistory.org/history/history.htm

Access historical background, source material, and lesson plans at this impressive site and learn how Jim Crow laws deprived African Americans of their civil rights.
Resource Type: General Reference; Primary Source Collection; Lesson or Activity

****African American History and Heritage
www.afroamericanheritage.com/

Extensive collection of online resources for the history of the U.S. civil rights movement and current projects and events in Black History.
Resource Type: General Reference

****The Two Nations of Black America
www.pbs.org/wgbh/pages/frontline/shows/race/

"The Two Nations of Black America" discusses the divide in the black American community and features audio excerpts, charts, graphs and analysis, interviews, readings and links. Provocative and engaging.
Resource Type: Multimedia Presentation; General Reference

****Black Panthers
www.spartacus.schoolnet.co.uk/USApantherB.htm

This Spartacus Web site looks at the history of the Black Panther movement and includes biographies of leading figures such as Huey Newton, Bobby Seale, Fred Hampton, Eldridge Cleaver, H. Rap Brown, and Bobby Hutton.
Resource Type: General Reference; Primary Source Collection

****Jackie Robinson and other Baseball Highlights
http://memory.loc.gov/ammem/jrhtml/jrhome.html

The two impressive special presentations called 'Baseball, the Color Line,' and 'Jackie Robinson, 1860s–1960s,' draw on approximately 30 items—manuscripts, books, photographs, and ephemera—from the Library of Congress. It describes, among other things, the color line that segregated baseball for many years, the Negro Leagues, and Branch Rickey and Jackie Robinson—two men who played key roles in integrating the sport. The last two sections of the presentation explore Robinson's career as a Dodger and his civil rights activities.
Resource Type: Primary Source Collection; General Reference

****Alabama Christian Movement for Human Rights Scrapbook
www.teachersdomain.org/9-12/soc/ush/civil/acmhr/

The Reverend Fred Shuttlesworth helped organize the Alabama Christian Movement for Human Rights (ACMHR) in Birmingham, Alabama. The ACMHR organized demonstrations and boycotts to protest segregation in Birmingham's schools and businesses. Their site features many revealing primary source documents. Part of WGBH Civil Rights Special Collection.

Resource Type: Primary Source Collection; Lesson or Activity

****Religion & Ethics News Weekly: Spirituality and the Civil Rights Movement
www.pbs.org/wnet/religionandethics/index_flash.html

This PBS news magazine provides insightful coverage and analysis of the news, people, events and trends behind the headlines in the world of religion and ethics. The program explores how religion shapes both national and international events, and examines the challenges raised by difficult ethical issues. The Web site features individual show transcripts, an audio archive of past programs, full transcripts of interviews with notable guests, related articles dealing with significant issues in religion and ethics news, a list of related resources and an online pressroom featuring downloadable versions of the program, press kit, and quarterly newsletter, as well as detailed summaries of individual stories. See Martin Luther King Jr. as Pastor (January 13, 2006; Episode no. 920); interview of Civil Rights movement leader Rep. John Lewis (January 16, 2004; Episode no. 720): "What spiritual legacy did the civil rights movement give to the United States?"; The Legacy of Howard Thurman—Mystic and Theologian (January 18, 2002; Episode no. 520). Howard influenced Martin Luther King, Jr.

Resource Type: Multimedia Presentation; General Reference

****Documents from the Women's Liberation Movement
http://scriptorium.lib.duke.edu/wlm/

The scholarly materials in this online collection highlight various aspects of the Women's Liberation Movement in the United States and focus on the radical origins of this movement during the late 1960s and early 1970s.

Resource Type: Primary Source Collection

****Agents of Social Change
www.smith.edu/libraries/ssc

Smith College offers an online exhibit and several lesson plans drawn from its collections. The lesson plans are directed at middle and high school students and make use of both the text-based documents and visual images that can be found at the curriculum portion of the Web site. They highlight women's part in struggles for social change in the twentieth century including labor, socialism, civil liberties, peace, racial justice, urban reform, welfare rights, and women's rights.

Resource Type: Primary Source Collection; Lesson or Activity

***Timeline of the American Civil Rights Movement
www.infoplease.com/spot/civilrightstimeline1.html

This is an Infoplease.com annotated timeline of the Civil Rights Movement from the *Brown v. Board of Education* ruling in 1954 to the Selma (Alabama) March in 1965. It provides hyperlinked encyclopedic summaries of key events and brief biographies of key participants.

Resource Type: General Reference

***Skin Deep: 1945–1994

www.pbs.org/wgbh/peoplescentury/episodes/skindeep/

The PBS "People's Century" site is based on the 26-episode PBS television series and features a teacher's guide, a timeline, a thematic overview, and RealAudio excerpts. The highlights of the Web site are the first-person narratives, often by ordinary people who lived through turbulent times. The "Skin Deep: 1945–1994" episode probes the challenge to racial oppression in the United States and South Africa and features an interesting interview of Jim Zwerg, civil rights activist.
Resource Type: Multimedia Presentation; Lesson or Activity

***The Fight in the Fields: Cesar Chavez

www.pbs.org/itvs/fightfields/

This portrait of Chavez is presented in both English and Spanish and features audio excerpts from Chavez himself and an interview with his brother.
Resource Type: Multimedia Presentation; General Reference

***The Rosa Parks Portal

http://e-portals.org/Parks/

"The Rosa Parks Portal" is a search directory for Web sites and online news media about Rosa Parks.
Resource Type: General Reference

Civil Rights Movement Lesson Plans, Teacher Guides, Activities, and More

Little Rock Nine

www.kn.pacbell.com/wired/BHM/little_rock/

"Little Rock Nine" is an interactive WebQuest from the Pacific Bell Knowledge Network and explores racial desegregation in schools. Students are asked: "What, if anything, should be done to racially desegregate U.S. schools?" Activities are group-oriented and inquiry-based and are designed to promote critical thinking. There is a teacher's guide included.
Resource Type: Lesson or Activity
Grade Level: HS

Birmingham 1963

www.archives.state.al.us/teacher/rights/rights3.html

In this civil rights movement lesson plan from the Alabama Department of Archives & History students read Martin Luther King's "Letter from a Birmingham Jail" and other documents relating to King's incarceration in a Birmingham jail in April, 1963. Students are then asked to write a press release to be sent to each newspaper, radio station and television station in Alabama which will explain what happened in Birmingham. High school level resource.
Resource Type: Lesson or Activity; Primary Source Collection
Grade Level: HS

Justice Learning: Race & Education Lesson Plans

www.justicelearning.org/

"Justice Learning" uses audio from the *Justice Talking* radio show and articles from the *New York Times* to teach students about civil rights and conflicting values in American democracy.

This impressive Web site includes articles, editorials and oral debates from the nation's finest journalists and advocates. For each issue, the site includes curricular material from *The New York Times* Learning Network for high school teachers and detailed information about how each of the institutions of democracy (the courts, the Congress, the presidency, the press and the schools) affect the issue. A great teaching resource.

- Race & Education Lesson Plans: Whitewashing History: Exploring Topics of Civil Rights from 1948–1964
- Birmingham Blues: Exploring the History of the American Civil Rights Struggle through Poetry
- Civil Services: Exploring the Lasting Impact of the Civil Rights Movement
- Learning the Hard Way: Examining School Segregation Around the World
- Revisiting "Separate but Equal": Examining School Segregation 45 Years after *Brown v. Board of Education*

Resource Type: Lesson or Activity; Multimedia Presentation
Grade Level: HS

Martin Luther King, Jr. Papers Project: Lesson Plans
www.stanford.edu/group/King/

This project out of Stanford University disseminates historical information about Dr. King and the social movements in which he participated. Primary sources and lesson plans include:

- Martin Luther King, Jr.'s Letter from Birmingham Jail
- The Children's Crusade and the Role of Youth in the African American Freedom Struggle
- Martin Luther King, Jr. and Malcolm X: A Common Solution?
- Martin Luther King, Jr.'s Beyond Vietnam
- Personal Stories of Liberation from the Civil Rights Movement
- Teaching King and the Civil Rights Movement with Primary Source Documents

Resource Type: Lesson or Activity; Primary Source Collection
Grade Level: HS

The Murder of Emmett Till: Teacher's Guide
www.pbs.org/wgbh/amex/till/tguide/index.html

Provided by PBS, this lesson plan is centered around the murder of Emmett Till. Students are also asked to discuss segregation, violence, and the Great Migration. This lesson plan is broken into four parts and is intended for grades 7–12.
Resource Type: Lesson or Activity
Grade Level: MS, HS

Lesson Plan: Martin Luther King, Jr. and the Power of Nonviolence
http://edsitement.neh.gov/view_lesson_plan.asp?id=326

This thoughtful EDSITEment lesson introduces students to Martin Luther King, Jr.'s philosophy of nonviolence and the teachings of Mohandas K. Gandhi that influenced King's views. Students explore the relevance of political philosophy to personal life. Intended for grades 6–8.
Resource Type: Lesson or Activity
Grade Level: MS

Whitewashing History: Exploring Topics of Civil Rights from 1948–1964
www.nytimes.com/learning/teachers/lessons/20021216monday.html

In this *New York Times* lesson, students revisit issues of civil rights in the United States, using the national discussion of retiring Senator Throm Thurmond's 1948 Dixiecrat Presidential campaign.
Resource Type: Lesson or Activity
Grade Level: HS

Course Models: Civil Rights Movement
www.history.ctaponline.org/center/hsscm/index.cfm?Page_Key=1747

Part of the California History-Social Science content standards and annotated course, which include: Background information, focus questions, pupil activities and handouts, assessment, and references to books, articles, Web sites, literature, audio-video programs, and historic site. Intended for Grade 11.
Resource Type: Course Model
Grade Level: HS

Cesar Chavez: Model Curriculum
www.cde.ca.gov/be/pn/nr/documents/chavez020602.pdf

Standards-based model curriculum on the life and work of César E. Chávez. Curriculum is provided for K–12, consisting of biographies and lesson plans. Page requires the Adobe Reader in order to be viewed.
Resource Type: Course Model
Grade Level: ES, MS, HS

CEC: Have Minorities Gained Acceptance?
www.col-ed.org/cur/sst/sst69.txt

In this mini-lesson, students will examine magazines and advertisements in order to determine how "accepted" minorities are in today's culture.
Resource Type: Lesson or Activity
Grade Level: HS

The Civil Rights Movement: Lesson Plan
http://school.discovery.com/lessonplans/programs/freeatlast/

In this clear lesson plan, students will learn about ordinary men and women also struggled for their beliefs. Grades 6–8.
Resource Type: Lesson or Activity
Grade Level: MS

Jackie Steals Home
http://lcweb2.loc.gov/ammem/ndlpedu/lessons/98/robinson/intro.html

In this lesson, students analyze primary sources from *Jackie Robinson and Other Baseball Highlights, 1860s–1960s in American Memory*. Middle school and high school levels.
Resource Type: Lesson or Activity; Primary Source Collection
Grade Level: MS, HS

Rounding the Bases—Lesson Plan
http://memory.loc.gov/learn/lessons/00/base/index.html

This lesson challenges students to investigate the roles that race and ethnicity have played in the United States. Covering the period from 1860 to 1959, students are divided into groups each investigating a 20-year segment of time and use primary sources from the Library of Congress's American Memory collection to develop and defend a unique historical hypothesis about race and ethnicity. Students draw parallels between the changing role of race and ethnicity in the history of baseball to the changing role these factors played in broader American society. Designed for grades 9–12.
Resource Type: Lesson or Activity; Primary Source Collection
Grade Level: HS

Living Legacies—Commemorating People Who Have Positively Impacted Society
www.nytimes.com/learning/teachers/lessons/20030620friday.html

In this involved and thorough *New York Times* lesson, students explore the commemoration of Dr. Martin Luther King, Jr., research the positive impact another famous person has had on society and the images that best represent the actions and beliefs of that person, create an art exhibit honoring that person's legacy, and finally, write an essay analyzing the effect this individual has had on modern society.
Resource Type: Lesson or Activity
Grade Level: HS

Non-Violent Protest through the Ages
www.yale.edu/ynhti/curriculum/units/1987/3/87.03.02.x.html

This is a detailed Middle School teaching unit from the Yale–New Haven Teachers Institute. It focuses on the beliefs of Henry David Thoreau, Mohandas K. Gandhi and Dr. Martin Luther King and is designed to be used for classroom discussion as well as independent reading projects. Includes terms, activities, and teaching strategies.
Resource Type: Lesson or Activity
Grade Level: HS

Burning Hatred: Discussing the Constitutional Conflict Over Cross Burning
www.nytimes.com/learning/teachers/lessons/20021213friday.html

In this lesson, students examine the constitutionality of various forms of expression; they then take part in a mock trial on the issue of cross burning.
Resource Type: Lesson or Activity
Grade Level: HS

The Civil Rights Movement
www.lessonplanspage.com/SSCICivilRightsMovementWebProjectHS.htm

Designed by George Cassutto, this lesson plan aims to give students a general historical understanding of the events of the civil rights movement and its context in African American history. It encourages students to construct a Black history timeline. A matching activity is also included, in which students pair a historical event with its correct description.
Resource Type: Lesson or Activity
Grade Level: HS

Civil Rights Movement, 1954–1968

www.eduref.org/cgi-bin/printlessons.cgi/Virtual/Lessons/Social_Studies/US_History/USH0045.html

Written by Texas Teacher Kristine A. McIntosh, this Educator's Reference lesson plan uses a "hands-on" approach to Civil Rights. Activities include a student research paper and a Segregation exercise. Intended for grade 11.

Resource Type: Lesson or Activity
Grade Level: HS

Digital History Resource Guides

www.digitalhistory.uh.edu/resource_guides/

"Digital History Resource Guides" provide links to American history Web sites by period and provide historical overviews, readings (online textbook chapter, Reader's Companion) primary source documents (documents, maps, cartoons), teaching resources (chronologies, maps, quizzes), audiovisual resources, and additional resources. It is an excellent and comprehensive teaching resource.

Resource Type: Course Model
Grade Level: HS, College

All about Martin Luther King, Jr.: An Overview of his Life

www.enchantedlearning.com/history/us/MLK/

This "Enchanted Learning" site is aimed at young learners and provides an overview of Martin Luther King's Life. It has printable activities about King's life and achievements for both beginning and fluent readers.

Resource Type: Lesson or Activity; Test or Quiz
Grade Level: ES, MS

HistoryTeacher.net: AP United States History Quizzes 1920–1970

www.historyteacher.net/USQuizMainPage.htm

A teacher at the Horace Greeley High School in Chappaqua, New York, has produced a great general site for history teachers that offers AP-level U.S. history quizzes on many different periods and topics.

Resource Type: Test or Quiz
Grade Level: HS

The American Nation: Internet Activities

www.phschool.com/atschool/TAN/Survey/Teacher_Area/TAN1_T_BK_index.html

Prentice Hall's phschool.com offers Internet activities based on their *The American Nation* textbook chapters.

Resource Type: Lesson or Activity
Grade Level: MS

A History of the United States: Internet Activities and Student Self-Test Questions

www.phschool.com/atschool/history_us/Student_Area/HUS_S_BK_index.html

Prentice Hall's phschool.com offers Internet activities and interactive quizzes based on *A History of the United States* textbook chapters.

Resource Type: Lesson or Activity
Grade Level: HS

VIETNAM WAR ERA

*****The Wars for Vietnam 1945–1975
www.pbs.org/wgbh/amex/vietnam/index.html

Very good page for getting a sound factual overview of the events of the war. Well organized, with detailed info. Also has some primary sources/documents.
Resource Type: General Reference; Primary Source Collection

****Vietnam Yesterday and Today: Chronology of U.S.–Vietnam Relations
http://servercc.oakton.edu/~wittman/chronol.htm

An extensive timeline of the Vietnam war and the politics surrounding it from 1930 to present. A good place to obtain factual knowledge about specific events, groups, and individuals.
Resource Type: General Reference; Timeline

Figure 6.5: Vietnam Yesterday and Today

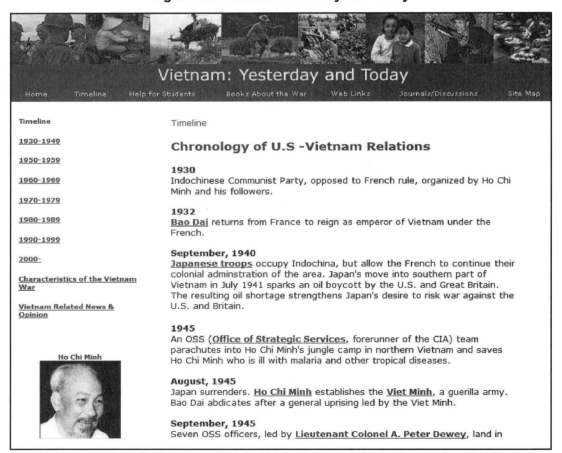

****The Wars for Vietnam
http://vietnam.vassar.edu/

This site was produced by students out of Vassar college and provides an overview of the

Vietnam war, primary documents and photos, and links to other related sites.
Resource Type: General Reference

****Battlefield: Vietnam
www.pbs.org/battlefieldvietnam/

A companion to the PBS video program, this site features a brief historical introduction, a battlefield timeline, an exposé on guerrilla tactics, a multimedia look at the siege of Khe Sanh, and other resources.
Resource Type: General Reference; Multimedia Presentation

****Spartacus—Vietnam War Index
www.spartacus.schoolnet.co.uk/vietnam.html

A large collection of topics including political and military figures, issues, events, organizations, and links to more sites. Clicking on a link for a particular subject leads to a separate page with detailed information. This is a very good collection of factual information.
Resource Type: General Reference

****The Vietnam War Photo Album
www.geocities.com/~nam_album/

A collection of photos taken by U.S. military servicemen of people, places, and things they thought should be remembered. The site is organized by military branch—Air Force, Army, Marine Corps, and Navy.
Resource Type: Primary Source Collection

****Vets with a Mission
www.vwam.com/index.html

Under the "history" tab there is a superb and very extensive collection of well-written information that deals with many topics in-depth. The site's coverage spans from the earliest history of Vietnam and the Vietnamese people to the present. There is also a collection of photos.
Resource Type: General Reference; Primary Source Collection

****1968 Democratic Party Convention Riots
http://historymatters.gmu.edu/d/6464

A primary source document (authored by Tom Hayden of SDS) that explains some of the reasoning behind the protest and revolts against the war and government/culture in general. Also discusses the role of race and civil rights during the period. Published by *History Matters*, an online U.S. history survey course by George Mason University.
Resource Type: Primary Source Collection

****CNN Perspective Series—Episode Eleven: Vietnam 1954–1968
www.cnn.com/SPECIALS/cold.war/episodes/11/

Includes a Spotlight on Dien Bien Phu and sections on changing media-military rules and the "living room" war.
Resource Type: Multimedia Presentation; General Reference

**** Vietnam Online
www.pbs.org/wgbh/pages/amex/vietnam/tease.html

Another PBS Online site, this features an introduction to the conflict, reflections of the participants, a timeline, a who's who, and more. Also has a teacher's guide.
Resource Type: Primary Source Collection; General Reference

****1968: The Whole World Was Watching
www.stg.brown.edu/projects/1968/

An engaging oral history project that features recollections of a group of Rhode Islanders regarding pivotal events and issues in 1968. Great example of a student project.
Resource Type: Primary Source Collection; Lesson or Activity

****Assignment Hanoi
www.pbs.org/hanoi/notebook.htm

Follow U.S. Ambassador and former P.O.W. Pete Peterson as he returns to the land of his captors on a "mission of reconciliation," through interviews, research on Vietnam's history before 1900, and investigation of an ambassador's duties. PBS
Resource Type: General Reference; Lesson or Activity

****The VietNam Pictures Archives
http://metalab.unc.edu/vietnam/vnpic.html

These archives consist of a number of JPEGs and GIFs, MIDI sequences, and RealAudio clips.
Resource Type: Primary Source Collection; Multimedia presentation.

***Statistics about the Vietnam War
www.vhfcn.org/stat.html

A large collection of statistics compiled by a veteran from a variety of credible sources, attempting to disprove several perceptions of the Vietnam War.
Resource Type: General Reference

****LBJ in the Oval Office
www.hpol.org/lbj/

At this audio-rich site, visitors listen to some President Lyndon Johnson's "most important speeches and secretly recorded conversations."
Resource Type: Multimedia Presentation

****Space Race
www.nasm.si.edu/exhibitions/gal114/gal114.htm

Visually engaging site that explores military origins of the space race and provides a gallery map and more. From the National Air and Space Museum.
Resource Type: Virtual Tour; General Reference

***The History of Televised Presidential Debates
www.museum.tv/debateweb/html/index.htm

Produced by the Museum of Broadcast Communications in Chicago, this engaging site

focuses on the Kennedy-Nixon debates of 1960 and televised debate history to 1996. Features lesson plans and activities.
Resource Type: Multimedia Presentation; Primary Source Collection

****John F. Kennedy Library and Museum
www.jfklibrary.org/

The museum offers speeches, official documents, photographs, and more from the presidency of John F. Kennedy.
Resource Type: Primary Source Collection; General Reference

****Revisiting Watergate
www.washingtonpost.com/wp-srv/national/longterm/watergate/front.htm

A 1997 *Washington Post* supplement marking the 25th anniversary of the Watergate burglary. Features include bios of the key figures involved in the affair and a discussion of the impact of the scandal.
Resource Type: General Reference

****AllPolitics: Watergate
www.cnn.com/ALLPOLITICS/1997/gen/resources/watergate/

A CNN-Time project that relies on *Time*'s coverage of the scandal, includes several video clips of interviews and other footage from the 25th anniversary of the scandal.
Resource Type: General Reference; Multimedia Presentation

****Watergate
http://watergate.info/

Well-organized overview of the Watergate scandal designed by an Australian schoolteacher.
Resource Type: General Reference; Primary Source Collection

Vietnam War Era Lesson Plans, Teacher Guides, Activities, and More

PBS Vietnam Online: Teacher's Guide
www.pbs.org/wgbh/amex/vietnam/tguide/index.html

A variety of useful classroom activities that take advantage of "PBS Vietnam Online" site in four different categories: History, Civics, Geography and Culture.
Resource Type: Lesson or Activity
Grade Level: HS

Teach Vietnam: Echoes from the Wall
www.teachvietnam.org/

The curriculum covers six modules: Escalating Involvement in the Vietnam War, Conflict on the Home Front, Those Who Served, The Vietnamese and Vietnam, The Wall as Healer, and The Legacy of the Vietnam War. Lesson plans may be accessed through the Teachers' Guide link on the Educators page.
Resource Type: Lesson or Activity
Grade Level: MS, HS

Teaching the Vietnam War
www.pbs.org/frontlineworld/educators/history_vietnam.html

Another good PBS lesson plan on Vietnam based around video clips that are available online.
Resource Type: Lesson or Activity
Grade Level: HS

Intervene or Interfere? Exploring Forty Years of United States Intervention in Foreign Affairs
www.nytimes.com/learning/teachers/lessons/20030407monday.html

In this topical lesson, students will research the motives, actions, and results of U.S. intervention in foreign affairs between the 1961 Bay of Pigs invasion and the 2003 invasion of Iraq; they then present their research to class for comparative analysis.
Resource Type: Lesson or Activity
Grade Level: HS

Vietnam WebQuest
http://people.heidelberg.edu/~bkreitzb/webquest.html

A WebQuest written by students from Heidelberg College for 10th-grade students that guides students through several Web sites on the Vietnam war.
Resource Type: Lesson or Activity
Grade Level: HS

Lesson Plan: Constitutional Issues—Watergate and the Constitution
www.archives.gov/education/lessons/watergate-constitution/

This National Archives and Records Administration lesson plan gives teachers a chance to explain the Watergate incident to students. The Teacher's guide has three different activities that stimulate discussions on the Constitution and the legal system. Grades 6–12.
Resource Type: Lesson or Activity
Grade Level: MS, HS

Lesson Plan: The Sixties
http://historymatters.gmu.edu/d/5803/

From the site: "This activity explores emotions of eagerness, frustration, betrayal, community, and compassion during the 1960s. Students will explore this entire document, including all the links, and write a five-page paper or an equivalent Web page (no frills necessary except links) where they take up a position and perspective chosen from the four options provided." Written by Eileen Walsh, Bemidji State University.
Resource Type: Lesson or Activity
Grade Level: HS, College

Teach Vietnam: Echoes from the Wall
www.teachvietnam.org/

This thorough curriculum covers six modules: Escalating Involvement in the Vietnam War, Conflict on the Home Front, Those Who Served, The Vietnamese and Vietnam, The Wall as

Healer, and The Legacy of the Vietnam War. Lesson plans may be accessed through the Teachers' Guide link on the Educators page.
Resource Type: Course Model
Grade Level: MS, HS

Digital History Resource Guides
www.digitalhistory.uh.edu/resource_guides/

"Digital History Resource Guides" provide links to American history Web sites by period and provide historical overviews, readings (online textbook chapter, Reader's Companion), primary source documents (documents, maps, cartoons), teaching resources (chronologies, maps, quizzes), audiovisual resources, and additional resources. It is an excellent and comprehensive teaching resource.
Resource Type: Course Model
Grade Level: HS, College

The American Century: Multiple Choice Quiz, Fill-in-the-Blank, Flashcards, American History Glossary, American History Appendix
http://wps.ablongman.com/long_carnes_an_11/0,7137,252269-,00.html

The Student Resources section of *The American Nation* companion Web site features introductions to chapters, interactive quizzes, flashcards, Web links, an American History Glossary, and an American History Appendix.
Resource Type: Test or Quiz; Lesson or Activity
Grade Level: MS

From Camelot to Watergate: Multiple Choice Quiz, Fill-in-the-Blank, Flashcards, American History Glossary, American History Appendix
http://wps.ablongman.com/long_carnes_an_11/0,7137,252320-,00.html

The Student Resources section of *The American Nation* companion Web site features introductions to chapters, interactive quizzes, flashcards, Web links, an American History Glossary, and an American History Appendix.
Resource Type: Test or Quiz; Lesson or Activity
Grade Level: MS

Society in Flux: Multiple Choice Quiz, Fill-in-the-Blank, Flashcards, American History Glossary, American History Appendix
http://wps.ablongman.com/long_carnes_an_11/0,7137,252372-,00.html

The Student Resources section of *The American Nation* companion Web site features introductions to chapters, interactive quizzes, flashcards, Web links, an American History Glossary, and an American History Appendix.
Resource Type: Test or Quiz; Lesson or Activity
Grade Level: MS

Views of JFK: Lesson Plan
http://school.discovery.com/lessonplans/programs/jfk-aportrait/

In this lesson plan, students will learn that personal interviews that are conducted now, in

modern times, and with people who lived through Kennedy's administration, can add insights into how Americans view JFK. Grades 6–8.
Resource Type: Lesson or Activity
Grade Level: MS

The Cuban Missile Crisis: Lesson Plan

http://school.discovery.com/lessonplans/programs/cubanmissile/

In this lesson plan, students research and write a news article about a Cold War event. Grades 8–12.
Resource Type: Lesson or Activity
Grade Level: MS, HS

Watergate: Lesson Plan

http://school.discovery.com/lessonplans/programs/watergate/

In this lesson plan, students conduct an interview with a Watergate-era adult and present a summary of their interview.
Resource Type: Lesson or Activity
Grade Level: MS, HS

The World in Uncertain Times, 1950–Present Practice Test

www.phschool.com/curriculum_support/brief_review/us_history/tests.html?unit=7&number=35

High school level quiz on Cold War America from Prentice Hall.
Resource Type: Test or Quiz
Grade Level: HS

The World in Uncertain Times, 1950–Present Document-Based Essay

www.phschool.com/curriculum_support/brief_review/us_history/essay_questions/unit7.cfm

From the site: "This Prentice Hall DBQ is designed to test your ability to work with historical documents and is based on the accompanying documents" (1–6).
Resource Type: Lesson or Activity
Grade Level:HS

HistoryTeacher.net: AP United States History Quizzes 1920–1970

www.historyteacher.net/USQuizMainPage.htm

A teacher at the Horace Greeley High School in Chappaqua, New York, has produced a great general site for history teachers that offers AP-level U.S. history quizzes on many different periods and topics.
Resource Type: Test or Quiz
Grade Level: HS

The American People: Reform and Rebellion During the Turbulent Sixties

http://wps.ablongman.com/long_nash_ap_6/0,7361,592970-,00.html

PowerPoint presentation on Cold War America in the 1960s as part of the online companion to *The American People*. Click on PowerPoint Presentations and then Chapter 28.
Resource Type: Lesson or Activity
Grade Level: HS

The American People: Discontent and Disorder, 1969–1980
http://wps.ablongman.com/long_nash_ap_6/0,7361,592970-,00.html

PowerPoint presentation on Cold War America in the 1960s as part of the online companion to *The American People*. Click Chapter 29.
Resource Type: Lesson or Activity
Grade Level: HS

Vietnam: Blank Map
http://wps.ablongman.com/long_nash_ap_6/0,7361,592970-,00.html

The companion Web site to *The American People* offers blank maps related to various topics in American history. The maps can be printed or placed in a PowerPoint presentation.
Resource Type: Maps
Grade Level: HS

The American Nation: Internet Activities
www.phschool.com/atschool/TAN/Survey/Teacher_Area/TAN1_T_BK_index.html

Prentice Hall's phschool.com offers Internet activities based on their *The American Nation* textbook chapters.
Resource Type: Lesson or Activity
Grade Level: MS

A History of the United States: Internet Activities and Student Self-Test Questions
www.phschool.com/atschool/history_us/Student_Area/HUS_S_BK_index.html

Prentice Hall's phschool.com offers Internet activities and interactive quizzes based on *A History of the United States* textbook chapters.
Resource Type: Test or Quiz
Grade Level: HS

POST–VIETNAM WAR ERA

****Vietnam—Echoes of the War
www.cnn.com/SPECIALS/2000/vietnam/

CNN page covering how the war has influenced America and Indochina today. Also has a history link (top right corner) with a good timeline for basic understanding of the war, a who's who, and maps.
Resource Type: General Reference

****Guerrilla Wars: 1956–1989
www.pbs.org/wgbh/peoplescentury/episodes/guerrillawars/

The "People's Century" is based on a 26-episode television series and features a teacher's guide, a timeline, a thematic overview, and RealAudio excerpts. The highlights of the Web site are the first-person narratives, often by ordinary people who lived through turbulent times. This section discusses guerrilla war movements in Vietnam, Afghanistan, and elsewhere.
Resource Type: Multimedia Presentation; Lesson or Activity

****The Gulf War
www.pbs.org/wgbh/pages/frontline/gulf/index.html

This "Frontline" site offers a comprehensive and engaging history of the Gulf War from the perspective of those who participated. Major categories include Oral Histories, War Stories, and Weapons and Technology; there are maps, a chronology, images, essays, discussions of Gulf Syndrome, and more.
Resource Type: Primary Source Collection; Multimedia Presentation

*****Cold War: From Yalta to Malta
http://cnn.com/SPECIALS/cold.war/

This CNN Perspectives series explores the Cold War experience. Included are interactive maps, rare video footage, declassified documents, biographies, picture galleries, timelines, interactive activities, a search function, book excerpts, an educator's guide and more.
Resource Type: General Reference; Multimedia Presentation

****Episode Nineteen: Freeze 1977–1981
www.cnn.com/SPECIALS/cold.war/episodes/19/

Features sections on the Carter-Brezhnev years, John Paul II toppling the communist domino, politics of European security, and missile diplomacy.

****Episode Twenty: Soldiers of God 1975–1988
www.cnn.com/SPECIALS/cold.war/episodes/20/

This presentation talks about the Afghan Civil War and the crumbling detente, with sections on the Olympic games, Afghan legacy, and Russian pain.

****Episode Twenty Two: Star Wars 1980–1988
www.cnn.com/SPECIALS/cold.war/episodes/22/

Includes excerpts of interviews, a transcript of Reagan's "Star Wars" speech, and a section on war games.

****Fast Forward: 1980–1999
www.pbs.org/wgbh/peoplescentury/episodes/fastforward/

The "People's Century" site is based on the 26-episode PBS television series and features a teacher's guide, a timeline, a thematic overview, and RealAudio excerpts. The highlights of the Web site are the first-person narratives, often by ordinary people who lived through turbulent times. Fast forward probes the impact of communications technology and business globalization on the traditional world order.
Resource Type: Primary Source Collection; General Reference

****The Reagan Years
www.cnn.com/SPECIALS/2001/reagan.years/

This site is a CNN.com special report on the Reagan Presidency, with many remembrances from Reagan's political colleagues.
Resource Type: General Reference; Primary Source Collection

Post–Vietnam War Era Lesson Plans, Activities, and More

Has the Wall Truly Tumbled Down?
www.nytimes.com/learning/teachers/lessons/19991110wednesday.html?searchpv=learning_lessons

The New York Times has created this lesson plan to spur debate on the division in Berlin. Students will learn about the wall itself and what Berlin is like now that the wall is down. Recommended for grade 11.
Resource Type: Lesson or Activity
Grade Level: HS

The American People: The Revival of Conservatism, 1980–1992
http://wps.ablongman.com/long_nash_ap_6/0,7361,592970-,00.html

PowerPoint presentation on Cold War America from 1980 to 1992 as part of the online companion to *The American People*. Click on PowerPoint Presentations and then Chapter 30.
Resource Type: Lesson or Activity
Grade Level: HS

The World in Uncertain Times, 1950–Present Practice Test
www.phschool.com/curriculum_support/brief_review/us_history/tests.html?unit=7&number=35

High school level multiple-choice quiz on Cold War America from Prentice Hall.
Resource Type: Test or Quiz
Grade Level: HS

The World in Uncertain Times, 1950–Present Document-Based Essay
www.phschool.com/curriculum_support/brief_review/us_history/essay_questions/unit7.cfm

From the site: "This Prentice Hall DBQ is designed to test your ability to work with historical documents and is based on the accompanying documents (1–6)."
Resource Type: Lesson or Activity
Grade Level:HS

POST–COLD WAR ERA

****Roe v. Wade 25 Years Later
www.cnn.com/SPECIALS/1998/roe.wade/

The CNN Archives feature special reports on many key world and American events, issues, and personalities. A CNN.com special report on the ongoing abortion debate in America.
Resource Type: General Reference; Multimedia Presentation

****U.S. and Quest for Peace in Middle East
www.usembassy-israel.org.il/publish/peace/peace1.htm

Produced by the United States Information Service, this site has texts, transcripts, speeches, a photo gallery, and links and is updated daily. A lot of information on recent events.
Resource Type: Primary Source Collection; General Reference

****AIDS at 20
www.nytimes.com/library/national/science/aids/aids-index.html

Provides 350+ *New York Times* articles on the AIDS epidemic as well as video, fact-sheets, reports and nine articles specifically related to AIDS in Africa.
Resource Type: Primary Source Collection

****The Clinton Years
www.pbs.org/wgbh/pages/frontline/shows/clinton/

PBS examines President Clinton's years in office in this engaging study.
Resource Type: Primary Source Collection; General Reference

****Clinton Accused
www.washingtonpost.com/wp-srv/politics/special/clinton/clinton.htm

A *Washington Post* report that covers the impeachment of the President and offers photos, documents, articles, and more.
Resource Type: Primary Source Collection; Multimedia Presentation

****The Pilgrimage of Jesse Jackson
www.pbs.org/wgbh/pages/frontline/jesse/

This PBS offering features interviews, speeches, a chronology and more.
Resource Type: Primary Source Collection; Multimedia Presentation

****The Affirmative Action and Diversity Project: A Web Site for Research
http://aad.english.ucsb.edu/

This scholarly site, by a member of the English department at the University of California Santa Barbara, is an academic resource and contains a substantial amount of information on California politics and debate over California's Classification by Race, Ethnicity, Color, or National Origin. The materials at the site are also helpful for putting the 2003 Supreme Court decision on affirmative action (at the University of Michigan) in historical perspective.
Resource Type: Primary Source Collection; General Reference

****From Yalta to Malta Episode Twenty Four: Conclusions
www.cnn.com/SPECIALS/cold.war/episodes/24/

This CNN Perspectives series explores the Cold War experience. Included are interactive maps, rare video footage, declassified documents, biographies, picture galleries, timelines, interactive activities, a search function, book excerpts, an educator's guide and more. Features a section on what the war cost, memories from the Cold War, and an excerpt from the book *After the Cold War*.
Resource Type: General Reference; Multimedia Presentation

****People's Century
www.pbs.org/wgbh/peoplescentury/

This PBS site is based on a 26-episode television series and features a teacher's guide, a time-line, a thematic overview, and RealAudio excerpts. The highlights of the Web site are the first-person narratives, often by ordinary people who lived through turbulent times.
Resource Type: Primary Source Collection; General Reference

Post–Cold War Era Lesson Plans

****Justice Learning: Civic Education in the Real World
www.justicelearning.org/

"Justice Learning" uses audio from the *Justice Talking* radio show and articles from *The New York Times* to teach students about reasoned debate and the often-conflicting values inherent in American democracy. The Web site includes articles, editorials, and oral debate from the nation's finest journalists and advocates. All of the material is supported by age-appropriate summaries and additional links. In addition, for each covered issue, the site includes curricular material from the *New York Times* Learning Network for high school teachers and detailed information about how each of the institutions of democracy (the courts, the Congress, the presidency, the press, and the schools) affect the issues.
Resource Type: General Reference; Multimedia Presentation; Lesson or Activity
Grade Level: HS

****CNN: Education
www.cnn.com/EDUCATION/

CNN: Education provides teachers with instructional materials for integrating current events across the curriculum. A student section keeps students in grades 6–12 aware of the latest news of interest to them. Lesson plans, background material, profiles, links to useful Internet sites, and forums for interaction with other teachers are also included.
Resource Type: General Reference; Lesson or Activity
Grade Level: MS, HS

The World in Uncertain Times, 1950–Present: Practice Test
www.phschool.com/curriculum_support/brief_review/us_history/tests.html?unit=7&number=35

High school level multiple-choice quiz on Cold War America from Prentice Hall.
Resource Type: Test or Quiz
Grade Level: HS

The World in Uncertain Times, 1950–Present Document Based Essay
www.phschool.com/curriculum_support/brief_review/us_history/essay_questions/unit7.cfm

From the site: "This Prentice Hall DBQ is designed to test your ability to work with historical documents and is based on the accompanying documents (1–6)."
Resource Type: Lesson or Activity
Grade Level:HS

9/11 AND TERRORISM

*****Frontline Teacher Center—Roots of Terrorism
www.pbs.org/wgbh/pages/frontline/teach/terror/

Excellent PBS site with lots of classroom activities and links for background information on terrorism and its development. Content includes timelines, maps, facts, people, content on Islam, and more. High quality site with plenty of facts and data.
Resource Type: General Reference; Lesson or Activity

*****The September 11 Digital Archive
http://911digitalarchive.org/

A tremendous resource for firsthand accounts—audio, video, and still-clips—from the 9/11 tragedy. Huge collection from the Center for History and New Media sheds much light on the impact of 9/11, though there is not much background information on terrorism.
Resource Type: Primary Source Collection

Figure 6.6: The September 11 Digital Archive

THE SEPTEMBER 11 DIGITAL ARCHIVE

SAVING THE HISTORIES OF SEPTEMBER 11, 2001

STORIES
Tell your story and read
the tales of others [En Español]

E-MAIL
Contribute and read e-mail

STILL IMAGES
Submit and view photos and art

MOVING IMAGES
Contribute and view videos,
animations, and digital creations

AUDIO
Listen to the voices and
experiences of 9/11

DOCUMENTS
Read fliers, reports, interviews,
and other materials

GUIDE TO WEBSITES
A portal to websites and
online resources

9/11 FAQS
Frequently Asked Questions
about the September 11 attacks

ABOUT THIS SITE
Contact us, contributor &
visitor information,
partners

The September 11 Digital Archive uses electronic media to collect, preserve, and present the history of the September 11, 2001 attacks.

 For the anniversary of the 9/11 attacks, the September 11 Digital Archive has overlaid a select group of photographs and stories from Ground Zero in New York on an interactive map. Clicking on blue markers (photos) or red markers (stories) shows details from the September 11 Digital Archive.

 Featured Collection -- Ground One: Voices from Post-911 Chinatown aims to provide an in-depth portrait of the ways in which the identity of a community, largely neglected by national media following 9/11, has been indelibly shaped by that day.

 Visit our sister project: The Hurricane Digital Memory Bank uses electronic media to collect, preserve, and present the stories, images, and responses of the devastating 2005 hurricane season.

****Library of Congress September 11th Documentary Project
http://memory.loc.gov/ammem/collections/911_archive/

Another collection of accounts, reactions, pictures, and opinions by the American people in the wake of the attacks. Captures the attitudes, emotions, and feelings of the people following the incident.
Resource Type: Primary Source Collection

****CNN: Fighting Terror
www.cnn.com/SPECIALS/2004/fighting.terror/index.html

Much information on Bin Laden and Al Qaida, mostly directly related to 9/11 and the war in

Iraq. Helpful site for understanding the current situation in Iraq.
Resource Type: General Reference

****Global Policy Forum: Iraq
www.globalpolicy.org/security/issues/irqindx.htm

Extensive and well-organized list of almost everything you might want to know about Iraq and the various factors linking it to the United States and the current Iraqi war.
Resource Type: General Reference

****Close Up Foundation: Domestic Terror
www.closeup.org/terror.htm

Another well-organized site that discusses the presence of terrorism and 9/11, and how this presence and the precautions we must take because of it can affect American people and their lives. Covers pre-9/11 (Unabomber, Oklahoma City, Flight 800) as well as much info about U.S. legislation regarding terrorism. Tons of info here, lots of detail and data.
Resource Type: General Reference

****The Avalon Project: 9/11 Collection
www.yale.edu/lawweb/avalon/sept_11/sept_11.htm

A staggeringly enormous collection of primary sources and government documents on terrorism, 9/11, and more. Fortunately it has a search feature; there is an amazing amount of material here!
Resource Type: Primary Source Collection

****History News Network: Terrorism
http://hnn.us/articles/299.html

Includes selections from essays on 9/11 from the *Journal of American History* and sections on the history of terrorism, the Afghans, and America's role in the Middle East (written by credible writers who are professors or field experts). Also has info on less recent terrorist topics.
Resource Type: General Reference

****The September 11th Sourcebooks
www.gwu.edu/~nsarchiv/NSAEBB/sept11/index.html

A dense collection of declassified primary sources on the 9/11 attacks from the National Security Archives. This site is especially useful for research on government policy. The first volume in the series seems to be the most directly useful and relevant.
Resource Type: Primary Source Collection

****The Washington Post: Attack Map and Database Search
www.washingtonpost.com/wp-dyn/world/issues/terrordata/

Allows user to find basic information and facts on terrorism. Allows searching from pulldown menus by organization, location, terrorist's name, or incident (also has a standard type-in search). Useful for any terrorist attack except for 9/11—for some reason there is little about 9/11 on this site.
Resource Type: General Reference

*****CNN.com: Archives
www.cnn.com/SPECIALS/

"CNN.com Archives" feature special reports on many key World and American events, issues, and personalities.
Resource Type: General Reference; Multimedia Presentation

****America Remembers
www.cnn.com/SPECIALS/2002/america.remembers/

The site contains pictures, articles, stories, videos, and a comprehensive overview of not only the day of 9/11, but also the days to follow, and the days leading up to it. The main categories of the site are: September 11, 2001, which includes a timeline of the day; Faces of September 11, which includes direct quotes and stories from people involved in September 11; and The Cleanup, which has photographs and clips. Other categories are: Fighting Terror, which has links to articles on the war against terrorism, the rescues of people, recovery, investigation, and even information on anthrax; and A Changed World, with comments on chances for new attacks, the way Bush dealt with the war, and how much Americans were changed by September 11.
Resource Type: General Reference; Multimedia Presentation

****Middle East: Centuries of Conflict
www.cnn.com/SPECIALS/2001/mideast/

Part of the "CNN.com Archives," this site is an excellent introduction to strife in the Middle East—past and present.
Resource Type: General Reference; Multimedia Presentation

****War Against Terror
www.cnn.com/SPECIALS/2001/trade.center/

Part of the "CNN.com Archives," this site is an excellent introduction to the issue of terrorism as it relates to 9/11.
Resource Type: General Reference; Multimedia Presentation

9/11 and Terrorism Lesson Plans, Activities, and More

Online News Hour: Teacher Resources on 9/11
www.pbs.org/newshour/bb/military/terroristattack/teachers/

Yet another good PBS site for teachers (and students), with many links and content for students at a variety of levels. Covers a broad range of related topics.
Resource Type: Lesson or Activity
Grade Level: HS

PBS: The Center of the World
www.pbs.org/wgbh/amex/newyork/tguide/index.html

A PBS teacher's guide for middle school students with ideas about teaching 9/11. The main page contains ideas and questions for teachers to give to students for brainstorming about the events, but there are several links within the text that could be helpful for giving a basic background on the situation.

Resource Type: Lesson or Activity
Grade Level: MS

EDSITEment: On the Homefront
http://edsitement.neh.gov/view_lesson_plan.asp?id=224

This lesson plan from the National Endowment for the Humanities contains ideas and resources for relating the war on terror with World War II. Issues are framed within the context of domestic support and the homefront. Plenty of useful resources to work with.
Resource Type: Lesson or Activity
Grade Level: MS

Defining Terrorism
www.pbs.org/newshour/extra/teachers/lessonplans/terrorism/terrorism1.html

This lesson poses the question, "What is a terrorist?" Students will have an opportunity to explore the debate over legitimate and illegitimate uses of force and the distinction between terrorists and freedom fighters. Students will explore a framework for analyzing political violence and terrorism, apply this framework to historical and contemporary case studies, and develop a working definition of terrorism.
Resource Type: Lesson or Activity
Grade Level: HS

Remembering September 11
www.pbs.org/newshour/extra/teachers/lessonplans/terrorism/sept11_test.html

This lesson plan serves as a basis for discussion and reflection on the one year anniversary of September 11, 2001. It consists of four parts which can be used separately or together.
Resource Type: Lesson or Activity
Grade Level: HS

Changing of the Guard: Examining the Role of the United States in Democratic Transitions Around the World
www.nytimes.com/learning/teachers/lessons/20030428monday.html

In this lesson, students research case studies of U.S.-led regime changes around the world. They then examine the possible future democratization of Iraq through the historical lens of past experience.
Resource Type: Lesson or Activity
Grade Level: MS, HS

Intervene or Interfere? Exploring Forty Years of United States Intervention in Foreign Affairs
www.nytimes.com/learning/teachers/lessons/20030407monday.html

In this lesson, students will research the motives, actions, and results of U.S. intervention in foreign affairs between the 1961 Bay of Pigs invasion and the 2003 invasion of Iraq; they then present their research to class for comparative analysis.
Resource Type: Lesson or Activity
Grade Level: MS, HS

Give Peace a Chance: Exploring Non-Violent Alternatives to Terrorism
www.nytimes.com/learning/teachers/lessons/20021106wednesday.html

In this lesson, students reflect on the 1979 occupation of the American Embassy in Iran. They then research the nations that are believed to currently pose a threat of terrorism toward the United States and speculate on ways in which these nations' conflicts with the United States could be solved through non-violent means.
Resource Type: Lesson or Activity
Grade Level: MS, HS

Frontline Teacher Center Roots of Terrorism
www.pbs.org/wgbh/pages/frontline/teach/terror/resources/

A page within the PBS site that contains numerous links to other terrorism resources, both within PBS and beyond.
Resource Type: Lesson or Activity
Grade Level: HS

CHAPTER 7

Prehistory and Ancient World History

PREHISTORY

*****Evolution
www.pbs.org/wgbh/evolution/

The PBS "Evolution" Web site complements a seven-part, eight-hour television broadcast series. This rich and impressive site features video clips from the series, simulations, animations, interactive timelines, expert commentary, primary sources, and extensive links to evolution-related learning resources worldwide. Among the special educational features are a free, 40-page teacher's guide, an eight-session course for high school teachers, four 15-minute videos that highlight the teaching of evolution in real classrooms around the country, online lessons that use multimedia formats to enhance students' understanding of evolution, and a multimedia library that provides Web access to more than 150 multimedia resources and concepts.
Resource Type: General Reference; Course Model

*****Becoming Human
www.becominghuman.org/

Presented by the Institute of Human Origins, "Becoming Human" is an impressive site that explores human evolution "in a broadband documentary experience" with video, articles, news and debates in paleoanthropology, and a Web guide (see Figure 7.2). Watch an introductory video overview of evolution with guide Donald Johanson, read paleoanthropology news and book reviews, and visit the learning center for educational activities and lessons. The site also features a glossary of terms and recommended web sites.
Resource Type: General Reference: Multimedia Presentation

****University of California Museum of Paleontology Online Exhibits
www.ucmp.berkeley.edu/

These are very helpful exhibits for students from the University of California Museum of Paleontology. The main exhibit sections include: History of Life through Time, which focuses on the ancestor/descendant relationships; Tour of Geologic Time, to learn how the Earth has changed; Understanding Evolution, which includes discussion of evolutionary theory; The

Figure 7.1: University of California Museum of Paleontology Online Exhibits

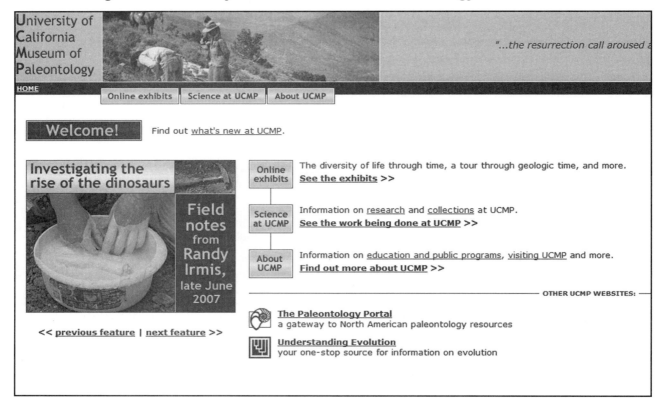

Paleontology Portal, on the fossil record of North America; K–12 Resources, or activities and lessons specifically for K–12 teachers and their students; Mystery Fossil, with a different fossil each month to identify; and Special exhibits, a collection of miscellaneous exhibits that UCMP has put together over the years.

Resource Type: Course Model

****The Story of Africa: Early History
www.bbc.co.uk/worldservice/africa/features/storyofafrica/index_section2.shtml

This BBC site features Africa's top historians and analyzes the events and characters that have shaped the continent from the origins of humankind to the end of South African apartheid. In this section you can listen to *Origins of Mankind* from the BBC *Story of Africa* series.

Resource Type: General Reference; Multimedia Presentation

****Secrets of Easter Island
www.pbs.org/wgbh/nova/easter/

This PBS Nova site follows a team of archaeologists as they try to discover how hundreds of giant stone statues that dominate Easter Island's coast were moved and erected. Learn about the first inhabitants and the stone statues and view panoramic images of the island.

Resource Type: General Reference; Multimedia Presentation

Figure 7.2: Becoming Human

****Mysteries of Çatalhöyük

www.smm.org/catal/

At Çatalhöyük, archaeologists are excavating the remains of a Neolithic town that was one of the world's largest settlements 9,000 years ago. This visually rich site is aimed at kids and provides a gallery, timeline, maps, activities, and a virtual tour.

Resource Type: General Reference; Multimedia Presentation

****Ice Mummies

www.pbs.org/wgbh/nova/icemummies/

This PBS companion Web site compliments a show about sacrificial mummies in Peru originally broadcast in November 1998. It includes articles on mummies and lost empires as well as images, accounts, audio, maps, and a teacher's guide.

Resource Type: General Reference; Lesson or Activity

****Hunting Hominids

http://exn.ca/hominids/wherethebonesare.cfm

This kid-friendly five-part series from Discovery School focuses on the fossil rich region of Eritrea. It explores Eritrea's natural environment, the plethora of hand axes in the area, and the evolution of hominids in Africa.

Resource Type: General Reference

****BBC History: Archaeology

www.bbc.co.uk/history/archaeology/index.shtml

This informative and engaging site from the BBC invites you to go "inside archaeology" to learn more about archaeological sites on land and sea. There are presentations on excavations, reconstructions, battlefields, as well as a timeline and treasure gallery. The Multimedia Zone has several simulations: Hunt the Ancestor, Iron Age Life, Diver's Quest, Wetwang Chariot, and Roundhouse.

Resource Type: General Reference; Multimedia Presentation

****The Human Origins Program

www.mnh.si.edu/anthro/humanorigins/index.htm

Hosted by the Smithsonian Institution, this site offers a Hall of Human Ancestors featuring movies of fossil skulls in the Smithsonian's collection. The Resource Guide explains various subjects of human evolution and there is a Q&A section. Current Topics section is not up to date, however, and only covers topics through 2002.

Resource Type: General Reference; Multimedia Presentation

****The Talk Origins Archive: Exploring the Creation/Evolution Controversy

www.talkorigins.org/

Talk Origins is a newsgroup devoted to the discussion and debate of biological and physical origins. Most discussions center on the creation/evolution controversy, but other topics of discussion include the origin of life, geology, biology, catastrophism, cosmology and theology. The Talk Origins Archive is a collection of articles and essays.

Resource Type: General Reference

****Genesis: Ideas of Origin in African Sculpture

www.metmuseum.org/special/se_event.asp?Occurrenceld={36C7412C-EEF8-11D5-9414-00902786BF44}

The Metropolitan Museum of Art's "Genesis: Ideas of Origin in African Sculptur" explores the following questions: How did the world begin? What is our ancestry? What is the source of agriculture, kingship, and other societal institutions? The exhibition explores how artists in distinct African cultures have interpreted these ideas and sought to answer these questions, with a focus on classical sculptural form, the ci wara antelope headdress of the Bamana

people. You can see videos illustrating headdress performances and read the transcript of a lecture presented in conjunction with this exhibition.
Resource Type: Multimedia Presentation; Art History

****The Metropolitan Museum of Art: Timeline of Art History
www.metmuseum.org/home.asp

There is much quality material for art students, educators, and enthusiasts at the The Metropolitan Museum of Art web site. Start with the "Metropolitan Museum of Art: Timeline of Art History," a chronological, geographical, and thematic exploration of the history of art from around the world. Each timeline page includes representative art from the Museum's collection, a chart of time periods, a map of the region, an overview, and a list of key events. The timelines—accompanied by world, regional, and sub-regional maps—provide a linear outline of art history, and allow visitors to compare and contrast art from around the globe at any time in history. For early art visit World Regions 8000–2000 BCE, Themes and Cultures presents past and present cultures with special features on the Met's collections and exhibitions.
Resource Type: Multimedia Presentation; Lesson or Activity

****The Cave of Lascaux
www.culture.gouv.fr:80/culture/arcnat/lascaux/en/

This multimedia and multilingual site from the French government offers a visual tour of the famous cave art at Lascaux. It also provides historical background on Lascaux as well as technical information, a bibliography, a quiz, and more.
Resource Type: General Reference; Multimedia Presentation

****Radiocarbon WEB-info
www.personal.psu.edu/users/w/x/wxk116/habitat/

"Radiocarbon WEB-info" offers a comprehensive look at radiocarbon dating techniques. In addition to the explanation of the radiocarbon dating method, the site offers recommended links, K–12 resources, and more. Produced by Tom Higham of the Radiocarbon Laboratory, University of Waikato, New Zealand.
Resource Type: General Reference

****Art History Resources on the Web: Prehistoric
http://witcombe.sbc.edu/ARTHprehistoric.html

Professor Chris Witcombe of the Art Department at Sweet Briar College has perhaps the best-organized gateway to art history sites on the Web. His directory is full of useful and regularly updated links and is divided into many categories. He also includes a list of museums and galleries and research resources. This section of "Art History Resources on the Web" contains many links to sites on prehistoric art.
Resource Type: General Reference; Course Model

****Art of the First Cities: The Third Millennium B.C. from the Mediterranean to the Indus
www.metmuseum.org/special/se_event.asp?OccurrenceId={9B8FB8E8-AE97-11D6-945F-00902786BF44}

The Metropolitan Museum of Art's "Art of the First Cities: The Third Millennium B.C. from the Mediterranean to the Indus" explores through art the emergence of the world's first city-states and empires in Syria and Mesopotamia during the third millennium B.C. The site also relates these developments to artistic and cultural developments from the eastern Aegean to the Indus

valley and Central Asia. Famous sites of the ancient world covered include the Royal Graves of Ur, the palace and temples of Mari, the citadel of Troy, and the great cities of the Indus Valley civilization. The exhibition includes approximately 400 works of extraordinary sculpture, jewelry, seals, relief carving, metalwork, and cuneiform tablets. There is a special, in-depth feature designed to complement the exhibition, an essay from the exhibition catalog, and samples from the accompanying Audio Guide.
Resource Type: General Reference; Art History

****Evolution of Modern Humans
http://anthro.palomar.edu/homo2/default.htm

This site offers a Web tutorial on human evolution complete with graphs, charts, and more. There are interactive quizzes, crossword puzzles, and additional information. The information at this site is more up-to-date than at some comparable sites.

****The Midwestern United States 16,000 Years Ago
www.museum.state.il.us/exhibits/larson/larson_top.html

The Illinois State Museum online exhibit "The Midwestern United States 16,000 Years Ago" provides information on the glaciation of the Midwestern United States. Plants and Animals of the Late Pleistocene, and Late Pleistocene Extinctions are among the links. You can also visit a cave in central Missouri to examine paleontological material. There are recommended books, Web sites, and lesson plans.
Resource Type: General Reference; Images Collection

****The Museum of Antiquities
http://museums.ncl.ac.uk/archive/

"The Museum of Antiquities" is a virtual gallery of special exhibits, including Hadrian's Wall and Flints and Stones, with nice images and explanatory text. The Museum of Antiquities is the principal museum of archaeology in northeast England.
Resource Type: General Reference; Image Collection

****Conversation for Exploration
www.lauralee.com/index.cgi

This talk show attempts to answer fundamental questions—Who are we? Where did we come from? Where are we going? What are we doing here, anyway?—and invites researchers in a range of fields to share their work. Listen to interviews on Navajo Stories and Reincarnation within Families, or search their database of 500 interviews. Consider listening to Jordan Maxwell who talks about how ancient and prehistoric concepts of religion and theology impact modern-day laws, religion, and government.
Resource Type: General Reference: Multimedia Presentation

***Human Origins and Evolution Homebase
www.indiana.edu/~origins/

Produced by Professor Jeanne Sept, this informative site revolves around courses in archaeology and the like at Indiana University. There are numerous, well-organized links to topics such as: Africa, Evolution, and Archaeology.
Resource Type: General Reference

***The Long Foreground: Human Prehistory
www.wsu.edu/gened/learn-modules/top_longfor/lfopen-index.html

Part of a student module at Washington State University, this site offers presentations on three learning topics: Overview of Human Evolution, Hominid Species Timeline, and Human Physical Characteristics. It features a clear and interesting step-by-step guide to the subjects with plenty of images and concise explanatory text.
Resource Type: General Reference; Lesson or Activity

***Ancient Britain
http://freespace.virgin.net/ancient.ways/ancient.htm

"Ancient Britain" offers an interactive map that leads the visitor to images, and descriptions of ancient British sites.
Resource Type: General Reference; Images Collection

***Flint and Stones: Real Life in Prehistory
http://museums.ncl.ac.uk/flint/menu.html

This site, aimed at a young audience, focuses on the inhabitants of Britain and north west Europe. A shaman guide escorts visitors to the Stone Age world who also meet an archeologist, take a food quiz, and learn about prehistory misconceptions.
Resource Type: General Reference; Lesson or Activity

***Stone Age Habitats
www.abotech.com/Articles/Kowalski01.htm

"Stone Age Habitats" provides an image-laden guide to Stone Age living conditions.
Resource Type: General Reference; Image Collection

***Stone Age Reference Collection
www.hf.uio.no/iakh/forskning/sarc/iakh/lithic/sarc.html

This site is a useful portal to Stone Age links. Categories include Technology, Study Methods, Raw Materials, and Online Publications. Developed for the teaching department of the Institute of Archaeology (I.A.K.K.) at the University of Oslo, Norway.
Resource Type: General Reference; Links Collection

***Creation Science
http://emporium.turnpike.net/C/cs/

A group of Christian scientists and engineers have created a large introductory site to creationism. Basic questions are answered through various articles. Little visual appeal, but the site provides clear and succinct articles.
Resource Type: General Reference

***The Cave of Chauvet
www.culture.gouv.fr/culture/arcnat/chauvet/en/

"The Cave of Chauvet" is an informative multimedia cave art site from the French government. Learn about the cave's discovery, authentication, and preservation via a photographic tour.
Resource Type: General Reference; Multimedia Presentation

***Neandertals: A Cyber Perspective
http://sapphire.indstate.edu/~ramanank/index.html

This Web site blends images and text to create an informative site on this extinct branch of the *Homo* species. Catergories: Tools, Hunting and Diet, Linguistic Capabilities, Architecture, Care for the Injured, Fate of the Neandertal, Burial & Ritual, Art, Morphology, Fate of Neandertals, Neandertal Remains, References. Links, and Further Reading.
Resource Type: General Reference

***Ice Ages
www.museum.state.il.us/exhibits/ice_ages/

A brief but informative site by the Illinois State Museum on the What? When? Why? of the Ice Ages. The exhibit was produced by the Illinois State Museum Director, R. Bruce McMillan.
Resource Type: General Reference

***Earth Mysteries
http://witcombe.sbc.edu/earthmysteries/EMIntro.html

This informative site is designed as an introduction to the mysteries of megaliths, druids, and more. The Stonehenge section is one of the most popular Stonehenge pages on the Web. "Earth Mysteries" is written and presented by Chris Witcombe of Sweet Briar College.
Resource Type: General Reference: Art History

***Various Theories of Origins of Life
www.religioustolerance.org/evolutio.htm

The Ontario Consultants on Religious Tolerance provides an overview of theories of life. Little visual content, but content is clear and well organized and site serves as a useful introduction to the topic.
Resource Type: General Reference

***Ice Age Art
www.humanities-interactive.org/ancient/iceage/index.html

"Ice Age Art" is an interesting site with varied material on Ice Age art. The site offers an image gallery, a presentation on art and evolution, Academic Research ice art game, a teacher's guide, and more.
Resource Type: General Reference; Image Collection

***Paleolithic Virtual Museum
http://vm.kemsu.ru/en/palaeolith/'

Few images, but much helpful background information by Russian/European researchers. Provides information on caves in Russia, Spain, France, and South America. Also offers hypertext essay on portable art as well as Web resources.
Resource Type: General Reference

Human Prehistory: An Exhibition
http://users.hol.gr/~dilos/prehis.htm

Features a gallery-style exhibition with good color photos, caricatures, and a step-by-step

guide. Covers Darwin and Palaeolithic and Neolithic Ages.
Resource Type: General Reference, Image Collection

***Creation Stories From Around the World
www.gly.uga.edu/railsback/CS/CSIndex.html

A 50-page online book from University of Georgia with links to various chapters. There are two Hebrew stories, a brief and accessible creation myth, and stories from Japan, China, Cherokees, and other regions/cultures.
Resource Type: General Reference

***Dig
www.digonsite.com/

"Dig" is an archaeology magazine for kids. Has an Ask Dr. Dig feature where popular questions on ancient world are answered. The site offers an archeology IQ quiz, guides for teachers and parents, and features other resources.
Resource Type: General Reference; Lesson or Activity

****Mr. Dowling's Electronic Passport: Prehistory
www.mrdowling.com/602prehistory.html

"Mr. Dowling's Electronic Passport" helps kids browse the world in his virtual classroom. He introduces many civilizations with clear explanations, engaging graphics for kids, and "cool links." His study guides, homework assignments, and exams are free and available for you to print or to edit.
Resource Type: General Reference; Course Model

****Bill Moyers: Genesis
www.pbs.org/wnet/genesis/

Based on the popular PBS series, the site contains a resource guide, program descriptions, biographies of participants, links to discussion groups and audio excerpts from the program's interviews.
Resource Type: General Reference

***Common Themes, East & West: Creation Myths & Sacred Narratives of Creation
www.mythinglinks.org/ct~creation.html

Created by by Kathleen Jenks, Ph.D., this broad gateway contains links to scholarly articles, Web sites, and more. (Some links to external sites are broken.) For Hindu, Japanese, Mesopotamian, Greek, Roman, and Norse traditions, see Creation Myths—Page Two. For North America and Meso-America, see Creation Myths—Page Three.
Resource Type: General Reference; Links Collection

***World Scripture: A Comparative Anthology of Sacred Texts
www.euro-tongil.org/ws/

Go to Chapter 1 and click on Traces of God's Existence. You'll find a brief introduction and then a slew of short quotes from varied religious texts on the existence and nature of God. The rest of the sections from the chapter are organized the same way. Very convenient way of comparing/contrasting religious texts on varied topics.
Resource Type: General Reference: Primary Source Collection

***Agricultural Revolution
www.wsu.edu/gened/learn-modules/top_agrev/agrev-index.html

This learning module provides seven informative and well-illustrated lessons on early agriculture, including The Earth as a Solar-driven System, Emergence of Agriculture, and Social Consequences.
Resource Type: General Reference; Lesson or Activity

***Web Geological Time Machine
www.ucmp.berkeley.edu/help/timeform.html

This site introduces the visitor to prehistoric geology and prehistoric sites around the world. It is essentially a hyperlinked timeline.
Resource Type: General Reference; Timeline

Prehistory Lesson Plans, Teacher Guides, Activities, and More

Evolution: Teacher's Guide
www.pbs.org/wgbh/evolution/

This rich and impressive PBS Web site features videos, simulations, animations, interactive timelines, expert commentary, primary sources, and extensive links to evolution-related learning resources worldwide. There is a also a free 40-page teacher's guide available and an eight-session course for high school teachers.
Resource Type: Course Model
Grade Level: MS, HS

Course Models: Early Humankind and the Development of Human Societies
www.history.ctaponline.org/center/hsscm/index.cfm?Page_Key=1426

This course model is produced in collaboration with the California Department of Education and is aimed at 6th-graders. Its lessons and resources aim to have students describe what is known through archaeological studies of the early physical and cultural development of humankind from the Paleolithic era to the agricultural revolution.
Resource Type: Course Model
Grade Level: MS

BBC History: Archaeology
www.bbc.co.uk/history/archaeology/index.shtml

In the "BBC Inside Archaeology" section, there are several engaging multimedia simulations: Hunt the Ancestor, Iron Age Life, Diver's Quest, Wetwang Chariot, and Reconstructing an Iron-Age Roundhouse.
Resource Type: Lesson or Activity; Multimedia Presentation
Grade Level: LS, MS

BBC History: Ages of Treasure Timelines
www.bbc.co.uk/history/archaeology/excavations_techniques/launch_tl_ages_treasure.shtml

From the Palaeolithic to the Norman Conquest, explore archaeological sites and treasures from the past, and then test yourself on the eras and events in the Ages of Treasure game.

Resource Type: Timeline; Multimedia Presentation
Grade Level: MS, HS

BBC History: Iron Age Tasks
www.bbc.co.uk/history/ancient/british_prehistory/ironage_tasks_gallery.shtml

This BBC section explores Iron Age Britons and their daily tasks. The images demonstrate that they at least were skilled artists and craft workers.
Resource Type: Virtual Tour
Grade Level: LS, MS

Science Safari Teaching Guide: The First People
www.pbs.org/safarchive/4_class/45_pguides/pguide_702/4572_firstpeople.html

Use bone measurements to make inferences about people who lived long ago, and learn more about cave paintings. PBS Scientific American.
Resource Type: Lesson or Activity
Grade Level: MS

Stonehenge: Solving Ancient Mysteries
www.thirteen.org/edonline/lessons/stonehenge/index.html

How do we learn about the past? What clues help us piece together a picture of life long ago? In this high school lesson, students become detectives as they investigate a mystery at Stonehenge, featured on the Thirteen/WNET New York program, "Secrets of the Dead: Murder at Stonehenge." They learn about archaeologists and anthropologists and the tools and methods they use to gather and interpret scientific evidence. They research current archaeological excavations and contact the scientists working at these digs. As a culminating activity, students advise a colleague on how to proceed with the excavation of a mysterious skeleton.
Resource Type: Lesson or Activity
Grade Level: HS

The Dawn of Humanity: Searching for Clues to Human Origins by Exploring African Geography and History
www.nytimes.com/learning/teachers/lessons/20020807wednesday.html

In this *New York Times* lesson, students learn about recent archaeological challenges to theories of human origins. They then research the history and geography of various African regions to create proposals for future excavations.
Resource Type: Lesson or Activity
Grade Level: MS, HS

Mr. Donn's Ancient History Page: Early Man
http://ancienthistory.mrdonn.org/EarlyMan.html

Don Donn of the Corkran (Maryland) Middle School provides a complete unit with daily lesson plans and unit test for 6th-graders. There are also links to multiple K–12 lesson plans and activities.
Resource Type: Course Model
Grade Level: MS

The World's History: The Dry Bones Speak

http://cwx.prenhall.com/bookbind/pubbooks/spodek2/chapter1/deluxe.html

The online guide to Howard Spodek's *The World's History* features quizzes (multiple-choice questions, true/false questions, interactive review questions), primary sources, maps, a bulletin board, a live chat, Web links, and faculty resources for each chapter/topic.
Resource Type: Course Model
Grade Level: HS, College

The World's History: From Village Community to City-State

http://cwx.prenhall.com/bookbind/pubbooks/spodek2/chapter2/deluxe.html

The online guide to Howard Spodek's *The World's History* features quizzes (multiple-choice questions, true/false questions, interactive review questions), primary sources, maps, a bulletin board, a live chat, Web links, and faculty resources for each chapter/topic.
Resource Type: Course Model
Grade Level: HS, College

Western Civilization: Stone and Wood

http://wps.prenhall.com/hss_king_westernciv_2/0,6774,207261-,00.html

The online study companion to Margaret King's *Western Civilization: A Social and Cultural History* has many features: Chapter learning objectives, online quizzes, writing activities, essay questions, Web links, built-in search engines, and faculty modules that include Power-Point outlines, presentation graphics, and lecture hints and activities.
Resource Type: Course Model
Grade Level: HS, College

University of California Museum of Paleontology Student Resources

www.ucmp.berkeley.edu/education/students.php

The UMCP offers several helpful K–12 teaching unit. Here are a few recommendations: Understanding Evolution (for grades K–12) helps students understand what evolution is, and how it works. Paleontology Portal provides a tool that allows you to map the ages of rocks in your own state and view related fossils. Getting Into the Fossil Record (for grades 5–10) helps students gain a basic understanding of fossils while Understanding Geologic Time (for grades 5–10) explores geologic time, Earth's history, dating techniques, and the geologic time scale.
Resource Type: Course Model
Grade Level: LS, MS, HS

Atlantis Quest

http://drb.lifestreamcenter.net/Lessons/Atlantis/index.htm

This WebQuest was created by Carolyn O. Burleson, Los Angeles Unified School District, for grades 9–12 English or Social Studies. Students will have to determine what is fact and what is fiction and create a multimedia presentation to present their findings.
Resource Type: Lesson or Activity
Grade Level: MS, HS

Mystery of the First Americans: The Dating Game
www.pbs.org/wgbh/nova/first/radiocarbon.html

Play this PBS Nova Shockwave game to see how scientists use radiocarbon dating to learn about ancient people.
Resource Type: Game
Grade Level: MS, HS

Could You Survive Today As a Hunter Gatherer?
http://museums.ncl.ac.uk/flint/foodquiz.html

Among the plants pictured at the site you have to pick which ones you can eat.
Resource Type: Game
Grade Level: LS, MS

Mammal Adaptation Game
www.museum.state.il.us/exhibits/larson/pdfs/Animal_Adaptation_Migration_Extinction.pdf

Play the "Mammal Adaptation Game" to learn how mammals are adapted to their environments and what happens when their environment changes. PDF document.
Resource Type: Game
Grade Level: LS

ANCIENT HISTORY: GENERAL RESOURCES

****BBC: Civilisations
www.bbc.co.uk/religion/interactive/civilisations/

This Flash-generated BBC site allows users to examine key events in the development of any given ideology or religion and its diffusion across the world. It uses Web technology to reveal the sweep of historical forces and the rise and fall of great empires and ideas over 5,000 years and is customizable. You will need the Flash player to use "Civilisations."
Resource Type: General Reference; Multimedia Presentation

*****Internet Ancient History Sourcebook
www.fordham.edu/halsall/ancient/asbook.html

"Internet History Sourcebooks" are wonderful collections of public domain and copy-permitted historical texts for educational use by Paul Halsall. The site and its documents are well organized, and the breadth of materials is impressive. Some external links are broken as the site does not appear to be actively maintained.
Resource Type: Primary Source Collection

****Internet Global History Sourcebook
www.fordham.edu/halsall/global/globalsbook.html

"Internet History Sourcebooks" are wonderful collections of public domain and copy-permitted historical texts for educational use by Paul Halsall. The site and its documents are well organized, and the breadth of materials is impressive. "Global History Sourcebook" is

dedicated to exploration of interaction between world cultures and the ways new cultural forms emerge. Some external links are broken as the site does not appear to be actively maintained.
Resource Type: Primary Source Collection

*****Exploring Ancient World Cultures
http://eawc.evansville.edu/index.htm

An online course supplement for students and teachers of the ancient and medieval worlds. Chapters are built around eight "cultures": Near East, India, Egypt, China, Greece, Rome, Early Islam, and Medieval European. Contains a chronology, essays, images, and links to related sites. Glossary is linked to the Argos project. Some links are broken.
Resource Type: General Reference; Lesson or Activity

*****Tradition and Memory: World Cultures to 1500
www.wsu.edu/~dee/110/110.HTM

A terrific overview of Ancient and Medieval History can be found at this online course, based at Washington State University. It offers clear and informative lecture notes, maps, a photo gallery, timelines, links to relevant sites, and more.
Resource Type: General Reference; Course Model

****ABZU: Ancient Near East Internet Resources
www.etana.org/abzu/

This is a guide to Internet materials on the study and public presentation of the Ancient Near East. Provides access to online exhibits, links, and access to electronic journals.
Resource Type: General Reference; Links Collection

****The Archeological Adventure
http://library.thinkquest.org/3011/

This student-created site shows how researchers find ancient ruins. Included are guided tours, a glossary of terms, interactive forums, and articles (with an audio component). Feature topics include Troy and Egypt.
Resource Type: Multimedia Presentation; Lesson or Activity

****Antiquity Online
http://fsmitha.com/h1/

A 30-chapter world history book that compares ancient religions, empires, cultures, and the like. Contains links, photos, and good maps.
Resource Type: General Reference; Course Model

****Collection: Collapse of Ancient Civilizations
www.learner.org/exhibits/collapse/

Part of the Annenberg/CPB exhibits, this site focuses on the fall of ancient civilizations in four areas: Maya, Mesopotamia, Chaco Canyon (U.S. southwest), and Mali and Songhai. Nice images and interesting presentation.
Resource Type: General Reference; Image Collection

****Mr. Donn's Ancient History Page

http://members.aol.com/donnandlee/index.html

Teacher Don Donn of the Corkran (Maryland) Middle School provides complete units on various historical topics with daily lesson plans and resources. This site is a rich resource on teaching ancient history from a 6th-grade teacher. Includes lessons, maps, links, tests, and games.
Resource Type: Course Model

****Diotima: Women & Gender in the Ancient World

www.stoa.org/diotima/

"Diotima" highlights gender in the ancient Mediterranean and helps instructors teach courses about women and gender in the ancient world. It offers course materials, essays, a bibliography, images, and good links to related sites. Also has a search feature and a section on biblical studies.
Resource Type: General Reference; Course Model

****Secrets of Lost Empires

www.pbs.org/wgbh/nova/lostempires/

This PBS site revolves around the question of how humans built inspiring structures, such as at Stonehenge, ancient Rome, and Inca Mexico. Some excellent pictures and articles, as well as interesting Q&A discussions with experts.
Resource Type: General Reference

****Historical Collections—Antiqua Medicina: From Homer to Vesalius

www.healthsystem.virginia.edu/internet/library/historical/artifacts/antiqua/

This interesting exhibit on ancient medicine was prepared in conjunction with the Colloquium Antiqua Medicina: Aspects in Ancient Medicine at the University of Virginia's McLeod Hall.
Resource Type: General Reference

****Turning the Pages

www.bl.uk/onlinegallery/ttp/ttpbooks.html

"Turning the Pages" is an award-winning interactive display system developed by The British Library to increase public access and enjoyment of some of its most valuable treasures. Visitors are able to virtually "turn" the pages of manuscripts in an incredibly realistic way, using touch-screen technology and animation. There are currently fifteen treasures on display in Turning the Pages including the Leonardo Notebook, the Golden Haggadah, and Sultan Baybars' Qur'an.
Resource Type: Multimedia Presentation; Primary Source Collection

****Cleopatra: A Multimedia Guide to the Ancient World

www.artic.edu/cleo/index.html

"Cleopatra" is an interactive guide to the Ancient Art collection of the Art Institute of Chicago. "Stories" accompany the objects and there are lesson plans for grades 4–12.
Resource Type: Multimedia Presentation; Lesson or Activity

****Mr. Dowling's Electronic Passport
www.mrdowling.com/index.html

"Mr. Dowling's Electronic Passport" helps kids browse the world in his virtual classroom. He introduces you to many civilizations with clear explanations, engaging graphics for kids, and "cool links." His study guides, homework assignments, and exams are free and available for you to print or to edit.
Resource Type: General Reference; Course Model

****World Mysteries
www.world-mysteries.com/

Explore lost civilizations, ancient ruins, sacred writings, unexplained artifacts, and science mysteries. Introduced are "alternative theories," subject experts, books, and resources on the Internet. World-Mysteries.com is a non-profit Web site.
Resource Type: General Reference

****History of Money from Ancient Times to the Present Day
www.ex.ac.uk/~RDavies/arian/llyfr.html

This award-winning site is based on a book with the same title and contains a chronology and a collection of essays on various themes regarding monetary history. Of special interest is the detailed chronology of money in its social and political context from the very earliest times onwards. The sources at this site are also useful in trying to determine how much a specified amount of money at a certain period of time would be worth today. There are also helpful essays, such as Origins of Money and Banking, Money in North American History, The Vikings and Money in England, Democracy and Government Control of the Money Supply, Third World Money and Debt in the Twentieth Century, Warfare and Financial History, and Britain and Monetary Union. Finally, there are links to related resources and even links to "financial thrillers."
Resource Type: General Reference

Ancient History: General Resources Lesson Plans, Teacher Guides, Activities, and More

World Civilizations: The Global Experience—Lesson Plans
www.phschool.com/advanced/lesson_plans/hist_stearns_2001/

Focus Lessons for "World Civilizations" highlight important ideas and concepts in each chapter, as well as the relevant sections in the program's ancillaries. The lessons, written by an experienced AP teacher, suggest strategies for assessing how well your students understand the important points in each chapter, and also provide test-taking tips that will help your students prepare for and take the AP World History test successfully.
Resource Type: Lesson or Activity
Grade Level: HS

Seven Wonders of the Ancient World
http://7wonders.mrdonn.org/list.html

Don Donn of the Corkran (Maryland) Middle School provides a complete unit with daily

lesson plans and unit test for 6th-graders. There are also links to multiple K–12 lesson plans and activities.
Resource Type: Course Model
Grade Level: MS

***The History Guide
www.historyguide.org/ancient/ancient.html

These lectures serve as the basis of a western civilization and an upper level European history course. The lectures on Ancient and Medieval European history are concise, informative, and feature useful links.
Resource Type: Course Model

BBC History Games: Dig Deeper Quiz
www.bbc.co.uk/history/archaeology/excavations_techniques/launch_gms_dig_deeper.shtml

Test your knowledge of ancient history and archaeology and complete a section of jigsaws.
Resource Type: Test or Quiz
Grade Level: MS

BBC History: Ages of Treasure Timelines
www.bbc.co.uk/history/archaeology/excavations_techniques/launch_tl_ages_treasure.shtml

From the Palaeolithic to the Norman Conquest, explore British archaeological sites and treasures from the past, then test yourself on the eras and events in the Ages of Treasure game.
Resource Type: Timeline; Test or Quiz
Grade Level: MS

Treasures of the Sunken City
www.pbs.org/wgbh/nova/teachers/activities/2417_sunken.html

This online PBS game involves students in identifying the Seven Wonders of the Ancient World.
Resource Type: Game
Grade Level: LS

Primary Source Materials and Document Based Questions
www.kn.pacbell.com/wired/fil/pages/listdocumentpa.html

An Internet hotlist on Document-Based Questions. Many useful links here.
Resource Type: Lesson or Activity; Primary Source Collection
Grade Level: HS

Prentice Hall Web Site Study Guides
www.prenhall.com/craig/

These Web sites are specifically designed to accompany Prentice Hall's *The Heritage of World Civilizations* series.
Resource Type: Course Model
Grade Level: HS

MESOPOTAMIA

****The British Museum: Mesopotamia
www.mesopotamia.co.uk/

The British Museum's various online offerings are impressive and its Ancient Civilizations Web site highlights achievements of some remarkable world civilizations and explores cross-cultural themes of human development. The British Museum offers a very slick and informative visual presentation of Mesopotamian art and culture.

Resource Type: General Reference; Multimedia Presentation

Figure 7.3: The British Museum: Mesopotamia

****Internet Ancient History Sourcebook: Mesopotamia
www.fordham.edu/halsall/ancient/asbook03.html

"Internet History Sourcebooks" are wonderful collections of public domain and copy-permitted historical texts for educational use by Paul Halsall. This Sourcebook is full of useful primary source documents on Mesopotamia. Some external links are broken as the site does not appear to be actively maintained.

Resource Type: Primary Source Collection

****ABZU: Mesopotamia
www.etana.org/abzu/

"ABZU" is a guide to Internet materials on the study and public presentation of the Ancient Near East. Provides access to online exhibits, links, and access to electronic journals. "ABZU" supplies a helpful index of resources for the study of ancient Mesopotamia.
Resource Type: General Reference

****History Links 101: Ancient Mesopotamia
www.historylink101.com/ancient_mesopotamia.htm

At "History Links 101" you'll find many links to Mesopotamian art, daily life, maps, research, art, and biographies.
Resource Type: General Reference; Links Collection

****Collection: Collapse of Ancient Civilizations
www.learner.org/exhibits/collapse/

Part of the Annenberg/CPB exhibits, this site focuses on the fall of ancient civilizations in four areas: Maya, Mesopotamia, Chaco Canyon (U.S. Southwest), and Mali and Songhai. Nice images and interesting presentation.
Resource Type: General Reference; Image Collection

****Mr. Dowling's Electronic Passport: Mesopotamia
www.mrdowling.com/603mesopotamia.html

"Mr. Dowling's Electronic Passport" helps kids browse the world in his virtual classroom. He introduces you to many civilizations with clear explanations, engaging graphics for kids, and "cool links." His study guides, homework assignments and exams are free and available for you to print or to edit.
Resource Type: General Reference; Course Model

Mesopotamia Lesson Plans, Teacher Guides, Activities, and More

Course Models: The Beginnings of Civilization in Mesopotamia, Egypt, and Kush
www.history.ctaponline.org/center/hsscm/index.cfm?Page_Key=1432

This course model is produced in collaboration with the California Department of Education and is aimed at 6th-graders. Students analyze the geographic, political, economic, religious, and social structures of the early civilizations of Mesopotamia, Egypt, and Kush.
Resource Type: Course Model
Grade Level: MS

Mesopotamia Web Site Staff Room
www.mesopotamia.co.uk/staff/main.html

The British Museum site on Mesopotamia offers a "Challenge"—an activity that allows pupils to practice certain skills (historical, analytical, mathematical, observational) within the context of a theme or topic relevant to Mesopotamia.
Resource Type: Lesson or Activity
Grade Level: LS, MS

Mr. Donn's Ancient History Page: Mesopotamia
http://ancienthistory.mrdonn.org/Mesopotamia.html#Top

Don Donn of the Corkran (Maryland) Middle School provides a complete unit with daily lesson plans and unit test for sixth graders. There are also links to multiple K–12 lesson plans and activities.
Resource Type: Lesson or Activity
Grade Level: MS

You Be the Judge: Hammurabi's Code
www.phillipmartin.info/hammurabi/homepage.htm

Using Hammurabi's Code, you decide the proper punishment for shoddy workmen, straying wives, and abusive landlords.
Resource Type: Lesson or Activity
Grade Level: MS

Accessing Women's Lives in Mesopotamia
www.womeninworldhistory.com/lesson2.html

Provides useful information on a neglected topic. From the Women in World History Curriculum.
Resource Type: Lesson or Activity
Grade Level: MS, HS

Create Your Own Sumerian City-State: A Problem-Based Activity
www.teachtheteachers.org/projects/CHamman/index.htm

A 6th-grade WebQuest activity: "This is your Mesopotamia City Designing Supervisor. I have invited you all here to do one thing and that is to Design A Sumerian City-State."
Resource Type: Lesson or Activity
Grade Level: MS

Classroom and Museum Lessons Plans: Mesopotamia
www-oi.uchicago.edu/OI/MUS/ED/TRC/MESO/lessonsmeso.html

From the Oriental Institute of the University of Chicago. The First Cities Lesson Plans: Ancient Jobs in Mesopotamia.
Resource Type: Lesson or Activity
Grade Level: MS

Ancient History Simulations: Akbar's Dilemma
http://socialstudies.com/c/@jULJ7g_Qi8o32/Pages/article.html?article@TCM251A+af@donn

Students will identify the role religion played in the everyday lives of ordinary Mesopotamians. They will recognize that Mesopotamian religion stressed ritual for the here and now as opposed to any concern for the afterlife.
Resource Type: Lesson or Activity
Grade Level: MS

BBC History: Mesopotamia Gallery

www.bbc.net.uk/history/ancient/cultures/mesopotamia_gallery.shtml

By 3000 B.C., the Mesopotamians had already invented the wheel, developed writing, and created the world's first cities and monumental architecture. Find out more about the many aspects of Mesopotamia's rich legacy through these BBC images.

Resource Type: Lesson or Activity; Virtual Tour

Grade Level: MS, HS

The World's History: River Valley Civilizations

http://cwx.prenhall.com/bookbind/pubbooks/spodek2/chapter3/deluxe.html

The online guide to Howard Spodek's *The World's History* features quizzes (multiple-choice questions, true/false questions, interactive review questions), primary sources, maps, a bulletin board, a live chat, Web links, and faculty resources for each chapter/topic. This chapter focuses on the civilizations that developed in the Nile valley of Egypt and the Indus River valley of India/Pakistan.

Resource Type: Course Model

Grade Level: HS, College

The World's History: Dawn of the Empires

http://cwx.prenhall.com/bookbind/pubbooks/spodek2/chapter5/deluxe.html

The online guide to Howard Spodek's *The World's History* features quizzes (multiple-choice questions, true/false questions, interactive review questions), primary sources, maps, a bulletin board, a live chat, Web links, and faculty resources for each chapter/topic. The empires in this chapter come from three different regions: Mesopotamia, Egypt and Greece.

Resource Type: Course Model

Grade Level: HS, College

Brief Review in Global History and Geography: Document-Based Essays and Practice Tests

www.phschool.com/curriculum_support/brief_review/global_history/

PH@School's "Brief Review in Global History and Geography" Web site provides multiple-choice questions from actual Regents exams. You can also practice your test-taking skills on document-based essay questions (DBQs), with the option of e-mailing answers directly to your teacher for review.

Resource Type: Lesson or Activity; Test or Quiz

Grade Level: HS

Map of Political Change in Mesopotamia

http://darkwing.uoregon.edu/~atlas/europe/interactive/map34.html

Requires Shockwave plug-in.

Resource Type: Map

Grade Level: MS, HS

EGYPT

****Mark Millmore's Ancient Egypt
www.eyelid.co.uk/

Mark Millmore's site is user-friendly, comprehensive, updated daily, and features a great section on temples and pyramids. In it you can explore the ancient monuments using interactive maps, photos, drawings, and paintings. The Rebuilding Temples shows how these shrines have appeared to ancient eyes. There is a basic description of hieroglyphic writing and you can send a friend their name as an eCard using the hieroglyphic translator.
Resource Type: General Reference; Image Collection

****Egypt WWW Index
http://ce.eng.usf.edu/pharos/index.html

"Egypt WWW" features a broad set of links covering History, Egyptology, Art, Culture and Tradition, and many other Egypt-related topics.
Resource Type: General Reference; Links Collection

****The British Museum: Ancient Egypt
www.ancientegypt.co.uk/menu.html

The British Museum's various online offerings are impressive and its Ancient Civilizations Web site highlights achievements of some remarkable world civilizations and explores cross-cultural themes of human development. The Ancient Egypt section offers great images, simulations, and games to make the study of Ancient Egypt enticing for students.
Resource Type: General Reference; Multimedia Presentation

****Egypt's Golden Empire
www.pbs.org/empires/egypt/index.html

The resources offered here are designed to help you use the PBS "Egypt's Golden Empire" video series and companion Web site in secondary social studies, civics, religion, and language arts classes. There are three lesson plans, a timeline, an interactive map, a heiroglyph translator, and more.
Resource Type: General Reference; Lesson or Activity

****World Cultures to 1500: Egypt
www.wsu.edu/~dee/MESO/MESO.HTM

A terrific overview of Ancient and Medieval History can be found at this online course, based at Washington State University. It offers clear and informative lecture notes, maps, a photo gallery, timelines, links to relevant sites, and more. Click Contents.
Resource Type: General Reference; Course Model

****ABZU: Egypt
www.etana.org/abzu/

"ABZU" is a guide to Internet materials on the study and public presentation of the Ancient

Near East. Provides access to online exhibits, links, and access to electronic journals. "ABZU" provides a helpful index of resources for the study of ancient Egypt.
Resource Type: General Reference; Links Collection

****Theban Mapping Project
www.thebanmappingproject.com/

An impressive site that focuses on the Theban Necropolis, the Valley of the Kings, the tomb of Rameses II, and Egyptology. It offers maps, a timeline, a Q&A section, and updates on the KV5 (Rameses tomb) archeological expedition.
Resource Type: General Reference; Map

****Egypt: Secrets of an Ancient World
www.nationalgeographic.com/pyramids/

This fine National Geographic Society presentation reveals the interior organization and a number of facts about the construction of the pyramids. There is also a timeline, news stories, a quiz game on daily life in Ancient Egypt, and lesson plans on Mummies.
Resource Type: General Reference; Lesson or Activity

****The Quest for Immortality: Treasures of Ancient Egypt
www.nga.gov/exhibitions/2002/egypt/index.htm

This National Gallery of Art exhibition covers the period of the New Kingdom (1550–1069 B.C.) through the Late Period (664–332 B.C.). It is divided into six sections: Journey to the Afterworld, The New Kingdom, The Royal Tomb, Tombs of Nobles, The Realm of the Gods, and The Tomb of Thutmose III.
Resource Type: Virtual Tour; Art History

****Guardian's CyberJourney: Egypt
www.guardians.net/egypt/egol1.htm

"Guardian's CyberJourney" provides useful images, virtual tours, discussions, and commentary on Ancient Egypt. Also features an interview with Dr. Zahi Hawass, Secretary of the State for the Giza Monuments.
Resource Type: General Reference; Virtual Tour

****Pyramids—The Inside Story
www.pbs.org/wgbh/nova/pyramid/

This attractive PBS site provides a nice blend of images and history of the pyramids and offers insights into excavations and mysteries.
Resource Type: General Reference; Image Collection

****At the Tomb of Tutankhamen
www.nationalgeographic.com/egypt/

This Flash-generated *National Geographic* exhibit focuses on King Tut's tomb and Egyptian "mysteries." It also offers links and resources.
Resource Type: Multimedia Presentation

****Mr. Dowling's Electronic Passport: Ancient Egypt
www.mrdowling.com/604egypt.html

"Mr. Dowling's Electronic Passport" helps kids browse the world in his virtual classroom. He introduces you to many civilizations with clear explanations, engaging graphics for kids, and "cool links." His study guides, homework assignments and exams are free and available for you to print or to edit.
Resource Type: General Reference; Course Model

****Egyptology Resources
www.newton.cam.ac.uk/egypt/

This site is set up with the assistance of the Newton Institute at the University of Cambridge to provide a Web resource for Egyptological information.
Resource Type: General Reference

****Treasures of the Sunken City
www.pbs.org/wgbh/nova/sunken/

This PBS "Nova" site examines the remains of sunken Alexandria. Features a map of underseas Alexandria, film clips, a teacher's guide, and more.
Resource Type: Multimedia Presentation; Lesson or Activity

***Splendors of Ancient Egypt
http://www2.sptimes.com/Egypt/

"Splendors of Ancient Egypt" provides an interactive tour of Ancient Egypt. This site is based on a Florida International Museum exhibit and features a selection of artifacts from the 2,800-year rule of the pharaohs, and a gallery of photographs and words by *St. Petersburg Times* travel editor, Robert Jenkins.
Resource Type: General Reference; Virtual Tour

***Institute of Egyptian Art and Archaeology
http://academic.memphis.edu/egypt/

The University of Memphis "Institute of Egyptian Art and Archaeology" offers an interactive tour of Egypt and an exhibit of their artifacts. The Institute also provides a timeline of Ancient Egypt as well as articles and text on new projects.
Resource Type: Image Collection; Art History

***Ancient Egyptian Virtual Temple
http://showcase.netins.net/web/ankh/

Learn about Egyptian temples via the great images this site has to offer. Many images in many categories.
Resource Type: General Reference; Image Collection

***The Egypt Museum in Cairo
www.emuseum.gov.eg/

The Institute of Egyptian Art and Archaeology maintains a collection of over eleven hundred ancient Egyptian antiquities. This site provides a "color" tour of Ancient Egypt and an interactive map.

Resource Type: Image Collection; Art History

Egypt Lesson Plans, Teacher Guides, Activities, and More

Ancient Egypt Lesson Plans for Teachers

www.dia.org/education/egypt-teachers/index.html

Sponsored by the Detroit Institute of Art, the site features cross-curricular lesson plans by local teachers for enriching the study of Ancient Egypt at the elementary and middle school levels.

Resource Type: Lesson or Activity

Grade Level: LS, MS

Mr. Donn's Ancient History: Ancient Egypt

http://ancienthistory.mrdonn.org/AncientEgypt.html

Don Donn of the Corkran (Maryland) Middle School provides a complete unit with daily lesson plans and unit test for 6th-graders. There are also links to multiple K–12 lesson plans and activities.

Resource Type: Course Model

Grade Level: MS

Inside the Great Pyramid

www.pbs.org/wgbh/nova/pyramid/explore/khufuenter.html

In this PBS activity you will crawl through Khufu's narrow passageways and navigate your way through to the King's burial chamber. This tour requires a QuickTime plug-in.

Resource Type: Lesson or Activity

Grade Level: MS, HS

BBC History: Khufu's Pyramid Complex

www.bbc.co.uk/history/ancient/egyptians/complex_gallery.shtml

King Khufu (2609–2584 B.C.), the second king of the Fourth Dynasty, made elaborate provisions for his own death and his afterlife. His body was to be entombed within a pyramid, the most perfect pyramid Egypt had ever seen. Explore the Great Pyramid's complex reconstruction through these BBC images to discover more about the various structures.

Resource Type: Lesson or Activity; Virtual Tour

Grade Level: MS, HS

Scaling the Pyramids

www.pbs.org/wgbh/nova/pyramid/geometry/

Learn from PBS "Nova" about the construction of the pyramids with a click through map and build models to scale. This section is part of a larger PBS site where you can wander through the chambers and passageways of the Great Pyramid, and learn about the pharaohs for whom these monumental tombs were built.

Resource Type: Lesson or Activity; Virtual Tour

Grade Level: LS, MS

Egypt's Greatest Leaders
www.pbs.org/empires/egypt/educators/lesson4.html

In this lesson, students will learn about seven of Egypt's most famous pharaohs. They will discuss leadership styles and draw conclusions about the success of each of these pharaohs. After learning about the personality and life of each pharaoh, students will break into groups to create in-depth projects about one of the seven pharaohs they have learned about and will teach others in the class about this leader. PBS, Grades 6–12.

Resource Type: Lesson or Activity
Grade Level: MS, HS

A Day in the Life of an Egyptian
www.pbs.org/empires/egypt/educators/lesson6.html

The focus of this lesson is to teach students about the daily lives of ancient Egyptians from every social class. Life varied dramatically for people based upon where they were in the social order, and students will examine how people from all walks of life lived. Students will use creative means to present what they have learned about the lives of Egyptians from all social classes. PBS, Grades 6–12.

Resource Type: Lesson or Activity
Grade Level: MS, HS

Tombs and the Afterlife
www.pbs.org/empires/egypt/educators/lesson2.html

This lesson focuses on the concept of the afterlife and the importance of pleasing the gods and goddesses, the significance of tombs and tomb building, and the burial customs and traditions of the ancient Egyptians. After learning about all of these concepts, students will design a tomb, create a model of it, and complete a short written assignment explaining the design and contents of the tomb. PBS, Grades 6–12.

Resource Type: Lesson or Activity
Grade Level: MS, HS

The Curse of Tut: Fact or Myth?
www.tqnyc.org/NYC00112/

A fun site for kids to learn about the fascinating life of King Tut. See pictures in the Tomb or solve the Lock Key Puzzle to see Tut smile. Students can learn the facts behind the myth and decide for themselves about the truth of the curse. Teachers will appreciate the spatial reasoning required to solve the Lock Key puzzle. Bibliography includes print and Web resources.

Resource Type: Lesson or Activity
Grade Level: LS, MS

The Clickable Mummy
www.akhet.co.uk/clikmumm.htm

Click on different parts of the mummy to view interesting facts and information about the mummification process.

Resource Type: Lesson or Activity
Grade Level: MS

Oasis of the Ancestors

www.pbs.org/safarchive/4_class/45_pguides/pguide_304/4534_oasis.html

People in the ancient Middle East relied on song, poetry, story, and symbols to share ideas and information. Students will study hieroglyphics of yesterday and today.

Resource Type: Lesson or Activity

Grade Level: MS

Tomb of the Pyramid Builders

www.pbs.org/safarchive/4_class/45_pguides/pguide_304/4534_tomb.html

Graveyards of the workers who built the pyramids were found on the Gaza Plateau and will tell archaeologists more about life in ancient Egypt. The activities included give you ideas for conducting your own dig.

Resource Type: Lesson or Activity

Grade Level: MS

This Just In! Nile Network News Update

www.thirteen.org/edonline/lessons/nile/index.html

In this elementary school lesson plan, students will conduct research on the large number of engineering, scientific, architectural and artistic contributions of the ancient Egyptians. They will share their findings by producing a TV news broadcast presentation.

Resource Type: Lesson or Activity

Grade Level: LS

BBC History: God and Goddesses of Ancient Egypt Gallery

www.bbc.co.uk/history/ancient/egyptians/gods_gallery.shtml

The deities in this BBC gallery are just 12 out of a possible 2,000 gods and goddesses who were worshipped in ancient Egypt. Some of them were major deities wielding great religious, temporal and political power, others being not much more than demons and genies, or living creatures chosen by ordinary Egyptians to be their personal gods.

Resource Type: Lesson or Activity; Virtual Tour

Grade Level: MS

BBC History Games: The Mummy Maker

www.bbc.co.uk/history/ancient/egyptians/launch_gms_mummy_maker.shtml

Test your knowledge of history with an interactive challenge. Enter the embalmer's workshop and prepare a body for burial.

Resource Type: Game

Grade Level: MS

BBC History Games: Pyramid Challenge

www.bbc.co.uk/history/ancient/egyptians/launch_gms_pyramid_builder.shtml

As the vizier, or head of state, you are about to undertake the most important building project of your career—building the king's pyramids.

Resource Type: Game

Grade Level: MS

BBC History: Ancient Egypt Timeline

www.bbc.co.uk/history/ancient/egyptians/timeline.shtml

Chart the ebb and flow of power on the banks of the Nile over 3,000 years with this interactive BBC timeline.
Resource Type: Timeline
Grade Level: MS

The Paper Boat

www.pbs.org/safarchive/4_class/45_pguides/pguide_1004/44104_boat.html

Using household materials and similar but more modern methods, you can make your own paper, similar to papyrus the Egyptians used 5,000 years ago. PBS *Scientific American* activity.
Resource Type: Lesson or Activity
Grade Level: LS, MS

BBC History: Animals of Ancient Egypt Gallery

www.bbc.co.uk/history/ancient/egyptians/animal_gallery.shtml

Animals of all kinds were important to the Ancient Egyptians, and featured in the daily secular and religious lives of farmers, craftsmen, priests and rulers. Explore their images in this BBC gallery.
Resource Type: Virtual Tour
Grade Level: MS

The World's History: River Valley Civilizations

http://cwx.prenhall.com/bookbind/pubbooks/spodek2/chapter3/deluxe.html

The online guide to Howard Spodek's *The World's History* features quizzes (multiple-choice questions, true/false questions, interactive review questions), primary sources, maps, a bulletin board, a live chat, Web links, and faculty resources for each chapter/topic. This chapter focuses on the civilizations that developed in the Nile valley of Egypt and the Indus River valley of India/Pakistan.
Resource Type: Course Model
Grade Level: HS, College

The World's History: Dawn of the Empires

http://cwx.prenhall.com/bookbind/pubbooks/spodek2/chapter5/deluxe.html

The online guide to Howard Spodek's *The World's History* features quizzes (multiple-choice questions, true/false questions, interactive review questions), primary sources, maps, a bulletin board, a live chat, Web links, and faculty resources for each chapter/topic. The empires in this chapter come from three different regions: Mesopotamia, Egypt and Greece.
Resource Type: Course Model
Grade Level: HS, College

Western Civilization: Armies and Empires

http://wps.prenhall.com/hss_king_westernciv_2/0,6774,207339-,00.html

The online study companion to Margaret King's *Western Civilization: A Social and Cultural History* has many features: Chapter learning objectives, online quizzes, writing activities,

essay questions, Web links, built-in search engines, and faculty modules that include Power-Point outlines, presentation graphics, and lecture hints and activities.
Resource Type: Course Model
Grade Level: HS

Brief Review in Global History and Geography: Document Based Essays and Practice Tests
www.phschool.com/curriculum_support/brief_review/global_history/

PH@School's "Brief Review in Global History and Geography" Web site provides multiple-choice questions from actual Regents exams. Students can also practice their test-taking skills on document-based essay questions (DBQs), with the option of e-mailing answers directly to a teacher for review.
Resource Type: Lesson or Activity; Test or Quiz
Grade Level: HS

GREECE

****Ancient Greece
www.ancientgreece.com/

An informative and well-illustrated guide to Ancient Greece, covering art and architecture, politics, Olympics, geography, mythology, peoples, war, history, and other topics.
Resource Type: General Reference; Image Collection

****The Perseus Digital Library
www.perseus.tufts.edu/

A worthwhile digital library for Greek and Classical resources that offers a search function (see Figure 7.4). It has FAQs, essays, a historical overview, and an extensive library of art objects and the like.
Resource Type: General Reference; Image Collection

****The Ancient Greek World
www.museum.upenn.edu/Greek_World/quicktime-north.html

An online exhibit by the University of Pennsylvania Museum of Archaeology and Anthropology that explores the land, time, economy, daily life, and religion of Ancient Greece.
Resource Type: General Reference; Image Collection

****The Ancient City of Athens
www.stoa.org/athens/

A good photo archive of Athens' architectural remains (but slow to load). Also a useful resource for students of classical art, archeology, civilization, language, and history.
Resource Type: General Reference; Image Collection

Figure 7.4: The Perseus Digital Library

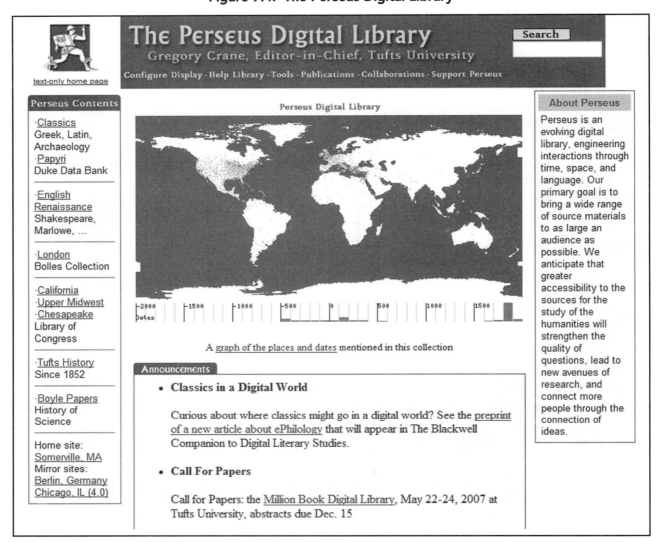

****Exploring Ancient World Cultures: Greece

http://eawc.evansville.edu/grpage.htm

Part of the "Exploring Ancient World Cultures" site, this page provides an introduction to Ancient Greece and includes essays, images, a quiz, and more. Some links are broken at this site.
Resource Type: General Reference; Lesson or Activity

****World Cultures to 1500: Bureaucrats and Barbarians: Minoans, Myceneans, and the Greek Dark Ages

www.wsu.edu/~dee/MINOA/MINOA.HTM

A terrific overview of Ancient and Medieval history can be found at this online course, based at Washington State University. It offers clear and informative lecture notes, maps, a photo gallery, timelines, links to relevant sites, and more. Click Contents.
Resource Type: Course Model

****World Cultures to 1500: Ancient Greece
www.wsu.edu/~dee/GREECE/GREECE.HTM

This site provides more excellent introductory material on Ancient Greece from Professor Richard Hooker, including clear and informative lecture notes, maps, a photo gallery, timelines, links to relevant sites, and more. Click Contents.
Resource Type: General Reference; Course Model

****Historical Collections—Antiqua Medicina: From Homer to Vesalius
www.healthsystem.virginia.edu/internet/library/historical/artifacts/antiqua/

This interesting exhibit was prepared in conjunction with the Colloquium Antiqua Medicina: Aspects in Ancient Medicine at the University of Virginia's McLeod Hall. This site offers an interesting and intelligent presentation on ancient medicine.
Resource Type: General Reference

****Mr. Dowling's Electronic Passport: Ancient Greece
www.mrdowling.com/701greece.html

"Mr. Dowling's Electronic Passport" helps kids browse the world in his virtual classroom. He introduces you to many civilizations with clear explanations, engaging graphics for kids, and "cool links." His study guides, homework assignments, and exams are free and available for you to print or to edit.
Resource Type: General Reference; Course Model

****Acropolis360
www.acropolis360.com/

"Acropolis360" is a full-sceen 360-degree virtual tour of the Athens Acropolis containing maps, 3-D reconstructions, 360-degree Quicktime panoramas, text information, sounds, music, and voice commentary.
Resource Type: Virtual Tour

****Oedipus the King: Introduction to Greek Drama
www.pbs.org/empires/thegreeks/educational/lesson4.html

There are some excellent resources as part of this PBS activity. The core information about Greek drama and playwrights can be found on this Web site under the following headings: How Salamis was remembered—Aeschylus' The Persians (Event Page: 472 B.C.—The earliest surviving tragedy); The Origins of Theatre—The First Actor (Event Page: 534 B.C.—Thespis becomes world's first actor); The Origins of Theatre—The First Plays (continued); The Different Types of Greek Drama and their importance; and The Great Playwrights of Athens' "Golden Age."
Resource Type: General Reference; Lesson or Activity

****Greek Medicine
www.nlm.nih.gov/hmd/greek/index.html

This site by the History of Medicine Division of the National Library of Medicine explores ancient Greek medicine, provides a timeline and vocabulary, and discusses Hippocrates, Aristotle, and other Greek physicians.
Resource Type: General Reference

****The Olympic Games in the Ancient Hellenic World
http://minbar.cs.dartmouth.edu/greecom/olympics/

This site has a complicated registration procedure, but tells much of the history, the mythology, and how and where the games were performed in Ancient Greece.
Resource Type: General Reference

****The Real Story of the Olympics
www.museum.upenn.edu/new/olympics/olympicintro.shtml

This site is from the University of Pennsylvania Museum of Archaeology and Anthropology and asks: Were the ancient Olympic games better than ours? More fair and square? More about sports and less about money? Are modern games more sexist? More political?
Resource Type: General Reference

****Alexander the Great
www.hackneys.com/alex_web/index.htm

This site provides information about Alexander the Great, his life, his family, his conquests, and his battles, including links to various Alexander the Great sites and resources on the Web.
Resource Type: General Reference

****Herodotus Project
www.losttrails.com/pages/Hproject.html

"Herodotus Project" is a free serialized translation of Inquiries by the Greek historian Herodotus along with extensive black-and-white photography of the locations and artifacts mentioned in the book. This site is updated monthly with photographic tours that are hyperlinked with the text.
Resource Type: Primary Source Collection; Virtual Tour

Greece Lesson Plans, Teacher Guides, Activities, and More

Mr. Donn's Ancient History Page: Early and Classical Greece Units
http://ancienthistory.mrdonn.org/AncientGreece.html

Don Donn of the Corkran (Maryland) Middle School provides a complete unit with 17 daily lesson plans and unit test for 6th-graders. There are also links to multiple K–12 lesson plans and activities.
Resource Type: Course Model
Grade Level: LS, MS, HS

Ancient Greek Olympics
http://members.aol.com/MrDonnUnits/GreekOlympics.html

This four-day unit by Don Donn includes lesson plans for teachers and activities for students.
Resource Type: Lesson or Activity
Grade Level: MS

"The Daily Athenian": A Greek Newspaper Project
www.pbs.org/empires/thegreeks/educational/lesson2.html

Working in small groups, students will produce sections of a historical newspaper or journal for publication in democratic Athens. Using the resources of a PBS Web site (as well as books and other resources listed in the Research Links & Resources Page), students pick an approximate date and research stories for the newspaper. This section has been tailored for a newspaper about Athens during the time of Pericles, because of the greater amount of information available for that period. However, with some adaptation and additional research, it would be possible to compile newspapers for early or later periods. Grades 5–12.
Resource Type: Lesson or Activity
Grade Level: MS, HS

Oedipus the King: Ancient Greek Drama
www.pbs.org/empires/thegreeks/educational/lesson4.html

Read Sophocles' famous work and explore what it reveals about ancient Greek culture. Grades 5–12. The goal of this activity is to gain an insight into Greek tragedy and such concepts such as fate, hubris, and (dramatic) irony.
Resource Type: Lesson or Activity
Grade Level: MS, HS

Interview a Famous Greek
www.pbs.org/empires/thegreeks/educational/lesson3.html

Students will research and then role play famous ancient Greek citizens in a talk-show format and assemble an Ancient Grecian Hall of Fame. Grades 5–12.
Resource Type: Lesson or Activity
Grade Level: MS, HS

Two Faces of Greece: Athens and Sparta
www.pbs.org/empires/thegreeks/educational/lesson1.html

Compare Athenian and Spartan culture from a variety of perspectives and through creative presentation ideas. Grades 5–12.
Resource Type: Lesson or Activity
Grade Level: MS, HS

The World's History: Dawn of the Empires
http://cwx.prenhall.com/bookbind/pubbooks/spodek2/chapter5/deluxe.html

The online guide to Howard Spodek's *The World's History* features quizzes (multiple-choice questions, true/false questions, interactive review questions), primary sources, maps, a bulletin board, a live chat, Web links, and faculty resources for each chapter/topic. The empires in this chapter come from three different regions: Mesopotamia, Egypt, and Greece.
Resource Type: Course Model
Grade Level: HS, College

An Ancient Odyssey: Exploring Ancient Greek Mythology and History through Geography
www.nytimes.com/learning/teachers/lessons/20021023wednesday.html

In this *New York Times* lesson, students identify both the traditional myths and historical facts that are associated with geographical locations in ancient Greece. They then create a "Travel to Ancient Greece" display to present their findings.
Resource Type: Lesson or Activity
Grade Level: MS, HS

Western Civilization: The Greek Polis
http://wps.prenhall.com/hss_king_westernciv_2/0,6774,207415-,00.html

The online study companion to Margaret King's *Western Civilization: A Social and Cultural History* has many features: Chapter learning objectives, online quizzes, writing activities, essay questions, Web links, built-in search engines, and faculty modules that include Power-Point outlines, presentation graphics, and lecture hints and activities.
Resource Type: Course Model
Grade Level: HS

Western Civilization: The School of Hellas
http://wps.prenhall.com/hss_king_westernciv_2/0,6774,207485-,00.html

The online study companion to Margaret King's *Western Civilization: A Social and Cultural History* has many features: Chapter learning objectives, online quizzes, writing activities, essay questions, Web links, built-in search engines, and faculty modules that include Power-Point outlines, presentation graphics, and lecture hints and activities.
Resource Type: Course Model
Grade Level: HS

Brief Review in Global History and Geography: Document-Based Essays and Practice Tests
www.phschool.com/curriculum_support/brief_review/global_history/

PH@School's "Brief Review in Global History and Geography" Web site provides multiple-choice questions from actual Regents exams. You can also practice your test-taking skills on document-based essay questions (DBQs), with the option of e-mailing answers directly to your teacher for review.
Resource Type: Lesson or Activity; Test or Quiz
Grade Level: HS

ROME

****Illustrated History of the Roman Empire
www.roman-empire.net/

This Web site offers a comprehensive history of the Roman Empire and contains interactive maps of Roman Italy, the Roman Empire, and the City of Rome. Categories include: The Founding, The Kings, The Republic, Early Emperors, The Decline, The Collapse, Constantinople, Religion, Society, and The Army.
Resource Type: General Reference; Map

Figure 7.5: Illustrated History of the Roman Empire

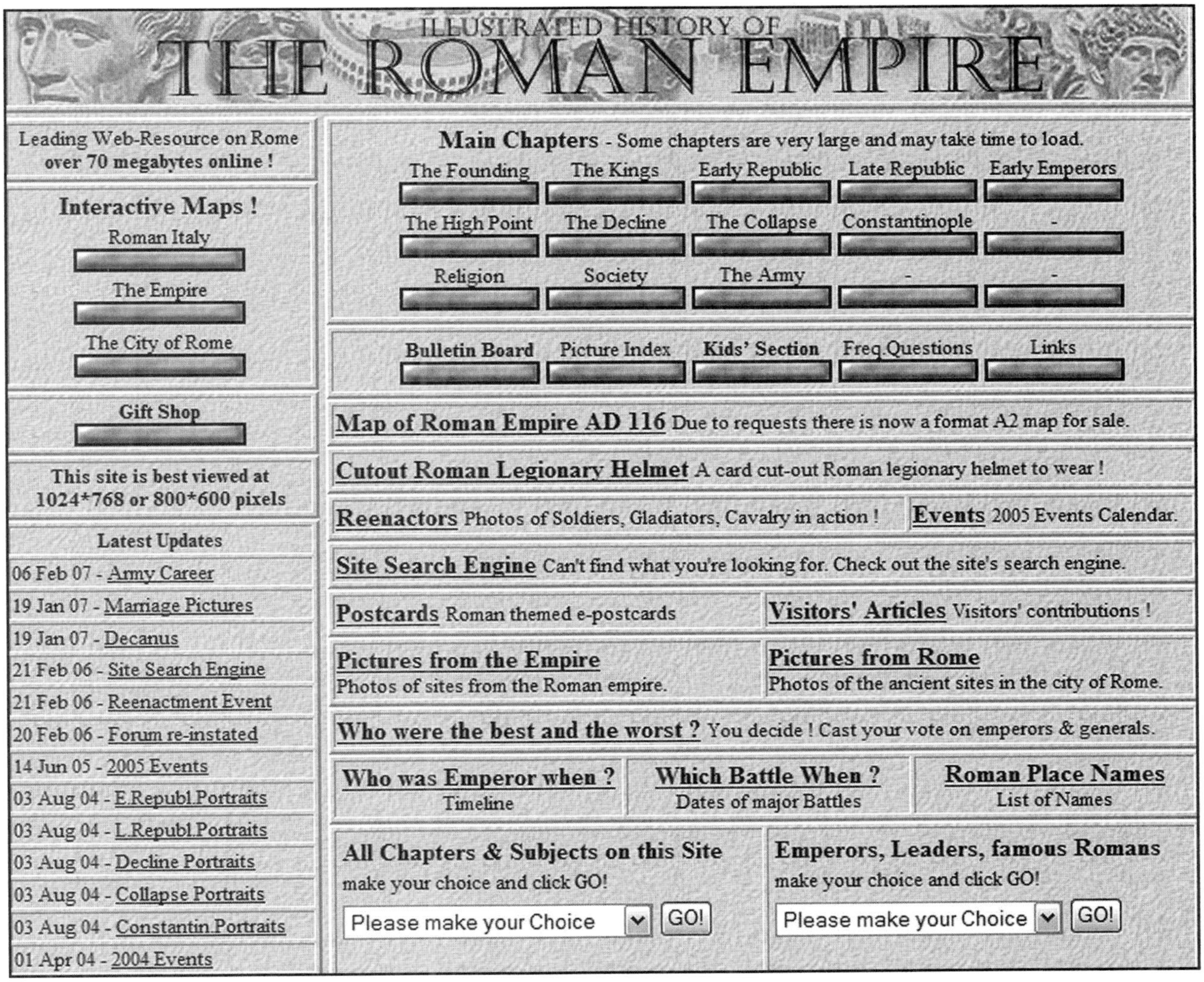

****The Roman Empire in the 1st Century
www.pbs.org/empires/romans/index.html

Meet the Emperors of Rome, read the words of poets and philosophers, learn about life in the first century A.D., and then try your skills in their Emperor of Rome game! Features many classroom resources and a timeline.
Resource Type: General Reference: Lesson or Activity

****The Rome Project
http://intranet.dalton.org/groups/Rome/index.html

"The Rome Project" offers an annotated index of Internet resources covering aspects of ancient Roman history and culture. It has links to sites that feature primary sources photographs and reconstructions. There are also articles relating to specific aspects of Rome and a clickable map of the Roman Empire.
Resource Type: General Reference: Links Collection

****Forum Romanum
www.forumromanum.org/

Forum Romanum is maintained by David Camden, a Ph.D. candidate in Classics at Harvard University, who has put together an award-winning site on Ancient Rome that includes a virtual tour, a Dictionary of Mythology, a picture index, and much information on History, Life, Language, and Literature.
Resource Type: General Reference; Multimedia Presentation

****The Perseus Digital Library
www.perseus.tufts.edu/

A worthwhile digital library for Greek and Classical resources that offers a search function. It has FAQs, essays, a historical overview, and an extensive library of art objects and the like.
Resource Type: General Reference; Virtual Tour

****World Cultures to 1500: Ancient Rome
www.wsu.edu/~dee/ROME/ROME.HTM

This site provides more excellent introductory material on Ancient Rome from Professor Richard Hooker, including clear and informative lecture notes, maps, a photo gallery, timelines, links to relevant sites, and more. Click Contents.
Resource Type: Course Model

****Mr. Dowling's Electronic Passport: Ancient Rome
www.mrdowling.com/702rome.html

"Mr. Dowling's Electronic Passport" helps kids browse the world in this virtual classroom. He introduces you to many civilizations with clear explanations, engaging graphics for kids, and "cool links." His study guides, homework assignments, and exams are free and available for you to print or to edit.
Resource Type: General Reference; Course Model

**** Explore Byzantium
http://byzantium.seashell.net.nz/

The Byzantine Empire bridged the gap between ancient and early modern Europe. From its inception as the eastern half of the partitioned Roman Empire in the fourth century A.D. through to its final disappearance in the fifteenth century, Byzantium played the role of an economic, political, and cultural superpower. At "Explore Byzantium" students will find a historical overview, timelines, maps, articles, and bibliographic material. The site also features an extensive photographic gallery, which details some of the surviving examples of Byzantine architecture and public art—from Italy through to the empire's heartland in modern Greece and Turkey.
Resource Type: General Reference; Virtual Tour

****BBC History: Hadrian's Wall Gallery
www.bbc.co.uk/history/ancient/romans/hadrian_gallery.shtml

Hadrian's Wall was a Roman frontier built in the years A.D. 122–130 by order of the Emperor Hadrian. It was 73 miles long and ran from Wallsend-on-Tyne in the east to Bowness on the

Solway Firth in the west. Explore these BBC photographs.
Resource Type: Virtual Tour

****BBC History: Roman Mosaics

www.bbc.co.uk/history/ancient/romans/mosaics_gallery.shtml

The floors of Roman buildings were often richly decorated with mosaics, many capturing scenes of history and everyday life. Explore these mosaics through these BBC images.
Resource Type: Virtual Tour

***Map of Roman Empire Expansion

http://darkwing.uoregon.edu/~atlas/europe/interactive/map26.html

This animated map of the Roman Empire shows the growth of the Empire from 200 B.C.E. to 100 C.E. Requires Shockwave plug-in.
Resource Type: Maps, Multimedia Presentation

***Gladiator: The Real Story

www.exovedate.com/the_real_gladiator.html

Briefly explains the historical inaccuracies in the popular *Gladiator* film.
Resource Type: General Reference;

Rome Lesson Plans, Teacher Guides, Activities, and More

The Roman Empire: For Educators

www.pbs.org/empires/romans/educators/

This PBS site offers a wide range of classroom activities, lesson plans, video clips, and interactive features that showcase some of the most intriguing and historically significant people, places, and events from first century Rome. Some of the activities include When in Rome, Getting to Know the Emperors of Rome, and Religion in Politics and Daily Life.
Resource Type: Course Model
Grade Level: MS, HS

Course Models: Stoicism and Civic Duty

www.history.ctaponline.org/center/hsscm/index.cfm?Page_Key=1532

Part of the California History-Social Science content standards and annotated course, which includes: background information, focus questions, pupil activities and handouts, an assessment, and references to books, articles, Web sites, literature, audiovisual programs, and a historic site. Grade 7.
Resource Type: Course Model
Grade Level: MS

Mr. Donn's Ancient History Page: Ancient Rome

http://members.aol.com/donnandlee/index.html#ROME

Don Donn of the Corkran (Maryland) Middle School provides a complete unit with 17 daily lesson plans and a unit test for 6th-graders. There are also links to multiple K–12 lesson plans and activities.

Resource Type: Lesson or Activity
Grade Level: MS

Slavery in Ancient Rome
www.lr.k12.nj.us/Site/cherokee/library/webquest/underwood/slavery.htm

In this WebQuest, you are part of a group which has been appointed by the Senate of Rome to investigate the life of a slave. You must investigate the following areas using resources available on the Internet and in print format: Sale of slaves, Punishment of slaves, Life of a city slave, and Life of a country slave.
Resource Type: Lesson or Activity
Grade Level: MS

Course Models: East Meets West—Rome
www.history.ctaponline.org/center/hsscm/index.cfm?Page_Key=1470

Part of the California History-Social Science content standards and annotated course, which includes: background information, focus questions, pupil activities and handouts, an assessment, and references to books, articles, Web sites, literature, audiovisual programs, and a historic site. Grade 6.
Resource Type: Course Model
Grade Level: MS

Rome's Rise to Power
http://school.discovery.com/lessonplans/programs/risetopower/

In this lesson plan, students will learn that the current American system of government at the national level both resembles and differs from the system of government in Rome from about 510 to 264 B.C. and that Ancient Rome experienced several forms of government. Grades 6–8.
Resource Type: Lesson or Activity
Grade Level: MS

The World's History: Rome and the Barbarians
http://cwx.prenhall.com/bookbind/pubbooks/spodek2/chapter6/deluxe.html

The online guide to Howard Spodek's *The World's History* features quizzes (multiple-choice questions, true/false questions, interactive review questions), primary sources, maps, a bulletin board, a live chat, Web links, and faculty resources for each chapter/topic. Much of the history in this chapter is the story of how Rome, a single city-state on the Italian peninsula, came to dominate the Mediterranean world and adjacent territories followed by their effort to maintain control of their conquests.
Resource Type: Course Model
Grade Level: HS, College

Western Civilization: Our Sea
http://wps.prenhall.com/hss_king_westernciv_2/0,6774,207552-,00.html

The online study companion to Margaret King's *Western Civilization: A Social and Cultural History* has many features: Chapter learning objectives, online quizzes, writing activities,

essay questions, Web links, built-in search engines, and faculty modules that include Power-Point outlines, presentation graphics, and lecture hints and activities.
Resource Type: Course Model
Grade Level: HS

Western Civilization: Pax Romana
http://wps.prenhall.com/hss_king_westernciv_2/0,6774,207629-,00.html

The online study companion to Margaret King's *Western Civilization: A Social and Cultural History* has many features: Chapter learning objectives, online quizzes, writing activities, essay questions, Web links, built-in search engines, and faculty modules that include Power-Point outlines, presentation graphics, and lecture hints and activities.
Resource Type: Course Model
Grade Level: HS

Ideas for Projects—Ancient Rome
www.historyforkids.org/crafts/rome.htm

This site is produced by Dr. Karen Carr, an associate professor of History at Portland State University. Also provides suggestions for lesson plans, scavenger hunts, and hands-on crafts.
Resource Type: Lesson or Activity
Grade Level: LS, MS

Brief Review in Global History and Geography: Document-Based Essays and Practice Tests
www.phschool.com/curriculum_support/brief_review/global_history/

PH@School's "Brief Review in Global History and Geography" Web site provides multiple-choice questions from actual Regents exams. You can also practice your test-taking skills on document-based essay questions (DBQs), with the option of e-mailing answers directly to your teacher for review.
Resource Type: Lesson or Activity; Test or Quiz
Grade Level: HS

CHINA

****World Cultures: Ancient China
www.wsu.edu/~dee/ANCCHINA/ANCCHINA.HTM

A terrific overview of Ancient and Medieval History can be found at this online course, based at Washington State University. It offers clear and informative lecture notes, maps, a photo gallery, timelines, links to relevant sites, and more. Click Contents.
Resource Type: General Reference: Course Model

****Internet East Asia History Sourcebook
www.fordham.edu/halsall/eastasia/eastasiasbook.html

"Internet History Sourcebooks" are wonderful collections of public domain and copy-permitted historical texts for educational use by Paul Halsall. The site and its documents are

well organized and the breadth of materials is impressive. "Internet East Asia History Source-book" is a subset of texts derived from the three major online Sourcebooks, along with added texts and web site indicators. Some external links are broken as the site does not appear to be actively maintained.
Resource Type: Primary Source Collection

****Fairbank Chinese History Virtual Library
www.cnd.org/fairbank/

"Fairbank Chinese History Virtual Library" was founded to facilitate easy access to sources of modern Chinese historical information on the Internet. It covers the Qing Dynasty to the present and features outlines, articles, pictures, and more. Some links are broken.
Resource Type: General Reference

****Ask Asia
http://askasia.org/

This site features resources, cultural information, activities, links, and guides for educators and students alike. The instructional resources section features a rich collection of readings, lesson plans, and many other teaching aids developed by educators and scholars.
Resource Type: General Reference: Course Model

****Mr. Dowling's Electronic Passport: Chinese History
www.mrdowling.com/613chinesehistory.html

"Mr. Dowling's Electronic Passport" helps kids browse the world in his virtual classroom. He introduces you to many civilizations with clear explanations, engaging graphics for kids, and "cool links." His study guides, homework assignments, and exams are free and available for you to print or to edit.
Resource Type: General Reference; Course Model

****Takla Makan Mummies: Mysterious Mummies of China
www.pbs.org/wgbh/nova/chinamum/

In the late 1980s, perfectly preserved 3,000-year-old mummies began appearing in a remote Chinese desert. They had long reddish-blond hair, European features, and didn't appear to be the ancestors of modern-day Chinese people. Archaeologists now think they may have been the citizens of an ancient civilization that existed at the crossroads between China and Europe. PBS "Nova" Online presentation.
Resource Type: Multimedia Presentation: Lesson or Activity

****BuddhaNet
www.buddhanet.net/

An interesting and broad site that includes Q&As, historical background, vivid images, and more. BuddhaNet is a Buddhist information service and a communication link for Buddhists. It operates Australia's first and only Buddhist bulletin board system (BBS).
Resource Type: General Reference

****Buddhism
www.wsu.edu/~dee/BUDDHISM/BUDDHISM.HTM

Part of a Washington State University course on World Civilizations, this site provides excellent background material.
Resource Type: General Reference; Course Model

****Asian Studies WWW Virtual Library
http://coombs.anu.edu.au/WWWVL-AsianStudies.html

A popular gateway to resources on Asia edited by Dr. T. Matthew Ciolek and co-editors of the AS WWW VL Project.
Resource Type: Links Collection

****Academic Info: Chinese History
www.academicinfo.net/chinahist.html

An annotated list of online resources on Chinese history in three basic categories: General Links; Subjects, Eras & Studies; Chinese Religion & Philosophy.
Resource Type: Links Collection

****China the Beautiful
www.chinapage.org/china.html

A large site on China that includes art, music, literature, and history. Classical Chinese Art, Calligraphy, Poetry, History, Literature, Painting and Philosophy. There is also an open reader Forum.
Resource Type: General Reference

***Encyclopedia of the Orient
http://i-cias.com/e.o/

Covers North Africa and the Middle East and includes several hundred topics in brief, encyclopedia-style. Also contains some useful teaching-oriented images and maps.
Resource Type: General Reference

***History of China
www-chaos.umd.edu/history/welcome.html

Brief overviews of Chinese dynasties and historical periods with links and color maps.
Resource Type: General Reference

***Daily Life in Ancient China
http://members.aol.com/Donnclass/Chinalife.html

This is a student-developed site on Life in Ancient China for the 6th-grade classroom. Offers timelines and examples of poetry and art.
Resource Type: General Reference; Lesson or Activity

China Lesson Plans, Teacher Guides, Activities, and More

Asia for Educators
http://afe.easia.columbia.edu/

This site from Columbia University offers an online curriculum about East Asia including lectures, discussion questions, handouts and supplementary materials. Some excellent teaching

resources are to be found here. I suggest you explore the teaching units under "history to 1800" and "history, 1800 to present."
Resource Type: Course Model
Grade Level: LS, MS, HS

Mr. Donn's Ancient History Page: Ancient and Modern China
http://members.aol.com/MrDonnHistory/K12east.html#CHINA

Don Donn of the Corkran (Maryland) Middle School provides a complete unit with 17 daily lesson plans and unit test for 6th–graders. There are also links to multiple K–12 lesson plans and activities.
Resource Type: Course Model
Grade Level: LS, MS, HS

Course Models: Chinese Culture and Society
www.history.ctaponline.org/center/hsscm/index.cfm?Page_Key=1535

Part of the California History-Social Science content standards and annotated course that includes background information, focus questions, pupil activities and handouts, an assessment, and references to books, articles, Web sites, literature, audiovisual programs, and a historic site. Grade 7.
Resource Type: Course Model
Grade Level: MS

Course Models: Ancient China
www.history.ctaponline.org/center/hsscm/index.cfm?Page_Key=1461

Part of the California History-Social Science content standards and annotated course which includes background information, focus questions, pupil activities and handouts, an assessment, and references to books, articles, Web sites, literature, audiovisual programs, and a historic site. Grade 6.
Resource Type: Course Model
Grade Level: MS

The World's History: Ancient China
http://cwx.prenhall.com/bookbind/pubbooks/spodek2/chapter7/deluxe.html

The online guide to Howard Spodek's *The World's History* features quizzes (multiple-choice questions, true/false questions, interactive review questions), primary sources, maps, a bulletin board, a live chat, Web links, and faculty resources for each chapter/topic. This chapter emphasizes the foundations of empire and the alternation between periods of dynastic strength and disorganization.
Resource Type: Course Model
Grade Level: HS, College

In Celebration of the Silk Road
http://score.rims.k12.ca.us/activity/silkroad/

As a member of the Council of National Treasures, you have been selected to travel to the province of Xinjiang, China, to represent your country at the First International Celebration

of the Silk Road. Once you have drawn or been assigned the name of the country your team will represent, you need to start making preparations for your trip, display, and press conference. For full credit, the display should be eye-catching, historically accurate, and must follow guidelines.
Resource Type: Lesson or Activity
Grade Level: MS

Searching for China WebQuest
www.kn.pacbell.com/wired/China/ChinaQuest.html

This WebQuest combines an understanding of Chinese History with current Sino-American relations. Students must research China and make policy recommendations to the U.S. government. Impressive activity, but some links are broken.
Resource Type: Lesson or Activity
Grade Level: HS

Discovering China: The Middle Kingdom
http://library.thinkquest.org/26469/?tqskip1=1&tqtime=0808

This ThinkQuest student-produced presentation offers a compact history of China, with special focus on the Cultural Revolution.
Resource Type: Lesson or Activity
Grade Level: HS

The Mongols
www.gananda.k12.ny.us/library/mshslibrary/mongolwq.htm

Genghis Khan, the Forbidden City, the Taj Mahal or Xanadu are all related to the Mongols. In this WebQuest, your job will be to learn about their culture and their effect on other cultures.
Resource Type: Lesson or Activity
Grade Level: MS, HS

Monsoon Winds to the "Land of Gold"
http://ias.berkeley.edu/orias/Spice/textobjects/overview.htm

This integrated unit introduces students to the trading networks and geographic factors that influenced the maritime spice trade from Southeast Asia to the Roman Empire and Han China during the period from 100 BC to 100 AD. Students work in cooperative groups in a series of activities to learn how the ancient world was unified by this sea trade.
Resource Type: Lesson or Activity
Grade Level: MS

Women and Confucianism
www.womeninworldhistory.com/lesson3.html

Students examine sayings by Confucius and evaluate the implications of Confucian ideas about women on the cultures of China, Japan, Korea, and Vietnam.
Resource Type: Lesson or Activity
Grade Level: MS, HS

India & China
www.intranet.csupomona.edu/~inch/welcome.html

This Web site introduces the content, approach, texts, and topics used in a three-year professional development program on India and China for school teachers. The site features a variety of segments from the program such as the two Summer Institutes. A photo gallery is added to provide a more human glimpse of the spirit and scope of the program. Also provided here are links to select Internet sites on or about Asia.
Resource Type: Course Model
Grade Level: LS, MS, HS

Ethics and Chinese Thought
www.globaled.org/curriculum/confu1.html

How do the Analects embody the ethical framework of Confucian thought? How do you know what is "right" and "wrong" behavior? Students participate and discuss.
Resource Type: Lesson or Activity
Grade Level: MS

Mandate of Heaven
http://acc6.its.brooklyn.cuny.edu/~phalsall/texts/shu-jing.html

Brief Zho-era document with questions for analysis. Middle school level.
Resource Type: Lesson or Activity
Grade Level: MS

Legalist Policies of the Qin
http://acc6.its.brooklyn.cuny.edu/~phalsall/texts/ssuma2.html

Brief primary source with questions for analysis. Middle school level.
Resource Type: Lesson or Activity
Grade Level: MS

Banpo Village: Gone, But Not Forgotten
http://score.rims.k12.ca.us/activity/banpo/

In this activity, you portray a renowned scholar of neolithic society who has received the opportunity through the Chinese Ministry of Culture to compete in the Battle of the Scholars in discovering the behind the cultural artifacts and physical remains found at Banpo neolithic village site near Xi'an, China.
Resource Type: Lesson or Activity
Grade Level: MS

The Three Doctrines & Legalism
http://members.aol.com/DonnAnCiv/Behavior.html

Lesson from teacher Don Donn. Give each student a handout (included on the Web site) that lists seven questions. Direct students to write down how they feel an individual would answer these questions if they were, in turn, a Buddhist, a Taoist, a follower of Confucianism, or a loyal citizen governed by Legalism.
Resource Type: Lesson or Activity
Grade Level: MS

The World's History: A Polycentric World
http://cwx.prenhall.com/bookbind/pubbooks/spodek2/chapter4/deluxe.html

The online guide to Howard Spodek's *The World's History* features quizzes (multiple-choice questions, true/false questions, interactive review questions), primary sources, maps, a bulletin board, a live chat, Web links, and faculty resources for each chapter/topic. This chapter completes the introduction to the seven areas where "primary" culture developed—the Yellow River of China, the Niger River valley of West Africa, Mesoamerica, and the Pacific coastal plain of South America and the adjacent Andes.
Resource Type: Course Model
Grade Level: HS, College

Ideas for Projects—Ancient China
www.historyforkids.org/crafts/china.htm

This site is produced by Dr. Karen Carr, an associate professor of History at Portland State University. The site provides suggestions for lesson plans, scavenger hunts, and hands-on crafts.
Resource Type: Lesson or Activity
Grade Level: LS, MS, HS

Brief Review in Global History and Geography: Document-Based Essays and Practice Tests
www.phschool.com/curriculum_support/brief_review/global_history/

PHSchool's "Brief Review in Global History and Geography" Web site provides multiple-choice questions from actual Regents exams. You can also practice your test-taking skills on document-based essay questions (DBQs), with the option of e-mailing answers directly to your teacher for review.
Resource Type: Lesson or Activity; Test or Quiz
Grade Level: HS

INDIA

****World Cultures to 1500: India
www.wsu.edu/~dee/ANCINDIA/ANCINDIA.HTM

This introduction is from Professor Richard Hooker's online course, "Traditions and Memory: World Cultures to 1500." Go to Contents for clear, contextual information on Indian history and religion as well as a glossary of Indian terms and historical maps.
Resource Type: General Reference; Course Model

****Ancient India—The British Museum
www.ancientindia.co.uk/#

The British Museum's online offerings are impressive. The Ancient Civilizations websites highlights achievements of some remarkable world civilizations and explores cross-cultural themes of human development. Explore the people, culture, beliefs, and history of ancient India using animations, 3-D models, and objects from the British Museum's collections.
Resource Type: General Reference; Multimedia Presentation

****Exploring Ancient World Cultures: India
http://eawc.evansville.edu/inpage.htm

Another fine introduction to Ancient India, though some links are broken. The most interesting features are an article entitled "The Historical Context of *The Bhagavad Gita* and Its Relation to Indian Religious Doctrines," and an online translation of *The Bhagavad Gita*. You can also find a whole slew of images of Harrapa.
Resource Type: General Reference; Lesson or Activity

****Ramayana
www.maxwell.syr.edu/moynihan/programs/sac/Outreach/ramayana/oral.asp

"Ramayana" provides insights into many aspects of Indian culture. This site includes a brief (and long) synopsis of the Rama story as well as many images, such as the "God Posters" or images of Hindu gods in the style of popular Indian posters and calendars. Consider the five lessons on "Moral Dilemmas." They include useful questions for the classroom to help students understand the moral dilemmas in the story and define outcomes and consequences. There is also an article on The Oral Tradition and the Many "Ramayanas."
Resource Type: General Reference; Image Collection

****History of the Sikhs
www.sikh-history.com/

The purpose of this Web site is to provide details about Sikhism. The site appears with mesmerizing music and has many categories, which are Sikh Gurus and Gursikhs, Great Sikh warriors and martyrs, major historical events, modern Sikh personalities, and famous Sikh institutes. There are many engaging features at this site, including a discussion forum, an education site that provides basic instruction of the Punjab alphabet and language, a selection of literature and poetry and links to several other sources of Punjab reading material, a news site, a greeting card site. This unique feature offers an extensive selection of photographs and Sikh art that can be personalized, either in English or Punjab, put to a selection of music, and emailed to your friends and family.
Resource Type: General Reference

****Harappa
www.harappa.com/

This is a very helpful site for learning about the Indus Valley and the Indus culture. It has many slide shows, pictures, photographs, and details concerning the culture and heritage and places of the Indus Valley. Three are six category links named Images, Indus News 3, Movies, Sound, Indus Valley, and Bazaar.
Resource Type: General Reference: Multimedia Presentation

****Mr. Dowling's Electronic Passport: India and the Himalayas
www.mrdowling.com/612india.html

"Mr. Dowling's Electronic Passport" helps kids browse the world in his virtual classroom. He introduces you to many civilizations with clear explanations, engaging graphics for kids, and "cool links." His study guides, homework assignments and exams are free and available for you to print or to edit.
Resource Type: General Reference; Course Model

***BBC: India Facts
http://news.bbc.co.uk/2/hi/south_asia/country_profiles/1154019.stm

A concise "fact box" that includes information on India's population, religions, languages, etc.
Resource Type: General Reference

***"Hindu-Muslim Violence Imperils India"—TIME.com
www.time.com/time/world/article/0,8599,213670,00.html

A good description of the historical significance of the holy site in Ayodhya, and how extreme violence has been justified by both Hindus and Muslims in the name of preserving holy sites for their people.
Resource Type: General Reference

***"Religious Tension Hangs Heavy in Sacred Hindu City"—Christian Science Monitor
www.csmonitor.com/2002/0522/p07s01-wosc.html

An excellent article about the fear among Indians in Mathura, a town with its own disputed holy site.
Resource Type: General Reference

***"Analysis: Why Is Gujarat So Violent?"—BBC News
http://news.bbc.co.uk/2/hi/south_asia/1856049.stm

A brief overview of the history of violence in the state of Gujarat. Also addresses the rise of Hindu nationalism in the past 20 years.
Resource Type: General Reference

***Architecture of India
www.boloji.com/architecture/index.htm

Rated as the Web's Best Site for "Architecture of India" by Encyclopaedia Britannica.
Resource Type: General Reference; Art History

India Lesson Plans, Teacher Guides, Activities, and More

Classroom Activities about India
http://home.att.net/~tisone/units.html

Classroom activities about India are written by Fullbright scholars who traveled to India in 1998. Some of the lesson topics (Arranged Marriages, Education in India) compare/contrast Indian and American cultures and should appeal to students. In the Arranged Marriages lesson you'll find interesting Indian advertisements for brides. What is Sacred? compares and contrasts the places considered sacred in U.S. and Indian culture. Eye for an Eye is about teaching Modern Indian History through the film Gandhi. Education in India examines four Indian schools the scholars visited. There is also a Self-Directed Exploration of Hindu Mythology aimed at younger students.
Resource Type: Course Model
Grade Level: MS, HS

AskAsia Lesson Plans: India

www.askasia.org/teachers/

"AskAsia" features resources, cultural information, activities, links, and guides for educators and students alike. The instructional resources section features a rich collection of readings, lesson plans, and many other teaching aids developed by educators and scholars.

Resource Type: Course Model

Grade Level: LS, MS, HS

Daily Life in Ancient India

http://members.aol.com/donnclass/Indialife.html

Teacher Don Donn of the Corkran (Maryland) Middle School provides complete units on various historical topics with daily lesson plans and resources. The numerous lesson plans and resources available at this popular site were developed by Mr. Donn and other contributors. Lessons cover: The Mysterious Indus Civilization 3000–1500 B.C.E., Aryan Civilization Daily Life 1500–500 B.C.E., Vedic Period 1500–1000 B.C.E., Epics Period 1000–500 B.C.E., and Age of Empires Daily Life 500 B.C.E.–700 C.E. Lessons are most appropriate for students in grades 5–8.

Resource Type: Lesson or Activity

Grade Level: MS

India & China

www.intranet.csupomona.edu/~inch/welcome.html

This Web site introduces the content, approach, texts, and topics used in a three-year professional development program on India and China for school teachers. The site features a variety of segments from the program such as the two Summer Institutes. A photo gallery is added to provide a more human glimpse of the spirit and scope of the program. Also provided here are links to select Internet sites on or about Asia.

Resource Type: Course Model

Grade Level: LS, MS, HS

INDOLink: Kids Corner

www.indolink.com/Kidz/stories.html

In this Kids Corner section of the "INDOlink" site, there are stories from Indian mythology, famous people and more. For a young audience.

Resource Type: Lesson or Activity

Grade Level: LS

Experiencing India's Caste System

http://teachers.eusd.k12.ca.us/mguerena/castewebquest/index.htm

After taking on the role of a person from Ancient India (3,000 years ago) including status in a specific caste, students create three journal entries and share them with the class. There are links to sites on caste, a glossary of terms, as well as an Inspiration worksheet on caste. Grade 6 WebQuest.

Resource Type: Lesson or Activity

Grade Level: MS

The Ramayana in Southeast India

www.ias.berkeley.edu/orias/SEARama/RamaStandards.htm

Grade 6 students are instructed to write a shadow puppet scene drawn from a Southeast Asian variant of the Ramayana to perform in class and to work collaboratively on a class sewing project to construct a Ramayana story cloth in the tradition of Southeast Asia.

Resource Type: Lesson or Activity
Grade Level: MS

Ramayana: An Enduring Tradition

www.globaled.org/curriculum/story1.html

During a 1997 summer institute, program participants designed related material to provide an entry for teachers and students into the study of this tradition. The institute was funded by the National Endowment for the Humanities; the American Forum for Global Education and Syracuse University collaborated on the program.

Resource Type: Lesson or Activity
Grade Level: MS

Ramayana: Connecting Communication Arts and Social Studies

www.globaled.org/curriculum/story1.html

These lessons are taken from *Spotlight on Ramayana: An Enduring Tradition*, a curriculum guide published by the American Forum.

Resource Type: Lesson or Activity
Grade Level: MS

AskAsia: Instructional Resources

www.askasia.org/teachers/resources/

The instructional resources section features a rich collection of readings, lesson plans, and many other teaching aids developed by educators and scholars.

Resource Type: Course Model
Grade Level: LS, MS, HS

India/Pakistan Dispute over Kashmir

http://members.aol.com/MrDonnGeo/Kashmir.html

This is a four-day mini-unit debate for grade 9 from teacher Don Donn.

Resource Type: Lesson or Activity
Grade Level: HS

The World's History: Hinduism and Buddhism

http://cwx.prenhall.com/bookbind/pubbooks/spodek2/chapter9/deluxe.html

The online guide to Howard Spodek's *The World's History* features quizzes (multiple-choice questions, true/false questions, interactive review questions), primary sources, maps, a bulletin board, a live chat, Web links, and faculty resources for each chapter/topic. Professor Spodek identifies the categories historians can deal with: The sanctification of time, of space, of language and literature, of artistic and cultural activity, as well as the creation of religious organizations.

Resource Type: Course Model
Grade Level: HS, College

The World's History: India
http://cwx.prenhall.com/bookbind/pubbooks/spodek2/chapter8/deluxe.html

The online guide to Howard Spodek's *The World's History* features quizzes (multiple-choice questions, true/false questions, interactive review questions), primary sources, maps, a bulletin board, a live chat, Web links, and faculty resources for each chapter/topic. India developed into a single loosely-unified but persistent cultural region through the operation of what Professor Spodek calls "intermediate" institutions. He discusses political disunity in this chapter and the forces of cultural unity in the next.
Resource Type: Course Model
Grade Level: HS, College

The World's History: River Valley Civilizations
http://cwx.prenhall.com/bookbind/pubbooks/spodek2/chapter3/deluxe.html

The online guide to Howard Spodek's *The World's History* features quizzes (multiple-choice questions, true/false questions, interactive review questions), primary sources, maps, a bulletin board, a live chat, Web links, and faculty resources for each chapter/topic. This chapter focuses on the civilizations which developed in the Nile valley of Egypt and the Indus River valley of India/Pakistan.
Resource Type: Course Model
Grade Level: HS, College

Brief Review in Global History and Geography: Document-Based Essays and Practice Tests
www.phschool.com/curriculum_support/brief_review/global_history/

PH@School's "Brief Review in Global History and Geography" Web site provides multiple-choice questions from actual Regents exams. Students can also practice their test-taking skills on document-based essay questions (DBQs), with the option of e-mailing answers directly to the teacher for review.
Resource Type: Lesson or Activity: Test or Quiz
Grade Level: HS

Water: A Key to Understanding India
www.globaled.org/curriculum/water.html

This lesson is from a curriculum guide entitled *A South Asia Curriculum, Teaching about India*.
Resource Type: Lesson or Activity
Grade Level: HS

AFRICA

****The Story of Africa
www.bbc.co.uk/worldservice/africa/features/storyofafrica/index.shtml

This BBC site features Africa's top historians and analyzes the events and characters that have shaped the continent from the origins of humankind to the end of South African apartheid. Among the topics covered are the rise and fall of empires and kingdoms, the power of religion, the injustices of slavery, and the expansion of trade between Africa and other continents. Features audio segments.

Resource Type: General Reference

Figure 7.6: The Story of Africa

****Wonders of the African World**
www.pbs.org/wonders/

In this PBS production, Harvard University professor Henry Louis Gates Jr. challenges the widespread Western view of Africa as the primitive "dark continent" civilized by white

colonists. The series covers Black Pharaohs, Meroe, Gedi, the Swahili People, Zanzibar, the Ashanti and Dahomey (Benin) Kingdoms, Aksum, Gondar, the Churches of Lalibela, the Dogon, Grand Mosque of Djenne, Empires of Mali & Ghana, the Tuareg, Great Zimbabwe, a 1,000-year-old South African city—Mapangubwe, the Shona People, and more. Includes a kids' activity page, teachers' lesson plans, and audio clips.
Resource Type: General Reference; Lesson or Activity

****Internet African History Sourcebook

www.fordham.edu/halsall/africa/africasbook.html

Part of Paul Halsall's excellent series of Internet Sourcebooks, "Internet African History Sourcebook" has full-text sources for African history arranged by topics that include the Black Athena Debate, human origins, Egypt, Ethiopia, Islam in Africa, West African kingdoms, Great Religion, the slave trade, and more. Some external links are broken as the site does not appear to be actively maintained.
Resource Type: Primary Source Collection

****African Voices

www.mnh.si.edu/africanvoices/

The Smithsonian Institution's National Museum of Natural History provides a thematic exploration of Africa. The themes revolve around issues of wealth, working, and living conditions in Africa. The history-oriented sections focus on the slave trade, colonialism, and other subjects. The Learning Center offers a helpful list of African resources.
Resource Type: General Reference

****World Cultures to 1500: Civilizations in Africa

www.wsu.edu/~dee/CIVAFRCA/CIVAFRCA.HTM

A terrific overview of Ancient and Medieval History can be found at this online course, based at Washington State University. It offers clear and informative lecture notes, maps, a photo gallery, timelines, links to relevant sites, and more. Click Contents.
Resource Type: General Reference; Course Model

****Mr. Dowling's Electronic Passport: Ancient Africa

www.mrdowling.com/609ancafr.html

"Mr. Dowling's Electronic Passport" helps kids browse the world in his virtual classroom. He introduces you to many civilizations with clear explanations, engaging graphics for kids, and "cool links." His study guides, homework assignments and exams are free and available for you to print or to edit.
Resource Type: General Reference; Course Model

****South of the Sahara

www-sul.stanford.edu/depts/ssrg/africa/history.html

"South of the Sahara" is maintained by the history department at Stanford University and contains an annotated directory of resources on the history of Sub-Saharan Africa. One can search by topics, countries, or just view the Africa Guide.
Resource Type: General Reference

Africa Lesson Plans, Teacher Guides, Activities, and More

The Road to Timbuktu
www.pbs.org/wonders/Classrm/lesson5.htm

Explore the geography of Africa and research the history of West African kingdoms like Timbuktu. PBS Classroom.
Resource Type: Lesson or Activity
Grade Level: HS

Holy Land
www.pbs.org/wonders/Classrm/lesson4.htm

Identify the achievements and rich heritage of Ethiopians—particularly their religious heritage—and compare these to modern-day public misconceptions about Ethiopian life. PBS Classroom.
Resource Type: Lesson or Activity
Grade Level: HS

Mr. Donn's Ancient History Page: Africa
http://africa.mrdonn.org/lessons.html#Top

Don Donn of the Corkran (Maryland) Middle School provides a complete unit with 17 daily lesson plans and unit test for 6th-graders. There are also links to multiple K12 lesson plans and activities.
Resource Type: Course Model
Grade Level: MS

Slave Kingdoms
www.pbs.org/wonders/Classrm/lesson3.htm

Ghana was the first European sub-Saharan slave port, and some scholars say that the African trade routes could not have started without the support of Ghana's ruling class. One of America's leading scholars on African American culture and history retraces his family roots to Ghana and explores the psychological impact of the slave trade on his identity as an African American. Students are directed to create a newspaper about Ghana's history, culture, and role in the slave trade.
Resource Type: Lesson or Activity
Grade Level: HS

Lost Cities of the South
www.pbs.org/wonders/Classrm/lesson6.htm

Complete a South African Web scavenger hunt and create class presentations about South Africa and Zimbabwe.
Resource Type: Lesson or Activity
Grade Level: HS

African Arts and Music
www.pbs.org/wnet/africa/tools/music/goals.html

Create original art, make African crafts, listen to selections of African music, and explore

numerous Web sites that depict images of many different kinds of art forms native to Africa. PBS. Grades 3–5.
Resource Type: Lesson or Activity
Grade Level: LS

Fight for Freedom
http://pbskids.org/bigapplehistory/parentsteachers/early_lesson3.html

Research slavery around the world today and find out more about institutions working to end slavery. Grades 4–8.
Resource Type: Lesson or Activity
Grade Level: LS, MS

Assessing Africa: Examining Issues in Africa and Responses by Local Countries and the International Community
www.nytimes.com/learning/teachers/lessons/20030709wednesday.html

In this *New York Times* lesson, students research important issues in Africa and how the concerns are being addressed both nationally and internationally. They then prepare briefing presentations for the American President to influence concerns of foreign policy.
Resource Type: Lesson or Activity
Grade Level: MS, HS

The World's History: A Polycentric World
http://cwx.prenhall.com/bookbind/pubbooks/spodek2/chapter4/deluxe.html

The online guide to Howard Spodek's *The World's History* features quizzes (multiple-choice questions, true/false questions, interactive review questions), primary sources, maps, a bulletin board, a live chat, Web links, and faculty resources for each chapter/topic. This chapter completes the introduction to the seven areas where "primary" culture developed—the Yellow River of China, the Niger River valley of West Africa, Mesoamerica, and the Pacific coastal plain of South America and the adjacent Andes.
Resource Type: Course Model
Grade Level: HS, College

Brief Review in Global History and Geography: Document-Based Essays and Practice Tests
www.phschool.com/curriculum_support/brief_review/global_history/

PH@School's "Brief Review in Global History and Geography" Web site provides multiple-choice questions from actual Regents exams. You can also practice your test-taking skills on document-based essay questions (DBQs), with the option of e-mailing answers directly to your teacher for review.
Resource Type: Lesson or Activity; Test or Quiz
Grade Level: HS

MESOAMERICA

*****The Sport of Life and Death: The Mesoamerican Ballgame
www.ballgame.org/

"The Sport of Life and Death: The Mesoamerican Ballgame" was voted Best Overall Site for 2002 by Museums and the Web and has won a slew of other web awards. The site is based on a traveling exhibition and bills itself as "an online journey into the ancient spectacle of athletes and gods." The Web site features dazzling special effects courtesy of Macromedia Flash technology and its overall layout and organization are superb. Not just stylish, the site's content is excellent and engaging as well. For instance, there are helpful interactive maps, timelines, and samples of artwork in the Explore the Mesoamerican World section. The focus of the site, however, is the Mesoamerican ballgame, the oldest organized sport in history. The sport is explained through a beautiful and engaging combination of images, text, expert commentary, and video. Visitors can even compete in a contest! A must-see for middle school or 9th-grade world history teachers.
Resource Type: Multimedia Presentation; Lesson or Activity

Figure 7.7: The Sport of Life and Death: The Mesoamerican Ballgame

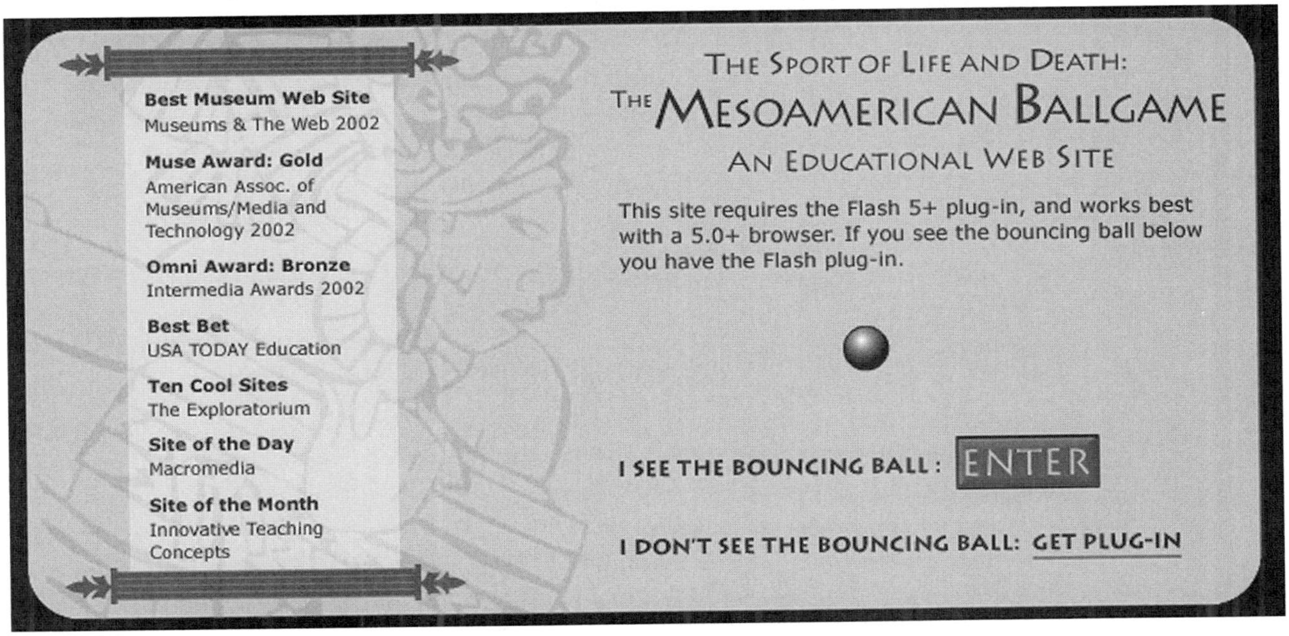

****Ancient Mesoamerican Civilization
www.angelfire.com/ca/humanorigins/index.html

This is a broad site by the University of Minnesota Department of Anthropology that supplies information regarding Mesoamerican Civilizations. The primary groups addressed are the Maya, Mixtec, Zapotec, and Aztec. Major topics include Writing Systems, Government, Religion, the Mayan Calendar, and more.
Resource Type: General Reference

****GB's Online Mesoamerica
http://pages.prodigy.com/GBonline/mesowelc.html

A popular Web site for students of Native American languages and culture, "GBN's Online Mesoamerica" is linked to by over 500 related sites and has over 9,000 visitors per month. Major features include Ancient Writing, Archeological Sites, Native Issues, Pre-Columbian Art, and the Mesoamerican Calendar.
Resource Type: General Reference

****Maya Adventure
www.sci.mus.mn.us/sln/ma/top.html

The Science Museum of Minnesota presents "Maya Adventure," a Web site that highlights science activities and information related to ancient and modern Maya culture. "Maya Adventure" includes images from the Science Museum's anthropological collections and activities developed by the Science Museum's education division. Featured in the project is information from two exhibits about the Maya developed by the Science Museum of Minnesota: "Cenote of Sacrifice" and "Flowers, Saints and Toads."
Resource Type: General Reference; Virtual Tour

****Mystery of the Maya
www.civilization.ca/civil/maya/mminteng.html

Based on the IMAX film of the same name, this kid-oriented site from the Canadian Museum of Civilization features slide shows, info, links, and more. There is a synopsis of the film, a feature on the People of the Jaguar, and a lot of information on Maya civilization.
Resource Type: General Reference; Multimedia Presentation

****Mayan Architecture
www.mayadiscovery.com/ing/archaeology/default.htm

"Mayan Architecture" is an informative site that covers different architectural styles and periods. Specific architectural characteristics are explained and illustrated.
Resource Type: General Reference; Image Collection

****Why do Civilizations Collapse?
www.learner.org/exhibits/collapse/

Part of the Annenberg/CPB exhibits, this site focuses on the fall of ancient civilizations in four areas: Maya, Mesopotamia, Chaco Canyon (U.S. Southwest), and Mali and Songhai. Nice images and interesting presentation.
Resource Type: General Reference

Mesoamerica Lesson Plans, Teacher Guides, Activities, and More

Mr. Donn's Ancient History Page
http://members.aol.com/donnandlee/index.html#ROME

Don Donn of the Corkran (Maryland) Middle School provides a complete unit with 17 daily lesson plans and unit test for 6th-graders on Incas, Mayans, and Aztecs. There are also links to multiple K–12 lesson plans and activities.

Resource Type: Lesson or Activity
Grade Level: MS

Conquistadors Teaching Guide: Different Views of the World
www.pbs.org/opb/conquistadors/teachers/teachers.htm

Was the fall of the Aztec Empire inevitable? Was Cortes a hero or a villain? What would the world be like today if the Aztecs had been the "conquistadors" and conquered Europe? Contains complete PBS lesson plans.
Resource Type: Lesson or Activity
Grade Level: MS

Conquistadors Teaching Guide: The What Ifs of History
www.pbs.org/opb/conquistadors/teachers/teachers.htm

Why do you think that such a well-governed and peaceful empire, which stretched 2,500 miles from Ecuador south to Chile, could have been conquered by only 200 Spanish Conquistadors? What is the legacy of the Incas? Contains complete PBS lesson plans.
Resource Type: Lesson or Activity
Grade Level: MS

Course Models: Meso-America and the Andes
www.history.ctaponline.org/center/hsscm/index.cfm?Page_Key=1508

Part of the California History-Social Science content standards and annotated course, this site includes background information, focus questions, pupil activities and handouts, an assessment, and references to books, articles, Web sites, literature, audiovisual programs, and an historic site.
Resource Type: Course Model
Grade Level: MS

The World's History: A Polycentric World
http://cwx.prenhall.com/bookbind/pubbooks/spodek2/chapter4/deluxe.html

The online guide to Howard Spodek's *The World's History* features quizzes (multiple-choice questions, true/false questions, interactive review questions), primary sources, maps, a bulletin board, a live chat, Web links, and faculty resources for each chapter/topic. This chapter completes the introduction to the seven areas where "primary" culture developed—the Yellow River of China, the Niger River valley of West Africa, Mesoamerica, and the Pacific coastal plain of South America and the adjacent Andes.
Resource Type: Course Model
Grade Level: HS, College

Mystery of the First Americans: The Dating Game
www.pbs.org/wgbh/nova/first/radiocarbon.html

Play this PBS "Nova" Shockwave game to see how scientists use radiocarbon dating to learn about ancient people.
Resource Type: Game
Grade Level: MS

Extension Activity: Exploring Aztec Religion
www.phschool.com/atschool/TAN/1877/Student_Area/TAN1877_SC2_ACT_index.html

Create a visual presentation of what you've learned about Aztec Religion using information that you have found on the site and Aztec graphics that you have printed. Grades 6–8.
Resource Type: Lesson or Activity
Grade Level: MS

Brief Review in Global History and Geography: Document-Based Essays and Practice Tests
www.phschool.com/curriculum_support/brief_review/global_history/

PH@School's "Brief Review in Global History and Geography" Web site provides multiple-choice questions from actual Regents exams. You can also practice your test-taking skills on document-based essay questions (DBQs), with the option of e-mailing answers directly to your teacher for review.
Resource Type: Lesson or Activity; Test or Quiz
Grade Level: HS

CHAPTER 8

The Origins of World Religions

JUDAISM

*****Heritage: Civilization and the Jews
www.pbs.org/wnet/heritage/index.html

A great general site featuring an interactive timeline, primary sources, lesson plans, teacher sources, images, and more (see Figure 8.1).
Resource Type: General Reference; Lesson or Activity

****Jewish History Sourcebook
www.fordham.edu/halsall/jewish/jewishsbook.html

"Internet History Sourcebooks" by Paul Halsall are wonderful collections of public-domain and copyright-permitted historical texts for educational use.
Resource Type: Primary Source Collection

****Judaism and Jewish Resources
http://shamash.org/trb/judaism.html

"Judaism and Jewish Resources" is a good starting point for Jewish resources on the Web.
Resource Type: Lesson or Activity

****Ancient Hebrews: A Virtual Museum
http://score.rims.k12.ca.us/activity/ancient_hebrews/

This virtual museum explores the land, the people and leaders, and the beliefs of the ancient Hebrews.
Resource Type: Virtual Tour

****Canaan & Ancient Israel
www.museum.upenn.edu/Canaan/index.html

This exhibit explores the identities of these peoples in prehistorical times through the material remains that they have left behind.
Resource Type: Virtual Tour

****The Hebrews: A Learning Module
www.wsu.edu:8080/~dee/HEBREWS/HEBREWS.HTM

Part of a university course on World Civilizations, here you'll find lecture notes, maps, timelines, and a photo gallery that provide excellent background material.
Resource Type: Course Model

****Messiah
www.livius.org/men-mh/messiah/messiah00.html

This site was written and is maintained by Jona Lendering, professor of Mediterranean archaeology and history at Amsterdam Free University, The Netherlands. It is a scholarly but accessible discussion of the concept of messiah in Jewish history.
Resource Type: General Reference

Figure 8.1: Messiah

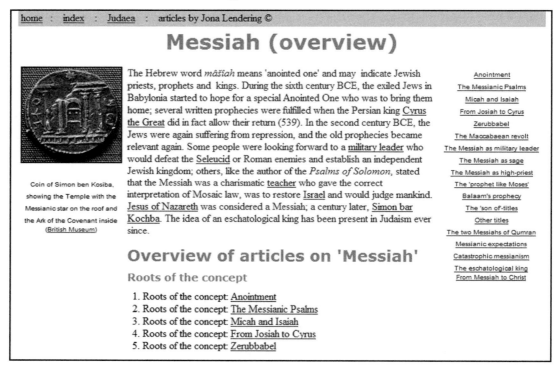

****IOUDAIOS-L Basic Bibliography
http://ccat.sas.upenn.edu/ioudaios/biblio/basic.html

Provides helpful introductory readings that will orient non-specialists to the study of Judaism in the Greco-Roman period.
Resource Type: General Reference

****Internet Resources for the Study of Judaism and Christianity
http://ccat.sas.upenn.edu/~jtreat/rs/resources.html

A well-organized list of several sites on the Internet useful for the study of Judaism and Christianity.
Resource Type: General Reference

***Jewish Virtual Library
www.jewishvirtuallibrary.org/index.html

The American-Israeli Cooperative Enterprise (AICE), a nonprofit organization designed to strengthen the U.S.-Israel relationship, produces this site which features the Virtual Israel Experience.
Resource Type: Virtual Tour

***Jerusalem 3000: Three Millenia of History
www.usm.maine.edu/~maps/exhibit1/

Provides an interesting tour of Jerusalem through the ages.
Resource Type: Virtual Tour

****Global Connections
www.pbs.org/globalconnections

"Global Connections" provides the background information needed to understand events occurring in the Middle East. The site includes original materials created in conjunction with the Centers for Middle Eastern Studies at Harvard and UCLA. The site also aggregates and contextualizes the rich resources available throughout public broadcasting, including material from *Frontline*, *Online NewsHour*, *NOW with Bill Moyers*, *Morning Edition*, *Talk of the Nation*, and many others. Designed with educators in mind, the site is also useful for those curious to better understand the Middle East and its relationship with the West.
Resource Type: Course Model

****Middle East: Centuries of Conflict
www.cnn.com/SPECIALS/2001/mideast/

The CNN Archives feature special in-depth reports on key current events, issues and personalities. Most special reports supply historical overviews, articles, photographs, timelines or chronologies, video clips, maps, interviews, sources and more. This special is an excellent introduction to strife in the Mideast—past and present.
Resource Type: Lesson or Activity

Judaism Lesson Plans, Teacher Guides, Activities, and More

The Torah Tells
http://rims.k12.ca.us/score_lessons/torah_tells/

This lesson was developed to show students about how the Bible is used as an archaeological resource to supplement the artifacts and other writings that have been found in the Near East. The quotes were selected by Biblical scholars at Hebrew Union College.
Resource Type: Lesson or Activity
Grade Level: MS

The Israel Geography Game
www.j.co.il/

This Flash game will help you learn about the history and geography of 101 locations in Israel.

Resource Type: Game
Grade Level: MS

Mapping the Middle East
www.pbs.org/wgbh/globalconnections/mideast/educators/nations/lesson1.html

In this PBS lesson plan, students will learn how the countries of the Middle East were created. They will understand the influence of various political and geographic factors in their creation. Grades 9–12.
Resource Type: Lesson or Activity
Grade Level: HS

Canaan & Ancient Israel: Activities
www.museum.upenn.edu/Canaan/Activities.html

Activities for children (ages 8–12) to do at home or in the classroom. These can be used in preparation for a museum gallery visit, after a visit, or even just for fun. Activities labeled "visit activity" are best done during a gallery visit. The activities are divided along the themes of the exhibit.
Resource Type: Lesson or Activity
Grade Level: LS, MS

The World's History: Judaism and Christianity
http://cwx.prenhall.com/bookbind/pubbooks/spodek2/chapter10/deluxe.html

The online guide to Howard Spodek's *The World's History* features quizzes (multiple-choice questions, true/false questions, interactive review questions), primary sources, maps, a bulletin board, a live chat, Web links, and faculty resources for each chapter/topic.
Resource Type: Course Model
Grade Level: HS

Course Models: Ancient Hebrews and Greeks
www.history.ctaponline.org/center/hsscm/index.cfm?Page_Key=1443

Part of the California History-Social Science content standards and annotated course, which includes: background information, focus questions, pupil activities and handouts, assessment, and references to books, articles, Web sites, literature, audiovisual programs, and historic site. Grade 6.
Resource Type: Course Model
Grade Level: MS

Western Civilization: Pagans, Jews and Christians
http://wps.prenhall.com/hss_king_westernciv_2/0,6774,207697-,00.html

The online study companion to Margaret King's *Western Civilization: A Social and Cultural History* has many features: Chapter learning objectives, online quizzes, writing activities, essay questions, Web links, built-in search engines, and faculty modules that include Power-Point outlines, presentation graphics, and lecture hints and activities.
Resource Type: Course Model
Grade Level: HS

Unmasking the Middle East: Examining the Political, Religious and Ethnic Relationships Among Middle Eastern Countries
www.nytimes.com/learning/teachers/lessons/20030416wednesday.html

In this *New York Times* lesson, students explore many of the countries in the Middle East, developing research-based posters and a "spider web" illustrating the relationships among the countries. They then write letters to fictional peers in Middle Eastern countries.
Resource Type: Lesson or Activity
Grade Level: MS, HS

Peace Signs: Exploring the 'Roller Coaster Ride' of the Israeli-Palestinian Peace Process
www.nytimes.com/learning/teachers/lessons/20030507wednesday.html

In this *New York Times* lesson, students review their prior knowledge about the peace process in Israel and examine recent steps towards peace. They then research key figures, events and policies since Israel's statehood in 1948 and determine how they impacted the peace process, illustrating their effects as if the process were a roller coaster. Finally, students reflect on how the proposed road map for peace might change the path of the roller coaster they created.
Resource Type: Lesson or Activity
Grade Level: MS, HS

Brief Review in Global History and Geography: Document-Based Essays and Practice Tests
www.phschool.com/curriculum_support/brief_review/global_history/

PH@School's "Brief Review in Global History and Geography" Web site provides multiple-choice questions from actual Regents exams. You can also practice your test-taking skills on document-based essay questions (DBQs), with the option of e-mailing answers directly to your teacher for review.
Resource Type: Lesson or Activity; Test or Quiz
Grade Level: HS

CHRISTIANITY

*****From Jesus to Christ: The First Christians (PBS)
www.pbs.org/wgbh/pages/frontline/shows/religion/

Part of PBS's *Frontline* series, this site explores archeological clues to Jesus' life, paints a portrait of his world, examines the gospels and first Christians, and discusses why Christianity succeeded (see Figure 8-2). There are also maps, a timeline, an anthology of primary sources, a discussion forum, and a biblical quiz.
Resource Type: General Reference; Course Model

****Anno Domini: Jesus Through the Centuries
www.virtualmuseum.ca/Exhibitions/Annodomini/introduction-en.html

The virtual edition of "Anno Domini: Jesus Through the Centuries" is the result of a lengthy and fruitful partnership between The Provincial Museum of Alberta, Alberta Community

Development, and the Canadian Heritage Information Network (CHIN). It provides an exhibit that explores Jesus through several themes.
Resource Type: General Reference; Multimedia Presentation

****World Cultures to 1500: Early Christianity
www.wsu.edu/~dee/CHRIST/CHRIST.HTM

A terrific overview of Ancient and Medieval History can be found at this online course, based at Washington State University. It offers clear and informative lecture notes, maps, a photo gallery, timelines, links to relevant sites, and more. Click Contents.
Resource Type: Course Model

Figure 8.2: World Cultures to 1500: Early Christianity

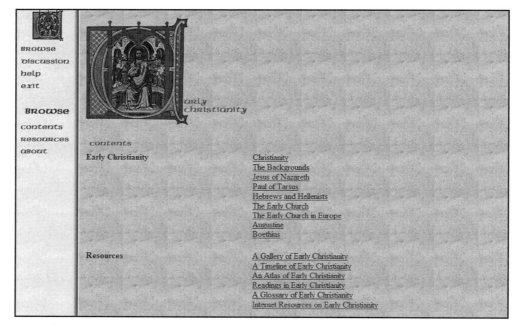

****The Ecole Initiative
http://www2.evansville.edu/ecoleweb/

An encyclopedia of pre-Reformation church history that contains a useful archive of primary source material. Sections of the Encyclopedia include: Translations of Judæo-Christian and Islamic Primary Sources to 1500; Short Essays on Numerous Topic; Long Essays on Major Topics and Figures; IMAGES—Judæo-Christian Iconography and Religious Art; Timeline with Geographical Cross-Index.
Resource Type: General Reference; Primary Source Collection

****Ad Hoc: Resources for Teaching and Research relating to the History of Christianity
www.yale.edu/adhoc/research_resources/links.htm

"Ad Hoc" offers a well chosen selection of Internet sites and electronic sites relating to history of Christianity. From Yale University.
Resource Type: General Reference

****Resource Pages for Biblical Studies
www.torreys.org/bible/

A lengthy set of links useful to scholars of early Christian writings and the Christian social world. The pages are intended as a resource for serious, scholarly studies.
Resource Type: General Reference

****Review of Biblical Literature
www.bookreviews.org/

"Review of Biblical Literature" is published by the Society of Biblical Literature, a nonprofit professional association for scholars in the field of biblical studies and supplies a comprehensive review of biblical literature and related studies.
Resource Type: General Reference

****Dead Sea Scrolls Exhibit
www.ibiblio.org/expo/deadsea.scrolls.exhibit/intro.html

An exhibit at the Library of Congress. The Library's exhibition describes the historical context of the scrolls and the Qumran community; it also relates the story of their discovery 2,000 years later.
Resource Type: General Reference; Primary Source Collection

****Messiah
www.livius.org/men-mh/messiah/messiah00.html

This site was written and is maintained by Jona Lendering, professor of Mediterranean archaeology and history at Amsterdam Free University, The Netherlands. It is a scholarly but readable discussion of the concept of Messiah in Jewish history.
Resource Type: General Reference

****ICLnet: Guide to Early Church Documents
www.iclnet.org/pub/resources/christian-history.html

A useful research resource on early Christian texts, featuring canonical documents, creeds, the writings of the Apostolic Fathers and other historical texts relevant to church history.
Resource Type: Primary Source Collection

****Internet Resources for the Study of Judaism and Christianity
http://ccat.sas.upenn.edu/~jtreat/rs/resources.html

A well-organized list of several sites on the Internet useful for the study of Judaism and Christianity. Compiled by Jay C. Treat of the University of Pennsylvania.
Resource Type: General Reference

****All in One: Biblical Resource Sites
http://ntgateway.com/multibib/resource.htm

Has a series of search functions to help you find varied biblical resources. Conceived by Dr Mark Goodacre, Department of Theology, University of Birmingham, U.K.
Resource Type: General Reference

****Interactive Bible Research
www.studyandteach.com/

This site tries to bring thousands of different interpretations of the Bible together, with the opportunity for the visitor to participate in forums and to vote for their preferred interpretations. The Bible is organized by verse and identifies nine research categories in which these verses can be discussed.
Resource Type: General Reference

****Journal of Biblical Studies
http://journalofbiblicalstudies.org/

"Journal of Biblical Studies" is an electronic journal dedicated to the field of Biblical Studies in general, including: Archaeology, linguistics, exegesis, history, and textual issues. Articles are in PDF format.
Resource Type: General Reference

****Bible Notes
www.biblenotes.net/

The entire Holy Bible is summarized with review notes and key points. When not stated, the verses are from The Holy Bible, New International Version (NIV). All verses and references are given in standard form of Book, Chapter: Verse.
Resource Type: General Reference; Primary Source Collection

****New Testament Gateway
www.ntgateway.com/
An award-winning directory of Internet resources related to the New Testament. Browse or search annotated links on everything from the Greek New Testament to Jesus in Film.
Resource Type: General Reference

****Bible History Online Images and Resources
www.bible-history.com/

A rich site on Bible History, its goal is to aid students and teachers of the Scriptures with Biblical and historical information for the purpose of furthering the gospel of Jesus Christ.
Resource Type: General Reference

****The Christian Catacombs of Rome
www.catacombe.roma.it/welcome.html

An extensive site, in many languages, that offers a historic and visual tour of Christian catacombs.
Resource Type: General Reference; Virtual Tour; Video Tutorial

Christianity Lesson Plans, Teacher Guides, Activities, and More

The World's History: Judaism and Christianity
http://cwx.prenhall.com/bookbind/pubbooks/spodek2/chapter10/deluxe.html

The online guide to Howard Spodek's *The World's History* features quizzes (multiple-choice

questions, true/false questions, interactive review questions), primary sources, maps, a bulletin board, a live chat, Web links, and faculty resources for each chapter/topic.
Resource Type: Course Model
Grade Level: HS

Western Civilization: Pagans, Jews and Christians
http://wps.prenhall.com/hss_king_westernciv_2/0,6774,207697-,00.html

The online study companion to Margaret King's *Western Civilization: A Social and Cultural History* has many features: Chapter learning objectives, online quizzes, writing activities, essay questions, Web links, built-in search engines, and faculty modules that include Power-Point outlines, presentation graphics, and lecture hints and activities.
Resource Type: Course Model
Grade Level: HS

Western Civilization: The Spiritual Sword
http://wps.prenhall.com/hss_king_westernciv_2/0,6774,207908-,00.html

The online study companion to Margaret King's *Western Civilization: A Social and Cultural History* has many features: Chapter learning objectives, online quizzes, writing activities, essay questions, Web links, built-in search engines, and faculty modules that include Power-Point outlines, presentation graphics, and lecture hints and activities.
Resource Type: Course Model
Grade Level: HS

Brief Review in Global History and Geography: Document-Based Essays and Practice Tests
www.phschool.com/curriculum_support/brief_review/global_history/

PH@School's "Brief Review in Global History and Geography" Web site provides multiple-choice questions from actual Regents exams. You can also practice your test-taking skills on document-based essay questions (DBQs), with the option of e-mailing answers directly to your teacher for review.
Resource Type: Lesson or Activity; Test or Quiz
Grade Level: HS

ISLAM

****Frontline: Muslims
www.pbs.org/wgbh/pages/frontline/shows/muslims/

This PBS site examines Islam through stories of diverse Muslims. The Frequently Asked Questions is like Islam 101 as it concisely explains the basic principles of Islam, including the most widely accepted definition of jihad. This site provides an abundance of fascinating facts about Islamic history, basic beliefs, and various other topics through its portrayal and interviews of various Muslims.
Resource Type: General Reference

****Turning the Pages

www.bl.uk/onlinegallery/ttp/ttpbooks.html

"Turning the Pages" is an award-winning interactive display system developed by The British Library to increase public access and enjoyment of some of its most valuable treasures. Visitors are able to virtually "turn" the pages of manuscripts in an incredibly realistic way, using touch-screen technology and animation. There are currently fifteen treasures on display in Turning the Pages, including Sultan Baybars' Qur'an.

Resource Type: Multimedia Presentation

Figure 8.3: Turning the Pages

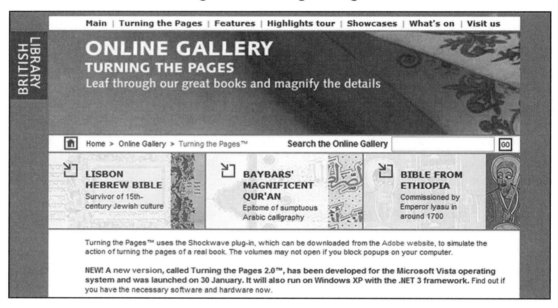

****Global Connections

www.pbs.org/wgbh/globalconnections/

"Global Connections" provides the background information needed to understand events occurring in the Middle East. The site includes original materials created in conjunction with the Centers for Middle Eastern Studies at Harvard and UCLA. The site also aggregates and contextualizes the rich resources available throughout public broadcasting, including material from *Frontline, Online NewsHour, NOW with Bill Moyers, Morning Edition, Talk of the Nation,* and many others. Designed with educators in mind, the site is also useful for those curious to better understand the Middle East and its relationship with the West.

Resource Type: Course Model

****World Cultures to 1500: Islam

www.wsu.edu/~dee/ISLAM/ISLAM.HTM

A terrific overview of Ancient and Medieval History can be found at this online course, based at Washington State University. It offers clear and informative lecture notes, maps, a photo gallery, timelines, links to relevant sites, and more. Click Contents.

Resource Type: General Reference; Course Model

****Middle East Network Information Center (MENIC): Islam

http://menic.utexas.edu/Society_and_Culture/Religion_and_Spirituality/Islam/

MENIC is a public service of the Center for Middle Eastern Studies at the University of Texas at Austin. Amongst its many features, MENIC provides an index to numerous links on the Arabic world.

Resource Type: General Reference

****Middle East: Centuries of Conflict

www.cnn.com/SPECIALS/2001/mideast/

The CNN Archives feature special in-depth reports on key current events, issues and personalities. Most special reports supply historical overviews, articles, photographs, timelines or chronologies, video clips, maps, interviews, sources and more. This special is an excellent introduction to strife in the Mideast—past and present.

Resource Type: General Reference; Multimedia Presentation

****ArabNet—The Resource for the Arab World in the Middle East and North Africa

www.arab.net/

This site provides excellent general information on Arab countries, including history, geography, and culture. It also has a set of useful links and special features.

Resource Type: General Reference

****Internet Islamic History Sourcebook

www.fordham.edu/halsall/islam/islamsbook.html

"Internet History Sourcebooks" by Paul Halsall are wonderful collections of public-domain and copyright-permitted historical texts for educational use. This Sourcebook's documents are well organized and the breadth of the collection is impressive.

Resource Type: Primary Source Collection

****The True Religion

http://thetruereligion.org/modules/news/

Offers an invitation to discover Islam that features many articles about past and current Islamic events and issues.

Resource Type: General Reference

****Muslim Scientists and Islamic Civilization

http://cyberistan.org/islamic/

Much of the site focuses on Islamic contributions to learning, but there are many helpful history-related sections and features.

Resource Type: General Reference

****The Islam Page

www.islamworld.net/

The Islam page has a thorough introduction to the religion for non-Muslims.

Resource Type: General Reference

****Islamic World: Islamic History Sites
www.islamic-world.net/links/islamic_history_sites.htm

Contains a useful set of links to sites on Islamic History.
Resource Type: General Reference

***Mr. Dowling's Electronic Passport: Crusades and the Rise of Islam
www.mrdowling.com/606islam.html

"Mr. Dowling's Electronic Passport" helps kids browse the world in his virtual classroom. He introduces you to many civilizations with clear explanations, engaging graphics for kids, and "cool links." His study guides, homework assignments, and exams are free and available for you to print or to edit.
Resource Type: Course Model

***Submission
www.submission.org/god-bible.html

A general site on Islam that also has comparisons of passages from the Bible and Koran.
Resource Type: General Reference

Islam Lesson Plans, Teacher Guides, Activities, and More

The Fascinating World of Islam
www.pbs.org/empires/islam/lesson2.html

Students will have the opportunity to learn about aspects of the world of Islam by using various research tools. They will then work with classmates in creating an ABC Book of Islam based on their research. Grades 6–12.
Resource Type: Lesson or Activity
Grade Level: MS, HS

An Introduction to Islam and Muhammed
www.pbs.org/empires/islam/lesson1.html

Students will compare the major monotheistic belief systems of the world, use vocabulary sheets to help understand new vocabulary, and prepare a parallel timeline. Grades 6–12.
Resource Type: Lesson or Activity
Grade Level: MS, HS

Exploring Islamic Lands
www.thirteen.org/edonline/lessons/landofislam/index.html

In this high school lesson, students explore what it's like to be a teenager living today in an Islamic country in the Middle East. They will begin by gaining background information about the religion and the region from which it sprang by using the PBS series *Islam: Empire of Faith* and other resources. Once students gain a historical understanding, they choose a particular modern-day Middle Eastern country to explore in depth using resources such as the Library of Congress Web site and e-pals. In the end, they will create a personal narrative of what it's like to live in that country.

Resource Type: Lesson or Activity
Grade Level: HS

How Many Wives?

www.pbs.org/wgbh/globalconnections/mideast/educators/women/lesson3.html

Students will learn that religious texts are often used to establish cultural norms and rules of behavior. These ancient texts, however, are open to interpretation.
Resource Type: Lesson or Activity
Grade Level: HS

Muslim Women Through Time

www.pbs.org/wgbh/globalconnections/mideast/educators/women/lesson2.html

Students will learn that monolithic cultures and accurate stereotypes of Muslim women do not exist. A combination of factors affects the role of Muslim women as a group and individually over time.
Resource Type: Lesson or Activity
Grade Level: HS

Islam in the United States

www.suite101.com/welcome.cfm/islam_in_the_us

This Web site could be used to find resources and also fun activities on the subject of Islam. This site would be most useful to a teacher looking for activities, or to someone studying Islam who wants to find helpful information and use different kinds of media pertaining to Islam. The layout is a bit confusing, but this site includes ratings for links and descriptions to Islam-related sites.
Resource Type: Lesson or Activity
Grade Level: HS

Twenty-Five Most Frequently Asked Questions About Islam

www.islam-usa.com/25ques.html

By Dr. Athar, a physician, an Islamic writer and speaker. He is author of over 60 articles and five books on Islam.
Resource Type: Lesson or Activity
Grade Level: HS

Top Ten Misconceptions about Islam

www.jannah.org/articles/misc.html

By Huma Ahmad. A brief discussion of common misconceptions.
Resource Type: Lesson or Activity
Grade Level: HS

The Islamic Quiz

http://islam.org/Quiz/New/selectquiz.htm

Tough set of questions on Islamic history.
Resource Type: Test or Quiz
Grade Level: MS, HS

The World's History: Islam
http://cwx.prenhall.com/bookbind/pubbooks/spodek2/chapter11/deluxe.html

The online guide to Howard Spodek's *The World's History* features quizzes (multiple-choice questions, true/false questions, interactive review questions), primary sources, maps, a bulletin board, a live chat, Web links, and faculty resources for each chapter/topic.
Resource Type: Course Model
Grade Level: HS

Brief Review in Global History and Geography: Document-Based Essays and Practice Tests
www.phschool.com/curriculum_support/brief_review/global_history/

PH@School's "Brief Review in Global History and Geography" Web site provides multiple-choice questions from actual Regents exams. You can also practice your test-taking skills on document-based essay questions (DBQs), with the option of e-mailing answers directly to your teacher for review.
Resource Type: Lesson or Activity; Test of Quiz
Grade Level: HS

Maps of Muslim World
www.muslimsonline.com/babri/mapsmuslim.htm

The site contains maps of Central Asia, South Asia, Southeast Asia, East Asia, and finally Africa. Each of these maps shows where the Muslim population is concentrated. One can also choose a link entitled "Muslim Minorities," which lists many articles about Islam's history and mythology. The last link is to "Muslims Online," a larger Web site which contains search engines, homepages, and links to Muslim organizations. From this site a student can learn about the religion of Islam; however, the site might be quite confusing to someone who is not familiar with the topic.
Resource Type: Map
Grade Level: HS

BUDDHISM AND HINDUISM

****Buddhanet
www.buddhanet.net/

An interesting and broad site that includes Q&As, historical background, vivid images, and more (see Figure 8.4). Some of the major categories include Buddhist Studies, e-Book Library, Buddhanet Audio, Archived File Library, World Buddhist Directory, BuddhaZine (a kind of Buddha-devoted magazine), and Meditation. It integrates the complexities of the religion with the basics very well and has so many subtopics that it is difficult not to find what one is looking for. Some of the special features include audio files of chanting, a photo documentary of Buddhism, teacher's guides, and crossword puzzles and games.
Resource Type: General Reference; Multimedia Presentation

Figure 8.4: Buddhanet

****BBC Religion and Ethics: Buddhism
www.bbc.co.uk/religion/religions/buddhism/index.shtml

"BBC Religion and Ethics: Buddhism" covers the basics: Introduction, Customs, Worship, History, Beliefs, and Holy Days. Go into Subdivisions for essays on Buddhist branches: Theravada, Mahayana, Pure Land, Tibetan, Zen, Korean Zen (Son). Special features: Four Noble Truths, Buddhism in Britain, and Sacred Mandala Sand Painting.
Resource Type: General Reference

****World Cultures to 1500: Buddhism
www.wsu.edu/~dee/BUDDHISM/BUDDHISM.HTM

A terrific overview of Ancient and Medieval History can be found at this online course, based at Washington State University. Go to Contents for clear, contextual information on the Origins of Buddhims, The Chinese Transformation, and Japanese Buddhism. Under Resources you'll find links, including one to the text of the The Dhammapada.
Resource Type: Course Model

****BBC Religion & Ethics: Hinduism
www.bbc.co.uk/religion/religions/hinduism/index.shtml

This BBC presentation provides sections on Customs, Worship, History, Holy Days, and Beliefs. There is also a Features section that provides interesting articles including reports on Hindu thoughts on homeschooling and organ donation. There is a Glossary as well.

Resource Type: General Reference

****The Hindu Universe—History
www.hindunet.org/hindu_history/

A good introduction to Hinduism and its history, this is a searchable site and offers audio (national anthem), images (maps, charts), and plain text. It has many links to more specialized areas of Hindu history and offers chats and forums. There is even an entire section on biographies.

Resource Type: General Reference

****Ramayana
www.maxwell.syr.edu/moynihan/programs/sac/Outreach/ramayana/index.asp

"Ramayana" provides insights into many aspects of Indian culture. This site includes a brief (and long) synopsis of the Rama story as well as the Story of Rama in Bengali Scrolls. Consider the five lessons on Moral Dilemmas. They include useful questions for the classroom to help students understand the moral dilemmas in the story and define outcomes and consequences. There is also an article on The Oral Tradition and the Many Ramayanas.

Resource Type: General Reference

****History of the Sikhs
www.sikh-history.com/

The purpose of this Web site is to provide details about Sikhism. The site appears with mesmerizing music and has categories on Sikh Gurus and Gursikhs, Great Sikh warriors and martyrs, major historical events, modern Sikh personalities, and famous Sikh institutes. There are many engaging features at this site, including a discussion forum, an education site that provides basic instruction of the Punjab alphabet and language, a selection of literature and poetry and links to several other sources of Punjab reading material, a news site, and a greeting card site. This unique feature offers an extensive selection of photographs and Sikh art that can be personalized, either in English or Punjab, put to a selection of music, and emailed to your friends and family.

Resource Type: General Reference

****The Dalai Lama: A Spiritual Leader in Exile
www.cnn.com/SPECIALS/2001/dalai.lama/

Part of CNN.com's In-Depth Specials, this site offers news reports, interviews, photo essays, links, and other resources. There are three videos of the Dalai Lama meeting with President Bush, but these are restricted to paid RealOne SuperPass members.

Resource Type: General Reference; Multimedia Presentation

****Frontline: Dreams of Tibet
www.pbs.org/wgbh/pages/frontline/shows/tibet/

This site has four main sections: Understanding Tibetan Buddhism, ascending the roof of the world, interviews, and China in Tibet. There is a great selection of reports and readings as

well as a historical chronology and links to other sites. The interviews feature a mix of political and Hollywood figures.
Resource Type: General Reference

****Dalai Lama: Public Talks in Boston & New York City
www.beliefnet.com/dalailama/

To watch selected highlights from his Central Park and Boston talks, click on a topic link. Choose T1 if you are viewing at school or on a high speed connection. At the same site are interviews with the Dalai Lama as well as related resources including a guided meditation.
Resource Type: Multimedia Presentation

****Asia Today: Buddhism in the U.S. (2001)
www.asiasource.org/news/at_mp_02.cfm?newsid=54751

Access a collection of articles, links to temples and Buddhist associations, online Buddhist publications, and general links with this special report. Unfortunately some of the links to essays are broken, but there are several active ones.
Resource Type: General Reference

Ethnic Buddhism and Other Obstacles to the Dhamma in the West
www.buddhanet.net/bsq14.htm

In this commentary, V. A. Gunasekara outlines Buddhism basics and the history of Buddhism in the West and argues that misconceptions about Buddhism are in danger of "transforming the universal message of Buddhism into a parochial cult."
Resource Type: General Reference

American Buddhism's Racial Divide
www.beliefnet.com/story/7/story_732_1.html

"Buddhists in the United States are split into two camps: Asian Americans and 'New Buddhists.' Can they be brought together?" This article attempts to answer the question.
Resource Type: General Reference

****"Hindu-Muslim Violence Imperils India," TIME.com
www.time.com/time/world/article/0,8599,213670,00.html

A good description of the historical significance of the holy site in Ayodhya, and how extreme violence has been justified by both Hindus and Muslims in the name of preserving holy sites for their people.
Resource Type: General Reference

****"Religious Tension Hangs Heavy in Sacred Hindu City," Christian Science Monitor
http://csmonitor.com/2002/0522/p07s01-wosc.html

An excellent article about the fear among Indians in Mathura, a town with its own disputed holy site.
Resource Type: General Reference

****"Analysis: Why Is Gujarat So Violent?" BBC News
http://news.bbc.co.uk/2/hi/south_asia/1856049.stm

A brief overview of the history of violence in the state of Gujarat. Also addresses the rise of Hindu nationalism in the past 20 years.
Resource Type: General Reference

****Human Rights Watch Report: State Participation in Gujarat Violence
http://hrw.org/reports/2002/india/

A very thorough report about the history of Muslim-Hindu violence in Gujarat. Select excerpts to use with students, or allow them to explore the linkable subsections of the report themselves. Students can visit the Gujarat riots photo gallery at: www.hrw.org/photos/2002/india/
Resource Type: General Reference; Multimedia Presentation

***Essentials of Buddhism
www.buddhaweb.org/

Brief information, but it is recommended by New York State High School Regents Exam Prep Center as an excellent resource for students.
Resource Type: General Reference

***"Religion, as ever, is the poison in India's blood"
http://books.guardian.co.uk/departments/politicsphilosophyandsociety/story/0,6000,664342,00.html

An article from the Saturday March 9, 2002 edition of *The Guardian*.
Resource Type: General Reference

Buddhism and Hinduism Lesson Plans, Teacher Guides, Activities, and More

AskAsia Lesson Plans
www.askasia.org/teachers/

"AskAsia" provides 59 lesson plans searchable by grade level, era of history, or region. There are also 116 background essays, maps, and images.
Resource Type: Lesson or Activity
Grade Level: LS, MS, HS

Classroom Activities about India
http://home.att.net/~tisone/units.html

"Classroom Activities about India" are written by Fullbright scholars who traveled to India in 1998. Some of the lesson topics (Arranged Marriages, Education in India) compare/contrast Indian and American cultures and should appeal to students. In the Arranged Marriages lesson you'll find interesting Indian advertisements for brides. What is Sacred? compares and contrasts the places considered sacred in U.S. and Indian culture. Eye for an Eye is about teaching Modern Indian History through the film *Gandhi*. Education in India examines four Indian schools the scholars visited. There is also a Self-Directed Exploration of Hindu Mythology aimed at younger students.
Resource Type: Lesson or Activity
Grade Level: HS

INDOlink: Kids Corner
www.indolink.com/Kidz/stories.html

In this Kids Corner section of the "INDOlink" site, there are stories from Indian mythology, Stories of India's Great People, Stories about India's Festivals, and more.
Resource Type: Lesson or Activity
Grade Level: MS

Experiencing India's Caste System
http://teachers.eusd.k12.ca.us/mguerena/castewebquest/index.htm

After taking on the role of a person from Ancient India (3,000 years ago) including status in a specific caste, students create three journal entries and share them with the class. There are links to sites on caste, a glossary of terms, and an Inspiration worksheet on caste. Grade 6 WebQuest.
Resource Type: Lesson or Activity
Grade Level: MS

Deciphering Buddha Imagery
www.pbs.org/wgbh/nova/tibet/buddha.html

Before you can honor a Buddha you have to recognize him—and there are many depictions in Buddhist art that resemble The Enlightened One. This site uses Flash animation to help you understand the meanings of the five most common hand gestures, or mudras, used in Buddhist art. Engaging way to present Buddha icons.
Resource Type: Lesson or Activity
Grade Level: HS

Daily Life in India
http://k12east.mrdonn.org/India.html

Don Donn of the Corkran (Maryland) Middle School provides a complete unit with daily lesson plans and unit test for 6th-graders. There are also links to multiple K–12 lesson plans.
Resource Type: Lesson or Activity
Grade Level: MS

Muslim-Hindu Conflict in India
www.pbs.org/wnet/religionandethics/teachers/lp_conflict2.html

Students investigate the causes and consequences of the deep-rooted conflict between Muslims and Hindus in India—particularly in the province of Gujarat. Students will consider the larger questions of whether religious beliefs can ever legitimize violence or whether religious conflict is an inevitable human experience. Part of BBC Religion & Ethics Lesson Plan.
Resource Type: Lesson or Activity
Grade Level: HS

The Tibet Question (WebQuest)
http://score.rims.k12.ca.us/activity/tibet_question/

An interesting project with many useful links on the Tibet issue: "An international news agency is doing a special on The Tibet Question. They will be interviewing members of the Tibetan groups, Chinese and US government officials, representatives of human rights

organizations and Chinese scholars. You will be assigned to one of these groups in preparation for this news special."
Resource Type: Lesson or Activity
Grade Level: HS

The Ramayana in Southeast India
www.ias.berkeley.edu/orias/SEARama/RamaStandards.htm

Grade 6 students are instructed to write a shadow puppet scene drawn from a Southeast Asian variant of the *Ramayana* to perform in class and to work collaboratively on a class sewing project to construct a Ramayana story cloth in the tradition of Southeast Asia.
Resource Type: Lesson or Activity
Grade Level: MS

Bhutan, the Last Shangri-La: Buddhism and Ecology
www.pbs.org/edens/bhutan/Bhu_teach_1.htm

In this PBS lesson plan, students will use the Internet, watch video clips, write a paragraph, make a chart (and more) to find out which countries observe Buddhism as their main religion, learn about Buddhist attitudes toward ecology, and write and perform or tell an allegory similar in scope to the story of the Four Harmonious Friends.
Resource Type: Lesson or Activity
Grade Level: HS

Ramayana: Connecting Communication Arts and Social Studies
www.globaled.org/curriculum/story1.html

These lessons are taken from *Spotlight on Ramayana: An Enduring Tradition*, a curriculum guide published by the American Forum.
Resource Type: Lesson or Activity
Grade Level: MS

Look for Symbol in Sculpture: Fudô Myô-ô
www.metmuseum.org/explore/symbols/html/el_symbols_fm.htm

In this Met Museum activity, you roll your cursor over the image to identify a symbol and to discover what it means. Fudô Myô-ô, a Buddhist deity from Japan, guards the Buddhist faith and helps believers who pray for assistance.
Resource Type: Lesson or Activity
Grade Level: MS

The World's History: Hinduism and Buddhism
http://cwx.prenhall.com/bookbind/pubbooks/spodek2/chapter9/deluxe.html

The online guide to Howard Spodek's *The World's History* features quizzes (multiple-choice questions, true/false questions, interactive review questions), primary sources, maps, a bulletin board, a live chat, Web links, and faculty resources for each chapter/topic. Professor Spodek identifies the categories historians can deal with: the sanctification of time, of space, of language and literature, of artistic and cultural activity, as well as the creation of religious organizations.

Resource Type: Course Model
Grade Level: HS

The World's History: Indian Empires
http://cwx.prenhall.com/bookbind/pubbooks/spodek2/chapter8/deluxe.html

The online guide to Howard Spodek's *The World's History* features quizzes (multiple-choice questions, true/false questions, interactive review questions), primary sources, maps, a bulletin board, a live chat, Web links, and faculty resources for each chapter/topic. India developed into a single loosely-unified but persistent cultural region through the operation of what Professor Spodek calls "intermediate" institutions. He discusses political disunity in this chapter and the forces of cultural unity in the next.
Resource Type: Course Model
Grade Level: HS

The World's History: River Valley Civilizations
http://cwx.prenhall.com/bookbind/pubbooks/spodek2/chapter3/deluxe.html

The online guide to Howard Spodek's *The World's History* features quizzes (multiple-choice questions, true/false questions, interactive review questions), primary sources, maps, a bulletin board, a live chat, Web links, and faculty resources for each chapter/topic. This chapter focuses on the civilizations which developed in the Nile valley of Egypt and the Indus River Valley of India/Pakistan.
Resource Type: Course Model
Grade Level: HS

Brief Review in Global History and Geography: Document-Based Essays and Practice Tests
www.phschool.com/curriculum_support/brief_review/global_history/

PH@School's "Brief Review in Global History and Geography" Web site provides multiple-choice questions from actual Regents exams. You can also practice your test-taking skills on document-based essay questions (DBQs), with the option of e-mailing answers directly to your teacher for review.
Resource Type: Lesson or Activity; Test or Quiz
Grade Level: HS

India & China
www.intranet.csupomona.edu/~inch/

This Web site introduces the content, approach, texts and topics used in a three-year professional development program on India and China for schoolteachers. The site features a variety of segments from the program such as the two Summer Institutes. A photo gallery is added to provide a more human glimpse of the spirit and scope of the program. Also provided here are links to select internet sites on or about Asia.
Resource Type: Course Model
Grade Level: MS

CHAPTER 9

Medieval and Early Modern Europe

MEDIEVAL EUROPE

****The Decameron Web
www.brown.edu/Departments/Italian_Studies/dweb/dweb.shtml

This impressive site is an interactive project by Brown University students designed to prompt investigation and discussion of the *Decameron* texts—stories from people escaping Florence at the time of the Plague (see Figure 9.1). There is plenty of excellent historical and literary material here: 300-plus documents, maps and images, essays, a bibliography, and more. There are also excellent teaching materials.
Resource Type: General Reference; Course Model

*****NetSERF: The Internet Connection for Medieval Resources
www.netserf.org/

"NetSERF" is a great gateway to Medieval Era Web sites. Edited by Dr. Andrea R. Harbin, a professor at George Washington University, "NetSERF" provides access to an impressive annotated list of scholarly (and not so scholarly) resources on Medieval times. It also includes a downloadable medieval glossary of some 1,500 terms.
Resource Type: General Reference

*****Labyrinth: Medieval Resources
www.georgetown.edu/labyrinth/labyrinth-home.html

This Georgetown University site offers great access to free access electronic resources in medieval studies. There is plenty to choose from here. Among the offerings are bibliographies, a searchable index, links to special topics, and full-text versions of medieval works. Moreover, "Labyrinth" provides connections to databases, services, texts, and images on other servers. A great general resource.
Resource Type: General Reference

****The End of Europe's Middle Ages: Fourteenth and Fifteenth Centuries
www.ucalgary.ca/applied_history/tutor/endmiddle/

Produced at the University of Calgary, "The End of Europe's Middle Ages" is designed to

Figure 9.1: The Decameron Web

assist those students engaged in Renaissance, Reformation and Early Modern studies who lack a background in medieval European history. The tutorial is presented in a series of chapters that summarize the economic, political, religious and intellectual environment of the fourteenth and fifteenth centuries.

Resource Type: General Reference

****Internet Medieval Sourcebook
www.fordham.edu/halsall/sbook.html

"Internet History Sourcebooks" are wonderful collections of public domain and copy-permitted historical texts for educational use by Paul Halsall. The site and its documents are well organized and the breadth of materials is impressive. "Internet Medieval Sourcebook" is great resource for medieval primary sources and is a must-stop for a research project. Unfortunately, some external links are broken as the site does not appear to be actively maintained any longer.

Resource Type: Primary Source Collection

****The Reformation Guide
www.educ.msu.edu/homepages/laurence/reformation/index.htm

"The Reformation Guide" is intended to provide easy access to Internet information available on the Reformation period. The extensive external links at this site are organized by topics such as: Martin Luther, John Calvin, Zwingli, Radical Reformation, English Reformation, Scottish Reformation, Counter Reformation, Reformation Gallery—People, and Reformation Gallery—Places. There is also an excerpt from David Hall's book *Savior or Servant?*, entitled "Reformation to Revolution: 1500–1650." A good starting point for research.

Resource Type: Links Collection

****Martin Luther: The Reluctant Revolutionary
www.pbs.org/empires/martinluther/

In this interactive PBS site visitors learn about Luther's confrontation with the great powers of Europe and meet characters from his time. Among the interesting offering at this site are Luther trivia, 10 Things You Didn't Know, Day in the Life of a Monk, and Martin Luther *v.* Martin Luther King. There are two lesson plans as well.
Resource Type: General Reference; Lesson or Activity

****Project Wittenberg
www.iclnet.org/pub/resources/text/wittenberg/wittenberg-home.html

"Project Wittenberg" is an excellent research site by and about Martin Luther and Lutherans. Included are commentaries, statements of faith, theological treatises, biographies, links, and more. "Project Wittenberg" documents are posted in their original languages, in English translation, and in other languages as they are available.
Resource Type: Primary Source Collection

****The Online Medieval and Classical Library
http://omacl.org/

Part of the Berkeley Digital Library, OMACL is a nice collection of important literary works of Classical and Medieval civilization. You can browse or search easily by author, title, genre, and even language. Clear and easy-to-navigate site.
Resource Type: Primary Source Collection

****Tudor History
www.tudorhistory.org/

History enthusiast Lara E. Eakins runs this rich and frequently updated site. Sections incude: The Tudor Monarchs, The Six Wives of Henry VIII, Who's Who in Tudor History, Topics in Tudor History, Chronologies of People and Events, Architecture, Electronic Texts, Genealogical Trees, Glossaries of Words and Terms, Reference Maps, Bibliography, Image Gallery Index, Ask or Help Answer Questions, Student Help, and Links of Interest.
Resource Type: General Reference

****Le Poulet Gauche
www.lepg.org/index.html

"Le Poulet Gauche" is a detailed guide to the history, culture, and daily life of sixteenth-century France. Most of the site deals with social issues, but the Wars of Religion section outlines how such conflict "destroyed a generation." Features a map of the territorial divisions of France along religious and political lines.
Resource Type: General Reference

****Voices of the Powerless
www.bbc.co.uk/radio4/history/voices/voices_reformation.shtml

This site is a companion to the BBC radio show in which Melvyn Bragg explores the lives of the ordinary working men and women of Britain at six critical moments over the last

1,000 years. These episodes are an intriguing glimpse into social history. This particular audio-episode deals with the upheavals and turmoil of the sixteenth century that transformed many aspects of religious life.
Resource Type: Multimedia Presentation

****Spartacus Internet Encyclopedia
www.spartacus.schoolnet.co.uk/

This encyclopedia-style resource concentrates on British history from the medieval era on. Contains overviews, essays, images, and subtopics such as Medieval World and British History. Good general resource and starting point for research.
Resource Type: General Reference

****Explore Byzantium
http://byzantium.seashell.net.nz/

"Explore Byzantium" is an excellent introduction to the Byzantine era. You will find a historical overview, timelines, maps, articles, a bibliography, and more. The site features an impressive photographic gallery of Byzantine architecture and public art and interesting essays.
Resource Type: General Reference

****Tudor Encyclopedia
www.spartacus.schoolnet.co.uk/Tudors.htm

"Tudor Encyclopedia" is a Spatacus collection of hypertexted articles on the Tudor period. In addition to 60 biographies, there are many articles. No multimedia features and few images, but as secondary content the collection is strong.
Resource Type: General Reference

****The Camelot Project
www.lib.rochester.edu/camelot/cphome.stm

"The Camelot Project" at the University of Rochester is good resource for information on the Arthurian age. The site offers a nice blend of images, links, and bibliographies. Go straight to the FAQs for a quick overview of Arthurian legends.
Resource Type: General Reference

****The Bayeux Tapestry
www.hastings1066.com/

This is a visually rich site that provides plenty of color photos of the tapestry as well as explanatory text. Great way to present the Tapestry to students.
Resource Type: Virtual Tour

****Wars of Independence
www.bbc.co.uk/history/scottishhistory/independence/index.shtml

This BBC Web site includes a helpful overview of the Anglo-Scottish conflict plus detailed biographies of William Wallace and Robert the Bruce.
Resource Type: General Reference

****The Gutenberg Bible at the Ranson Center
www.hrc.utexas.edu/exhibitions/permanent/gutenberg/

The Harry Ransom Humanities Research Center at the University of Texas at Austin has created this engaging site about the Bible and the printing process. Of special note is the Anatomy of a Page section where varied pages in the Gutenberg Bible are explored and explained.
Resource Type: General Reference; Primary Source Collection

****Church and State
www.bbc.co.uk/history/trail/church_state/

This engaging BBC site focuses on the development of the Church and State in Britain and is organized under four main headings: Monarchs and Leaders, Nations, Church and Reformation, and Documents. Of special note for teachers are the activities and quizzes.
Resource Type: General Reference; Course Model

****Battle of Hastings 1066
http://battle1066.com/index.html

This mammoth Web site contains 950,000 words and over 300 graphics, images, and pictures. The contents are well organized. The site answers fundamental questions: Why did the Battle Happen?, The Buildup to the Battle, Harold's Battle Force, William's Battle Force, The Battle, The Aftermath, and Norman Rule After 1066. Clear and informative site.
Resource Type: General Reference; Image Collection

****Secrets of the Norman Invasion
www.secretsofthenormaninvasion.com/

An avid Norman enthusiast has put together a popular site with articles, documents, and images about the landing of the Normans in England. In it he depicts and explains the Bayeux Tapestry. He also provides several Domesday maps that relate to the area where the Normans landed in 1066.
Resource Type: General Reference; Primary Source Collection

****Vikings: The North Atlantic Saga
www.mnh.si.edu/vikings/

This Smithsonian Institution National Museum of Natural History site was created around an exhibit commemorating the 1000th anniversary of the Viking landing in the New World (see Figure 9.2). Besides a cool Flash-generated introduction, the site contains extensive documentation on the contents of the exhibit, as well as a Virtual Viking Voyage—a multimedia presentation including 3-D animations of ship-building, runes and sagas, video interviews with leading experts in the field, and detailed histories of Viking settlements and journeys from Scandinavia to Newfoundland.
Resource Type: General Reference; Multimedia Presentation

****ORB: The Online Reference Book for Medieval Studies
www.the-orb.net/

This is an academic site, geared towards medieval scholars. Among its best features are a medieval encyclopedia and annotated links to online reference, teaching, and translation resources. Note: Last update was in 2002.
Resource Type: General Reference

Figure 9.2: Vikings: The North Atlantic Saga

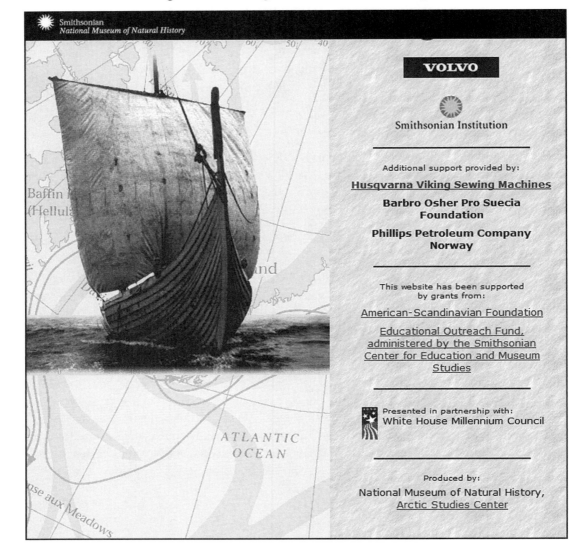

****BBC History: The Norman Conquest
www.bbc.co.uk/history/british/normans/

This BBC site offers background, articles, multimedia, a chat forum, and other information regarding the Norman Conquest. There are interesting presentations, such as the War and Technology Gallery, The Bayeux Tapestry, and a Battle of Hastings animated game.
Resource Type: General Reference; Course Model

****Art History Resources on the Web
http://witcombe.sbc.edu/ARTHLinks.html

Professor Chris Witcombe of Sweet Briar College has perhaps the best-organized collection of art history links on the Web. Check out the Art in Late Antiquity, Early Medieval Art, and Gothic Art sections. A good starting point for art history research.
Resource Type: Art History

****Web Gallery of Art
www.wga.hu/index.html

"Web Gallery of Art" is a virtual museum and searchable database of European painting and sculpture of the Gothic, Renaissance, and Baroque periods (1150–1800). It contains over 15,400 reproductions. Biographies, commentaries, and guided tours are available. Furthermore, a search engine allows you to find pictures in the collection using various search criteria. The guided tours make it easier to visit the Gallery and to understand the artistic and historical relationship between the artworks and artists included in the collection.
Resource Type: Art History

****The Ecole Initiative
http://www2.evansville.edu/ecoleweb/

This hypertext of Early Church history features documents, images, a glossary, and a chronology. Among the best features of the site are the numerous topical essays as well and extensive links to images and translated documents. Unfortunately, some external links are broken and it is not clear if the site is actively maintained.
Resource Type: General Reference

****De Re Militari: The Society for Medieval Military History
www.deremilitari.org/

This an academic association, representing scholars interested in medieval warfare. It offers an online resources section, with articles, primary texts and book reviews. You can some book chapters here as well. Check the What's New section for the latest additions to the site.
Resource Type: General Reference

***The Britannia Lexicon
www.britannia.com/history/resource/gloss.html

"The Britannia Lexicon" offers a glossary of "strange" words used during the Middle Ages. It is helpful if you need the meaning of terms associated with the period. Alphabetical listing, but no search function unfortunately.
Resource Type: General Reference

****Voices of the Powerless: Norman Conquest in York
www.bbc.co.uk/radio4/history/voices/voices_york.shtml

This site is a companion to the BBC radio show in which Melvyn Bragg explores the lives of the ordinary working men and women of Britain at six critical moments over the last 1,000 years. This particular audio-episode deals with the decade following the conquest of the north of England and "so-called harrying of the north." These episodes are an intriguing glimpse into British social history.
Resource Type: Multimedia Presentation

Voices of the Powerless: The Peasants' Revolt
www.bbc.co.uk/radio4/history/voices/voices_revolt.shtml

This audio-episode deals with the Peasants' Revolt that began in the Essex village of Fobbing in May 1381.
Resource Type: Multimedia Presentation

****Mr. Dowling's Electronic Passport: Middle Ages
www.mrdowling.com/703middleages.html

"Mr. Dowling's Electronic Passport" helps kids browse the world in his virtual classroom. He introduces young readers to many civilizations with clear explanations, engaging graphics for kids, and "cool links." His study guides, homework assignments, and exams are free and available for you to print or to edit.
Resource Type: General Reference; Course Model

***BBC History: Battle of Hastings Video
www.bbc.co.uk/history/interactive/audio_video/

This engaging video is from Simon Schama's *A History of Britain*. Play episode 2: The Battle of Hastings.
Resource Type: Multimedia Presentation

BBC History: Black Death Video
www.bbc.co.uk/history/interactive/audio_video/

Play a clip from 'King Death'—episode 5. In this episode, the Black Death sweeps through Britain, claiming 300 victims a day in London alone.
Resource Type: Multimedia Presentation

BBC History: Blood of the Vikings Video
www.bbc.co.uk/history/interactive/audio_video/

In *Blood of the Vikings*, Julian Richards investigates Viking Britain using archaeological evidence and the latest genetics research.
Resource Type: Multimedia Presentation

***The Catholic Encyclopedia
www.newadvent.org/cathen/index.html

"The Catholic Encyclopedia" is a good introductory resource. It features short bios on numerous historic individuals associated with the Catholic Church.
Resource Type: General Reference

Medieval Europe Lesson Plans, Teacher Guides, Activities, and More

Mr. Donn's Middle Ages History Page
http://worldhistory.mrdonn.org/middleages.html

Don Donn of the Corkran (Maryland) Middle School provides a complete teaching unit with 17 daily lesson plans and unit test for 6th-graders. There are also links to multiple K–12 lesson plans and activities.
Resource Type: Lesson or Activity
Grade Level: LS, MS

BBC History Games: Anglo Saxon Coins
www.bbc.co.uk/history/ancient/anglo_saxons/launch_gms_saxon_coins.shtml

BBC has devised a fun way for kids to learn about Anglo-Saxon coins and the stories behind them. Play 'Coins' and test your knowledge.

Resource Type: Game
Grade Level: LS, MS

BBC History: Kings and Queens Through Time
www.bbc.co.uk/history/british/launch_tl_kings_queens.shtml

This animated timeline provides a fun way to learn how to put the kings and queens of England, and later the United Kingdom, in chronological order. There are four periods to explore: The Plantagenets and the Houses of Lancaster and York, the Tudors and Stuarts, and the House of Hanover, and the Windsors.
Resource Type: Test or Quiz
Grade Level: LS, MS, HS

BBC History: Build a Medieval Arch animation
www.bbc.co.uk/history/british/launch_ani_build_arch.shtml

Play this educational animation to find out how medieval masons built cathedral arches—without the benefits of modern technology.
Resource Type: Multimedia Presentation
Grade Level: MS, HS

Norman Conquest School Site
www.normanconquest.co.uk/

This site has useful worksheets, quizzes, and activities for the students.
Resource Type: Lesson or Activity
Grade Level: LS, MS

Using Computer Technology to Teach Medieval Texts
www.unc.edu/student/orgs/cams/techtoteach/

This site focuses more on general strategies than on specific activities. The site has five main parts: Creating Hypertext, On-line Discussions, CD-ROMs, Internet Resources, and Sample Lesson Plans. There are a few sample lesson plans.
Resource Type: General Reference; Course Model
Grade Level: HS, College

Course Models: Medieval Europe
www.history.ctaponline.org/center/hsscm/index.cfm?Page_Key=1496

Part of the California History-Social Science content standards, this comprehensive annotated course includes background information, focus questions, pupil activities and handouts, assessment, and references to books, articles, Web sites, literature, audiovisual programs, and historic site. Grade 7.
Resource Type: Course Model
Grade Level: MS

The Medieval Arms Race
www.pbs.org/wgbh/nova/lostempires/trebuchet/race.html

A PBS "Nova" site, it describes and illustrates some of the major weapons and strategies used in what became a medieval arms race. Clear, easy to follow, and appropriate for young students.

Resource Type: Lesson or Activity
Grade Level: LS, MS

Destroy the Castle

www.pbs.org/wgbh/nova/lostempires/trebuchet/destroy.html

This animated Nova Science activity challenges students to engineer a trebuchet that can knock down a castle wall. Fun and engaging.
Resource Type: Lesson or Activity
Grade Level: LS, MS

The Black Plague

http://scorescience.humboldt.k12.ca.us/fast/teachers/Plague/Pindex.html

In this simulation activity, visitors travel as a Pilgrim or as a Trader/Voyager. In doing so they learn about the plague in modern times as the Middle Ages. Travelers can keep track of what they are find out along the way. Engaging SCORE activity for middle schoolers.
Resource Type: Game
Grade Level: MS

Battle of Hastings Essay Outline

www.spartacus.schoolnet.co.uk/NORQ2.htm

In this well-structured Spartacus activity, students develop an essay about the Battle of Hastings Spartacus provides resources and even topic sentences to help students along.
Resource Type: Lesson or Activity
Grade Level: MS

Jousting Game

www.tudorbritain.org/joust/

Kids will enjoy this simulation that provides them with an opportunity to take part in a joust.
Resource Type: Game
Grade Level: LS, MS

Western Civilization: A Social and Cultural History

http://wps.prenhall.com/hss_king_westernciv_2/0,6774,207260-,00.html

The online study companion to Margaret King's *Western Civilization: A Social and Cultural History* has many excellent teaching resources: Chapter learning objectives, online quizzes, writing activities, essay questions, Web links, built-in search engines, and faculty modules that include PowerPoint outlines, presentation graphics, lecture hints, and activities. Clink on Jump to . . . at the top and pick by chapter.
Resource Type: Course Model
Grade Level: HS, College

A Medieval Cartoon

www.learningcurve.gov.uk/snapshots/snapshot12/snapshot12.htm

A good primary-source activity, students try to unravel the meaning of this medieval cartoon. From the National Archives Learning Curve.

Resource Type: Lesson or Activity
Grade Level: MS

BBC History: Ages of Treasure Timeline

www.bbc.co.uk/history/archaeology/excavations_techniques/launch_tl_ages_treasure.shtml

This engaging animated timeline of archaeological sites and treasures is a great way to test yourself on eras and events from the Palaeolithic to the Norman Conquest.

Resource Type: Multimedia Presentation; Game
Grade Level: MS, HS

The World's History: Establishing World Trade Routes, 1100–1500

http://cwx.prenhall.com/bookbind/pubbooks/spodek2/chapter12/deluxe.html

The online guide to Howard Spodek's *The World's History* is an excellent teaching resource and features quizzes (multiple-choice questions, true/false questions, interactive review questions), primary sources, maps, a bulletin board, a live chat, Web links, and faculty resources for each chapter/topic.

Resource Type: Course Model
Grade Level: HS, College

Medieval England

www.historylearningsite.co.uk/Year%207.htm

This "History Learning Site" resource offers an impressive number of hypertexted essays, many accompanied by photos, on various medieval England topics. They represent teaching materials for younger audiences. Topics include the Battle of Hastings, the Bayeux Tapestry, castles, feudalism, the lifestyle of the medieval peasant, the Domesday Book, the medieval church, the Magna Carta, the Black Death, the Crusades, and much more.

Resource Type: Lesson or Activity
Grade Level: LS, MS

Castles

www.schoolshistory.org.uk/Castles.htm

"Schools History" is a great resource for history lessons and various teaching resources. This section provides a brief introduction to the development of Castles and fortifications. It covers Roman fortifications in Britain, Anglo-Saxon forts, Stone Keep Castles, and features images to illustrate key changes.

Resource Type: Lesson or Activity
Grade Level: LS, MS

BBC History Trail: Church and State

www.bbc.co.uk/history/trail/church_state/

This great teaching site focuses on the development of the Church and State in Britain and is organized under four main headings: Monarchs and Leaders, Nations, Church and Reformation, and Documents. Of special note for teachers are the activities and quizzes. In this "trail" students discover how the Palace of Westminster and other churches reveal the history of Britain.

Resource Type: Lesson or Activity
Grade Level: MS

AP European History Web Links and Primary Source Documents
www.historyteacher.net/APEuroCourse/APEuro_Main_Weblinks_Page.htm

Historyteacher.net offers thousands of links to great Web sites and primary source documents. Just pick a topic and go to that page where you will find a large number of links that can be used for research and study. You will also be directed to in-depth, detail-linked class assignments on several topics.
Resource Type: Course Model
Grade Level: HS, College

Web Guide for AP World History
http://apcentral.collegeboard.com/apc/public/courses/teachers_corner/4484.html

"Web Guide for AP World History" includes some 500 Web links that are categorized and annotated to compliment the AP World History course. The Web Guide is organized into five sections: Foundations, 1000–1450, 1450–1750, 1750–1914, and 1914–present. The thematic and analytical sections follow the structure of the AP World History course. Visitors must register through the College Board. This is a must-stop if you teach the AP World History course.
Resource Type: Course Model
Grade Level: HS, College

Brief Review in Global History and Geography: Document-Based Essays and Practice Tests
www.phschool.com/curriculum_support/brief_review/global_history/essay_questions/dbq3.cfm

PH@School's "Brief Review in Global History and Geography" Web site provides multiple-choice questions from actual Regents exams. These are very useful to practice test-taking skills on document-based essay questions (DBQs). There is even the option of e-mailing answers directly to a teacher for review. When Cultures Collide explores cultural diffusion among Medieval Europe, China, and the Middle East.
Resource Type: Test or Quiz
Grade Level: HS

RENAISSANCE AND REFORMATION

****Renaissance
www.learner.org/exhibits/renaissance/

This informative Annenberg/CPB site introduces the visitor to the intellectual, political, technological, and economic forces that drove cultural rebirth in Europe, and in Italy in particular. There are five sections: Out of the Middle Ages, Exploration and Trade, Printing and Thinking, Symmetry, Shape, Size, and Focus on Florence. Out of the Middle Ages covers the plague, a new middle class, and the resurgence of cities. Exploration and Trade discusses the beginning of trade in the period and the impact of explorers. Printing and Thinking focuses on the demand for books, the emergence of humanism, and how thinking changed in the Renaissance. Symmetry, Shape, Size covers proportions in architecture, as well as painting and music. This interactive site also has a role-playing trade game and a learning module. Related Resources include Web links and book recommendations.
Resource Type: General Reference; Lesson or Activity

****World Cultures to 1500: Early Modern Italian Renaissance
www.wsu.edu/~dee/REN/REN.HTM

This online course by Professor Thomas Hooker, based at Washington State University, offers a terrific overview of Ancient and Medieval History, including the Renaissance. It offers clear and informative lecture notes, maps, a photo gallery, timelines, links to relevant sites, and more. The Early Modern Italian Renaissance topics include: The Idea of the Renaissance, The Backgrounds to the Italian Renaissance, Humanism, Renaissance Neo-Platonism, Pico della Mirandola, Niccoló Machiavelli, Leonardo da Vinci, and Architecture and Public Space. Resources include: A Gallery of the Italian Renaissance, A Timeline of the Italian Renaissance, An Atlas of the Italian Renaissance, Italian states and cities, Readings in the Italian Renaissance, Leonardo da Vinci: "The Painter," Niccoló Machiavelli: *The Prince*, Michelangelo Buonarotti, *Selected Poetry*, Pico della Mirandola: "Oration on the Dignity of Man," A Glossary of the Italian Renaissance, and Internet Resources on the Italian Renaissance.
Resource Type: General Reference; Course Model

****World Cultures to 1500: Discovery and Reformation
www.wsu.edu/~dee/REFORM/REFORM.HTM

Topics include: Reformation The Northern Renaissance, Martin Luther, Ulrich Zwingli, John Calvin, Protestant England, Counter-Reformation, and Religious Wars (Thirty Years War). Resources include: Readings in Reformation Culture, A Glossary of Reformation Terms and Concepts, Reformation and Northern Renaissance Gallery, and Internet Resources on the Reformation.
Resource Type: General Reference; Course Model

****BBC: Reformation
www.bbc.co.uk/history/british/tudors/reformation_overview_01.shtml

This clear, engaging, and interactive BBC section provides a nice introduction to the Protestant Reformation in England and offers some unique features. You can learn about Henry VIII's need for an heir that triggered the English Reformation and chart the legacy of Henry's split with Rome. (British visitors can also discover how to trace the history of their local church.) Guest scholars review the events which lead up to the introduction of a simpler Protestant faith and answers questions such as: What happened after Henry decided Rome was unnecessary? What might it have been like to live through the Reformation? So, what exactly happened, and what lasting impact did the Reformation have? In all, there is plenty of background information on the Reformation and related links, as well as special galleries devoted to English cathedrals. You can even join a discussion board. Ideal site for students.
Resource Type: General Reference

****Internet Modern History Sourcebook
www.fordham.edu/halsall/mod/modsbook.html

"Internet History Sourcebooks" are wonderful collections of public domain and copy-permitted historical texts for educational use by Paul Halsall. The site and its documents are well organized and the breadth of materials is impressive. "Internet Modern History

Sourcebook" contains thousands of sources in dozens of categories. Subjects covered include the Late Middle Ages, the Italian Renaissance, and the Early Reformation, as well as dozens of other topics. Note: Some external links are broken as the site does not appear to be actively maintained.

Resource Type: Primary Source Collection

****The End of Europe's Middle Ages
www.ucalgary.ca/applied_history/tutor/endmiddle/

The University of Calgary's "End of Europe's Middle Ages" is a very useful overview for those who wish to study the Renaissance, Reformation, and Early Modern periods. It is really geared at beginners, or those who lack background in medieval European history. The site is essentially a series of well-organized chapters that summarize the economic, political, religious and intellectual environment of the fourteenth and fifteenth centuries. Section titles are: Economy, Feudal Institutions, New Monarchies, Holy Roman Empire, Italy's City-States, Eastern Europe, Ottoman Turks, The Church, Literature, Intellectual Life, Visual Arts, and Music. In each section there are useful internal links to definitions of historical terms as well as external links to supplemental primary sources.

Resource Type: General Reference

****Printing: Renaissance & Reformation
www.sc.edu/library/spcoll/sccoll/renprint/renprint.html

"Printing: Renaissance & Reformation" is part of "An Exhibit for History 101: European Civilization I," a course offered at the University of South Carolina. Originally exhibited in fall 1995 at the Thomas Cooper Library, the items in this exhibit of early printing are more than four hundred years old and each is accompanied by concise explanatory text.

Reference Type: General Reference

****Center for Reformation and Renaissance Studies
www.crrs.ca/

Hosted at the University of Toronto, the CRRC is a research center with a library devoted to the study of the period from approximately 1350 to 1700. Its Web site contains links to sites useful for researchers working in the Renaissance and the Reformation and more. It offers FICINO, an international electronic seminar and bulletin board for the circulation and exchange of information about the Renaissance and Reformation. There are also exhibitions from its Rare Book collections, such as Music in Medieval and Early Modern Europe and Textual Conversations—interactions between Renaissance authors, printers, readers and texts. There are even two fully searchable databases containing information from approximately 170 prompt-books for productions of Shakespeare's *Romeo and Juliet*.

Resource Type: General Reference; Primary Source Collection

****Investigating the Renaissance
www.artmuseums.harvard.edu/Renaissance/index.html

This interesting Harvard University Art Museum site uses digital imaging techniques to examine three Renaissance paintings: Portrait of a Man, The Virgin and Child, and The Last

Judgement. The site explains and demonstrates how Infrared light, ultraviolet light and X-rays can provide valuable information on a painting's condition, on earlier stages of its production, and on later alterations. Very impressive site.
Resource Type: Multimedia Presentation

****Turning the Pages
www.bl.uk/onlinegallery/ttp/ttpbooks.html

"Turning the Pages" is an award-winning and impressive interactive display system developed by The British Library. Visitors are able to virtually "turn" the pages of manuscripts in a realistic way, using touch-screen technology and animation. There are currently 15 treasures on display in "Turning the Pages," including the Leonardo Notebook. Most of the pages in the Notebook were written by Leonardo in 1509, but cover much of his career and range in topics from mechanics to the flight of birds. A great multimedia presentation.
Resource Type: Multimedia Presentation

****Mr. Dowling's Electronic Passport: Renaissance
www.mrdowling.com/704renaissance.html

"Mr. Dowling's Electronic Passport" helps kids browse the world in his virtual classroom. He introduces students to many civilizations with clear explanations, engaging graphics for kids, and "cool links." His study guides, homework assignments and exams are free and available for you to print or to edit. Renaissance topics are: The Dawn of a New Age, Humanism, Gutenberg, City-States in Italy, The Medicis, Social Levels, Renaissance Art, The Renaissance Spreads, Machiavelli, Exploration, and Magellan.
Resource Type: General Reference; Lesson or Activity

****The Digital Michelangelo Project
http://graphics.stanford.edu/projects/mich/

Researchers from Stanford University and the University of Washington are attempting to advance the technology of 3-D scanning and help humanities studies by creating a digital archive of some important cultural artifacts. The project focuses on some of Michelangelo's sculptures, including the famous David statue. Check out two photographic essays about a physical replica of the David, and download ScanView, a program that lets you "fly around" models of Michelangelo's statues. Impressive and engaging.
Resource Type: Multimedia Presentation; Academic Research

****Art History Resources on the Web
http://witcombe.sbc.edu/ARTHLinks.html

Professor Chris Witcombe of Sweet Briar College has perhaps the best-organized collection of art history links on the Web. His Renaissance links are divided into two sections, 15th-Century Renaissance Art and 16th-Century Renaissance Art. Topics include: Examples of Renaissance art, Special Topics (via the Metropolitan Museum of Art's Timeline of Art History), and Artists in 14th, 15th, and 16th Century Northern Europe, Spain and Italy (via the Web Gallery of Art). A good starting point for research.
Resource Type: Art History

****The Metropolitan Museum of Art Presents Timeline of Art History
www.metmuseum.org/toah/splash.htm

This interactive timeline is a chronological, geographical, and thematic exploration of the history of art from around the world, as illustrated by the Metropolitan Museum of Art's collection. Each timeline page includes representative art from the Museum's collection, a chart of time periods, a map of the region, an overview, and a list of key events. The timelines, accompanied by world, regional, and sub-regional maps, provide a linear outline of art history, and allow visitors to compare and contrast art from around the globe at any time in history. Europe 1400–1600 includes coverage of Renaissance Florence and central Italy, Renaissance Venice and northern Italy, Rome and southern Italy, and the Low Countries. First launched in 2000, the Timeline now extends from prehistory (20,000 B.C.) to the present day.
Resource Type: Art History

****Web Gallery of Art
www.wga.hu/index.html

"Web Gallery of Art" is a virtual museum and searchable database of European painting and sculpture of the Gothic, Renaissance, and Baroque periods (1150–1800). It contains over 15,400 reproductions. Biographies, commentaries, and guided tours are available. Furthermore, a search engine allows you to find pictures in the collection using various search criteria. The guided tours make it easier to visit the Gallery and to understand the artistic and historical relationship between the artworks and artists included in the collection.
Resource Type: Art History

****Medici: Godfathers of the Renaissance
www.pbs.org/empires/medici/

This PBS site shows how the Renaissance unfolded through key dates of the Medici family, as well as the Church, politics and culture. There is an overview of the Renaissance, profiles of the Medici leaders, a chart of the Medici family tree, an interactive timeline, an interactive tour of Florence, a quiz to see which Renaissance figure you most resemble, a reading list, and links. You can also see great art from the Renaissance. Engaging site for high school students in particular.
Resource Type: Multimedia Presentation; Art History

****The Medici Archive Project
www.medici.org/

"The Medici Archive Project" provides fully searchable on-line database of historical data in the Medici Granducal Archive. The Project contains almost three million letters online. There is a helpful essay that explains the importance of the document in question. A valuable site for researchers.
Resource Type: Primary Source Collection

****Leonardo da Vinci: Master Draftsman
www.metmuseum.org/special/Leonardo_Master_Draftsman/draftsman_splash.htm

This comprehensive site by the Metropolitan Museum of Art accompanies an exhibit of drawings by Leonardo da Vinci. The drawings can be examined closely with the help of a zoom

feature and the site includes audio commentary, a scholarly bibliography, an introductory essay, and even a discourse on da Vinci's left-handedness. Impressive and detailed site.
Resource Type: Multimedia Presentation; Art History

****Luminarium: 16th century Renaissance English Literature
www.luminarium.org/lumina.htm

"Luminarium" contains searchable texts and supplemental materials for Medieval, Renaissance, and seventeenth-century British literature. For each author listed there is a set of links (mostly external) that lead to biographical information, secondary sources, texts, and more. A guestbook, a powerful search engine, and a bookstore are relatively new additions to the site. This is a valuable resource to anyone interested in Renaissance literature.
Resource Type: Primary Source Collection

****Renaissance Connection
www.renaissanceconnection.org/

"Renaissance Connection" is an Allentown Art Museum's (Allentown, Pennsylvania) interactive educational Web site and explores Renaissance visual arts and innovations. There is a collection of online activities and resources for middle school students and teachers to help visitors design their own innovations, investigate Renaissance artworks in depth, and discover how past innovations impact life today. Fun, educational site for students.
Resource Type: Multimedia Presentation; Lesson or Activity

****Treasures in Full: Gutenberg Bible
http://portico.bl.uk/treasures/gutenberg/homepage.html

At this British Library site you can learn about Gutenberg, how he produced the Bible, and the texts he printed. The Texts section allows you to view the digital versions of two slightly different copies for comparison. Other resources include a timeline, a links section, a glossary, and further reading in References.
Resource Type: General Reference; Primary Source Collection

****Treasures of the World: Mona Lisa
www.pbs.org/treasuresoftheworld/a_nav/mona_nav/mnav_level_1/3technique_monafrm.html

Part of the PBS *Treasures of the World* series, Mona Lisa is cast as a masterwork of art in an engaging story of crime and discovery. The section revolves around the Mona Lisa's disappearance in 1911, but its true focus lies in Leonardo's technique and the myth of Mona Lisa. Visitors should gain a greater appreciation of the Da Vinci masterpiece.
Resource Type: General Reference; Art History

****Michelangelo Buonarroti
http://michelangelo.com/buon/bio-index2.html?http://www.michelangelo.com/buon/bio-early.html

This biographical resource on the Renaissance artist Michelangelo Buonarroti discusses his life and achievements and offers links to many of his great works. The site has three major sections: Early Life, Mid Years, and Final Days and each section highlights key events of Michelangelo's life as well as his most important works. This is a concise and useful overview aimed at high school students.
Resource Type: General Reference

***Creating French Culture: The Path to Royal Absolutism
www.loc.gov/exhibits/bnf/bnf0001.html

"Creating French Culture: Treasures from the Bibliothèque Nationale de France" (via the Library of Congress) traces the political and cultural history of France from Charlemagne to Charles de Gaulle through more than 200 "treasures" from the Bibliothèque nationale de France. "The Path to Royal Absolutism: The Renaissance and Early 17th Century" scans the political and cultural history of France from 1498 to 1661, from Louis XII's accession to the throne to Louis XIV's assumption of power. Nice blend of text and images.
Resource Type: Multimedia Presentation

***The Cervantes Project
www.csdl.tamu.edu/cervantes/V2/index.html

"The Cervantes Project," headed by Professor Eduardo Urbina at Texas A&M University, presents the work of Cervantes in online editions. Along with a biography of Cervantes, the Cervantes Digital Library enables visitors to read full-text searchable versions of his works and there are both Spanish and English language versions of Don Quixote. The Don Quixote dictionary will help visitors reading the work in English with the classical Spanish terms.
Resource Type: Primary Source Collection

***Renaissance and Baroque Architecture: Architectural History 102
www.lib.virginia.edu/dic/colls/arh102/index.html

Professor C. W. Westfall's course on Renaissance and Baroque Architecture at the University of Virginia features a collection of over 500 topically organized images. Section include: Italy in the 15th Century—Introduction, Brunelleschi's Legacy and Beyond, Florence in the 15th Century, The Sixteenth Century—Bramante and Roman Architecture, and many more. Teachers, scholars, students, and the general public are free to use these images for educational purposes.
Resource Type: Image Collection; Art History

***Art and Artists in the Renaissance
www.arthistory.sbc.edu/artartists/renaissance.html

Professor Chris Witcombe of the Art Department at Sweet Briar College provides well-organized background information and examples on Renaissance arts and artists for classroom viewing and discussion. His brief but helpful essays address fundamental questions such What is Art? and What is an Artist? And he discusses The Renaissance and the Rise of the Artist and Renaissance art and "grazia."
Resource Type: Art History

***Artists by Movement: The High Renaissance
www.artcyclopedia.com/history/high-renaissance.html

This site provides an overview of famous Renaissance artists, most from the Italian Renaissance. See a list of famous works, and the museums in which they appear, and then study the images. Concise and informative.
Resource Type: General Reference; Art History

***Christian Classics Ethereal Library: John Calvin

www.ccel.org/c/calvin/

This site offers a concise but useful introduction to one of the most important figures of the Reformation as well as translations of the theologian's writings.
Resource Type: General Reference

***The Spiritual Program: The Protestant Reformation

www.newgenevacenter.org/west/reformation.htm

A "personal journey" by a teacher, pastor, systems analyst (and even a carpenter), this site provides a brief, clear and well organized introduction to the Protestant Reformation—from a Christian perspective. Sections include: Early Efforts at Reform of the Church, Growing Conditions for Reform, Luther precipitates the challenge, the Catholic Counter Reformation, The Wars of Religion (The Thirty Years War), the Puritan Revolution in England, and more.
Resource Type: General Reference

***Elizabeth I

www.luminarium.org/renlit/eliza.htm

Part of the "Luminarium" site, this section offers detailed information on Elizabeth I. There is an introduction to The Life of Elizabeth I by Britannia.com, The Works of Elizabeth I, Essays and Articles, an Image gallery, Additional Sources and Elizabeth I in the Bookstore. See also the section on Henry IV.
Resource Type: General Reference; Primary Source Collection

***Reformation Ink

http://homepage.mac.com/shanerosenthal/reformationink/index.html

This site serves to make "important and hard to find" primary source Reformation documents readily accessible. The Classics section is broad in scope and includes articles and links from authors spanning from the Reformation to the early twentieth century.
Resource Type: Primary Source Collection

***Oliver Cromwell's Internet Portal

www.olivercromwell.org/

If Cromwell is your topic, here is a good place to start. The Cromwell Association and the Cromwell Museum in Huntingdon have organized much relevant material under the following headings: Calendar of Key Events, Oliver Cromwell's Antecedents, Oliver Cromwell as Politician, Oliver Cromwell's Military Career, Oliver Cromwell's Views on Religion, Words Said About Oliver Cromwell, Words Said By Oliver Cromwell, English Civil Wars, and Cromwell: A Select Bibliography of Books and Articles. There is also a picture gallery.
Resource Type: General Reference; Primary Source Collection

***The Thirty Years War

www.pipeline.com/%7Ecwa/TYWHome.htm

The Web site provides a concise summary and year-by-year history of the Thirty Years War. It provides overviews of military and diplomatic developments of the Thirty Years War. There is

discussion of various phases (Bohemian, Palatinate, Danish, Swedish, and French) as well as the The Peace of Westphalia.
Resource Type: General Reference

Renaissance and Reformation Lesson Plans, Teacher Guides, Activities, and More

Renaissance Secrets
www.open2.net/renaissancesecrets/index.html

"Renaissance Secrets" is an interactive BBC Web site that explores select events of the late Middle Ages and the Renaissance and discusses the process and art of writing history. The four main topics covered at the site include Venice as a "secondhand" city, Renaissance hospitals, an assassination attempt on Elizabeth I, and Gutenberg's movable type printing. Visitors examine essays about historical evidence and knowledge and learn more about the historian's craft. An excellent site for students to learn how to "do" history.
Resource Type: General Reference; Lesson or Activity
Grade Level: MS, HS

Exploring Leonardo
www.mos.org/sln/Leonardo/LeoHomePage.html

A great site for students (grades 4–9) by the Boston Museum of Science, "Exploring Leonardo" is organized into four major learning areas (plus a resource center) and offers engaging lessons in science, art, history, and language arts. Inventor's Workshop focuses on some of Leonardo's futuristic inventions, Leonardo's Perspective introduces Leonardo's way of looking at the world and explores Renaissance techniques for representing the 3-D world on 2-D surfaces, What, Where, When? is a concise biography of Leonardo da Vinci, and Leonardo:

Figure 9.3: Exploring Leonardo

Right to Left explores Leonardo's penchant for writing in reverse. Cool interactive elements help students explore Size and Distance, Linear Perspective, Aerial Perspective and Gadget Anatomy. The site also has five lesson plans for hands-on classroom activities and three opportunities for students to communicate their ideas electronically.
Resource Type: Course Model; Lesson or Activity
Grade Level: LS, MS

Redefining the Sacred in Early Modern England
www.folger.edu/html/folger_institute/sacred/index.html

This site is drawn from the experiences of 16 college teachers who gathered at the Folger Shakespeare Library in 1998 for a collaborative investigation of the English Reformation. They focused on religious beliefs and controversies and discussed strategies for bringing that material to life in the classroom. Teachers should consult the classroom examples. These include books, manuscripts, and images reviewed in the summer institute.
Resource Type: Documents Collection; Course Model
Grade Level: MS, HS

Ye Olde Renaissance Map
www.twingroves.district96.k12.il.us/Renaissance/GeneralFiles/Map.html

This site was developed as a ThinkQuest project by teachers and students at Twin Groves Junior High School in Illinois. It is an interactive Renaissance museum that helps visitors discover towns, universities, cathedrals, and more. Try the Guild Hall project and start an apprenticeship or browse around to meet various Renaissance inhabitants of "Virtual Renaissance." Fun, engaging activity for students in grades 5–9.
Resource Type: Virtual Tour
Grade Level: MS, HS

Mrs. Donn's Ancient History Page: Renaissance and Reformation
http://members.aol.com/MrDonnHistory/World.html#REN

There are links to multiple K–12 lesson plans and activities on topics including: Age of Exploration, Medieval Times, Renaissance, Revolution, World Wars, and Ancient History.
Resource Type: Lesson or Activity
Grade Level: ES, MS, HS

The World's History: Demography and Migration, 1500–1750
http://cwx.prenhall.com/bookbind/pubbooks/spodek2/chapter14/deluxe.html

The online guide to Howard Spodek's *The World's History* features quizzes (multiple-choice questions, true/false questions, interactive review questions), primary sources, maps, a bulletin board, a live chat, Web links, and faculty resources for each chapter/topic.
Resource Type: Course Model
Grade Level: HS, College

Course Models: The Italian Renaissance
www.history.ctaponline.org/center/hsscm/index.cfm?Page_Key=1541

Part of the California History-Social Science content standards and annotated course which includes: background information, focus questions, pupil activities and handouts, assessments,

and references to books, articles, Web sites, literature, audiovisual programs, and historic sites. Grade 7.
Resource Type: Course Model
Grade Level: MS

The World's History: The Unification of World Trade, 1500–1776
http://cwx.prenhall.com/bookbind/pubbooks/spodek2/chapter13/deluxe.html

The online guide to Howard Spodek's *The World's History* features quizzes (multiple-choice questions, true/false questions, interactive review questions), primary sources, maps, a bulletin board, a live chat, Web links, and faculty resources for each chapter/topic.
Resource Type: Course Model
Grade Level: HS, College

SCIENTIFIC REVOLUTION, ENLIGHTENMENT, AND FRENCH REVOLUTION

*****Exploring the French Revolution
http://chnm.gmu.edu/revolution/

This great site is a collaboration of the Center for History and New Media (George Mason University) and the American Social History Project (City University of New York). It serves as a useful and lively introduction to the French Revolution as well as a repository of many key documents from the era (see Figure 9.4). Among its offerings are numerous essays, 245 images, 338 text documents, 13 songs, a timeline, a glossary, and short audiovisual lectures from leading historians. The site should help visitors understand the causes of the French Revolution and the reasons for its radicalization. Furthermore, there are commentaries on the French Revolution by Thomas Jefferson and other prominent Americans of the time. In all, "Exploring the French Revolution" is an engaging resource for learning and teaching about the French Revolution.
Resource Type: Multimedia Presentation; Course Model

****World Cultures to 1500: The European Enlightenment
www.wsu.edu:8080/~dee/ENLIGHT/ENLIGHT.HTM

This online course created by Professor Hooker at Washington State University offers a terrific introduction to the Enlightenment. It provides clear and informative lecture notes, a photo gallery, links to relevant sites, and more. Topics include: Pre-Enlightenment Europe, The Case of England, Seventeenth Century Enlightenment Thought, René Descartes, Blaise Pascal, The Scientific Revolution, The Eighteenth Century, The Philosophes, Jean-Jacques Rousseau, Women: Communities, Economies, and Opportunities, Absolute Monarchy and Enlightened Absolutism, and The Industrial Revolution of the Eighteenth Century. Resources include a Gallery of Seventeenth and Eighteenth Century Visual Culture, Enlightenment Reader, A Glossary of Enlightenment Terms and Concepts, and Internet Resources on the European Enlightenment. Professor Thomas Hooker argues that the Enlightenment should be dated to the new natural science of Isaac Newton, the social and political theories of thinkers such as Hobbes, the empirical psychology of John Locke, and the epistemological revolutions of Blaise Pascal and René Descartes.
Resource Type: General Reference; Course Model

Figure 9.4: Exploring the French Revolution

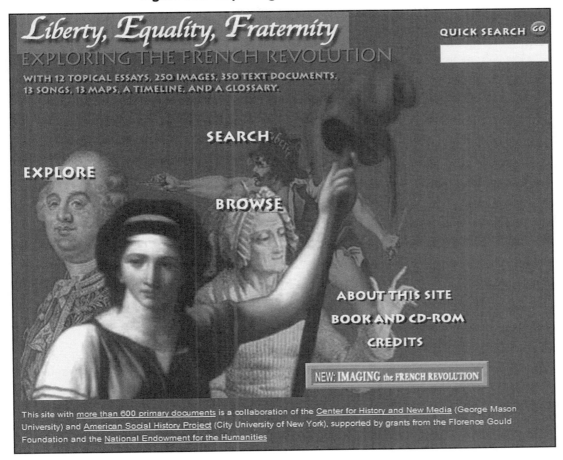

****The Galileo Project
http://galileo.rice.edu/

Hosted by Rice University, "The Galileo Project" provides detailed and thorough information about Galileo's family, career, and scientific inquiries. Included are a list of Galileo Project texts, an overview of the scientific community in the sixteenth and seventeenth centuries, Internet resources, a glossary, a bibliography, maps, a timeline, and even college projects.
Resource Type: General Reference

****Internet Modern History Sourcebook: Scientific Revolution/French Revolution
www.fordham.edu/halsall/mod/modsbook.html

"Internet History Sourcebooks" are wonderful collections of public domain and copy-permitted historical texts for educational use by Paul Halsall. The site and its documents are well organized and the breadth of materials is impressive. Subjects covered in the French Revolution section include Responses to the Revolution, Napoleon, and Napoleonic Wars. Subjects covered in the The Scientific Revolution include: Traditional Aristotelianism, New Medieval Analyses of motion, The Challenge: Astronomy in the 16th Century, Galileo Galilei: The Turning Point, Philosophy of Science: Induction/Deduction, The Creation of

Classical Physics, New Medical Theories, and Scientific Institutions. Some external links are broken as the site does not appear to be actively maintained.
Reference Type: General Reference

****The Scientific Revolution
http://web.clas.ufl.edu/users/rhatch/pages/03-Sci-Rev/SCI-REV-Home/

Professor Robert A. Hatch of the University of Florida has created a diverse and engaging introduction to the Scientific Revolution. He provides an overview and background to the Scientific Revolution, bibliographic essays, outlines, timelines, a glossary, biographies of major sources, well organized links to primary and secondary sources, manuscript and archive sources, and books online.
Resource Type: General Reference

Europe in Retrospect: The French Revolution
www.britannia.com/history/euro/1/2_2.html

This *Britannia Internet Magazine* site provides useful information on the history of Europe during the past 200 years and, in this chapter, the ideology of the French Revolution.
Resource Type: General Reference

****Napoleon
www.pbs.org/empires/napoleon/

A visually appealing and informative PBS site on Napoleon. The site offers concise summaries and expert commentary on the following topics: The Man and the Myth, Napoleon and Josephine, Politics in Napoleon's Time, and Napoleon at War. There are also interactive elements that students should find interesting, including the Interactive Battlefield Simulator: Could you win the battle of Waterloo? and video clips from the television series that this site supports. Teachers are provided with four lesson plans: Napoleon Becomes a Man of Destiny, Napoleon: Hero Or Tyrant? The Laws Live On, and Church and State. Finally, there is a discussion forum offering varied perspectives on Napoleon.
Resource Type: General Reference; Multimedia Presentation

****Napoleon.org
www.napoleon.org/en/home.asp

The comprehensive "Napoleon.org" site is produced by The Fondation Napoleon and has as its mission the encouragement of the study of and in interest in the history of the First and Second Empires. The Web site is bilingual (French/English), updated daily, and includes: a weekly newsletter, Essential Napoleon, Fun stuff (Napoleonic postcards, music, recipes, jigsaws, quizzes, wallpaper, screensaver), The Magazine (Napoleonic "What's On" events diary, Napoleonic press and book review pages, six Napoleonic itineraries, a guide to more than 100 Napoleonic museums and monuments, interviews, Napoleonic Directory), a Reading Room (20 articles in English, about 200 in French, Bibliographies, Timelines, Biographies), a Gallery including an image database (900 images) and two filmographies, a special dossier section with four "mini-sites," a collectors' corner, a general forum, a full-text search engine, and Foundation details. Well worth a visit.
Resource Type: General Reference; Primary Source Collection

****NapoleonSeries.org
www.napoleon-series.org/

A useful research site, "NapoleonSeries.org" is dedicated to the study of Napoleon Bonaparte, the Napoleonic Era, and the French Revolution. This site provides access to contemporary documents and serves as a vehicle for historians to share their work.
Resource Type: General Reference

***Catalog of the Scientific Community in the 16th and 17th Centuries
http://galileo.rice.edu/lib/catalog.html

This site offers a collection of 631 detailed biographies on members of the scientific community during the sixteenth and seventeenth centuries. The information was compiled by the late Richard S. Westfall, Professor in the Department of History and Philosophy of Science at Indiana University. There are key facts about each individual and their contributions to science. The information is concise and very well organized.
Resource Type: General Reference

Scientific Revolution, Enlightenment, and French Revolution Lesson Plans

Course Models: The French Revolution
www.history.ctaponline.org/center/hsscm/index.cfm?Page_Key=1587

Part of the California History-Social Science content standards and annotated course that includes: background information, focus questions, pupil activities and handouts, assessments, and references to books, articles, Web sites, literature, audiovisual programs, and historic sites. Grade 10.
Resource Type: Course Model
Grade Level: HS

Course Models: The Enlightenment and the Rise of Democratic Ideals
www.history.ctaponline.org/center/hsscm/index.cfm?Page_Key=1605

Part of the California History-Social Science content standards and annotated course that includes: background information, focus questions, pupil activities and handouts, assessments and references to books, articles, Web sites, literature, audiovisual programs, and historic sites. Grade 11.
Resource Type: Course Model
Grade Level: HS

The World's History: Political Revolutions in Europe and the Americas, 1688–1850
http://cwx.prenhall.com/bookbind/pubbooks/spodek2/chapter15/deluxe.html

The online guide to Howard Spodek's *The World's History* features quizzes (multiple-choice questions, true/false questions, interactive review questions), primary sources, maps, a bulletin board, a live chat, Web links, and faculty resources for each chapter/topic.
Resource Type: Course Model
Grade Level: HS

Napoleon: Church and State
www.pbs.org/empires/napoleon/n_clas/churchandstate.html

Study historic and present-day examples of the interplay between religion and government. Based on the PBS video, *Napoleon*. Grades 7–12.
Resource Type: Lesson or Activity
Grade Level: MS, HS

Hero or Tyrant?
www.pbs.org/empires/napoleon/n_clas/heroortyrant.html

Debate Napoleon's legacies and leadership style to determine if he was a hero or a tyrant. Use your view to produce a newspaper from 1815 which assesses Napoleon's career. Based on the PBS video, *Napoleon*. Grades 7–12.
Resource Type: Lesson or Activity
Grade Level: MS, HS

Napoleon Becomes a Man of Destiny
www.pbs.org/empires/napoleon/n_clas/destiny.html

Ask students to consider what has influenced their own lives and whether or not they believe in "destiny." Explore how the French Revolution, family, personality, historical events, and other factors influenced Napoleon's rise to power. Based on the PBS video, *Napoleon*. Grades 7–12.
Resource Type: Lesson or Activity
Grade Level: MS, HS

How Did the British React to July 1789?
www.learningcurve.gov.uk/snapshots/snapshot36/snapshot36.htm

Students look at primary source material from 1789, including a London newspaper report and personal letters, and then they examine the British reaction to the events that started the French Revolution. From the National Archives Learning Curve.
Resource Type: Lesson or Activity
Grade Level: MS, HS

The Laws Live On
www.pbs.org/empires/napoleon/n_clas/lawsliveon.html

Compare Napoleon's Civil Code with the U.S. Constitution and explore how guiding documents evolve over time. Based on the PBS video, *Napoleon*. Grades 7–12.
Resource Type: Lesson or Activity
Grade Level: MS, HS

EARLY MODERN BRITAIN

****Spartacus Internet Encyclopedia
www.spartacus.schoolnet.co.uk/

This Spartacus Educational resource concentrates mostly on British history from the medieval era and contains overviews, essays, images and subtopics such as: British History 1700–1900,

Slavery 1750–1870, RR 1780–1900, and Emancipation of Women 1750–1920. Offers a Tudor Encyclopedia, Biographies: 1485–1600, an Encyclopedia of British History, 1700–1900, an Encyclopedia of the English Civil War, an Encyclopedia of Politics in Britain: 1750–1950, Chartism Encyclopedia, Journalists and Newspapers 1700–1945, Parliamentary Reform 1700–1832, Peterloo Massacre, history timelines, online lessons, Web site reviews, two free online newsletters, and more. Good general resource and starting point for research.
Resource Type: General Reference

****Britannia: British History
www.spartacus.schoolnet.co.uk/

The Internet's "most comprehensive" treatment of the times, places, events and people of British history. This "Britannia" site features narrative histories of England, Wales, Scotland and London, as well as timelines, biographies, glossaries, bibliographies, historical documents, and much more. Well organized, clear, and detailed but some content is for Brittania's "British History Club" members only. (Cost is $20 per year.)
Resource Type: General Reference

****BBC: History
www.bbc.co.uk/history/

BBC's History section of the site offers an impressive array of exhibitions, activities, games, photo galleries and other resources. Major Sections of interest include: Ancient History, Archaeology, Church and State, Science and Discovery, Society and Conflict, War and Culture, and Historic Figures. There are also sections entitled Multimedia Room, Historic Figures, Timelines, Programmes, Reading Room, Talk History, For Kids, and History Trails. Great site for students.
Resource Type: General Reference; Multimedia Presentation

****The Victorian Web
www.victorianweb.org/

George P. Landow, Professor of English and Art History at Brown University, directs this broad and comprehensive resource for courses in Victorian literature. This award-winning site is full of material on Victorian era subtopics (Political, Social, Gender, Philosophy, Religion, Science, Technology, Visual Arts, Entertainment, etc.) and each section typically features a concise essay, some images, and internal links that lead to much more information. Furthermore, "Victorian Web" offers bibliographies, many related external links, and visitors are encouraged to contribute materials.
Resource Type: General Reference; Course Model

****Victoria Research Web
http://victorianresearch.org/

"Victoria Research Web" is a wide-ranging guide to research for students, teachers, and scholars pursuing interests in nineteenth-century British history and culture. The archives feature scholarly discussion by Victorianists around the world, while other features include a portal to dozens of reviews of books of nineteenth-century interest and even tips for planning a trip to Britain. Of interest to both the scholar and nonscholar.
Resource Type: General Reference

****Monuments and Dust: The Culture of Victorian London
www.iath.virginia.edu/london/

This Web site is from an international group of scholars who have put together a visual, textual, and statistical representation of Victorian London. Available are Texts, Data, Models, Maps, and Online Publications. The site includes extracts from Victorian editions of *The Times* and information on various cultural issues of the time. There is also a 3-D model of Crystal Palace, site of the Great Exhibition. An excellent research site with great multimedia features.
Resource Type: General Reference; Primary Source Collection

****Queen Victoria's Empire
www.pbs.org/empires/victoria/index.html

"Queen Victoria's Empire" by PBS is a good site to introduce students to Queen Victoria. They will learn about her family and the people and places that shaped her reign. Site features lesson plans and a game.
Resource Type: General Reference; Lesson or Activity

****Power, Politics, and Protest
www.learningcurve.gov.uk/politics/default.htm

This interactive U.K. National Archives Learning Curve exhibition investigates the political changes that took place during the nineteenth century. It contains eight different investigations of the political history of Britain between 1800 and 1914 (Radicals, Luddites, Captain Swing, Peterloo, Great Reform Act, the Chartists, White Slavery and the Suffragettes). It is an effective site for immersing students in investigative history and how individual actions impacted British history.
Resource Type: Lesson or Activity

****British Empire in 1815
www.bbc.co.uk/history/british/empire_seapower/britain_empire_01.shtml

Britain was firmly established by 1815 and, along with France, Russia, Ottoman Turkey, and China, was one of the world's great imperial powers. This BBC essay by Professor Andrew Porter explains how and features color maps, related articles, links, and more.
Resource Type: General Reference

****18th Century History
www.history1700s.com/

This site is mostly about the eventful eighteenth century and covers the period from approximately 1660 through 1840. It contains articles and resources that are useful for students and teachers. It also includes an e-text archive of various classic works available for download in text and pdf format.
Resource Type: General Reference; Lesson or Activity

****British Civil Wars
www.british-civil-wars.co.uk/

This impressive site includes timelines, 24 biographies of leading figures in the conflict, and descriptions of 62 battles and sieges. Sections include: Time Lines: chronological listings of

events during the period 1640–60, Biography: who's who in the Civil Wars and Commonwealth, Military: military history of the Civil Wars and Commonwealth. There are links to Web sites and online articles relevant to this period and a Booklist of the main reference books used in creating this site.
Resource Type: General Reference; Timeline

****EuroDocs: History of the United Kingdom—Primary Documents
http://eudocs.lib.byu.edu/index.php/History_of_the_United_Kingdom:_Primary_Documents

These links connect to Western European (mainly primary) historical documents and shed light on key historical happenings. The sources on the United Kingdom cover various chronological periods, such as 1689 to 1815 and 1816 to 1918.
Resource Type: Primary Source Collection

***English History and Heritage Guide
www.britainexpress.com/History/index.htm

Key periods in English history are covered here through informative and concise essays. Topics of interest include: The Tudor Era, Stuart Britain, Georgian Britain, The Victorian Age, and Timeline of English Monarchs. See also British Battles for accounts of some of the most influential battles fought on British soil. Each battle profile contains facts about the battle: who was involved and why, account of the battle, and results.
Resource Type: General Reference

***British Empire
www.britishempire.co.uk/

This site analyzes and describes the Empire and includes timelines, maps, photos of colonies, descriptions of battles, and more. Note that it is more of a "personal journey" than a rigorous academic site.
Resource Type: General Reference

***British Empire
http://www.ualberta.ca/~janes/EMPIRE.html

A professor at the University of Alberta in Edmonton, Canada, has created this Internet gateway. You'll find courses on various aspects of the British empire, including history and cultural studies. There are links to other sites, other gateways, libraries, writings and images of empire, and more. You can also find out about journals and discussion lists connected with British empire or Commonwealth studies. Some broken links.
Resource Type: Course Model

****Attending to Early Modern Women: Gender, Culture, and Change
www.crbs.umd.edu/atw/atw6/index.html

Compiled by an Arts and Humanities team at the University of Maryland Libraries, this site provides annotated links to useful resources for the study of women in early modern Europe (and the Americas), particularly those between the sixteenth and eighteenth centuries. The site offers searchable full-text resources, images, and sound recordings, though some resources are not free.
Resource Type: General Reference

****Early Modern Resources
www.earlymodernweb.org.uk/emr/

In 2000, a PhD student began "Early Modern Resources," a gateway site for the early modern period (c.1500–1800). It contains a wide range of links. Subject themes are Old and New Worlds; Material and symbolic cultures; Society, economy, and demography; Politics, rebellions and revolutions; Women, gender, and sexuality; Crime, law, and disorder; Religion, science, and philosophy; Literature, art, and performance; and Medicine and illness. Also includes links to General Resources, e-tests, e-journals, and more.
Resource Type: Links Collection

****The Garden, the Ark, the Tower, the Temple: Biblical Metaphors of Knowledge in Early Modern Europe
www.mhs.ox.ac.uk/gatt/

This Oxford University site describes how the biblical stories of the Garden of Eden, Noah's Ark, the Tower of Babel, and the Temple of Solomon provided explanations for the human condition and seemed to offer plans for escape into a better world. The searchable site aims to provide a broad picture of the role of biblical interpretation in early modern Europe and shows how stories from the Bible were used by early scientists and Reformation leaders as a story of the growth and decline of knowledge. Mostly text with a few hyperlinks, but there are some engaging images.
Resource Type: General Reference; Image Collection

Early Modern Britain Lesson Plans, Teacher Guides, Activities, and More

****Victorian Britain: Fair or Foul?
www.learningcurve.gov.uk/victorianbritain/default.htm

Was Victorian Britain fine or not? This well-structured U.K. National Archives Learning Curve Web site, written by teachers about aspects of life in Victorian Britain, debates this issue. Features documents, photographs, video and sound recordings.
Resource Type: Lesson or Activity Multimedia Presentation
Grade Level: MS, HS

***History Learning Site
www.historylearningsite.co.uk/

Useful student-oriented resources are offered here on many different historical periods and people, such as Tudor England, Stuart England, and Britain 1700 to 1900.
Resource Type: Lesson or Activity
Grade Level: MS, HS

History Learning Site
www.historylearningsite.co.uk/

This site covers many UK Key Stage 3 topics and contains a complete Modern World History course, together with numerous GCSE and Advanced Level History and Politics courses.
Resource Type: Course Model
Grade Level: HS

BBC History Trail: Victorian Britain

www.bbc.co.uk/history/trail/victorian_britain/index.shtml

Victorian Britain experienced dramatic economic growth but at great social cost. Discover more about the winners and losers in the race to prosperity. Find out how heroic cartoons and the novels of Charles Dickens can help the historian piece together a picture of the past.

Resource Type: Multimedia Presentation; Lesson or Activity
Grade Level: MS, HS

Tudor Hackney

www.learningcurve.gov.uk/tudorhackney/default.asp

This UK National Archives Learning Curve and Hacknet Archives site enables you to explore the world of 1601 through a virtual reality reconstruction of the Rectory House, which once stood on the west side of Hackney's Mare Street. The site uses video drama and virtual tours to provide insight into Tudor life in general, and how court and country could come to be linked in the web of intrigue and politics of the latter days of Elizabeth I.

Resource Type: Virtual Tour
Grade Level: MS, HS

Kings and Queens Through Time

www.bbc.co.uk/history/british/launch_tl_kings_queens.shtml

This Flash-based BBC website explores the Kings and Queens of England and later United Kingdom through an interactive timeline. There is also a game that tests one's ability to put monarchs in order.

Resource Type: Multimedia Presentation
Grade Level: MS, HS

Did God Really Help the English Defeat the Spanish Armada?

www.learningcurve.gov.uk/snapshots/snapshot39/snapshot39.htm

At Key Stage 3, this work fits into the unit on the Making of the United Kingdom and could be used as a straight account of events, illustrating English foreign relations. It could also be used to explore the role of propaganda in Elizabeth's reign. From the National Archives Learning Curve.

Resource Type: Lesson or Activity
Grade Level: MS

19th Century People: What Can We Tell From this Photograph?

www.learningcurve.gov.uk/snapshots/snapshot04/snapshot4.htm

Who were these people? What were they called?? The exercise aims to give pupils the opportunity to use two historical sources to answer these basic questions. From the National Archives Learning Curve. Key Stage 2–3.

Resource Type: Lesson or Activity
Grade Level: ES, MS

Past Pleasures: How Did the Victorians Have Fun?

www.learningcurve.gov.uk/snapshots/snapshot05/snapshot5.htm

Photographs and posters from Victorian Britain help students understand how leisure time was spent. From the National Archives Learning Curve. Key Stage 2–3.
Resource Type: Lesson or Activity
Grade Level: ES, MS

Great Victorian Achievements

www.bbc.co.uk/education/beyond/factsheets/victorians/victorians_home.shtml

In this BBC animation, the Victorian "train" to the twentieth century will stop and show you the great achievements of the Victorian age. When you arrive at your final destination, you can find out more about the great pioneers of the time.
Resource Type: Lesson or Activity
Grade Level: ES, MS

The Romantic Chronology

http://english.ucsb.edu:591/rchrono/

An attractive site featuring an interactive chronology of the Romance period.
Resource Type: Timeline
Grade Level: HS, College

Course Models: The Industrial Revolution

www.history.ctaponline.org/center/hsscm/index.cfm?Page_Key=1596

Part of the California History-Social Science content standards and annotated course that includes: background information, focus questions, pupil activities and handouts, assessments, and references to books, articles, Web sites, literature, audio-video programs, and historic sites. Grade 10.
Resource Type: Course Model
Grade Level: HS

A Victorian News Magazine

www.activehistory.co.uk/

Students will create a special feature news magazine that highlights Queen Victoria and her reign over England. Students will include stories about key events, people, and politics of the time. They will use proper writing techniques when creating news and feature stories as well as editorials. Magazines will focus on different decades of Victoria's life from 1819 to 1901. PBS, High School.
Resource Type: Lesson or Activity
Grade Level: HS

The Six Wives of Henry VIII

www.pbs.org/wnet/sixwives/

Meet the wives, get a portrait of life in Tudor times, explore Henry VIII and his fascinating life, access lessons and play matchmaker for the monarch himself with a fun interactive game.
Resource Type: Lesson or Activity; Game
Grade Level: ES, MS, HS

The World's History: The Industrial Revolution, 1740–1914

http://cwx.prenhall.com/bookbind/pubbooks/spodek2/chapter16/deluxe.html

The online guide to Howard Spodek's *The World's History* features quizzes (multiple-choice questions, true/false questions, interactive review questions), primary sources, maps, a bulletin board, a live chat, Web links, and faculty resources for each chapter/topic.
Resource Type: Course Model
Grade Level: HS, College

Inventions That Changed the World

www.pbs.org/empires/victoria/text.html

Students will create small group projects that illustrate the positive and negative impacts of the inventions of the Industrial Revolution, the ways this revolution shaped Victoria's reign as Queen of England, and the ways this invention contributed to the idea of a world economy.
Resource Type: Lesson or Activity
Grade Level: MS

BBC History Games: Battle of Waterloo

www.bbc.co.uk/history/british/empire_seapower/launch_gms_battle_waterloo.shtml

Play the game and take sides in the Battle of Waterloo. Then find out more about the battle, the tactics employed, and the consequences for Europe.
Resource Type: Game
Grade Level: ES, MS

BBC History Games: Elizabethan Spying

www.bbc.co.uk/history/british/tudors/launch_gms_spying.shtml

Play the game and see if you can crack the code that incriminated Mary, Queen of Scots.
Resource Type: Game
Grade Level: ES, MS

BBC History Games: Victorian Women's Rights

www.bbc.co.uk/history/british/victorians/launch_gms_womens_rights.shtml

Play the game to find out how women's rights evolved during the Victorian Age.
Resource Type: Game
Grade Level: ES, MS

BBC History: Kings and Queens Through Time

www.bbc.co.uk/history/british/launch_tl_kings_queens.shtml

In this animated timeline, you put the kings and queens of England, and later the United Kingdom, in their proper place. There are four periods to explore. The Plantagenets and the Houses of Lancaster and York are featured in the first period, the Tudors and Stuarts in the second, and the House of Hanover in the third. The timeline concludes with the Windsors.
Resource Type: Timeline
Grade Level: ES, MS

BBC History: Stephenson's Rocket Animation

www.bbc.co.uk/history/british/victorians/launch_ani_rocket.shtml

Play the animation to operate the Rocket, considered by many to be the forerunner of all steam locomotives, and a key factor in the advance of the Industrial Revolution.
Resource Type: Game
Grade Level: ES, MS

BBC History: Spinning Mill Animation

www.bbc.co.uk/history/british/victorians/launch_ani_spinning_mill.shtml

Play the animation to operate a steam-powered spinning mill.
Resource Type: Game
Grade Level: ES, MS

BBC History: The Changing British Population Animation

www.bbc.co.uk/history/british/launch_ani_population.shtml

Play the animation, and track how key events in British history have affected the size of the British population.
Resource Type: Game
Grade Level: ES, MS

BBC History: The Great Fire of London Animation

www.bbc.co.uk/history/british/civil_war_revolution/launch_ani_fire_london.shtml

View the animation to see contemporary etchings of the London skyline, showing the extent of the devastation. Afterwards, you could view the changing designs for St Paul's Cathedral, rebuilt in the aftermath of the fire.
Resource Type: Game
Grade Level: ES, MS

BBC History: The History of European Map Making Animation

www.bbc.co.uk/history/british/empire_seapower/launch_ani_mapmaking.shtml

Explore the changing European view of the world in the animated history of maps across the centuries. The Map Animation features images that are reproduced courtesy of the British Library.
Resource Type: Game
Grade Level: ES, MS

BBC History Games: The Gunpowder Plot

www.bbc.co.uk/history/british/civil_war_revolution/launch_gms_gunpowder_plot.shtml

Guy Fawkes was among a gang of Roman Catholic conspirators who wanted to blow up the House of Lords and assassinate King James VI of Scotland and I of England. As part of their plan, they stored gunpowder kegs in the cellars of the House of Lords. You must find those kegs before the fizzing fuse causes disaster!
Resource Type: Game
Grade Level: MS

Wales
www.ngfl-cymru.org.uk/7-0-0-0_vtc_vymru/7-3-0-0-ks3/40357.htm

At the Cymru's Virtual Teachers' Center, there are useful Key Stage 3 digital materials grouped under: Wales and Early Modern Britain 1500–1760 (Tudor Wales), and Wales and Industrial Britain.

Resource Type: Lesson or Activity
Grade Level: MS, HS

CHAPTER 10

Twentieth Century

GENERAL RESOURCES

*****Cold War: From Yalta to Malta
http://cnn.com/SPECIALS/cold.war/

This CNN Perspectives series explores the Cold War experience from many different angles. Included are interactive maps, rare video footage, declassified documents, biographies, picture galleries, timelines, interactive activities, a search function, book excerpts, an educator's guide and more. For instance, you can watch a video interview with George Kennan, tour a Cold War prison, play a Brinkmanship interactive game interview, and listen to an interview with Fidel Castro. Launched in September the site covers more than a 1,000 pages and was honored with a 1998 Sigma Delta Chi Award in the Online Journalism by the Society of Professional Journalists.
Resource Type: General Reference; Multimedia Presentation

****People's Century
www.pbs.org/wgbh/peoplescentury/

"People's Century" site is based on the 26-episode PBS television series and features a teacher's guide, a timeline, a thematic overview, and RealAudio excerpts. The highlights of the web site are the first-person narratives, often by ordinary people who lived through turbulent times.
Resource Type: Primary Source Collection; Lesson or Activity

****TIME Archive
www.time.com/time/magazine

TIME provides a searchable text collection of its magazine articles since 1923. An excellent source of both primary and secondary source information on the twentieth century. While there make sure to check out the *TIME* 100 of twentieth-century leaders.
Resource Type: Primary Source Collection

****Conversations With History
http://globetrotter.berkeley.edu/conversations/

In this University of California, Berkeley site, distinguished men and women from all over the world talk about their lives and their work. They reminisce about their participation in

great events in the twentieth century, and they share their perspectives on the past and reflect on what the future may hold. Guests include diplomats, statesmen, and soldiers; economists and political analysts; scientists and historians; writers and foreign correspondents; and activists and artists.
Resource Type: Oral History; Primary Source Collection

****Academy of Achievement
www.achievement.org/

"Academy of Achievement" features stories of "legendary achievers" of the twentieth century in arts, public service, sports, science, and other fields. Includes audio and video clips. Check out the Gallery of Achievement.
Resource Type: General Reference; Multimedia Presentation

****Famous Trials
www.law.umkc.edu/faculty/projects/ftrials/ftrials.htm

A professor of law at the University of Minnesota-Kansas City Law School has created an excellent Web site on famous trials. Most of these include background information on the case, biographies and photographs of trial participants, trial transcript excerpt and articles from newspapers that covered the trial. Trials from the twentieth century include: the Sacco-Vanzetti Trial (1921), Scopes Monkey Trial (1925), Scottsboro Trials (1931–37), Nuremberg Trials (1945–49), Rosenberg Trial (1951), Mississippi Burning Trial (1967), Chicago Seven Conspiracy Trial (1969–70) and the My Lai Court Martial (1970).
Resource Type: General Reference

****American Rhetoric
http://www.americanrhetoric.com

"American Rhetoric" is a massive multimedia site that contains an Online Speech Bank, Rhetorical Figures in Sound, and American Top 100 Speeches. The Online Speech Bank contains 291 active links to 5,000+ full text, audio and video (streaming) versions of public speeches, sermons, legal proceedings, lectures, debates, interviews, other recorded media events, and a declaration or two. Figures in Sound has 200+ short audio clips from well-known speeches, movies, sermons, popular songs, and sensational media events by famous (and infamous) politicians, actors, preachers, athletes, singers, and other noteworthy personalities. You'll also find significant American political speeches of the twentieth century and even Hollywood speeches. In all you'll find an impressive blend of actual and simulated historic speeches, debates, lectures, etc.
Resource Type: Multimedia Presentation; Primary Source Collection

****Historical Atlas of the 20th Century
http://users.erols.com/mwhite28/20centry.htm

An interesting and informative collection of information on the twentieth century. Atlas topics include General Trends in Living Conditions, Government, War, and Religion. Maps are often interactive, allowing you to zoom in on details. There are also essays, FAQs, and links.
Resource Type: Map

****Internet Modern History Sourcebook

www.fordham.edu/halsall/mod/modsbook.html

"Internet History Sourcebooks" are wonderful collections of public domain and copy-permitted historical texts for educational use by Paul Halsall. The site and its documents are well organized and the breadth of materials is impressive. Note: Some external links are broken as the site does not appear to be actively maintained.

Resource Type: Primary Source Collection

****20th Century History

http://history1900s.about.com/

Presents an extensive list of related sites and offers special weekly highlights. Links come with brief descriptions, but few are critically evaluated.

Resource Type: Links Collection

****Agents of Social Change

www.smith.edu/libraries/ssc

Smith College offers an online exhibit and several lesson plans drawn from its collections. The lesson plans are directed at middle and high school students and make use of both the text-based documents and visual images that can be found at the curriculum portion of the Web site. They highlight women's part in struggles for social change in the twentieth century including labor, socialism, civil liberties, peace, racial justice, urban reform, welfare rights, and women's rights.

Resource Type: Primary Source Collection; Lesson or Activity

***The 20th Century—a World History

www.fsmitha.com/h2/

"The 20th Century—a World History" is a hypertexted online book with colorful maps, recommended readings, and an index. It is written by a graduate in History from California State University.

Resource Type: General Reference

***WWW Virtual Library: International Affairs Resources

www2.etown.edu/vl/

"International Affairs Resources" is a well-organized and helpful gateway to over 2600 annotated links in international affairs, international studies, and international relations topics. It links to sites with detailed information for those interested in a global perspective. It is edited and maintained, by Wayne A. Selcher, Professor of International Studies at Elizabethtown College.

Resource Type: Links Collection

****Authentic History: Primary Resources from American Pop Culture

www.authentichistory.com/

"Authentic History" is useful as an educational tool and a digitial archive. It contains an impressive array of pictures, audio, and video from the antebellum period to the 9/11 terrorist attack. Collection is organized by decades and some include interpretive essays.

Resource Type: Primary Source Collection; Multimedia Presentation

***Historical Atlas of Europe: The Development of Europe's Modern States 1648–2001
http://home.versatel.nl/gerardvonhebel/

This site provides an overview of the political changes in Europe during the last 350 years.
Resource Type: Maps

History Net: Timeline
http://history1900s.about.com/library/time/bltime1990.htm

Timeline 1990–1999.
Resource Type: Timeline

General Resources Lesson Plans, Teacher Guides, Activities, Primary Sources, and More

Modern World History
www.johndclare.net/

A detailed review site for students of GCSE Modern World History. Includes material on the Treaty of Versailles, League of Nations, Road to WWII, Cold War, Russia 1917–1941 and Britain and World War II. Helpful revision sheets and essays on some 30 topics make this a useful study site.
Resource Type: Course Model
Grade Level: HS

History 20
www.sasked.gov.sk.ca/docs/history20/index.html

The Saskatchewan Social Studies Curriculum has developed a "resource hot sheet" dealing with topics identified in the History 20 (Modern World History) curriculum. The resource hot sheets can act as a primary or secondary reading or to assist in classroom discussions of a variety of topics. Each page has been supported with appropriate visual images, and where possible, first person accounts by individuals who were present during the event. In addition, there is a number of multimedia-learning objects including sound bites, mini-movies and Flash items.
Resource Type: Course Model
Grade Level: MS, HS

20th Century Heroes and Villains
www.learningcurve.gov.uk/heroesvillains/

This interactive UK National Archives Learning Curve provides documents and asks students to judge whether the figure in question is 'a hero or a villain?' The figures are: Winston Churchill, John F. Kennedy, Josef Stalin, Harry S. Truman, and Benito Mussolini.
Resource Type: Lesson or Activity
Grade Level: HS, College

GCSE History Pages
www.historygcse.org/

Main features of this UK site include interactive tests and quizzes, revision tips, practice exam papers with mark-schemes for self-assessment, revision notes, and structured lessons. Review site for students of GCSE Modern World History.
Resource Type: Course Model
Grade Level: HS

History Learning Site
www.historylearningsite.co.uk/

This site covers many UK Key Stage 3 topics and contains a complete Modern World History course, together with numerous GCSE and Advanced Level History and Politics courses.
Resource Type: Course Model
Grade Level: HS

Historical Presents: Uncovering Time Capsules of the Twentieth Century
www.nytimes.com/learning/teachers/lessons/20030519monday.html

In this *New York Times* lesson, students research events, trends, and phenomena of specific years in the twentieth century, then design "time capsules" to commemorate those years.
Resource Type: Lesson or Activity
Grade Level: MS, HS

The World's History: Technologies of Mass Production and Destruction, 1914–1990s
http://cwx.prenhall.com/bookbind/pubbooks/spodek2/chapter18/deluxe.html

The online guide to Howard Spodek's *The World's History* features quizzes (multiple-choice questions, true/false questions, interactive review questions), primary sources, maps, a bulletin board, a live chat, Web links, and faculty resources for each chapter/topic.
Resource Type: Course Model
Grade Level: HS

The World in Uncertain Times, 1950–Present Practice Test
www.phschool.com/curriculum_support/brief_review/us_history/tests.html?unit=7&number=35

High school level multiple-choice quiz on Cold War America from Prentice Hall.
Resource Type: Test or Quiz
Grade Level: HS

The World in Uncertain Times, 1950–Present Document-Based Essay
www.phschool.com/curriculum_support/brief_review/us_history/essay_questions/unit7.cfm

This Prentice Hall DBQ is designed to test your ability to work with historical documents and is based on the accompanying documents (1–6).
Resource Type: Lesson or Activity; Primary Source Collection
Grade Level: HS

WORLD WAR I

****Encyclopaedia of the First World War
www.spartacus.schoolnet.co.uk/FWW.htm

The Spartacus encyclopaedia provides a basic, but informative, overview of the following topics: Chronology, Outbreak of War, Countries, Allied Armed Forces, Important Battles, Technology, Political Leaders, British Home Front, Military Leaders, Life in the Trenches, Trench System, Trench War, Soldiers, War Heroes, Medals, War at Sea, War in the Air, Pilots, Aircraft, War Artists, Cartoonists and Illustrators, War Poets, Journalists, Newspapers and

Journals, Novelists, Women at War, Women's Organisations, Weapons and Machines, Inventors and the War, Theatres of War, and War Statistics.
Resource Type: General Reference

****The World War I Document Archive
www.lib.byu.edu/~rdh/wwi/index.html

"World War I Document Archive" from Brigham Young University is an important source of links to WWI primary documents, such as treaties and personal recollections.
Resource Type: Primary Source Collection

****The Great War and the Shaping of the 20th Century
www.pbs.org/greatwar/

This PBS site includes interviews, maps, an interactive timeline, education resources, and brief summaries of the series episodes. Among the multimedia highlights are dramatized audio recordings of letters and poems written by combatants and non-combatants, and streaming video of archival footage taken during World War I. There is also a section where historians comment on how the Great War is still having an effect upon the world.
Resource Type: Multimedia Presentation; Lesson or Activity

****Age of Hope
www.pbs.org/wgbh/peoplescentury/episodes/ageofhope/

"People's Century" site is based on the 26-episode PBS television series and features a teacher's guide, a timeline, a thematic overview, and RealAudio excerpts. The highlights of the Web site are the first-person narratives, and this section includes interesting first-hand accounts of life in the early twentieth century.
Resource Type: Primary Source Collection

****The Great War Society 1914–1918
www.worldwar1.com/tgws

An informative site for students and researchers that features numerous links to WWI topics. "The Great War Society" was founded by a group of researchers at the Hoover Institution of War.
Resource Type: General Reference; Links Collection

****Hellfire Corner—The Great War: 1914–1918
www.fylde.demon.co.uk/welcome.htm

"Hellfire Corner" is an informative English perspective on WWI battles. It is produced by an author of military books and contains articles, remembrances, general interest information, links and more.
Resource Type: General Reference

****Trenches on the Web
www.worldwar1.com/

Informative multimedia site with articles, a library, a timeline, and a searchable database. Teachers and students should go directly to the Learning and Research Center. Has an extensive collection of links.
Resource Type: General Reference

****Paths of Memory

www.lescheminsdelamemoire.net/lcdlm.asp

This multilingual European museum site has well-organized sections on the First World War, Spanish Civil War, and the Second World War. Use the interactive map of Europe to learn how about military operations and related information in select European countries.

Resource Type: General Reference; Multimedia Presentation

****David Lloyd George

www.llgc.org.uk/ardd/dlgeorge/dlg0002.htm

David Lloyd George became the British Prime Minister at the height of WWI and held that office until 1922. This image-rich exhibition commemorates the 50th anniversary of his death and focuses on both public and private aspects of his life. It features an extensive image collection.

Resource Type: General Reference; Image Collection

***Eyewitness to History: World War One

http://www.eyewitnesstohistory.com/w1frm.htm

This site features eyewitness accounts of a few key WWI events, such as the assassination of Francis Ferdinand and a German U-Boat attack. Excellent primary sources.

Resource Type: Primary Source Collection

World War I Lesson Plans, Teacher Guides, Activities, and More

Life in the Trenches

www.activehistory.co.uk/games/trenches/frameset.htm

This is a decision-making activity where students play the role of a British soldier in 1914. You must be a paid subscriber in order to access material.

Resource Type: Lesson or Activity
Grade Level: MS

The Great War

www.learningcurve.gov.uk/greatwar/

This interactive UK National Archives Learning Curve presentation provides seven different investigations that will tell the story of the Great War—the First World War, 1914–1918. The sources in these investigations have been chosen to highlight the role of important events, or communications from individuals that were key to the war.

Resource Type: Lesson or Activity
Grade Level: General Reference

World War I: A Soldiers Record—What Can You Tell?

www.learningcurve.gov.uk/snapshots/snapshot38/snapshot38.htm

This snapshot focuses on a Scottish World War I soldier, Donald Campbell. The main task requires pupils to decide whether he was a 'good solider.' This snapshot does not give a broad history of World War I; instead, it personalizes the conflict by helping students find out what happened to one solider. (This snapshot can form part of studies for Scheme of Work Unit 18,

and could also be a valuable activity for Modern World History classes investigating the First World War.)
Resource Type: Lesson or Activity
Grade Level: MS

BBC History: Western Front Animation
www.bbc.co.uk/history/worldwars/wwone/launch_ani_western_front.shtml

Pinpoint key locations along the Western Front, watch the general movements of both sides and view the battles of Ypres, Verdun and the Somme in detail.
Resource Type: Multimedia Presentation
Grade Level: HS

Britain 1906–1918
www.learningcurve.gov.uk/britain1906to1918/

This interactive UK National Archives Learning Curve exhibition provides six galleries studying the varied life of the British people in 1906–1918, plus a seventh gallery devoted to review and revision.
Resource Type: Lesson or Activity
Grade Level: MS, HS

BBC History Trials: Wars and Conflicts
www.bbc.co.uk/history/trail/wars_conflict/

Discover more about the personal experience of battle. For instance, make a virtual visit to the Somme and follow the development of weapons through the ages.
Resource Type: Virtual Tour
Grade Level: MS

BBC History: World War I Movies—The Human Experience
www.bbc.co.uk/history/worldwars/wwone/#the_human_experience

This BBC multimedia production involves contemporary photographs, dramatised diary readings and interviews with veterans exploring key themes of World War I. Each chapter may take a couple of minutes to download the first time you view it, so please be patient.
Resource Type: Multimedia Presentation
Grade Level: MS, HS

Fallen Heroes
http://fallenheroes.moonfruit.com/

This site is from the History Department of Tideway School in New Haven, East Sussex and is part of the National Curriculum for England and Wales. The highlight of this site is a visual tour of battlefields of the Western Front completed by students and teachers of Tideway School and reflects their Great War research.
Resource Type: Lesson or Activity
Grade Level: MS

Western Civilization: The Western Imperium
http://wps.prenhall.com/hss_king_westernciv_2/0,6774,208818-,00.html

The online study companion to Margaret King's *Western Civilization: A Social and Cultural History* has many features: Chapter learning objectives, online quizzes, writing activities, essay questions, Web links, built-in search engines, and faculty modules that include Power-Point outlines, presentation graphics, and lecture hints and activities.
Resource Type: Course Model
Grade Level: HS

Western Civilization: The Mighty Are Fallen
http://wps.prenhall.com/hss_king_westernciv_2/0,6774,208959-,00.html

The online study companion to Margaret King's *Western Civilization: A Social and Cultural History* has many features: Chapter learning objectives, online quizzes, writing activities, essay questions, Web links, built-in search engines, and faculty modules that include Power-Point outlines, presentation graphics, and lecture hints and activities.
Resource Type: Course Model
Grade Level: HS

The League of Nations Photo Archive
www.indiana.edu/~league/

"The League of Nations Photo Archive" is a newly announced resource that is sponsored jointly by the Center for the Study of Global Change, the United Nations Library, and the Indiana University Libraries. The League of Nations Overview of PhotoCollections organizes the photos into groups: Personalities, Assemblies, Councils, Delegations, Commissions, Conferences, the Secretariat, the Permanent Court of International Justice, the Bureau International du Travail, and miscellaneous photos.
Resource Type: Virtual Tour
Grade Level: HS

Art of the First World War
www.art-ww1.com/gb/index2.html

This site features 100 paintings from international collection to commemorate the 80th anniversary of the conflict. Visitors can examine the exhibit thematically per artillery, battlefield, suffering, etc.
Resource Type: Art History; Lesson or Activity
Grade Level: MS, HS

BBC History: 1916 Easter Uprising
www.bbc.co.uk/history/british/easterrising/

The 1916 Easter Rising and the War of Independence that followed in 1919–1921 transformed the political landscape in Ireland. You can explore the events leading up to 1916, the Insurrection itself and its aftermath, through essays, photographs, sound archive, music and newspapers from the period.
Resource Type: Lesson or Activity
Grade Level: HS

The Titanic
http://historyonthenet.com/Titanic/titanicmain.htm

History on the Net has a section on the *Titanic* that asks "Why did the *Titanic* sink?" This site also looks at many aspects of the ship and includes a worksheet, a bibliography and a Further Information section.
Resource Type: Lesson or Activity
Grade Level: MS

Free 20th Century History Quizzes
www.sheppardsoftware.com/content/history/20th_century_general.htm

Each quiz selects 20 questions at random from a total set of 600; therefore you can play an unlimited number of times. Quiz can be hard to view in some browsers.
Resource Type: Test or Quiz
Grade Level: MS

The World's History: Technologies of Mass Production and Destruction, 1914–1990s
http://cwx.prenhall.com/bookbind/pubbooks/spodek2/chapter18/deluxe.html

The online guide to Howard Spodek's *The World's History* features quizzes (multiple-choice questions, true/false questions, interactive review questions), primary sources, maps, a bulletin board, a live chat, Web links, and faculty resources for each chapter/topic.
Resource Type: Course Model
Grade Level: HS

Brief Review in Global History and Geography: Document-Based Essays and Practice Tests
www.phschool.com/curriculum_support/brief_review/global_history/

PH@School's "Brief Review in Global History and Geography" Web site provides multiple-choice questions from actual Regents exams. You can also practice your test-taking skills on document-based essay questions (DBQs), with the option of e-mailing answers directly to your teacher for review.
Resource Type: Lesson or Activity; Primary Source Collection
Grade Level: HS

World War I: Blank Map
http://wps.ablongman.com/long_nash_ap_6/0,7361,592970-,00.html

The companion Web site to *The American People* offers blank maps related to various topics in American history. The maps can be printed or placed in a PowerPoint presentation. Click on Blank Maps for Quizzes.
Resource Type: Map
Grade Level: HS

WWI in Cartoons
http://rutlandhs.k12.vt.us/jpeterso/uboatcar.htm

These poltical cartoons are from about 1900 to 1948 and represent a personal collection from a variety of American and European newspapers and magazines.

Resource Type: Primary Source Collection
Grade Level: HS

RUSSIAN REVOLUTION

****Red Flag
www.pbs.org/wgbh/peoplescentury/episodes/redflag/

Part of PBS's *The People's Century* television series, this site covers the Russian Revolution and its aftermath, providing text and audio interviews, a teacher's guide, and links to related sites.
Resource Type: General Reference; Lesson or Activity

****Alexander Palace Time Machine
www.alexanderpalace.org/palace/mainpage.html

"Alexander Palace Time Machine" presents a history of the Alexander Palace and the Romanovs, and includes biographies, diaries, letters, maps, and more. It is a nice blend of images, text, primary sources, and secondary sources.
Resource Type: General Reference

****Soviet Archives Exhibit
www.ibiblio.org/expo/soviet.exhibit/soviet.archive.html

This Library of Congress offering is unique in that it is the first public exhibit of declassified Soviet documents from 1917 to 1991. It covers both Soviet domestic and foreign policies. Of special interests are the documents detailing repressive activities and Soviet-American relations.
Resource Type: Primary Source Collection

****The Marx/Engels Internet Archive
http://www2.cddc.vt.edu/marxists/admin/intro/history/csf/index.htm

"The Marx/Engels Internet Archive" offers an extensive collection of writings from Karl Marx and Friedrich Engels, arranged in chronological order. In addition, there is a photo gallery and biographies.
Resource Type: Primary Source Collection

*** Russian and Soviet History—Internet Resources
http://slav-db.slav.hokudai.ac.jp/fmi/xsl/link-e.xsl

Click on "Russia-f" for an extensive list of links on Russian history. Visit the other sections of the site for links on Russian culture, economics, and other topics.
Resource Type: Links Collection

***Russian History
www.bucknell.edu/x17601.xml

This site from Bucknell University is one of the better American portals to Russian history. It offers an annotated list of Russian history resources, a chronology of Russian history, a Romanov and Rurik family chart, and a table of Peter I's administration.
Resource Type: General Reference

***Documents in Russian History: An Online Sourcebook
http://artsci.shu.edu/reesp/documents/about.htm

Seton Hall University has selected primary source documents useful for teaching Russian history. There are four documents from the period of the Russian Revolution. Also has recommended links.
Resource Type: Primary Source Collection

****The Russo-Japanese War Research Society
www.russojapanesewar.com/index.html

"The Russo-Japanese War Research Society" has dedicated this site to the research and documentation of the Russo-Japanese War of 1904–1905. Set in a newspaper format, the site provides a large amount of information on the conflict, as well as maps, charts, documents, a message board, and more.
Resource Type: General Reference

Russian Revolution Lesson Plans, Teacher Guides, Activities, and More

Course Models: The Russian Revolution
www.history.ctaponline.org/center/hsscm/index.cfm?Page_Key=1560

Part of the California History-Social Science content standards and annotated course. Materials include: background information, focus questions, pupil activities and handouts, assessment, and references to books, articles, Web sites, literature, audiovisual programs, and historic site. Grade 10.
Resource Type: Course Model
Grade Level: HS

The World's History: The Soviet Union and Japan, 1914–1997
http://cwx.prenhall.com/bookbind/pubbooks/spodek2/chapter19/deluxe.html

The online guide to Howard Spodek's *The World's History* features quizzes (multiple-choice questions, true/false questions, interactive review questions), primary sources, maps, a bulletin board, a live chat, Web links, and faculty resources for each chapter/topic.
Resource Type: Course Model
Grade Level: HS

Follow the Marx: Learning about Communism
www.nytimes.com/learning/teachers/lessons/20020909monday.html

In this *New York Times* lesson, students explore communism from historical and theoretical perspectives to present to fellow classmates at a teach-in.
Resource Type: Lesson or Activity
Grade Level: MS, HS

Western Civilization: States in Conflict
http://wps.prenhall.com/hss_king_westernciv_2/0,6774,209073-,00.html

The online study companion to Margaret King's *Western Civilization: A Social and Cultural History* has many features: Chapter learning objectives, online quizzes, writing activities,

essay questions, Web links, built-in search engines, and faculty modules that include Power-Point outlines, presentation graphics, and lecture hints and activities.
Resource Type: Course Model
Grade Level: HS

Free 20th Century History Quizzes
www.sheppardsoftware.com/content/history/20th_century_general.htm

Learn fascinating facts about the twentieth century. Each quiz selects 20 questions at random from a total set of 600. You can play an unlimited number of times.
Resource Type: Test or Quiz
Grade Level: MS

FASCIST ITALY AND NAZI GERMANY

****Mussolini: What Is Fascism?
www.fordham.edu/halsall/mod/mussolini-fascism.html

This is a primary source document in which Mussolini considers and explains the benefits of his fascist system and contrasts it with communism and democracy. The actual source of this, interestingly, is from an Italian encyclopedia article that Mussolini wrote.
Resource Type: Primary Source Collection

****Spartacus: Mussolini
www.spartacus.schoolnet.co.uk/2WWmussolini.htm

An excellent summary/biography of Mussolini's life and climb up the political ladder. Also briefly covers his military and social endeavours. There are many links within the text which can be explored for further information.
Resource Type: General Reference

Mussolini Timeline
http://cidc.library.cornell.edu/DOF/chron/chronmus.htm

Part of the "Fathers and Regimes" site, this is a detailed timeline of Mussolini's life from 1876 to 1946.
Resource Type: Timeline

*****The Rise of Adolf Hitler and the Nazis
www.bbc.co.uk/history/worldwars/wwtwo/hitler_01.shtml

A moderately sized and very readable BBC summary of the growth and formation of Hitler's career and the Nazi party. A great start for basic factual information and understanding.
Resource Type: General Reference

****Master Race: 1926–1945
www.pbs.org/wgbh/peoplescentury/episodes/masterrace/

Part of PBS's *People's Century* series, "Master Race" probes the Nazi takeover in Germany. In it, Germans talk candidly about the initial seduction of Nazism; Gypsies reminisce about

life before Hitler; and Jews recall their persecution. There are eyewitness interviews, a teacher's guide, links to related sites, and a chance to tell your own story.
Resource Type: General Reference; Primary Source Collection

****Spartacus: Hitler
www.spartacus.schoolnet.co.uk/GERhitler.htm

An extensive history of Hitler's life, including his rise to power, military achievements and failures, ideology, and what he left behind in his wake. Very comprehensive, and like all Spartacus articles, contains links within the text to relevant info.
Resource Type: General Reference

****WWII Germany Audio and Video
www.earthstation1.com/Germany_WWII.html

A compilation of primary source audio and video put on the Web. Includes a huge section dedicated to Hitler, as well as propaganda posters/broadcasts and more. This provides an excellent view into Nazi Germany.
Resource Type: Primary Source Collection; Multimedia Presentation

****History Place: The Rise of Adolf Hitler
www.historyplace.com/worldwar2/riseofhitler/index.htm

A very extensive history of Hitler from his beginnings to the very end. This is broken up chronologically into many sections and provides excellent information about his childhood in particular.
Resource Type: General Reference

*****Nazi Propaganda Gallery
www.bbc.co.uk/history/worldwars/wwtwo/nazi_propaganda_gallery.shtml

This page has six propaganda images. Clicking on an image brings about a detailed analysis and examination of the ideas, themes, and emotions that the Nazi party were trying to spread.
Resource Type: Primary Source Collection; Multimedia Presentation

****BBC: Hitler's Leadership Style
www.bbc.co.uk/history/worldwars/wwtwo/hitler_commander_01.shtml

An informative article on Hitler's strengths and weaknesses as a military leader and commander. Discusses his strategy, philosophies, and relations with his subordinates. Broken up into seven subsections.
Resource Type: General Reference

****Nazi Propaganda: 1933–1945
www.calvin.edu/academic/cas/gpa/ww2era.htm#Speech

This site contains primary source speeches and writings from major German figures such as Hitler. Also has visual material, propaganda links, examples of anti-Semitic material, and much more.
Resource Type: Primary Source Collection

****Nuremberg—The Doctor's Trial
www.ushmm.org/research/doctors/index.html

This informative presentation is part of a larger site—The United States Holocaust Memorial Museum—and contains the testimonies and evidence used during this trial against Nazi physicians who conducted scientific experiments on concentration camp prisoners. There are numerous primary source documents that describe the surgical atrocities.
Resource Type: General Reference; Primary Source Collection

****Spartacus: The Nazi Party
www.spartacus.schoolnet.co.uk/GERnazi.htm

This is a very solid overview of the formation and founding ideas of the Nazi party, and how the party functioned over time. Discusses founding members and rival parties as well.
Resource Type: General Reference

***Spartacus: German Fascism
www.spartacus.schoolnet.co.uk/GERfascist.htm

A summary of fascism and more specifically how Hitler's integrated it in Germany.
Resource Type: General Reference

***Spartacus: The Hitler Youth
www.spartacus.schoolnet.co.uk/GERyouth.htm

Provides a quick but informative basic summary of the role and purpose of the Hitler Youth in Nazi Germany.
Resource Type: General Reference

****Hitler's Bunker
http://dsc.discovery.com/guides/history/unsolvedhistory/hitler/hitler.html

A production of the Discovery Channel's *Unsolved History* series, this collection of photos helps one understand Hitler's final moments. Clicking on the photos reveals a description and analysis of the photo's subject and its relevance to Hitler and his final days. Also offers a quiz on the "last gasp" of World War II.
Resource Type: General Reference; Virtual Tour

****Oscar Schindler
www.oskarschindler.com/

Biography of the rescuer Oskar Schindler, who saved 1,200 Jews during the Holocaust and World War II. Stories of war crimes, survivors, and the entire Schindler's List.
Resource Type: General Reference

Fascist Italy and Nazi Germany Lesson Plans, Teacher Guides, Activities, and More

20th Century Heroes and Villains: Mussolini
www.learningcurve.gov.uk/heroesvillains/mussolini/default.htm

This site covers Mussolini's invasion of Abyssinia and the role of intervention from other nations at that point. The goal is to formulate an opinion on whether Mussolini was a hero or villain.

Resource Type: Lesson or Activity
Grade Level: MS, HS

Chamberlain and Hitler, 1938: What Was Chamberlain Trying to Do?
www.learningcurve.gov.uk/snapshots/snapshot31/snapshot31.htm

Chamberlain's account of his meeting with Hitler over the Sudetenland crisis of 1938 is the center of this activity. Is it unfair to criticize Chamberlain for misjudging Hitler? Students could try to construct the case for Chamberlain. From the UK National Archives. Key Stage 3–4.
Resource Type: Lesson or Activity
Grade Level: HS

Was Hitler a Passionate Lunatic?
www.learningcurve.gov.uk/snapshots/snapshot06/snapshot6.htm

This exercise is aimed at getting pupils to look at conflicting evidence and assessing their reliability. It can be used as an introduction to looking at the issue of appeasement and the decisions that were made in the run up to the outbreak of the war. From Learning Curve. Key Stage 3–4.
Resource Type: Lesson or Activity
Grade Level: HS

Assassinate Hitler: How Did the British Plan to Kill Hitler?
www.learningcurve.gov.uk/snapshots/snapshot17/snapshot17.htm

In 1944, the SOE (Special Operations Executive) drew up some plans to kill Hitler and as Head of SOE it is your job to decide which of two ways of killing Hitler should be given the go-ahead. From the Learning Curve (UK National Archives). Key Stage 3–4.
Resource Type: Lesson or Activity
Grade Level: HS

Lesson Plan: Hitler's Rise to Power
www.schoolhistory.co.uk/lessons/riseofhitler/teacher_notes.htm

The goal of this lesson plan is to allow students to attain their own opinion on how Hitler came to power. Web- and computer-based research is the main means of teaching in this lesson plan.
Resource Type: Lesson or Activity
Grade Level: MS, HS

Teacher's Guide: Master Race
www.pbs.org/wgbh/peoplescentury/teachers/tgmaster.html

Study the racial philosophies and ethnic cleansing policies of Nazi Germany through this PBS "People's Century" teacher's guide.
Resource Type: Lesson or Activity
Grade Level: HS

Nazi Designers of Death
www.pbs.org/wgbh/nova/teachers/activities/2204_nazidesi.html

Nearly 50 years after the Holocaust, discover how a British historian gathered powerful

evidence to show how Nazi death camps were planned and constructed. PBS activity for middle school students.
Resource Type: Lesson or Activity
Grade Level: MS

BBC History: Nazi Propaganda Gallery
www.bbc.co.uk/history/worldwars/wwtwo/nazi_propaganda_gallery.shtml

Professor David Welch uses six Nazi-era posters to explain how Hitler used propaganda as a vehicle of political salesmanship.
Resource Type: Lesson or Activity
Grade Level: MS, HS

STALIN AND COMMUNIST RUSSIA

****The Internal Workings of the Soviet System
www.loc.gov/exhibits/archives/intn.html

Part of the Library of Congress Soviet Archives Exhibit, this detailed section covers the Lenin/Stalin regimes. It includes information on the secret police, the great terror, forced labor camps, collectivization/industrialization, religion, and more. Primary source documents are integrated into the pages. A great breadth of information.
Resource Type: Primary Source Collection

***Stalin Biography
www.bbc.co.uk/history/historic_figures/stalin_joseph.shtml

From BBC *Historic Figures* series. Offers a basic biography of Joseph Stalin and a selection of relevant links to other articles, historical figures, timelines, and external Web sites. See articles entitled Humanising Stalin, and Stalin and the Betrayal of Stalingrad. See also essays on Lenin and Trotsky.
Resource Type: General Reference

****Seventeen Moments in Soviet History
www.soviethistory.org/

For each of the 17 events between 1917 and 1991, there is an informative short essay introducing the subject, and a selection of newsreel clips, songs and audio clips, images and translated texts to depict how contemporaries understood the events. 1929: Liquidation of the Kulaks as a Class; 1936: Year of the Stakhanovite; 1943: Stalin Welcomes the Orthodox Metropolitans to the Kremlin; 1947: End of Rationing.
Resource Type: General Reference; Multimedia Presentation

****Forced Labor Camps: An Online Exhibition
www.osa.ceu.hu/gulag/

Part of the Open Society Archives, at this site you can find highlights of their holdings related to the Gulag and other forced labor camps. Plenty of images and you can read documents to learn more about living conditions in the camp.
Resource Type: General Reference

****The Yalta Conference Documents
www.yale.edu/lawweb/avalon/wwii/yalta.htm

From the Avalon Project, this site contains the text of the document signed at the Yalta Conference in February of 1945 by Churchill, Stalin and Roosevelt. It deals with the establishment of the United Nations, the dismemberment of Germany, the occupation of Nazi controlled Europe and other topics.
Resource Type: Primary Source Collection

****The Race for the Superbomb: Stalin
www.pbs.org/wgbh/amex/bomb/peopleevents/pandeAMEX69.html

Part of a PBS site, this section discusses Stalin's role and decisions regarding the development of nuclear weapons at the close of World War II. Also covers some general information about Stalin's reign.
Resource Type: General Reference Lesson or Activity

***The Age of Totalitarianism: Stalin and Hitler
www.historyguide.org/europe/lecture10.html

From the *History Guide: Lectures on 20th Century History*. Offers a hyperlinked essay on the age of totalitarianism. After reading, go to table of contents and consult The Aftermath of the Bolshevik Revolution as well.
Resource Type: General Reference

****Soviet Dictatorship Introduction
http://chnm.gmu.edu/wwh/lessons/lesson11/lesson11.php?s=0

Essay that covers the Stalinist system of ruling, understanding Stalinism in a Soviet context, and the role of women in Stalin's society. From the Center for History and New Media, George Mason University.
Resource Type: General Reference

****"Stalin Compares Churchill to Hitler"
www.cnn.com/SPECIALS/cold.war/episodes/02/1st.draft/pravda.html

From CNN's "Cold War: From Yalta to Malta" site, this interview appeared in the March 14, 1946, edition of *Pravda* and came on the heels of Winston Churchill's Iron Curtain speech.
Resource Type: Primary Source

****"Sir Frank Roberts on Stalin"
www.cnn.com/SPECIALS/cold.war/episodes/01/interviews/roberts/

As British Foreign Secretary Ernest Bevin's principal private secretary, Frank Roberts negotiated face-to-face with Stalin over the Berlin blockade. Interesting primary source that is part of CNN's "Cold War: From Yalta" to Malta site.
Resource Type: General Reference

****"Pictorial essay: Death trenches bear witness to Stalin's purges"
www.cnn.com/WORLD/9707/17/russia.gulag.grave/index.html

CNN.com story from Karelia, a republic in northwest Russia, where excavators unearthed more than 9,000 bodies of political prisoners.
Resource Type: General Reference

****Joseph V. Stalin Archive

www.marxists.org/history/ussr/

Contains telegrams, letters, reports, and speeches by Stalin from 1913 to 1951. Also contains a biography, a few pictures, and external links.

Resource Type: Primary Source Collection

****Stalin and the Rise of Soviet Totalitarianism

www.stanford.edu/dept/CREES/Workshop2004.html

The Center for Educational Research at Stanford produced this set of annotated links as part of a conference for teachers on Stalin. Some excellent links to lesson plans.

Resource Type: General Reference; Lesson or Activity

***Joseph Stalin

www.spartacus.schoolnet.co.uk/RUSstalin.htm

Hypertext essay on Stalin from the Spartacus publishing company. Also contains brief commentaries on Stalin from contemporaries and historians. Good secondary source information.

Resource Type: General Reference

***"Stalin's Personal Files Released"

http://archives.cnn.com/2002/WORLD/europe/12/21/russia.stalin/index.html

CNN.com story about Kremlin's release of approximately 1,200 of Soviet dictator Josef Stalin's personal files to the Russian State Archive.

Resource Type: General Reference

***Sergei Khrushchev on Stalin

www.cnn.com/SPECIALS/cold.war/episodes/07/interviews/khrushchev/

Interesting text transcript and video interview of Sergei Khrushchev, son of Soviet Premier Nikita Khrushchev.

Resource Type: Primary Source

Stalin and Communist Russia Lesson Plans, Teacher Guides, Activities, and More

Heroes or Villains? Stalin

www.learningcurve.gov.uk/heroesvillains/g4/

This classroom activity, designed by the British National Archives, challenges students to research Stalin's efforts to industrialize the Soviet Union and to evaluate the costs and gains of this endeavor. The design of this thorough activity is similar to a WebQuest, with lots of online reproducible worksheets, charts, etc.

Resource Type: Lesson or Activity

Grade Level: HS

Soviet Women Under Stalin

http://chnm.gmu.edu/wwh/modules/lesson11/pdfs/sovietteachingmaterials.pdf

Produced by the Center for History and New Media, this interesting lesson plan focuses on how women were affected by Stalin's reign.

Resource Type: Lesson or Activity
Grade Level: HS; College

Red Flag—Teacher's Guide
www.pbs.org/wgbh/peoplescentury/teachers/tgred.html

A teacher's guide for the Russian Revolution and related topics such as Communism, Propaganda, Mass Movements, and more. Part of PBS Red Flag series. Requires the accompanying video.
Resource Type: Lesson or Activity
Grade Level: HS

TWENTIETH-CENTURY CHINA AND TIBET

See also Chapter 7: China

****Eye On China
http://edition.cnn.com/SPECIALS/2005/eyeonchina/

This wide-ranging CNN special report focuses on China's "swiftly evolving role in global politics and business, and the impact of the country's rapid modernization on its people and culture." Helpful blend of articles and features (see Figure 10.1).
Resource Type: General Reference; Multimedia Presentation

****The Office of Tibet
www.tibet.com/

The Office of Tibet, in London, is an official agency of the Dalai Lama and tries to draw the attention to the plight of the Tibetan people and the exiled Tibetan government. This is a good source of information for both twentieth-century history and current day affairs.
Resource Type: General Reference

****China Internet Information Center: Tibet
www.tibetinfor.com.cn/english/

This pro-China source has White Papers on Tibet and articles on the Human Rights Situation and Exposing the Trickery of the Dalai Lama. Read about China's "unprecedented progress" in human rights and the "peaceful liberation of Tibet Autonomous Region" and contrast it with the views of other sites in this list.
Resource Type: General Reference

****Dreams of Tibet
www.pbs.org/wgbh/pages/frontline/shows/tibet/

This PBS *Frontline* companion site examines Hollywood efforts on behalf of the Dalai Lama and provides a useful overview of Tibetan history. Has interesting interviews.
Resource Type: General Reference

Figure 10.1: Eye on China

****China's Communist Party
www.cnn.com/SPECIALS/2001/ccp80/

A CNN.com special report on 80 years of Communist rule in China, this site is packed with features. There are in-depth articles, profiles of leaders, a China timeline, and more.
Resource Type: General Reference; Multimedia Presentation

****Amnesty International: China Report 2005
http://web.amnesty.org/report2005/chn-summary-eng

The Amnesty International report summarizes: "There was progress towards reform in some areas, but this failed to have a significant impact on serious and widespread human rights violations perpetrated across the country."
Resource Type: General Reference

****Students for a Free Tibet**

www.studentsforafreetibet.org/index.php

"Students for a Free Tibet" promotes nonviolent direct action to campaign for Tibetans' fundamental right to political freedom. Go to the About Tibet section for Tibet history and culture and to Newsroom for Tibet news.

Resource Type: General Reference

China and Tibet Lesson Plans, Teaching Guides, Activities, and More

Competing National Stories in Tibet

www.yale.edu/macmillan/pier/resources/lessons/JFrazer.html

"Competing National Stories in Tibet" is a rich teaching unit. Many excellent teaching resources are available here.

Resource Type: Course Model
Grade Level: HS

****China: Roots of Revolution**

http://projects.edtech.sandi.net/kearny/roots/#Task

In this simulation activity, The State Department asks you to produce a documentary about China, which will be used to brief State Department employees who will be posted to China. Contains links to historical, economic, and human rights issues.

Resource Type: Lesson or Activity
Grade Level: HS

The Tibet Question WebQuest

http://score.rims.k12.ca.us/activity/tibet_question/

A WebQuest activity: "An international news agency is doing a special on 'The Tibet Question.' They will be interviewing members of the Tibetan groups, the Chinese and U.S. government officials, representatives of human rights organizations and Chinese scholars. You will be assigned to one of these groups in preparation for this news special."

Resource Type: Lesson or Activity
Grade Level: HS

What's Next for China and the US?

http://score.rims.k12.ca.us/activity/china/

In this SCORE activity, students research China and advise President Bush on foreign relations. Good simulation activity.

Resource Type: Lesson or Activity
Grade Level: HS

U.S.–Tibet Relations

http://cnnstudentnews.cnn.com/2001/fyi/lesson.plans/05/10/tibet.da/index.html

From CNN Student News, this lesson plan is based on a 2001 interview of Dalai Lama.

Resource Type: Lesson or Activity
Grade Level: HS

Human Rights Violations

http://cnnstudentnews.cnn.com/2000/fyi/teacher.resources/lesson.plans/03/28/china/index.html

In this CNN lesson plan from 2000, students examine and evaluate the state of human rights in China and the United States.

Resource Type: Lesson or Activity

Grade Level: MS, HS

COLD WAR ERA TOPICS

*****Cold War: From Yalta to Malta

http://cnn.com/SPECIALS/cold.war/

This CNN Perspectives series explores the Cold War experience from many different angles in 24 episodes. Included are interactive maps, rare video footage, declassified documents, biographies, picture galleries, timelines, interactive activities, a search function, book excerpts, an educator's guide and more. For instance, you can watch a video interview with George Kennan, tour a Cold War prison, play a Brinkmanship interactive game interview, and listen to an interview with Fidel Castro. Launched in September The site covers more than a 1,000 pages and was honored with a 1998 Sigma Delta Chi Award in the Online Journalism by the Society of Professional Journalists.

Resource Type: General Reference; Multimedia Presentation

****Episode One: Comrades 1917–1945

www.cnn.com/SPECIALS/cold.war/episodes/01

This presentation displays the United States and Russia as allies through video interview with George Kennan, a tour of a Cold War prison, historical documents, and more.

****Episode Two: The Iron Curtain 1945–1947

www.cnn.com/SPECIALS/cold.war/episodes/02/

This presentation displays the Iron Curtain through a Cold War military museum, a Brinkmanship interactive game, a video interview with George Kennan, a spotlight on the Oder-Niesse Line, a look at post Cold War U.S.-Russian relations, and more.

****Episode Three: The Marshall Plan 1947–1952

www.cnn.com/SPECIALS/cold.war/episodes/03/

Has a brinkmanship simulation, a feature on the birth of the CIA, an analysis of the IMF, discussion of the Czech coup in 1948, and more.

****Episode Four: Berlin 1948–1949

www.cnn.com/SPECIALS/cold.war/episodes/04/

Features a West German radio report, reflections of a Berlin mayor, a look at propaganda, a brinkmanship simulation, and more.

****Episode Five: Korea 1949–1953

www.cnn.com/SPECIALS/cold.war/episodes/05/

The special features of this site include spotlights on the Russian connection, the continuing divide between North and South Korea, a look at America's Korean War memorial, a brinkmanship game, interviews, and more.

****Episode Six: Reds 1948–1949
www.cnn.com/SPECIALS/cold.war/episodes/06

Based on the *Intensification of the Cold War*, this presentation features a look at the Red Scare then and now, the U.S. Communist Party, and totalitarianism, and it has an excerpt from Daniel Moynihan's "Secrecy."

****Episode Seven: After Stalin 1953–1956
www.cnn.com/SPECIALS/cold.war/episodes/07

This presentation features reflections by Krushchev's son and sections on Kremlin power struggles, NATO's importance, and a German radio report.

****Episode Eight: After Sputnik 1949–1961
www.cnn.com/SPECIALS/cold.war/episodes/08/

Explores the new arms race launched by the Soviet atomic bomb. There are features on espionage, Russia's space exploits, and an interactive timeline.

****Episode Nine: The Wall 1959–1963
www.cnn.com/SPECIALS/cold.war/episodes/09/

Explores shootings at the Berlin Wall, U.S. unpreparedness, and offers some reflections on the wall.

****Episode Ten: Cuba 1959–1968
www.cnn.com/SPECIALS/cold.war/episodes/10/

Features the ExComm files, the hotline between Kennedy and Khrushchev, contemporary Cuba and an interview with Fidel Castro.

****Episode Eleven: Vietnam 1954–1968
www.cnn.com/SPECIALS/cold.war/episodes/11/

Includes a Spotlight on Dien Bien Phu and sections on changing media-military rules and the "living room" war.

****Episode Twelve: MAD 1960–1972
www.cnn.com/SPECIALS/cold.war/episodes/12/

Examines "mutually assured destruction" and the escalating arms race.

****Episode Thirteen: Make Love, Not War: The Sixties
www.cnn.com/SPECIALS/cold.war/episodes/13/

Spotlights the draft, music, the "silent majority," and protests.

****Episode Fourteen: Red Spring: The Sixties
www.cnn.com/SPECIALS/cold.war/episodes/14/

Features the sexual revolution, the rehabilitation of communism, and a look at an expatriate Soviet artist.

****Episode Fifteen: China 1949–1972
www.cnn.com/SPECIALS/cold.war/episodes/15/

Spotlights Kissinger's secret talks with Mao, conflict between Beijing and Moscow, and "pingpong" diplomacy and US-China rapprochement.

****Episode Sixteen: Detente 1969–1975**
www.cnn.com/SPECIALS/cold.war/episodes/16/

Features a Brezhnev confidant, critiques of detente, and space cooperation.

****Episode Seventeen: Good Guys, Bad Guys 1967–1978**
www.cnn.com/SPECIALS/cold.war/episodes/17/

Examines African Renaissance, mercenaries for hire, and the Arab-Israeli peace process.

****Episode Eighteen: Backyard 1954–1990**
www.cnn.com/SPECIALS/cold.war/episodes/18/

This presentation talks about Central America, the Caribbean, and South America as battleground, examining the School of Americas, the plan to fund the Contras in Nicaragua, and conflicts in Mexico.

****Episode Nineteen: Freeze 1977–1981**
www.cnn.com/SPECIALS/cold.war/episodes/19/

Features sections on the Carter-Brezhnev years, John Paul II toppling the communist domino, politics of European security, and missile diplomacy.

****Episode Twenty: Soldiers of God 1975–1988**
www.cnn.com/SPECIALS/cold.war/episodes/20/

This presentation talks about the Afghan Civil War and the crumbling detente with sections on the Olympic games, Afghan legacy, and Russian pain.

****Episode Twenty One: Spies 1945–1990**
www.cnn.com/SPECIALS/cold.war/episodes/21/

Stories of dead spies, finding good spies, counterintelligence, and continuing espionage.

****Episode Twenty Two: Star Wars 1980–1988**
www.cnn.com/SPECIALS/cold.war/episodes/22/

Includes excerpts of interviews, a transcript of Reagan's Star Wars speech, and a section on war games.

****Episode Twenty Three: The Wall Comes Down 1989**
www.cnn.com/SPECIALS/cold.war/episodes/23/

Features a slide show of lifting the Iron Curtain in 1989 and sections on reformers in Hungary, the surprise of the fall of the Berlin Wall, and the chaos in Russia during the last years of the Cold War.

****Episode Twenty Four: Conclusions**
www.cnn.com/SPECIALS/cold.war/episodes/24/

Features a section on what the war cost, memories from the Cold War, and an excerpt from the book *After The Cold War*.

****People's Century**
www.pbs.org/wgbh/peoplescentury/

The site is based on a 26-episode television series and features a teacher's guide, a timeline, a

thematic overview, and RealAudio excerpts. The highlights of the Web site are the first-person narratives, often by ordinary people who lived through turbulent times.
Resource Type: Primary Source Collection; Lesson or Activity

****Young Blood: 1950–1975**
www.pbs.org/wgbh/peoplescentury/episodes/youngblood/

Focus is on youth movement in America in the 1960s.

****Brave New World: 1945–1961**
www.pbs.org/wgbh/peoplescentury/episodes/bravenewworld/

Site probes the changing world order after WWII and emergence of Cold War.

**** Freedom Now: 1947–1990**
www.pbs.org/wgbh/peoplescentury/episodes/freedomnow/

Covers the overthrow of colonial rule in Asia and Africa.

****Skin Deep: 1945–1994**
www.pbs.org/wgbh/peoplescentury/episodes/skindeep/

Probes the challenge to racial oppression in the United States and South Africa.

****Fallout: 1945–1995**
www.pbs.org/wgbh/peoplescentury/episodes/fallout/

Examines the atomic age in the Cold War era.

****Picture Power: 1939–1997**
www.pbs.org/wgbh/peoplescentury/episodes/picturepower/

Probes how television transformed society, culture, and politics.

****The Great Leap: 1943–1976**
www.pbs.org/wgbh/peoplescentury/episodes/greatleap/

Focus is on Chairman Mao and the communist takeover in China.

****Guerrilla Wars: 1956–1989**
www.pbs.org/wgbh/peoplescentury/episodes/guerrillawars/

Discusses guerrilla war movements in Vietnam, Afghanistan, and elsewhere.

****God Fights Back: 1978–1992**
www.pbs.org/wgbh/peoplescentury/episodes/godfightsback/

Examines religious fundamentalism in the East and West.

****People Power: 1971–1991**
www.pbs.org/wgbh/peoplescentury/episodes/peoplepower/

Examines the fall of communist rule in the Soviet Union.

****Fast Forward: 1980–1999**
www.pbs.org/wgbh/peoplescentury/episodes/fastforward/

Probes the impact of communications technology and business globalization on the traditional world order.

****Cold War International History Project

www.wilsoncenter.org/index.cfm?topic_id=1409&fuseaction=topics.home

"Cold War International History Project" features new evidence from Central and Eastern European archives of the Cold War in Asia. It also offers a CD-ROM on Bulgaria and the Cold War. You can also learn about the George Washington University, NEH-supported collaboration to train high school teachers in recent advances in Cold War historiography. The CWIHP Bulletin contains recently released and translated documents from former Communist-world archives, along with brief introductions by leading Cold War historians and archivists.

Resource Type: General Reference; Course Model

***Soviet Archives Exhibit

www.ibiblio.org/expo/soviet.exhibit/soviet.archive.html

This site, designed by the Library of Congress and hosted by ibiblio.org, contains declassified Soviet documents from 1917 to 1991, arranged as a museum exhibit of primary sources.

Resource Type: Primary Source Collection; Virtual Tour.

***Cold War Policies 1945–1991

http://history.acusd.edu/gen/20th/coldwar0.html

Written by a professor at the University of San Diego, this is part of a larger site from their history department. The major topics are Negotiation, Demonstration, Containment, Coercion, Detente, Confrontation, Glasnost, and Revolution. While basically a timeline of policies and events, it also included are primary sources, detailed maps, and links to other sites, such as Reagan and Gorbachev's pages.

Resource Type: General Reference; Course Model

***Castro Speech Database

http://www1.lanic.utexas.edu/la/cb/cuba/castro.html

This site includes speeches, interviews, etc. by Fidel Castro from 1959 to 1996. The collection is well organized and searchable.

Resource Type: Primary Source Collection

****The Wars for Vietnam

http://vietnam.vassar.edu/

This rich site was produced by students out of Vassar College and provides an overview of the Vietnam war, primary documents and photos, and links to other related sites.

Resource Type: General Reference

****Vietnam, Stories Since the War

www.pbs.org/pov/stories/

Another excellent PBS site; it contains background information on the Vietnam War, first-hand stories of veterans, an index, and a search function. Useful blend of primary source and secondary source information on the war.

Resource Type: General Reference

****Cambodian Holocaust
www.cybercambodia.com/dachs/

This site relates moving personal stories from the Cambodian genocide of the Khmer Rouge years. There are also photographs and suggested resources.
Resource Type: Primary Source Collection

****Vietnam: A Television History
www.pbs.org/wgbh/amex/vietnam/

Part of PBS's *American Experience* series, this informative site includes video clips of the war, background information, and much more.
Resource Type: General Reference; Multimedia Presentation

****The Face of Russia
www.pbs.org/weta/faceofrussia/

This informative PBS site attempts to answer the question: Who are the Russian People? There is a timeline, glossary, bibliography, media index, links, lesson plans, and a chat forum.
Resource Type: General Reference; Lesson or Activity

****K-19
www.nationalgeographic.com/k19/

Inspired by *National Geographic*'s *Widowmaker* film, this online feature delves into the history of K-19, and the Cold War politics and mechanical malfunctions that led to a Russian nuclear submarine disaster in the summer of 1961. This interactive site offers a director's commentary, K–19's schematic, movie stills, selected profiles of U.S. and Russian subs, a sunken submarine map, an exploration of the evolution of submarine technology and much more.
Resource Type: Multimedia Presentation; General Reference

Cold War Era Topics Lesson Plans, Teacher Guides, Activities, and More

The World in Uncertain Times, 1950–Present Practice Test
www.phschool.com/curriculum_support/brief_review/us_history/tests.html?unit=7&number=35

High school level multiple-choice quiz on Cold War America from Prentice Hall.
Resource Type: Test or Quiz
Grade Level: HS

The World in Uncertain Times, 1950–Present Document-Based Essay
www.phschool.com/curriculum_support/brief_review/us_history/essay_questions/unit7.cfm

This Prentice Hall DBQ is designed to test your ability to work with historical documents and is based on the accompanying documents.
Resource Type: Lesson or Activity; Primary Source Collection
Grade Level: HS

Intervene or Interfere? Exploring Forty Years of United States Intervention in Foreign Affairs
www.nytimes.com/learning/teachers/lessons/20030407monday.html

In this lesson, students will research the motives, actions, and results of U.S. intervention in

Figure 10.2: Intervene or Interfere?

foreign affairs between the 1961 Bay of Pigs invasion and the 2003 invasion of Iraq; they then present their research to class for comparative analysis.

Resource Type: Lesson or Activity
Grade Level: HS

MIDDLE EAST CRISIS

****Global Connections: Middle East
www.pbs.org/wgbh/globalconnections/index.html

"Global Connections" provides the background information needed to understand events occurring in the Middle East. The site includes original materials created in conjunction with the Centers for Middle Eastern Studies at Harvard and UCLA. The site also aggregates and contextualizes the rich resources available throughout public broadcasting, including material from *Frontline*, *Online NewsHour*, *NOW with Bill Moyers*, *Morning Edition*, *Talk of the Nation*, and many others. Designed with educators in mind, the site is also useful for those curious to better understand the Middle East and its relationship with the West.

Resource Type: General Reference; Course Model

****Middle East: Centuries of Conflict
www.cnn.com/SPECIALS/2003/mideast/

Part of the CNN.com Archives, this site is an excellent introduction to strife in the Middle East—past and present. The site uses text and multimedia to explore issues such as

Jerusalem, Jewish settlers, a Palestinian state, and Palestinian refugees. It also outlines "key players" and key documents and provides maps, galleries, a timeline, and a virtual tour of the region.
Resource Type: General Reference; Multimedia Presentation

****BBC News: Israel & the Palestinians
http://news.bbc.co.uk/1/hi/in_depth/middle_east/2001/israel_and_the_palestinians/default.stm

The BBC provides plenty of helpful contextual and current information on the Middle East crisis. Offers Top Stories on Israel and the Palestinians, profiles of key players, BBC audio and video, maps, country profiles, stories of ordinary citizens, key documents, timelines, profiles, Web links, and more.
Resource Type: General Reference; Multimedia Presentation

****The Israeli-Palestinian Conflict
www.washingtonpost.com/wp-dyn/world/issues/mideastpeace/

This is a *Washington Post* special report on the Israeli-Palestinian conflict in the Middle East. Click on One Land, Two Peoples for an interactive guide to the Middle East conflict. Also features a multimedia guide to the walls and barriers Israel is building in the West Bank. In Audio Perspectives, you can ask an Israeli lawyer and a Palestinian spokesman about Hamas. There are also several editorials and commentary from the *Washington Post*.
Resource Type: General Reference Multimedia Presentation

****CBC News: Middle East
www.cbc.ca/news/background/middleeast/index.html

A helpful overview of the Middle East conflict from the Canadian Broadcasting Corporation. The site features a timeline of recent developments, a brief history of the Mideast, FAQ on Israeli settlements, and studies of Mahmoud Abbas, Ariel Sharon, al-Aqsa Martyrs Brigades, Yasser Arafat, and others. Special features include a video: Inside the Mind of a Suicide Bomber. Also provides articles on the Gaza Strip, Hebron, Jerusalem, and Palestinian refugee camps as well as various commentaries on the conflict.
Resource Type: General Reference

****The Avalon Project at the Yale Law School: Middle East
www.yale.edu/lawweb/avalon/mideast/mideast.htm

A comprehensive collection of documents on the Middle East ranging from 1916 to 2003, arranged by date and searchable by period and keyword.
Resource Type: Primary Source Collection

****Center for Middle Eastern Studies
http://menic.utexas.edu/

Center for Middle Eastern Studies from the University of Texas provides an online guide to Middle East-related Web sites and databases that can be accessed via the Web. The editors visit and evaluate Web sites and then organize them into subject-based categories and subcategories. Useful research site.
Resource Type: General Reference; Links Collection

****Middle East Web Gateway
www.mideastweb.org/timeline.htm

"Middle East Web Gateway" is produced by a non-government organization in Israel and offers much in the way of news and views on the Middle East. Learn about the Israeli-Palestinian conflict "in a nutshell" and read various articles and editorials on the Middle East. Consult the reference section for maps, timeline, and a history of the Middle East.
Resource Type: General Reference; Links Collection

****ArabNet—The Resource for the Arab World in the Middle East and North Africa
www.arab.net/

This site provides excellent general information on Arab countries, including history, geography, and culture; it has a set of useful links and special features.
Resource Type: General Reference; Links Collection

****Israel at 50
www.cnn.com/SPECIALS/1998/israel/

A 1998 CNN.com special report on the Israeli people. Examines early days of Israel, internal conflicts among Israelis, the West Bank, and more. Features a virtual tour of Israel, an interactive timeline, as well as maps of the Jewish state throughout history.
Resource Type: General Reference; Multimedia Presentation

****Foundation for Middle East Peace (FMEP)
www.fmep.org/

Nonprofit organization dedicated to informing Americans about the Israeli-Palestinian conflict and assisting in a peaceful solution that brings security for both peoples. Provides documents, maps, charts, and much more.
Resource Type: General Reference; Primary Source Collection

****Israeli Ministry of Foreign Affairs: Guide to the Peace Process
www.israel-mfa.gov.il/mfa/peace process/guide to the peace process/

Provides links to ongoing developments in the Middle East peace process as well as diagrams on the structure of the negotiations. See also the History of Israel section, especially the Israeli perspective on the history of Jerusalem.
Resource Type: General Reference; Links Collection

****Middle East Conflict—Palestinian View (Palestine Daily)
www.palestinedaily.com/

Provides news on the Middle East conflict from a Palestinian perspective.
Resource Type: General Reference

****Muslims
www.pbs.org/wgbh/pages/frontline/shows/muslims/

This PBS addition examines Islam through interesting stories of diverse Muslims. The "Frequently Asked Questions" is like "Islam 101" as it concisely explains the basic principles of Islam, including the most widely accepted definition of 'jihad.' This site provides an

abundance of fascinating facts about Islamic history, basic beliefs, and various other topics through its portrayal and interviews of various Muslims.
Resource Type: General Reference; Lesson or Activity

****World Cultures to 1500: Islam
www.wsu.edu/~dee/ISLAM/ISLAM.HTM

A well-organized overview of Islamic history can be found at this online course, based at Washington State University. It offers clear and informative lecture notes, maps, a photo gallery, timelines, links to relevant sites, and more. Click Contents.
Resource Type: Course Model

****Heritage: Civilization and the Jews
www.pbs.org/wnet/heritage/index.html

A great general site on Jewish history from PBS featuring an interactive timeline, primary sources, lesson plans, teacher sources, images, and more. Organized chronologically, each section features concise historical documents (with contextual information) as well as film clips from the PBS series.
Resource Type: General Reference; Multimedia Presentation

***Internet Islamic History Sourcebook
www.fordham.edu/halsall/islam/islamsbook.html

"Internet History Sourcebooks" by Paul Halsall are wonderful collections of public-domain and copyright-permitted historical texts for educational use. "Islamic History Sourcebook" documents are well organized around several main categories, including The Western Intrusion, Islamic Nationalism, and The Islamic World since 1945. Note: Links are no longer actively maintained.
Resource Type: Primary Source Collection

Middle East Crisis Lesson Plans, Teacher Guides, Activities, and More

Global Connections: Lesson Plans
www.pbs.org/wgbh/globalconnections/mideast/educators/lessons.html

"Global Connections" aggregates and contextualizes the rich resources available throughout public broadcasting, including material from *Frontline, Online NewsHour, NOW with Bill Moyers, Morning Edition, Talk of the Nation*, and many others. Designed with educators in mind, the site is also useful for those curious to better understand the Middle East and its relationship with the West.

LESSON PLANS:
- **Israeli-Palestinian Peace Summit**
  Students will develop persuasive arguments for a given position or point of view regarding the Israeli-Palestinian conflict.
- **A Meeting of World Leaders**
  Students will gain an understanding of some of the background, motivation, and philosophy that shape political strategies proposed by world leaders to address the Palestinian-Israeli conflict.

- **Stereotypes: More Than Meets the Eye**
  Students will think critically about images and media that portray the Middle East.
- **Coup to Revolution: U.S. Foreign Policy in Iran**
  Students will learn that many factors shape U.S. foreign policy through the examination of one case study: Iran.
- **Middle East: Land, Resources, and Economics**
  Students will be able to describe major geographical features of the Middle East and explain how these features and other natural resources influence the economy of the area.
- **Oil Crisis: What Would You Do?**
  Students will understand the multiple dimensions of the role of oil in the economies and politics of both the United States and the Middle East.

Resource Type: Lesson or Activity
Grade Level: HS

Peace Signs: Exploring the 'Roller Coaster Ride' of the Israeli-Palestinian Peace Process
www.nytimes.com/learning/teachers/lessons/20030507wednesday.html

In this *New York Times* lesson, students review their prior knowledge about the peace process in Israel and examine recent steps towards peace. They then research key figures, events and policies since Israel's statehood in 1948 and determine how they impacted the peace process, illustrating their effects as if the process were a roller coaster. Finally, students reflect on how the proposed road map for peace might change the path of the roller coaster they created.
Resource Type: Lesson or Activity
Grade Level: MS, HS

Unmasking the Middle East: Examining the Political, Religious and Ethnic Relationships among Middle Eastern Countries
www.nytimes.com/learning/teachers/lessons/20030416wednesday.html

In this *New York Times* lesson, students explore many of the countries in the Middle East, developing research-based posters and a "spider web" illustrating the relationships among the countries. They then write letters to fictional peers in Middle Eastern countries.
Resource Type: Lesson or Activity
Grade Level: MS, HS

Understanding History, Religion, and Politics in Jerusalem and Beyond
www.pbs.org/pov/pov2001/promises/lessonplan.pdf

This lesson is based on the PBS program, *Promises*, and is designed to help students understand the reasons for the Israeli-Palestinian conflict and interpret a conflict from multiple perspectives.
Resource Type: Lesson or Activity
Grade Level: MS, HS

Whose Peace? Analyzing Perspectives on the Israeli-Palestinian Peace Process
www.nytimes.com/learning/teachers/lessons/20000517wednesday.html?searchpv=learning_lessons

In this *New York Times* lesson, students explore the perspectives of different groups of people involved in the Israeli-Palestinian peace process.
Resource Type: Lesson or Activity
Grade Level: MS, HS

The Fascinating World of Islam
www.pbs.org/empires/islam/lesson2.html

Students will have the opportunity to learn about aspects of the world of Islam by using various research tools. They will then work with classmates in creating an ABC Book of Islam based on their research. Grades 6–12.
Resource Type: Lesson or Activity
Grade Level: MS, HS

Exploring Islamic Lands
www.thirteen.org/edonline/lessons/landofislam/index.html

In this high school lesson, students explore what it's like to be a teenager living today in an Islamic country in the Middle East. They will begin by gaining background information about the religion and the region from which it sprang by using the PBS series *Islam: Empire of Faith* and other resources. Once students gain a historical understanding, they choose a particular modern-day Middle Eastern country to explore in depth using resources such as the Library of Congress Web site and e-pals. In the end, they will create a personal narrative of what it's like to live in that country.
Resource Type: Lesson or Activity
Grade Level: HS

Maps of Muslim World
www.muslimsonline.com/babri/mapsmuslim.htm

The site contains maps of Central Asia, South Asia, Southeast Asia, East Asia, and finally Africa. Each of these maps shows where the Muslim population is concentrated. One can also choose a link entitled Muslim Minorities, which lists many articles about Islam's history and mythology. The last link is to "Muslims Online," a larger Web site that contains search engines, homepages, and links to Muslim organizations. From this site a student can learn about the religion of Islam; however, the site might be quite confusing to someone who is not familiar with the topic.
Resource Type: Maps
Grade Level: HS

Twenty-Five Most Frequently Asked Questions about Islam
www.islam-usa.com/25ques.html

By Dr. Athar, a physician, an Islamic writer, and speaker. He is the author of over 60 articles and five books on Islam.
Resource Type: General Reference
Grade Level: HS

Top Ten Misconceptions about Islam
www.jannah.org/articles/misc.html

By Huma Ahmad at jannah.org, an introductory site on Islam.
Resource Type: General Reference
Grade Level: HS

The Islamic Quiz
http://islam.org/Quiz/New/selectquiz.htm

Tough set of questions on Islamic history.
Resource Type: Test or Quiz
Grade Level: HS

The World's History: Islam
http://cwx.prenhall.com/bookbind/pubbooks/spodek2/chapter11/deluxe.html

The online guide to Howard Spodek's *The World's History* features quizzes (multiple-choice questions, true/false questions, interactive review questions), primary sources, maps, a bulletin board, a live chat, Web links, and faculty resources for each chapter/topic.
Resource Type: Course Model
Grade Level: HS

BALKANS CRISIS

****BBC News—The Milosevic Trial
http://news.bbc.co.uk/2/hi/in_depth/europe/2001/yugoslavia_after_milosevic/

This informative BBC section offers a timeline and overview of the rise and fall of Milosevic and key trial questions. It also profiles Serbia's elite, killings of Kosovo, Milosevic's crumbling empire, and war crime trails. It offers individual and country profiles as well as excerpts from the trial.
Resource Type: General Reference; Primary Source Collection

****CNN Special Report: Focus on Kosovo
www.cnn.com/SPECIALS/1998/10/kosovo/

This 1998 CNN Special Report provides a review of the Balkans crisis as well as related images, video, maps, and background articles. Also contains a few primary source documents and an extensive set of links.
Resource Type: Primary Source Collection; Multimedia Presentation

****CNN Special Report: Kosovo Prospects for Peace
www.cnn.com/SPECIALS/2000/kosovo/

This 2000 CNN Special Report updates the Balkans crisis and reviews Milosovec's rule in Serbia. There is also a Kosovo Journal, plenty of maps and images, and background articles. Also contains an extensive set of links and transcripts of interactive chats with experts.
Resource Type: Primary Source Collection; Multimedia Presentation

****Keeping Peace with Kosovo
www.pbs.org/newshour/bb/europe/jan-june99/kosovo_index.html#

This is from a 1999 PBS *Online NewsHour* special. In addition to articles and maps, there are special reports on refugees, strikes in Yugoslavia, peacekeeping mission, and other topics.
Resource Type: Primary Source Collection; General Reference

****CBC News: The Balkans
www.cbc.ca/news/background/balkans/milosevic_timeline.html_

This Canadian Broadcasting Corporation site offers a detailed timeline of the Balkans crisis as well as related articles and external links.
Resource Type: General Reference

RELATED STORIES:

Srebrenica: Europe's Shame
www.cbc.ca/news/background/balkans/index_sr.html_
Features Flash presentation on mass graves.

The Bones of Srebrenica
www.cbc.ca/news/background/balkans/bones.html

Besieged Sarajevo
www.cbc.ca/news/background/balkans/sarajevo.html

****Washington Post: Milosevic on Trial
www.washingtonpost.com/wp-dyn/world/issues/balkans/

This *Washington Post* offering contains many articles as well as a multimedia presentation on the New Yugoslavia. Note: Video of Milosevic and some other features are no longer available.
Resource Type: General Reference; Multimedia Presentation

NPR Special Report: Milosevic on Trial
www.npr.org/news/specials/milosevic/milosevic.html_

National Public Radio has archived this informative 2002 audio report as well as several related stories.
Resource Type: General Reference

The Srebrenica Killings, 10 Years Later
www.npr.org/templates/story/story.php?storyId=4748459

Serbians Still Divided Over Srebrenica Massacre
www.npr.org/templates/story/story.php?storyId=4737583

The Balkans, 10 Years After the Dayton Accords
www.npr.org/templates/story/story.php?storyId=5021598

Ethnic Conflict Persists in Bosnia, 10 Years After Pact
www.npr.org/templates/story/story.php?storyId=5021170

***Center for Peace in the Balkans

www.balkanpeace.org/

This site features many articles and commentary and is critical of NATO and U.S. involvement in the Balkans. Major sections include Crisis in Balkans, War Crimes, Documents, Photo Gallery. Has some interesting and provocative features and articles: The Politics of the Srebrenica Massacre; 2000 years of Christianity; Balkans and bin-Laden; maps of History of Ethnic Cleaning; Balkans and 2004 U.S. election. Its views and opinions serve as a contrast to others in this list.
Resource Type: General Reference; Primary Source Collection

***Old Yugoslavia

www.usatoday.com/news/index/kosovo/kpi/bd/bd1.htm

This is an interactive map of both "old" (pre–1991) and "new" Yugoslavia.
Resource Type: Map

Balkans Crisis Lesson Plans, Teacher Guides, Activities, and More

Lesson Plans about Kosovo

www.nytimes.com/learning/general/specials/kosovo/lessons.html

These nine lesson plans are from the *New York Times* Learning Network and cover various elements of the Balkans Crisis. These lesson plans are standards-based and are well supported by articles, charts, graphs, and images.
Resource Type: Lesson or Activity
Grade Level: MS, HS

Srebrenica: A Cry from the Grave

www.pbs.org/wnet/cryfromthegrave/lessons/lessons.html

These are two lesson plans from the PBS site "Srebrenica: A Cry from the Grave." They explore human rights and ethnic identity.
Resource Type: Lesson or Activity
Grade Level: MS, HS

NATO and Its Role in Kosovo

http://sipa.columbia.edu/REGIONAL/ECE/teachers.html

This is a four-day lesson plan from West Babylon Senior High School. It contains articles, worksheets, and discussion questions.
Resource Type: Lesson or Activity
Grade Level: HS

Excerpts from Zlata's Diary: A Child's Life in Sarajevo

http://school.discovery.com/lessonplans/activities/childrenofwar/index.html

This is from a broader Discovery Channel lesson plan in which students read, analyze, and discuss children's war diaries. In addition to the lesson plan there is background on the Sarajevo conflict and a video on protecting children during wartime.
Resource Type: Lesson or Activity
Grade Level: MS, HS

Who's Who and What's What

www.nytimes.com/learning/students/quiz/kosovo.html

This is a *New York Times* quiz based on the "KOSOVO: A Bitter Struggle in a Land of Strife" article and images.

Resource Type: Lesson or Activity

Grade Level: HS

POST-COLD WAR

****The Gulf War

www.pbs.org/wgbh/pages/frontline/gulf/index.html

This "Frontline" site offers a comprehensive and engaging history of the Gulf War from the perspective of those who participated. Major categories include Oral Histories, War Stories, and Weapons and Technology and there are maps, a chronology, images, essays, a discussion of Gulf Syndrome, and more.

Resource Type: Primary Source Collection; Multimedia Presentation

****The History of the European Union

http://europa.eu.int/abc/history/index_en.htm

This Web site presents the chronology of important accomplishments of the EU and its institutions. Topics include Robert Schuman's declaration of 1950 to the first enlargement waves in the 1970s and the 1980s, the establishment of the Single Market in 1993 to the introduction

Figure 10.3: The History of the European Union

of the euro notes and coins on January 1, 2002, and the opening of enlargement negotiations with the countries of Eastern and Central Europe.
Resource Type: General Reference

****History of European Integration
www.eu-history.leidenuniv.nl/

Leiden University provides a well-organized directory of resources on the history of European Integration under the headings: Archives, Historical Documents, Bibliographies, Brussels, Journals, Cold War, Timelines, EU-Institutions, Non-EU Institutions, Discussion Groups, Oral Histories, Statistical Sources, Eurospeak and Federalism.
Resource Type: General Reference

****The Changing Face of Europe
www.cnn.com/SPECIALS/2000/eurounion/

A CNN.com special report on the European Union and how it is impacting all of Europe.
Resource Type: General Reference; Multimedia Presentation

****Collapse of the USSR: 10 Years On
http://news.bbc.co.uk/hi/english/static/in_depth/europe/2001/collapse_of_ussr/defalut.stm

"Countdown to Collapse" is a *BBC News* special presentation on the fall of the Soviet Union. Among its offerings is a timeline of events from 1985 to 1991 and an interactive map on how life has changed in the former Soviet Union. Special features at the site include eyewitness accounts in the form of *BBC News* articles and a photo gallery that provides images from the anti-Gorbachev coup of August 1991. Helpful overview and analysis
Resource Type: General Resource

****BBC Timeline of European Union
http://news.bbc.co.uk/2/hi/europe/358301.stm

BBC News offers a detailed timeline on the European Union highlighting select years from 1948 to the present. Additionally, the page features links to "Inside Europe" articles on related topics, such as the debate over a proposed new treaty for the European Union.
Resource Type: Timeline, General Resource

****AIDS at 20
www.nytimes.com/library/national/science/aids/aids-index.html

Provides 350-plus *New York Times* articles on the AIDS epidemic as well as video, factsheets, reports and nine articles specifically related to AIDS in Africa.
Resource Type: General Reference

****African Voices
www.mnh.si.edu/africanvoices/

The Smithsonian Institution's National Museum of Natural History provides a thematic exploration of Africa. The themes revolve around issues of wealth and the working and living conditions in Africa.
Resource Type: General Reference; Multimedia Presentation

****Africa
www.pbs.org/wnet/africa/

This PBS Web site focuses on African daily life and culture. There is a helpful Teacher Tools section and an Africa Challenge. The Africa for Kids section is designed for younger students.
Resource Type: General Reference; Lesson or Activity

****CNN Special Reports
www.cnn.com/SPECIALS/

The CNN Archives feature special reports on many key World and American events, issues, and personalities. They typically include CNN articles and video, among other features.
Resource Type: General Reference; Multimedia Presentation

****NATO at 50
www.cnn.com/SPECIALS/1999/nato/

A CNN.com special report on NATO's "midlife crisis."
Resource Type: General Reference; Multimedia Presentation

****Focus on Kosovo
www.cnn.com/SPECIALS/1998/10/kosovo/

A CNN.com special on the Kosovo crisis in the Balkans.
Resource Type: General Reference; Multimedia Presentation

****The Kashmir Conflict
http://edition.cnn.com/SPECIALS/2002/kashmir/index.html

A CNN.com special report on the conflict over Kashmir between India and Pakistan.
Resource Type: General Reference; Multimedia Presentation

****Asia's Row Over History
www.cnn.com/SPECIALS/2001/japan.history/

A CNN.com special report on the uproar in Asia after Japanese history textbooks whitewash Japanese atrocities in WWII.
Resource Type: General Reference; Multimedia Presentation

****China: 50 Years of Communism
http://news.bbc.co.uk/1/hi/special_report/1999/09/99/china_50_years_of_communism/456465.stm

This BBC Special Report (in association with CNN) looks back at the birth of the People's Republic and takes stock of what the future might hold for its people. Includes articles, a glossary, and more.
Resource Type: General Reference; Multimedia Presentation

****China's Communist Party
www.cnn.com/SPECIALS/2001/ccp80/

A CNN.com special report on 80 years of Communist rule in China.
Resource Type: General Reference; Multimedia Presentation

****Japan: A Nation in Crisis

www.cnn.com/SPECIALS/2001/jeconomy/

A CNN.com special report on the struggling Japanese economy and its impact on the nation.

Resource Type: General Reference; Multimedia Presentation

****Wars and Conflict: Northern Ireland

www.bbc.co.uk/history/recent/troubles/

A BBC history of the conflict in Northern Ireland.

Resource Type: General Reference; Multimedia Presentation

****Conflict and Hope in Northern Ireland

www.cnn.com/SPECIALS/2000/n.ireland/

A CNN.com special report on the Northern Ireland peace process.

Resource Type: General Reference; Multimedia Presentation

****Violence in Spain

http://edition.cnn.com/SPECIALS/2002/basque/

A CNN.com special report on continuing Basque violence.

Resource Type: General Reference; Multimedia Presentation

****War Without End

www.cnn.com/SPECIALS/2000/colombia.noframes/

A CNN.com special report on continuing civil insurgence and conflict in Columbia.

Resource Type: General Reference; Multimedia Presentation

****Two Koreas

www.cnn.com/SPECIALS/2001/korea/

A CNN.com special report on "reconciliation, engagement, and cooperation" between the Koreas.

Resource Type: General Reference; Multimedia Presentation

****Israel at 50

www.cnn.com/SPECIALS/1998/israel/

A 1998 CNN.com special report on the Israeli people.

Resource Type: General Reference; Multimedia Presentation

****Hong Kong: Between Two Worlds

www.cnn.com/WORLD/9706/hk97/

A 1997 CNN.com special report on the handover of Hong Kong from Britain to China.

Resource Type: General Reference; Multimedia Presentation

***The Next Millennium: Now What

www.cnn.com/SPECIALS/1999/future/index.html

CNN.com asks 14 experts to outline their vision of the next 1,000 years.

Resource Type: General Reference; Multimedia Presentation

The New York Times Learning Network
www.nytimes.com/learning/

This informative site offers detailed lesson plans and quizzes built around *New York Times* articles. Check out the Lesson Plan Archive and search by keyword, subject, or grade level. Social studies lesson plans are objective and standard-based and are well supported by charts, graphs, and images.
Resource Type: Lesson or Activity

CNN Education with Student News
www.cnn.com/EDUCATION/

"CNN Education" provides teachers with instructional materials for integrating current events across the curriculum. A student section keeps students in grades 6–12 aware of the latest news of interest to them. Lesson plans, background material, profiles, links to useful Internet sites, and forums for interaction with other teachers are also included.
Resource Type: Course Model

TV News Archive: Vanderbilt University, Nashville, Tennessee
http://tvnews.vanderbilt.edu/

This site contains a searchable database of news shows from 1968 to 2001. It offers 30,000 individual network evening news broadcasts. Note: You must be a registered user in order to search or use the videos.
Resource Type: Primary Source Collection; Multimedia Presentation

TIME Archive
www.time.com/time/magazine

"TIME Archive" provides a searchable text collection of its magazine articles since 1923. An excellent source of both primary and secondary source information on the 20th century.
Resource Type: Primary Source Collection

Post-Cold War Lesson Plans, Teacher Guides, Activities, and More

European Unity WebQuest
www.spartacus.schoolnet.co.uk/SPRINGwebquestUnity.htm

This WebQuest looks at the history of the European Unity movement and explores the contribution made to this debate.
Resource Type: Lesson or Activity
Grade Level: HS

The World in Uncertain Times, 1950–Present Practice Test
www.phschool.com/curriculum_support/brief_review/us_history/tests.html?unit=7&number=35
High school level quiz on Cold War America from Prentice Hall.
Resource Type: Test or Quiz
Grade Level: HS

The World in Uncertain Times, 1950–Present Document-Based Essay
www.phschool.com/curriculum_support/brief_review/us_history/essay_questions/unit7.cfm

From the site: "This Prentice Hall DBQ is designed to test your ability to work with historical documents and is based on the accompanying documents (1–6)."
Resource Type: Lesson or Activity
Grade Level:HS

TERRORISM

For 9/11 resources please go to Chapter 6, 9/11 and Terrorism.

***History News Network
http://hnn.us/articles/299.html

"History News Network" offers several informative articles and opinion pieces (written by credible writers—professors/field experts), such as Short History of Terrorism, The First Act of Terrorism in English America, Democracy: A Cure for Terrorism, and many others. They help put terrorism in historical perspective.
Resource Type: General Reference

****The Washington Post: Attack Map and Database Search
www.washingtonpost.com/wp-dyn/world/issues/terrordata/

Allows user to find basic information and facts on terrorism. Allows searching from pulldown menus by organization, location, terrorist's name, or incident (also has a standard type-in search). Useful for any terrorist attack except for 9/11—for some reason there is little about 9/11 on this site.
Resource Type: General Reference

*****Frontline Teacher Center—Roots of Terrorism
www.pbs.org/wgbh/pages/frontline/teach/terror/

Excellent PBS site with lots of classroom activities and links for background information on terrorism and its development. Content includes timelines, maps, facts, people, content on Islam, and more. High quality site with plenty of facts and data.
Resource Type: General Reference; Lesson or Activity

****War Against Terror
www.cnn.com/SPECIALS/2001/trade.center/

Part of the CNN.com Archives, this site is an excellent introduction to the issue of terrorism as it relates to 9/11.
Resource Type: General Reference; Multimedia Presentation

***Terrorism in the 20th Century
www.terrorism-research.com/history/recent.php

Provides a brief overview of terrorism in the twentieth century. This section is part of a broader site that outlines the evolution of terrorism and explains many of its components.
Resource Type: General Reference

***Teacher Oz: Terrorism

www.teacheroz.com/government.htm#terrorism

This section of "Teacher Oz's Kingdom of History" provides a useful links set of links dealing with terrorism and, more specifically, with the tragedy of September 11.
Resource Type: Links Collection

***Timeline of Terrorism

www.simplytaty.com/broadenpages/terrorism.htm

This section offers a detailed timeline of terrorism covers the 1970s to the 1980s and the 1990s to 2001.
Resource Type: Timeline

Terrorism Lesson Plans, Teacher Guides, Activities, and More

Frontline Teacher Center—Roots of Terrorism

www.pbs.org/wgbh/pages/frontline/teach/terror/resources/

Excellent PBS site with lots of classroom activities and links for background information on terrorism and its development. Content includes timelines, maps, facts, people, content on Islam, and more. High quality site with plenty of facts and data.
Resource Type: Lesson or Activity
Grade Level: HS

CHAPTER 11

History through a Different Lens

ART HISTORY

General Art History Resources

*****The Metropolitan Museum of Art
www.metmuseum.org/home.asp

There is much quality material for art students, educators, and enthusiasts at the the Metropolitan Museum of Art Web site (see Figure 11.1). Start with the Metropolitan Museum of Art Timeline of Art History, a chronological, geographical, and thematic exploration of the history of art from around the world. Each timeline page includes representative art from the Museum's collection, a chart of time periods, a map of the region, an overview, and a list of key events. The timelines—accompanied by world, regional, and sub-regional maps— provide a linear outline of art history, allowing visitors to compare and contrast art from around the globe at any time in history. There is plenty more here apart from the Timeline: Just for Fun has interactive activities for kids, A Closer Look examines the "hows and whys" behind Met objects (such as *George Washington Crossing the Delaware*), "Artist" enables visitors to access biographical materials on a selection of artists as well as general information about their work, and "Themes and Cultures" presents past and present cultures with special features on the Met's collections and exhibitions. (Many of these individual exhibitions are listed below.)
Resource Type: Multimedia Presentation; Lesson or Activity

****Art History Resources on the Web
http://witcombe.sbc.edu/ARTHLinks.html

Professor Chris Witcombe of the Art department at Sweet Briar College has perhaps the best organized gateway to art history sites on the Web. His directory is full of useful and regularly updated links and is divided into the following categories: Prehistoric Art, Ancient Near East, Ancient Egypt, Ancient Greece, Ancient Rome, Art in Early Europe, 15th-Century Renaissance Art, 16th-Century Renaissance Art, 17th-Century Baroque Art, Baroque Art, 18th-Century Art, 19th-Century Art, 20th-Century Art, 21st-Century Art, and Prints & Photography (see Figure 11.2). He also includes a list of museums and galleries and research resources. Professor Witcombe has also produced an exhibition exploring the perception of

Figure 11.1: Metropolitan Museum of Art's Timeline of Art History

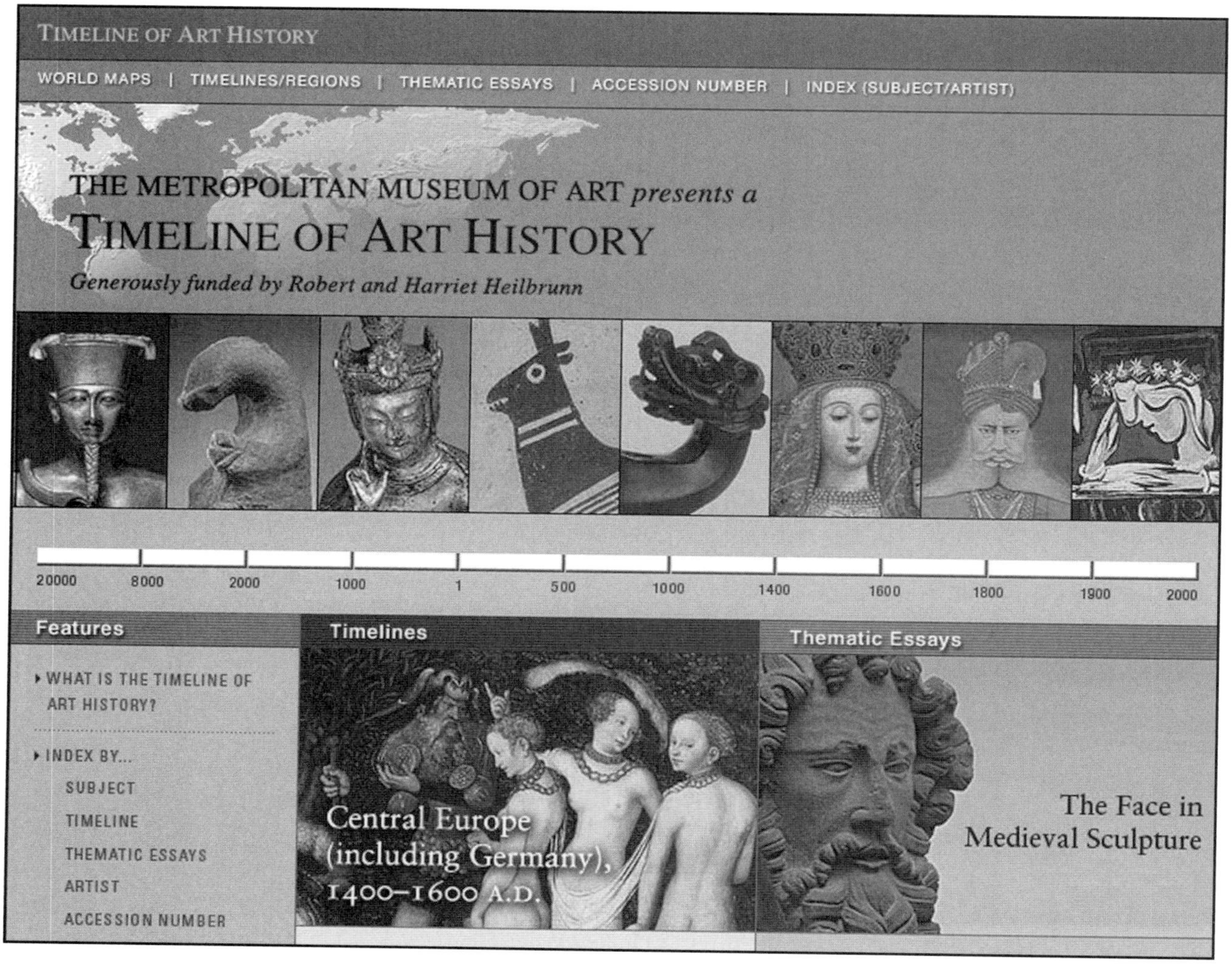

Focus on Metropolitan Museum of Art Timeline of Art History

If you are looking to create a slideshow on historic art, this is a great site to work with. Start with the Metropolitan Museum of Art **Timeline of Art History**, a chronological, geographical, and thematic exploration of the history of art from around the world. Each timeline page includes representative art from the Museum's collection, a chart of time periods, a map of the region, an overview, and a list of key events. The timelines—accompanied by world, regional, and subregional maps—provide a linear outline of art history, and allow visitors to compare and contrast art from around the globe at any time in history. There is plenty more at the Met site than just the Timeline: **Just for Fun** has interactive activities for kids, **A Closer Look** examines the "hows and whys" behind Met objects, **Artist** enables visitors to access biographical materials on a selection of artists as well as general information about their work, and **Themes and Cultures** presents past and present cultures with special features on the Met's collections and exhibitions. Sections of interest in **Ancient History** include: Art of the First Cities—The Third Millennium B.C. from the Mediterranean to the Indus, Egyptian Art in the Age of the Pyramids, The New Greek Galleries, The Legacy of Genghis Khan: Courtly Art and Culture in Western Asia, Genesis: Ideas of Origin in African Sculpture, In the Footsteps of Marco Polo: A Journey through the Met to the Land of the Great Khan, and The Glory of Byzantium.

Art and the identity of the artist through history and in contemporary society, entitled What is Art?.... What is an Artist?
Resource Type: General Reference; Course Model

Figure 11.2 Art History Resources on the Web

****Artcyclopedia: The Guide to Museum-Quality Art on the Internet**
www.artcyclopedia.com/

"Artcyclopedia" editors have compiled a comprehensive index of every artist represented at hundreds of museum sites, image archives, and other online resources. "Artcyclopedia" only provides references to sites on the Web where artists' works can be viewed online, and the vast majority of the artists in their database specialize in painting and sculpture. They have a searchable index of over 1,200 arts sites, and offer more than 32,000 links to an estimated 100,000 works by 7,500 renowned artists. A great resource for researching particular artists.
Resource Type: General Reference

****World Art Treasures
www.bergerfoundation.ch/index.html

The Jacques-Eduard Berger Foundation of Art and Civilisation offers "World Art Treasures," an impressive site for learning about art and artists through the ages. The site offers lectures and itineraries of the cultural tours, an Artists Slide Library, slides by Country, Region, and City, a Periods Slide Library, Essays, an Audio Section to listen to the different lectures, a Zoom function, and Puzzle, a chance to click on a piece of a masterwork and drag to correct place. Lectures and itineraries include Tell el Amarna, Capital of the Disk, Roman Portraits from Egypt, The Enchanted Gardens of the Renaissance, Sandro Botticelli, Caravaggio: The Night Prince, Johannes Vermeer, and more. There is also an interactive timeline.
Resource Type: General Reference; Multimedia Presentation

****The Getty Museum
www.getty.edu/

The J. Paul Getty Trust focus on the visual arts serves both general audiences and specialized professionals, and it offers an impressive array of services. For instance, the Getty Research Institute provides access to a range of online research tools. The Research Library is accessible to both on-site and remote users and provides access to the Library Catalog, a myriad of collections and other services. The Explore Art section allows you to browse many of the works of art on display at the Getty by name, object, theme, or topic. You can also view current or past exhibitions. Among the best are Jean-Antoine Houdon (1741–1828): Sculptor of the Enlightenment and Raphael at the Gallery. There are also lesson plans and ideas for discussion on many aspects of art and art history.
Resource Type: General Reference; Multimedia Presentation

****Voice of the Shuttle: Art & Art History
http://vos.ucsb.edu/browse.asp?id=3404

VoS is an extensive humanities database with many useful links to art history resources. Among their many art history categories are General Art Resources, Artists & Works By Chronology, Museums, Institutes, & Centers, Galleries & Exhibitions, Journals & Zines (Art & Art History), Depts. & Programs (Art & Art History), and Course Syllabi & Teaching Resources (Art & Art History).
Resource Type: General Reference

****Art History Research Center
www.harmsen.net/ahrc/

The Art History Research Center from Concordia University, Canada, is a tool for art historical research. It provides access to newsgroups, mailing lists, library catalogs, article indexes, online collections, art history & arts web servers, and links. There is also a short essay entitled "The Internet as a Research Medium for Art Historians."
Resource Type: General Reference

****About: Art History
http://arthistory.about.com/About_Art_History.htm

This About.com comprehensive gateway to Art History resources is managed by Shelley Esaak, who is a portrait artist, a freelance illustrator and graphic designer, a writer, and an educator. There are plenty of helpful annotated links in multiple categories: Articles & Resources, Famous Names in Art, Timelines of Art History, Movements and Schools, Different Types of Art, Art by Country or Region, Art by Culture or Group, Images/Picture Galleries, Contemporary Art, Find Museums/Galleries, Art Appreciation, Help/Advice for Students, Educator/Parent Resources, Reference and Reading, 60-Second Artist Profiles, Leonardo's Last Supper, Art History Glossary, The Art History Forum, and more. A broad and helpful site, though obtrusive ads are annoying.
Resource Type: General Reference

****The World Wide Web Virtual Library: History of Art
www.chart.ac.uk/vlib/

The "History of Art" virtual library is a gateway of links relating to Art History sponsored by CHArt, the Computers and History of Art Group. This site is aimed at everybody interested in art, but it has a special focus on the academic study of Art History. If you have an interest in art history and would like to find images online or to learn more about particular artists, the sites they list be of use to you.
Resource Type: General Reference

****Smithsonian American Art Museum
www.americanart.si.edu/index3.cfm

The Smithsonian American Art Museum (SAAM) is America's first federal art collection, dedicated to the art and artists of the United States. More than 7,000 American artists are represented, including major artists such as John Singleton Copley, John Singer Sargent, Georgia O'Keeffe, and others. The featured themes and topics of the collection include Colonial portraiture, nineteenth-century landscape, American impressionism, twentieth-century realism and abstraction, New Deal projects, sculpture, photography, prints and drawings, contemporary crafts, African American art, Latino art, and folk art. Today the collection consists of more than 40,000 artworks in all media, spanning more than 300 years of artistic achievement. The Smithsonian Online Exhibitions feature prize holdings from different eras in American history. The online version of American Art, the academic journal of the Smithsonian American Art Museum, has articles of interest to art historians.
Resource Type: General Reference; Multimedia Presentation

****Library of Congress: The American Memory
http://memory.loc.gov/ammem/index.html

The American Memory Collection from the Library of Congress contains primary source materials relating to the history and culture of the United States. The site offers more than seven million digital items from more than 100 historical collections. Included are multimedia collections of photographs, recorded sound, moving pictures, and digitized text. Select

collections to search, search for items across all collections, and explore teaching and learning ideas with American Memory.
Resource Type: Primary Source Collection

****Artchive
www.artchive.com/

Mark Harden's "Artchive" offers over 2,000 high quality scans of artwork for educational purposes. The museum is divided into several galleries: The Artchive, Glyphs Art Reviews, The Galleries, Theory and Criticism, Juxtapositions, Art CD-ROM Reviews, and Art Links. "Artchive" offers browser access in HTML format to the archive for all of the fine art scans. The Galleries is the entry point to the online exhibitions currently showing.
Resource Type: General Reference

****WorldArt Web Kiosk
http://worldart.sjsu.edu/

"WorldArt Web Kiosk" image database allows you to search over 35,000 images from throughout the world. Portfolios of art, architecture and sculpture arranged by geographic area or time period. Faculty, staff, and students of the California State University System created this database. Categories: American Paintings and Sculpture; Ancient Near Eastern Art; Arts of Africa, Oceania, and the Americas; Asian Art; European Paintings; European Sculpture and Decorative Arts; Egyptian Art; Greek and Roman Art; and Islamic Art.
Resource Type: General Reference; General Reference

****Art History Network
www.arthistory.net/index.html

"Art History Network" is a resource for Art History, Archaeology, and Architecture resources on the Web. Topics include Artist, Civilizations, Links: Journals & Magazines, Images & Virtual Tours, and General Resources. There are also links to discussion groups, chats, and a bookstore.
Resource Type: Art History

****Art Images for College Teaching
http://arthist.cla.umn.edu/aict/html/index.html

AICT is a free-use image resource for the educational community by art historian and visual resources curator Allan T. Kohl. AICT is intended primarily to disseminate images of art and architectural works in the public domain on a free-access, free-use basis to all levels of the educational community, as well as to the public at large.
Resource Type: General Reference

****The Incredible Art Department
www.princetonol.com/groups/iad/

This popular site is managed by two K–12 art teachers and offers plenty of links to curriculum resources, art education sites, art teacher listservs, art teacher Web sites, and more and features a "site of the month." You'll find many helpful lessons and ideas, including Art History games.
Resource Type: General Reference

****Reunion des Musees Nationaux (RMN), France
www.rmn.fr/fr/04editions/index-07agence-photo.html

The photo agency of the Reunion des Musées Nationaux (RMN), French National Organization of Art Museums, houses more than 100,000 color transparencies and 500,000 black-and-white negatives relating to works of art in France's national museums: paintings, sculptures, decorative arts, drawings and photographs. For the less proficient in French, this site also has an English version.
Resource Type: General Reference

****Nineteenth-Century Art Worldwide
www.19thc-artworldwide.org/

"Nineteenth-Century Art Worldwide" is the world's first scholarly, refereed e-journal devoted to the study of nineteenth-century painting, sculpture, graphic arts, photography, architecture, and decorative arts across the globe. The chronological scope of the journal is the "long" nineteenth century, stretching from the American and French Revolutions at one end to the outbreak of World War I at the other.
Resource Type: General Reference

****Mother of all Art and Art History Links Page
www.art-design.umich.edu/mother/

"Mother of all Art and Art History Links Page" is available courtesy of the School of Art & Design at the University of Michigan. It offers a gateway to Art History Departments, Research Resources, and Online Exhibitions.
Resource Type: Art History

****Art Guide: The Art Lovers Guide to Britain and Ireland
www.artguide.org/uk/

An extensive index to the art collections of Great Britain and Ireland. "Art Guide" is organized by artist, by museum, and geographically. The database currently contains more than 1,900 named artists, more than 650 museums, more than 4,500 individual listings, and comprehensive exhibitions listings. For each artist there is a list of their works and where they can be found and for each museum a list of outstanding works in the collection, and other information.
Resource Type: General Reference

****Site Officiel du Musée du Louvre
www.louvre.fr/llv/commun/home_flash.jsp

At the official Web site of the Louvre, there are virtual tours of many of the galleries and exhibitions. The site presents a selection of the works of art from each of the seven departments of the museum. There is also an English version.
Resource Type: Virtual Tour

***Spartacus: Encyclopedia of British Art, 1600–1950
www.spartacus.schoolnet.co.uk/art.htm

This Spartacus Educational UK resource offers brief essays and information on Art Institutions, Artists 1600–1750, Artists 1750–1900, Artists 1900–1950, and Architects.
Resource Type: General Reference

***AskArt.com
www.askart.com/AskART/index.aspx

AskArt.com offers extensive information on over 52,000 American artists. Artists searchable by name.
Resource Type: General Reference

***Hunt for Art History
www.huntfor.com/arthistory/

Part of HuntFor.com, "Hunt for Art History" provides a wealth of information about the arts. Selected periods and artists are profiled and there are artists' resources, lessons, and tutorials. This portal Web site was developed and maintained by computer and graphic art professionals.
Resource Type: General Reference; Lesson or Activity

Select Topics in Art History

****Egyptian Art in the Age of the Pyramids
www.metmuseum.org/explore/new_pyramid/pyramids/html/el_pyramid_intro.htm

The Metropolitan Museum of Art's "Egyptian Art in the Age of the Pyramids" is a comprehensive exhibition of Old Kingdom art. It includes approximately 250 objects from more than 30 museums in Egypt, Europe, and North America, and 41 are presented at this site. You can learn about the Old Kingdom in the introduction or explore the individual works by selecting one of the following themes: Pyramid complexes, tombs of officials, Images of Royalty, Images of Officials and their Families, Portraiture, Images of Artisans and Occupations, Objects, and Daily Life.
Resource Type: General Reference; Virtual Tour

****Art of the First Cities: The Third Millennium B.C. from the Mediterranean to the Indus
www.metmuseum.org/special/se_event.asp?OccurrenceId={9B8FB8E8-AE97-11D6-945F-00902786BF44}

The Metropolitan Museum of Art's "Art of the First Cities: The Third Millennium B.C. from the Mediterranean to the Indus" explores through art the emergence of the world's first city-states and empires in Syria and Mesopotamia during the third millennium B.C. The site also relates these developments to artistic and cultural developments from the eastern Aegean to the Indus valley and Central Asia. Famous sites of the ancient world covered include the Royal Graves of Ur, the palace and temples of Mari, the citadel of Troy, and the great cities of the Indus Valley civilization. The exhibition includes approximately 400 works of extraordinary sculpture, jewelry, seals, relief carving, metalwork, and cuneiform tablets. There is a special, in-depth feature designed to complement the exhibition, an essay from the exhibition catalogue, and samples from the accompanying Audio Guide.
Resource Type: General Reference; Virtual Tour

****The New Greek Galleries
www.metmuseum.org/explore/Greek/Greek1.htm

The Metropolitan Museum of Art's "The New Greek Galleries" is an extensive collection of Greek art. You can explore the galleries online by following four interconnected paths: a time-

line illustrated with signal works of art, a menu of eighteen art objects selected for this online preview and accompanied by explanatory text, a geographical map of the Mediterranean area where the works of art were produced, and a gallery map coupled with descriptions of the newly designed spaces and a selection of art objects.
Resource Type: General Reference; Virtual Tour

****Ancient Near East and the Ancient Mediterranean World
www.lib.uchicago.edu/e/dl/proj/neh2/

The University of Chicago Library preserves deteriorated research materials relating to the history, art, and archaeology of the Ancient Near East and the Ancient Mediterranean world. The project focuses on materials published between 1850 and 1950, drawn from two of the library's complimentary collections: the Ancient Near East and Classics Collections.
Resource Type: General Reference; Virtual Tour

****The Legacy of Genghis Khan: Courtly Art and Culture in Western Asia, 1256–1353
www.metmuseum.org/special/se_event.asp?OccurrenceId={36C74128-EEF8-11D5-9414-00902786BF44}

The Metropolitan Museum of Art's "The Legacy of Genghis Khan: Courtly Art and Culture in Western Asia, 1256–1353" features images, audio, and essays related to the exhibition. This exhibition displays more than 200 outstanding examples of illustrated manuscripts, the decorative arts, and architectural decoration. Accompanied by a catalogue.
Resource Type: General Reference; Virtual Tour

****Oriental Institute Virtual Museum
http://oi.uchicago.edu/OI/MUS/QTVR96/QTVR96_Tours.html

"Oriental Institute Virtual Museum" is a showcase of the history, art and archaeology of the ancient Near East. The Museum exhibits major collections of antiquities from Egypt, Mesopotamia, Iran, Syria, Palestine, and Anatolia. "Oriental Institute Virtual Museum" makes use of a series of Apple QuickTime VR panoramic movies to take you on a tour of each of the museum's galleries, accompanied by descriptions of each alcove and their artifacts. Where appropriate, links to related materials, such as the Museum's Highlights From The Collections, the Photographic Archives, and relevant Oriental Institute Archaeology and Philology projects elaborate on the most significant objects in greater detail.
Resource Type: General Reference; Virtual Tour

****Genesis: Ideas of Origin in African Sculpture
www.metmuseum.org/special/se_event.asp?OccurrenceId={36C7412C-EEF8-11D5-9414-00902786BF44}

The Metropolitan Museum of Art's "Genesis: Ideas of Origin in African Sculpture" explores the following questions: How did the world begin? What is our ancestry? What is the source of agriculture and of kingship, and other societal institutions? The exhibition explores how artists in distinct African cultures have interpreted these ideas and sought to answer these questions, with a focus on classical sculptural form, the ci wara antelope headdress of the Bamana people. You can see videos illustrating headdress performances and read the transcript of a lecture presented in conjunction with this exhibition.
Resource Type: General Reference; Virtual Tour

****Art and Oracle: A Scholarly Resource of African Art and Rituals of Divination
www.metmuseum.org/explore/oracle/index.html

The Metropolitan Museum of Art's "Art and Oracle: A Scholarly Resource of African Art and Rituals of Divination" features objects in color photographs, basic information, and explanatory text. There are 50 works—grouped into eight categories—from the "Art and Oracle" exhibition catalogue, an exhibition list sorted by African cultures, a group of divination objects in South African collections, a selection of related works from other parts of the world in the Met's collection, a map of sub-Saharan Africa, four essays on different aspects of divination in Africa, a glossary of principal terms, and a bibliography of sources on African divination. *Resource Type: General Reference; Virtual Tour*

****In the Footsteps of Marco Polo: A Journey through the Met to the Land of the Great Khan
www.metmuseum.org/explore/Marco/index.html

The Metropolitan Museum of Art's "In the Footsteps of Marco Polo" offers an interactive map, audio clips, activities and reading suggestions. Use the online Image Explorer to review the works of art you've seen on this journey through art from Venice to China. *Resource Type: General Reference; Virtual Tour*

****The Glory of Byzantium
www.metmuseum.org/explore/Byzantium/byzhome.html

The Metropolitan Museum of Art's "The Glory of Byzantium" includes many images from the Met's collection and can be accessed in a number of ways. You can explore Byzantine works of art, investigate a theme in Byzantine art, and probe the history of Byzantium. You can also view the works of art in a visual timeline. There is a glossary as well as a special resource area for teachers. *Resource Type: General Reference; Virtual Tour*

****Treasures from the Royal Tombs of Ur
http://oi.uchicago.edu/OI/UR/Ur_home.html

A presentation by the University of Pennsylvania Museum of Archaeology and Anthropology, this is an exhibition from the School of Art and Design at San Jose State University, featuring 157 Sumerian objects that were excavated by the British archaeologist Sir Leonard Woolley, director of the joint excavations of the British Museum and the University of Pennsylvania Museum at ancient Ur in the 1920s and 1930s. *Resource Type: General Reference; Virtual Tour*

****Web Gallery of Art
www.wga.hu/index.html

"Web Gallery of Art" is a virtual museum and searchable database of European painting and sculpture of the Gothic, Renaissance, and Baroque periods (1100–1850), currently containing over 15,400 reproductions. Biographies, commentaries, and guided tours are available. Furthermore, a search engine allows you to find pictures in the collection using various search criteria. The guided tours make it easier to visit the Gallery and to understand the artistic and historical relationship between the artwork and artists included in the collection. *Resource Type: General Reference; Virtual Tour*

****Cleopatra: A Multimedia Guide to the Ancient World
www.artic.edu/cleo/index.html

This is an interactive guide to the Ancient Art collection of the Art Institute of Chicago. Stories accompany the objects, and there are lesson plans for grades 4–12.
Resource Type: General Reference; Lesson or Activity

****Huntington Photographic Archive of Buddhist and Related Art
http://kaladarshan.arts.ohio-state.edu/default.html

The John C. and Susan L. Huntington Photographic Archive of Buddhist and Related Art of the College of the Arts, Ohio State University contains nearly 300,000 original color slides and black-and-white and color photographs of art and architecture throughout Asia. Countries covered in the collection include India, Afghanistan, Pakistan, Bangladesh, Sri Lanka, Nepal, China, Japan, Thailand, Indonesia, and Myanmar (Burma). Works range from approximately 2500 B.C.E. to the present, and documentation includes contemporary religious activities in various parts of Asia. The Archive documents the art and architecture of these countries in situ, as well as works of art found in most major Asian, European, and American museums. This broad, yet detailed collection contains predominantly Buddhist material, but also includes Hindu, Jain, Islamic, and other works.
Resource Type: General Reference; Primary Source Collection

****Pharaohs of the Sun: Akhenaten, Nefertiti, Tutankhamen
www.mfa.org/egypt/amarna/

"Pharaohs of the Sun: Akhenaten, Nefertiti, Tutankhamen," from the Museum of Fine Arts in Boston, captures the revolutionary epoch known as the Amarna Age (1353–1336 B.C.). This exhibition brings together over 250 objects from museums all over the world—from Cairo and Luxor to Paris, Berlin, and Boston. View 20 selected highlights that trace the story of Akhenaten, his city, and his legacy. Linked to each of these highlights are related objects with which you can explore the exhibition further.
Resource Type: General Reference; Virtual Tour

****Perseus: Greco-Roman
www.perseus.tufts.edu/cgi-bin/perscoll?collection=

The Perseus Classics collection integrates textual and visual materials on the Archaic and Classical Greek world and the Roman world. The collection contains extensive and diverse resources including primary and secondary texts, site plans, digital images, and maps. Art and Archaeology catalogs a wide range of objects: Over 1,500 vases, over 1,800 sculptures and sculptural groups, over 1,200 coins, hundreds of buildings from nearly 100 sites and over 100 gems.
Resource Type: General Reference; Primary Source Collection

****ABZU: Guide to Resources for the Study of the Ancient Near East Available on the Internet
www.etana.org/abzu/

ABZU is a guide to the study and public presentation of the Ancient Near East via the Internet and has been available on the Internet since October 5, 1994. The editor of ABZU is Charles

E. Jones, Research Archivist and Bibliographer at The Oriental Institute at the University of Chicago.
Resource Type: General Reference, Primary Source Collection

****Theban Mapping Project
www.thebanmappingproject.com/

An impressive site that focuses on the Theban Necropolis, the Valley of the Kings, the tomb of Rameses II, and Egyptology. It offers maps, a timeline, Q&As, and updates on the KV5 (Rameses tomb) archeological expedition.
Resource Type: Virtual Tour

****The Age of Enlightenment in the Paintings of France's National Museums
http://mistral.culture.fr/files/imaginary_exhibition.html

The Web site offers extensive historical background and information about painters of the Age of Enlightenment, as well as images of their paintings found in France's National Museums.
Resource Type: General Reference

****Creating French Culture: Treasures from the Bibliothèque Nationale de France
www.loc.gov/exhibits/bnf/bnf0001.html

"Creating French Culture: Treasures from the Bibliothèque Nationale de France" traces the history of power and culture from Charlemagne (742?–814) to Charles de Gaulle (1890–1970), through the prism of more than 200 "magnificent treasures."
Resource Type: General Reference; Virtual Tour

****Splendors of Christendom: Worldwide Tour of Churches, Cathedrals and Monasteries
www.christusrex.org/www1/splendors/splendors.html

Includes hundreds of images of works of art found in churches, cathedrals, and monasteries from around the world.
Resource Type: General Reference; Virtual Tour

****Lantern Slides of Classical Antiquity
www.brynmawr.edu/Admins/DMVRC/lanterns/

Bryn Mawr College has a large collection of slides and prints from classical antiquity. These images are not simply classroom aids now, but resources for scholarship.
Resource Type: General Reference

****Vatican Museums, Vatican City
http://mv.vatican.va/3_EN/pages/MV_Home.html

This site offers online tours of the collections of art and antiquities at the Vatican museums. Collections include the Gregorian Egyptian and Etruscan Museums, Raphael's Rooms, the Pinacoteca (Art Gallery), and the Ethnological Missionary Museum. Visitors can examine various rooms in the Vatican, including the Sistine Chapel. Visitors may also take a virtual tour of each room.
Resource Type: General Reference

****Poets, Lovers, and Heroes in Italian Mythological Prints
www.metmuseum.org/special/se_event.asp?OccurrenceId={065B077D-DB1B-423B-9412-D3B45235AD46}

The Metropolitan Museum of Art's "Poets, Lovers, and Heroes in Italian Mythological Prints" presents more than 100 woodcuts, engravings, and etchings that extol popular mythological tales. Themes consist of the ancient gods as patrons of music, poetry, and painting and as participants in music competitions; the heroic exploits of Hercules; and the legendary history of Rome.
Resource Type: General Reference; Virtual Tour

****Islamic Art
www.lacma.org/islamic_art/intro.htm

This Web site is conceived as a companion to the Islamic galleries at the Los Angeles County Museum of Art. Intended as a general introduction to Islamic art, it draws upon examples from the museum's comprehensive collection, which includes works from an area extending from southern Spain to Central Asia, ranging in date from the seventh through the nineteenth century.
Resource Type: General Reference

****American Photographs: The First Century
http://americanart.si.edu/collections/exhibits/helios/amerphotos.html

The Smithsonian American Art Museum offers a broad selection of photographs from The Charles Isaacs Collection of American Photography. The images include Civil War images by George Barnard and the Mathew Brady Studio, and Western landscapes by Timothy O'Sullivan and William Henry Jackson. There is a mix of familiar and lesser known photographers and styles of work in order to explore ideas about the influence of photographic culture in America during the years from 1839 to 1939.
Resource Type: Primary Source Collection

****Maecenas: Images of Ancient Greece and Rome
http://wings.buffalo.edu/AandL/Maecenas/

The photographs were taken primarily for use in teaching by a professor at the University of Buffalo and can be used for any purpose except a commercial one. This Web site has been assisted by grants from the Classical Association of the Empire State and the Classical Association of the Atlantic States.
Resource Type: Image Collection

****Ancient Near Eastern Art: New Light on an Assyrian Palace
www.metmuseum.org/explore/anesite/html/el_ane_newfirst.htm

The central gallery of the Raymond and Beverly Sackler Gallery for Assyrian Art recreates an audience hall in the palace of Ashurnasirpal II (r. 883–859 B.C.) at Nimrud in northern Iraq. Objects in an adjacent gallery illustrate the ivory carving and other art of the Assyrian empire and its neighbors. Learn more about the palace of Ashurnasirpal II, the city of Nimrud, and the stone reliefs and carved ivories of the Assyrian empire through the following sections: Map of Assyrian Empire, Excavations at Nimrud, Ivories from the Northwest Palace, and Reliefs. View a virtual reality reconstruction and a drawn rendering of the interior of the palace.
Resource Type: General Reference; Virtual Tour

****Investigating the Renaissance

www.artmuseums.harvard.edu/Renaissance/index.html

This interesting Harvard University Art Museum site uses digital imaging techniques to examine three Renaissance paintings: Portrait of a Man, The Virgin and Child, and The Last Judgment. The site explains and demonstrates how Infrared light, ultraviolet light and X-rays can provide valuable information on a painting's condition, on earlier stages of its production, and on later alterations.

Resource Type: General Reference; Multimedia Presentation

****The Digital Michelangelo Project

http://graphics.stanford.edu/projects/mich/

Researchers from Stanford University and the University of Washington are attempting to advance the technology of 3-D scanning and place this technology in the service of the humanities by creating a long-term digital archive of some important cultural artifacts. The project focuses on some of Michelangelo's sculptures, including the famous David statue. Check out two photographic essays about a physical replica of the David and download ScanView, a program that lets you "fly around" models of Michelangelo's statues.

Resource Type: General Reference; Multimedia Presentation

****The Museum of Antiquities

http://museums.ncl.ac.uk/archive/

The Museum of Antiquities is the joint museum of the Society of Antiquaries of Newcastle upon Tyne and the University of Newcastle upon Tyne. It is the principal museum of archaeology in northeast England and teaches about the history of the region, especially Hadrian's Wall and the Roman frontier. It has a renowned collection of artifacts, models, and archives relating to the Wall, and a full-scale reconstruction of the Temple to Mithras at Carrawburgh. Other displays illustrate the variety of life in the region from early prehistory to the seventeenth century. There is a virtual gallery of special exhibits, including Hadrian's Wall and Flints and Stones, with nice images and explanatory text. Also offers an Object of the Month.

Resource Type: General Reference; Virtual Tour

****The Biography Channel

www.biography.com/search/

Biographies of Impressionist artists such as Degas, Monet, Morisot, Pisarro, and Renoir are found here.

Resource Type: General Reference

****Leonardo da Vinci: Master Draftsman

www.metmuseum.org/special/Leonardo_Master_Draftsman/draftsman_splash.htm

This site by the Metropolitan Museum of Art accompanies an exhibit of drawings by Leonardo da Vinci. The drawings can be examined closely with a zoom feature and the site includes audio commentary, a scholarly bibliography, an introductory essay, and even a discourse of da Vinci's left-handedness.

Resource Type: General Reference; Multimedia Presentation

***Treasures of the World: Mona Lisa

www.pbs.org/treasuresoftheworld/a_nav/mona_nav/mnav_level_1/3technique_monafrm.html

Part of the PBS *Treasures of the World* series, Mona Lisa is cast as a masterwork of art in an engaging story of crime and discovery. The section revolves around the Mona Lisa's disappearance in 1911 but its true focus lies in Leonardo's technique and the myth of Mona Lisa. Visitors, particularly students, should gain a greater appreciation of the Da Vinci masterpiece.
Resource Type: General Reference

***Michelangelo Buonarroti

http://michelangelo.com/buon/bio-index2.html?http://www.michelangelo.com/buon/bio-early.html

This biographical resource on the Renaissance artist Michelangelo Buonarroti discusses his life and achievements and offers links to many of his great works. The site has three major sections—Early Life, Mid Years, and Final Days—and each section highlights key events of Michelangelo's life as well as his most important works. A concise and useful overview aimed at high school students.
Resource Type: General Reference; Lesson or Activity

***Renaissance and Baroque Architecture: Architectural History 102

www.lib.virginia.edu/dic/colls/arh102/index.html

Professor C. W. Westfall's course on Renaissance and Baroque Architecture at the University of Virginia features a collection of over 500 topically organized images. Section include: Italy in the 15th Century—Introduction, Brunelleschi's Legacy, Florence in the 15th Century, The 16th Century—Bramante and Roman Architecture, and many more. Teachers, scholars, students, and the general public are free to use these images for educational purposes.
Resource Type: General Reference; Virtual Tour

***Rodin-Web

www.rodin-web.org/

"Rodin-Web" purports to be the world's largest Web site on Auguste Rodin. It contains an overview of 220 public Rodin collections, biographical data, extensive bibliography, image database, links to useful resources, email network. "Rodin-Web" constitutes an art-historical database, an Internet guide, and an online forum at the same time.
Resource Type: General Reference

Art History Lesson Plans and Activities

Art History: A Preliminary Handbook

http://web.ubc.ca/okanagan/creative/links/arthistory.html

Dr. R. J. Belton of the Department of Fine Arts at Okanagan University College has produced this excellent guidebook to Art History. Sections include Why Study Visual Culture? Evaluation in Term Papers (Research, Thinking and Writing Skills), Further Basic Questions to Ask Yourself About the Work, Some Points for Writing Any Essay, and Academic Documentation in the Department of Fine Arts.
Resource Type: Lesson or Activity
Grade Level: College

Getty Center: Resources for Teachers
http://www.getty.edu/education/for_teachers/

K–12 teachers can get reference materials, lessons, and activities from the Getty Institute. In the Professional Development Opportunities section, Looking at Decorative Arts examines furniture, tapestries, porcelain, and scientific objects; Looking at Portraits offers lesson plans, suggested questions, and activities prompt discussion and activities about six different portraits; Language Through Art helps ESL students learn new vocabulary, and practice using it by looking at and describing portraits, landscapes, and narrative works of art. Art and Language Arts are lessons by Los Angeles-area elementary teachers that use artwork in the Getty Museum collection to teach students language and visual arts skills. ArtsEdNet includes lesson plans, curriculum ideas, an image gallery, and ArtsEdNet Talk, an online community of teachers and learners.
Resource Type: Course Model
Grade Level: LS, MS, HS

Eyes on Art
www.kn.pacbell.com/wired/art2/index.html

This interactive Pacific Bell site is devoted to helping students learn how to look at art. The Teacher's Guide section explains the rationale and criteria behind each of the student activities and offers ways to facilitate (students) getting the most out of the curriculum.
Resource Type: Course Model
Grade Level: MS, HS, College

National Gallery of Art
www.nga.gov/

The National Gallery of Art has over 120 free-loan education resources. Titles range in format from color slide programs and teaching packets, to videocassettes, CD-ROMs and DVDs. The varied program topics provide opportunities for use in non-art curricula such as social studies, literature, and foreign languages.
Resource Type: Course Model
Grade Level: LS, MS, HS

ARTSEDGE
http://artsedge.kennedy-center.org/

ARTSEDGE—the National Arts and Education Network—supports the placement of the arts at the center of the curriculum and advocates creative use of technology to enhance the K–12 educational experience. ARTSEDGE offers free, standards-based teaching materials for use in and out of the classroom, as well as professional development resources, student materials, and guidelines for arts-based instruction and assessment.
Resource Type: Course Model
Grade Level: LS, MS, HS

Odyssey Online
http://carlos.emory.edu/ODYSSEY/

"Odyssey Online" was developed to help educators teach using works of art from the ancient

Near East, Egypt, Greece, Rome and Africa. The Teacher Resource explains ways in which this project meets curriculum standards. Designed for elementary and middle school students.
Resource Type: Lesson or Activity
Grade Level: LS, MS

The Incredible Art Department
www.princetonol.com/groups/iad/

Art Lessons and Resources provide many helpful lessons and ideas, including Art History games.
Resource Type: Course Model
Grade Level: LS, MS, HS

teachart.net
http://teachart.net/

The Basics of Art section offers lesson plans and there is much more to explore. Its goal is to make learning about art and teaching about art "easy and fun."
Resource Type: Lesson or Activity
Grade Level: LS, MS HS

Portrait Detectives
www.liverpoolmuseums.org.uk/nof/portraits/

This online activity is for independent readers or an educator who enjoys reading aloud. It shows, interactively, how to discern which clues in any given portrait help to put it, its subject, and often the artist all in historical context. A wonderful way to introduce (or reinforce) the concept of critical thinking in art.
Resource Type: Lesson or Activity
Grade Level: LS, MS, HS

Renaissance Connection
www.renaissanceconnection.org/

"Renaissance Connection," the Allentown Art Museum's (Allentown, Pennsylvania) interactive educational Web site, explores Renaissance visual arts and innovations. There is a collection of online activities and resources for middle school students and teachers to help visitors design their own innovations, investigate Renaissance artworks in depth, and discover how past innovations impact life today. Fun, educational site for middle school students.
Resource Type: Lesson or Activity
Grade Level: MS

Writing in Art History
www.unc.edu/depts/wcweb/handouts/arthistory.html

A Web form all about writing an art history paper from the University of North Carolina at Chapel Hill. See also the included link on MLA Format citations.
Resource Type: Lesson or Activity
Grade Level: HS, College

Cultural "Art"-ifacts: Learning about World Cultures through Art
www.nytimes.com/learning/teachers/lessons/20030328friday.html

In this *New York Times* lesson, students explore how culture is reflected through art. After researching the art of a specific culture, students create replicas of art objects that reflect the ideals, values, and history of the culture.
Resource Type: Lesson or Activity
Grade Level: MS, HS

Art History Adventures
www.eduweb.com/insideart/

Educational Web Adventures develops award-winning online learning activities about art, history, and science. Their mission is to create exciting and effective learning experiences. Their "Art History Adventures" is a fun, educational experience appropriate for elementary school children. There are also Teachers' Resources.
Resource Type: Lesson or Activity
Grade Level: LS, MS

KinderArt
www.kinderart.com/

"KinderArt" is all about making art fun for kids and easy for adults who teach art to kids. Currently, there are over 1,000 art-incorporating ideas and lesson plans, as well as an extensive library section and many, many other features.
Resource Type: Lesson or Activity
Grade Level: LS, MS, HS

Art Teacher on the Net
www.artmuseums.com/

Offers ideas, lesson plans, and projects for teachers, parents, and group leaders. It is also a spot for the exchange of ideas between educators, as well as after-school and adult education project areas.
Resource Type: Lesson or Activity
Grade Level: LS, MS, HS

ArtsConnectEd
www.artsconnected.org/

From the Minneapolis Institute of Art and the Walker Art Center. This site includes an online art gallery, library, and interactive activities. The Classroom section features a searchable database of educational materials and a Teacher's Guide.
Resource Type: Course Model
Grade Level: LS, MS, HS

ORAL HISTORY

Oral History Association
http://alpha.dickinson.edu/oha/index.html

"Oral History Association" seeks to bring together all persons interested in oral history and provides both professional guidance and collegial environment for sharing information. It

offers an online newsletter, oral history evaluation guidelines, as well as links to oral history collections and centers across the United States. One can purchase the *Oral History Review* or educator guides via this site. The association also recognizes outstanding achievement in oral history through an awards program.
Resource Type: General Reference

Oral Histories
www.ohs.org.uk/

This UK Web site, run by the Oral History Society, provides practical advice on how to start an oral history project. The society offers a journal, conferences, and links to oral history organizations.
Resource Type: General Reference

The Library of Congress
www.loc.gov/index.html

While most Library of Congress online exhibitions are text-based, some have extensive audio and video clips, including oral histories. American history teachers should start with American Memory. The bulk of the LOC collections are to be found here. One can browse by topic or search by keyword. All of these exhibitions include guides as to how to work with the collections.
Resource Type: Primary Source Collection

American Rhetoric
www.americanrhetoric.com/

This is a massive multimedia site that contains an Online Speech Bank, Rhetorical Figures in Sound, and American Top 100 Speeches. The Online Speech Bank contains 291 active links to 5,000+ full text, audio and video (streaming) versions of public speeches, sermons, legal proceedings, lectures, debates, interviews, other recorded media events, and a declaration or two. Figures in Sound has 200+ short audio clips from well-known speeches, movies, sermons, popular songs, and sensational media events by famous (and infamous) politicians, actors, preachers, athletes, singers, and other noteworthy personalities. You'll also find significant American political speeches of the twentieth century and even Hollywood speeches. Links are arranged alphabetically by first name and checked for errors.
Resource Type: Primary Source Collection

H-Oralhist
www.h-net.msu.edu/~oralhist/

"H-Oralhist" is a discussion network for scholars and others involved in oral history studies and practice. It is affiliated with the Oral History Association and provides links to oral history projects by subject as well as websites with sound files.
Resource Type: General Reference

Oral History Projects and Lesson Plan Resources

"Telling Their Stories"—Oral History Archive Project of the Urban School
www.tellingstories.org/index.html

Visit "Telling Their Stories" and read, watch, and listen to perhaps the best student-created oral history project in the country. High school students at the Urban School of San Franciso have produced three impressive oral history interviews featured at this site: Holocaust Survivors and Refugees, World War II Camp Liberators, and Japanese-American Internees. Urban School students conducted, filmed, and transcribed interviews, created hundreds of movie files associated with each transcript, and then posted the full-text, full-video interviews on this public Web site. The National Association of Independent Schools (NAIS) has recognized Urban School's Telling Their Stories project with a Leading Edge Recognition award for excellence in technology integration. Teachers interested in conducting an oral history project can contact Urban School technology director Howard Levin and should consider attending his summer teacher workshop.

Resource Type: Lesson or Activity

Grade Level: HS

Figure 11.3: Telling Their Stories

American Century Project

www.americancenturyproject.org/

"American Century Project" is produced by Glen Whitman, author of *Dialogue with the Past: Engaging Students and Meeting Standards Through Oral History* (AltaMira Press, 2004). For this project students interview individuals who helped shape or witnessed events or periods

that form the American experience of the twentieth century. Interviewees have ranged from war veterans, civil rights activists, politicians, and restaurant waitresses to survivors of the Great Depression and the Holocaust. Whitman provides procedures for guiding students through oral histories and offers an archive of student projects. There are also workshops for educators.
Resource Type: Lesson or Activity
Grade Level: HS

1968: The Whole World Was Watching
www.stg.brown.edu/projects/1968/

"1968: The Whole World Was Watching" is an oral history project created by South Kingstown High School and Brown University's Scholarly Technology Group in Kingstown, Rhode Island. It features recollections of a group of Rhode Islanders regarding pivotal events and issues in 1968 and contains transcripts, audio recordings, and edited stories. The stories include references to the Vietnam War, the struggle for civil rights, as well as the assassinations of Martin Luther King, Jr., and Robert Kennedy.
Resource Type: Lesson or Activity
Grade Level: HS

Learning about Immigration through Oral History
http://historymatters.gmu.edu/d/18

Students compare and contrast the stories of these contemporary immigrants with those researched in the 1930s reflected in *American Life Histories, 1936–1940*, and other American Memory collections. Students engage in visual and information literacy exercises to gain an understanding of how to identify and interpret primary historical sources. From the Library of Congress American Memory site.
Resource Type: Lesson or Activity; Primary Source Collection
Grade Level: HS

Been Here So Long: Selections from the WPA American Slave Narratives
http://newdeal.feri.org/asn/asn00.htm

These three lessons use the American Slave Narratives gathered between 1936 and 1938 by journalists and other writers employed by the Federal Writers Project, part of the New Deal's Works Progress Administration (WPA). The lessons ask students to explore the slave narratives to gain an understanding of the experiences of African Americans in nineteenth-century America. They are also asked to consider the nature of oral history and personal narratives as historical evidence. From the New Deal Network Web site.
Resource Type: Lesson or Activity
Grade Level: HS

What Did You Do in the War, Grandma?
www.stg.brown.edu/projects/WWII_Women/tocCS.html

"What did you do in the war, Grandma?" is an Oral History of Rhode Island women during World War II written by students in the Honors English Program at South Kingstown High School in Kingstown, Rhode Island.

Resource Type: Lesson or Activity
Grade Level: HS

Voices of the Past

http://oldsegundo.com/webquests/voices_from_past/student-home.htm

In this oral history project for grades 6–12, students follow oral history processes to contact and interview a World War II veteran or person alive during the World War II era. Students produce indexed oral history archival tapes and then analyze and synthesize the information gained during the interview and research activities.
Resource Type: Lesson or Activity
Grade Level: MS, HS

Documenting the American South

http://docsouth.unc.edu/

"Documenting the American South" (DAS) is an impressive collection of sources by the University of North Carolina on Southern history, literature and culture from the colonial period through the first decades of the twentieth century. DAS supplies teachers, students, and researchers with a wide range of titles they can use for reference, studying, teaching, and research. Currently, DAS includes ten thematic collections of primary sources for the study of Southern history, literature, and culture including Oral Histories of the American South, True and Candid Compositions: Antebellum Writings, First-Person Narratives of the American South, and North American Slave Narratives.
Resource Type: Primary Source Collection
Grade Level: HS, College

Normandy

www.britannica.com/dday

"Normandy" is part of a World War II study guide by Britannica online. A key section is Veterans' Oral Histories and there are also combat videos, interactive charts and maps, a photo gallery, war documents, an activities guide, and more.
Resource Type: Primary Source Collection

Voices from the Dust Bowl

www.britannica.com/dday

This Library of Congress site documents the everyday life of residents in central California in 1940 and 1941. There are audio recordings, photographs, manuscript materials, publications, related sources, and more.
Resource Type: Primary Source Collection; Multimedia Presentation

Riding the Rails

www.pbs.org/wgbh/amex/rails/

Part of PBS's *American Experience* television series, this engaging site focuses on the plight of more than a quarter million teenagers living on the road in America. There are "tales from the rails," as well as hobo songs, a timeline, a teacher's guide, recommended resources, and more.
Resource Type: Primary Source Collection

The Great Depression and the 1990s

http://memory.loc.gov/learn/lessons/97/depress/overview.html

By using the American Memory's *American Life Histories, 1936–1940* documents, personal interviews, and the Library of Congress's online legislative information, students will be able to gain a better understanding of why the government takes care of its people and how this type of welfare state started. Armed with this knowledge, they can then evaluate the current need of government programs, such as welfare, Medicare, and Social Security, on the federal and state level.

Resource Type: Primary Source Collection

People's Century

www.pbs.org/wgbh/peoplescentury/

The site is based on a 26-episode television series and features oral histories from throughout the century. There is also a teacher's guide, a timeline, a thematic overview, and RealAudio excerpts.

Resource Type: Primary Source Collection

Studs Terkel: Conversations

www.studsterkel.org/

Produced by the Chicago Historical Society, this site explores the life and work of Studs Terkel, an important American oral historian. Galleries focus on interviews that Mr. Terkel did for his books and also the site also contains a multimedia interview with him.

Resource Type: Primary Source Collection

World War II Remembered

www.usd230.k12.ks.us/PICTT/index.html

Former Senator Bob Dole and historian Stephen Ambrose are among those who contribute to the site. It was created to preserve untold stories of those who lived during the World War II era.

Resource Type: Primary Source Collection

Vietnam, Stories Since the War

www.pbs.org/pov/stories/

Another well-done PBS site; it contains background information on the Vietnam War, first-hand stories of veterans, an index, and a search function.

Resource Type: Primary Source Collection

Cambodian Holocaust

www.cybercambodia.com/dachs/

This site relates personal stories from the Cambodian genocide of the Khmer Rouge years. There are photographs and suggested resources.

Resource Type: Primary Source Collection

The Gulf War

www.pbs.org/wgbh/pages/frontline/gulf/index.html

This "Frontline" site offers a comprehensive and engaging history of the Gulf War from the perspective of those who participated. Major categories include Oral Histories, War Stories, and Weapons and Technology and there are maps, a chronology, images, essays, a discussion of Gulf Syndrome, and more.

Resource Type: Primary Source Collection; General Reference

Go for Broke (Japanese American World War II Veterans)

www.goforbroke.org/

The educational Web site GoForBroke.org is one of the leading resources for educators, students, researchers and the general public to learn about the legacy of the Japanese American World War II veterans. It features streaming oral history videos, as well as lesson plans, student activities, glossaries, timelines, photos, and interactive maps.

Resource Type: Primary Source Collection; General Reference

CHAPTER 12

Focus on History Topics

MAPS AND GEOGRAPHY

*****Oddens' Bookmarks
http://oddens.geog.uu.nl/index.php

"Oddens' Bookmarks" was started in 1995 by Roelof Oddens, the curator of the Map Library of the Faculty of GeoSciences at Utrecht University, Utrecht, The Netherlands (see Figure 12.1). Today, it is perhaps the most extensive online map collection in the world. (The number of links in the database has grown from 6,500 in 1999 to over 22,000 in April 2004.) You can find almost any map you are searching for via this enormous site. The site is searchable by country, region, and category. Key sections include Maps and Atlases, Map Collections, Government Cartography, and Touristic Sites.
Resource Type: Map

*****Map History/History of Cartography
www.maphistory.info/

"Map History," managed by the former Map Librarian of the British Library, is hosted by the Institute of Historical Research, University of London, and forms part of the World Wide Web Virtual Library. Spread over about 100 pages, it provides a well-organized global overview of the history of cartography as well as over 1,500 links. The site provides reference information and Web articles, and it lists activities, opportunities, and resources for surfers and scholars. There are also leads to the collecting of early maps. Furthermore, there is a section aimed specifically at parents and teachers.
Resource Type: Map

*****National Geographic: Maps and Geography
www.maphistory.info/

You can always search for maps via their MapMachine Online Atlas, but the *National Geographic* Web site also provides interactive quizzes, games, expeditions and tours as well (see Figure 12.2). Xpeditions Atlas offers teacher-tested lessons plans sorted by standard and grade level as well as interactive lessons and a virtual museum called Xpeditions Hall. You can also get print-friendly and black-and-white maps in Xpeditions. The online "National

Figure 12.1: Oddens' Bookmarks

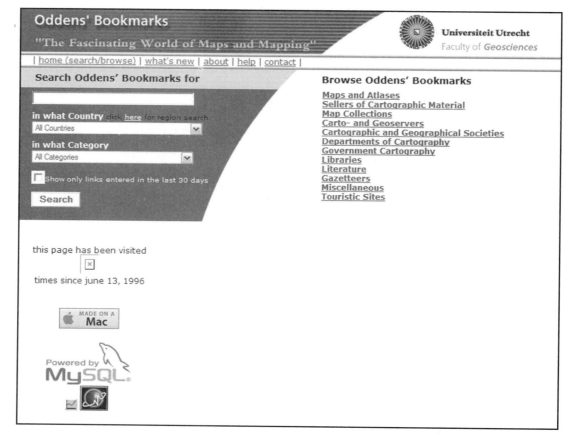

Geographic Atlas of the World" profiles 192 independent nations and in each entry you'll find key geographic, demographic, and economic data as well as a brief overview. Students will benefit from the Homework Help section where they can research pictures, articles, maps, and more for reports, presentations, and more. The GeoBee Challenge is a game that features five new geography-based questions every day. MapMachine provides physical and political characteristics of countries and includes aerial views. You can view nearly any place on Earth by population, climate, and more.
Resource Type: Map; Lesson or Activity

****Geography World
http://members.aol.com/bowermanb/101.html

A teacher from Pennsylvania has put together this resource. Check out the links to Maps and Globes as well as the Geography Quizzes area. (Site is slow to load.)
Resource Type: Maps; Course Model

****Open Directory: Geography
http://dmoz.org/Science/Social_Sciences/Geography/

The Open Directory Project on Geography contains 1,177 Web sites: Cartography (76), Dictionaries (4), Education (95), Geographic Information Systems (787), Geomatics (719),

Figure 12.2: National Geographic Maps and Geography

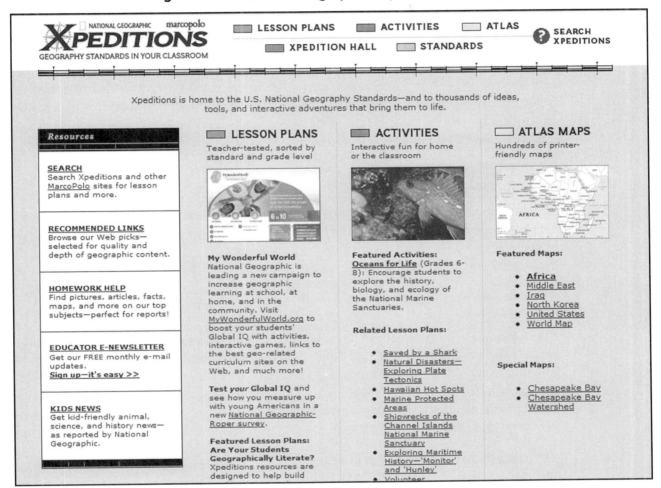

Human Geography (48), Navigation (55), Organizations (25), Physical Geography (22), Place Names (59), Publications (12), and Regional Planning (868).
Resource Type: Map

****SCORE Map Resources

http://score.rims.k12.ca.us/resources/grades/?g=6&q=Maps

The Schools of California Online Resources for Educators (SCORE) project is a terrific resource for teachers and students alike. (See description in Chapter 12, Best General History Resources.)
Resource Type: Maps; Lesson or Activity

****Animated Atlas

www.animatedatlas.com/index.html

"Animated Atlas" portrays history by animating maps. This site features a ten-minute interactive movie that is a geographic history of the United States, locating major events and the admission of every state. Also sells classroom videos.
Resource Type: Map

****Shock-ing Geography
http://people.depauw.edu/djp/shock_maps/

An interactive outline map site created by Daniel J. Pfeifer of Wake Forest University. Students can quiz themselves on physical, current political, and some historical map information. Historical maps are so far only for Europe 1763, World 1800, Europe 1815, and Europe 1914, but physical and current political maps cover most world areas. Instructors can have results of student self-quizzes emailed to them. Requires Shockwave software.
Resource Type: Map; Lesson or Activity

****OSSHE Historic Atlas Resource Library
http://darkwing.uoregon.edu/~atlas/

Extensive, colorful, and often interactive, the maps in this library cover Europe, Middle East, North Africa, and North America. The U.S. maps are limited in scope and can be slow to load if you don't have Shockwave software.
Resource Type: Map

****David Rumsey Map Collection
www.davidrumsey.com/

"David Rumsey Map Collection" has over 8,800 maps online and focuses on rare eighteenth- and nineteenth-century North and South America maps and other cartographic materials. Historic maps of the World, Europe, Asia and Africa are also represented. Collection categories include antique atlas, globe, school geography, maritime chart, state, county, city, pocket, wall, children's, and manuscript maps.
Resource Type: Map

****Historical Atlas of the 20th Century
http://users.erols.com/mwhite28/20centry.htm

An interesting and informative collection of information on the twentieth century. Atlas topics include: General Trends in Living Conditions, Government, War, and Religion. Maps are often interactive, allowing you to zoom in on details. There also are essays, FAQs, and links.
Resource Type: Map

****Periodical Historical Atlas of Europe
www.euratlas.com/summary.htm

"Periodical Atlas of Europe" features 21 online maps showing the countries of Europe at the end of each century from Year 1 to Year 2000. Also includes a few images of historical sites.
Resource Type: Map

****Perry-Castaneda Library Map Collection
www.lib.utexas.edu/maps/index.html

The PCL offers a diverse set of physical, political and historical maps.
Resource Type: Map

***The Effectiveness of GIS in High School Education
http://gis.esri.com/library/userconf/proc99/proceed/papers/pap203/p203.htm

GIS (Geographic Information Systems) is a powerful software mapping program. With GIS teachers have a dynamic mapping tool allowing them to create almost any required map, but the software also allows students to create, query and detect patterns involving demographic, historical, and scientific data. Experiments conducted in geography and special education courses in Boulder High School, Boulder, Colorado, provide some of the first empirical and case study data as to the effectiveness of GIS in teaching.
Resource Type: Map; Course Model

***A Nationwide Analysis of the Implementation of GIS in High School Education
http://gis.esri.com/library/userconf/proc99/proceed/papers/pap202/p202.htm

The survey provides some of the first comprehensive data on the geographic and curricular extent to which GIS is being implemented, why and how GIS is being implemented, forces that motivate teachers to adopt GIS, and the benefits and challenges of adoption of the technology.
Resource Type: Map; Course Model

***GEODESY
www.bgrg.com/geodesy/

GEODESY is a comprehensive and integrated application of remote sensing and geographic information systems for K–12 schools. Students and teachers using GEODESY learn to interpret and analyze geographic information about their local community.
Resource Type: Map; Course Model

***Quia: Shared Activities
www.quia.com/shared/

Has assorted links to geography quizzes and games. Also helps teachers create their own quizzes. You must be a paying member in order to use the site.
Resource Type: Games; Lesson or Activity

***Historical Atlas of Europe: The Development of Europe's Modern States 1648–2001
http://home.zonnet.nl/gerardvonhebel/

This site provides an overview of the political changes in Europe during the last 350 years.
Resource Type: Map

***Mapping.com
www.mapping.com/

A commercial site that has a good mix of links, geography quizzes, and a resources page. See Hot Links.
Resource Type: Map

Blank Maps or Outline Maps

****WorldAtlas.com: Blank Maps
http://worldatlas.com/webimage/testmaps/maps.htm

WorldAtlas.com offers a large selection of blank maps of various regions of the world as well

as map tests. All outline maps and map tests may be used (at no charge) for any educational application whatsoever.
Resource Type: Map

****Houghton Mifflin Eduplace Online Maps
www.eduplace.com/ss/maps/

Has freely usable blank outline maps. There are political and physical outline maps of the world and various smaller regions.
Resource Type: Map; Lesson or Activity

****About.com Blank and Online Maps
http://geography.about.com/od/blankmaps/Blank_and_Outline_Maps.htm

About.com offers collections of blank and outline maps to print out for educational or personal use at home or in the classroom.
Resource Type: Map; Lesson or Activity

****National Geographic: Maps and Geography
www.nationalgeographic.com/education/maps_photos/index.html

National Geographic offers outline maps in the Xpeditions Atlas section and gives you the option of modifying the maps to print with or without borders.
Resource Type: Lesson or Activity

RESEARCH

*****The Library of Congress
www.loc.gov/index.html

"The Library of Congress" is an outstanding site for American history research and general studies (see Figure 12.3). The LOC contains primary and secondary documents, exhibits, map collections, prints and photographs, sound recordings, and motion pictures. The LOC's American Memory Historical Collections, a must-see, contain the bulk of digitalized materials, but the Exhibitions Gallery is enticing and informative as well. The Learning Page provides a "teacher's eye view" of over seven million historical documents, photographs, maps, films, and audio recordings. Thomas is an ideal section for civics or constitutional history research, and the Global Gateway offers country profiles and much related information.
Resource Type: Primary Source Collection; Lesson or Activity

****National Archives and Records Administration
www.archives.gov/index.html

The National Archives and Records Administration offers federal archives, exhibits, classroom resources, census records, Hot Topics, and more. The NARA is a great resource for American history research, especially government records and constitutional history. The Constitution of the United States of America, the Declaration of Independence, and the Bill of Rights are all available here online, as well as many other original

Figure 12.3: The Library of Congress

documents. Most of the scanned images of these documents are high resolution and you can zoom in and examine them in great detail. The NARA offers 100 milestone documents that chronicle United States history from 1776 to 1965. In the Resources sections are Documents Analysis Worksheets, helpful in analysis of primary sources. Also, the Online Exhibit Hall has features on the New Deal, WWII, and photographs from 1864 to 1921.

Resource Type: Primary Source Collection

****The Internet History Sourcebooks
www.fordham.edu/halsall/

"Internet History Sourcebooks" are wonderful collections of public domain and copy-permitted historical texts for educational use by Paul Halsall (see Figure 12.4). The site and its documents are well organized and the breadth of materials is impressive. There are several Sourcebooks: Ancient History Sourcebook, Medieval Sourcebook, Modern History Sourcebook, Byzantine Studies Page, African, East Asian, Global, Indian, Islamic, Jewish, Lesbian and Gay, Science, Women's, Medieval Studies Course, Modern History Course, Chinese Studies Course, Medieval Webguide. Note: The Sourcebooks are no longer actively maintained, and you will invariably run into broken links.

Resource Type: Primary Source Collection

Figure 12.4: Internet History Sourcebooks

Focus on Internet History Sourcebooks

The Internet History Sourcebooks are a terrific resource for world history primary source documents, though not so useful in regards to American history. (Try the Library of Congress or the National Archives & Records Administration site first.)

Look at the top of the page and you will see links to all the **Internet History Sourcebooks**. On the left you will see links to special sections such as Medieval History, Film, and other topics. Professor Paul Halsall also offers guidance on homework and research in his Ancient History Help, Medieval History Help, and Modern History Help pages.

To get a feel for the Sourcebooks click on the **Ancient History Sourcebooks** link at the top of page. On the left you will see a list of Ancient History topics. The documents are organized under the categories listed here. Click on "Rome." You'll see that the documents are further organized into thematic topics. Select a topic and explore some of the related documents. Most documents are relatively brief. Some include introductory text and even teaching questions. Links to full texts of specified books are available through this site and recommended external links are listed under **Full Texts**. There is also a **Legal Texts** section on various aspects of the law in the ancient world—history law, law codes, etc.

Please explore other Sourcebooks. Keep in mind that the Sourcebooks are huge and you will invariably run into broken links—many more in some sections than others. Don't give up—you'll enjoy the great scope of these materials.

****The Avalon Project: Documents in Law, History and Diplomacy
www.yale.edu/lawweb/avalon/avalon.htm

A great research site from Yale University rich with primary source documents relating to world history. Searchable database is organized into three periods: pre-18th century, 19th century, and 20th century. Scan the Documents Collection. "The Avalon Project" groups documents per theme or topic, such as From Versailles to NATO; American Diplomacy: Bilateral Treaties 1778–1999; Cold War Diplomacy—Defense Treaties of the United States; and more.

Resource Type: Primary Source Collection

****American Rhetoric
www.americanrhetoric.com

This is a massive multimedia site that contains an Online Speech Bank, Rhetorical Figures in Sound, and American Top 100 Speeches. The Online Speech Bank contains 291 active links to 5,000+ full text, audio and video (streaming) versions of public speeches, sermons, legal proceedings, lectures, debates, interviews, other recorded media events, and a declaration or two. Figures in Sound has 200+ short audio clips from well-known speeches, movies, sermons, popular songs, and sensational media events by famous (and infamous) politicians, actors, preachers, athletes, singers, and other noteworthy personalities. You'll also find significant American political speeches of the 20th century and even Hollywood speeches. Links are arranged alphabetically by first name and checked for errors. In all you'll find an impressive blend of actual and simulated historic speeches, debates, lectures, etc. (I get a kick out of hearing *Law and Order's* Sam Waterston doing Abraham Lincoln.) There are some great video clips as well. If you have the Quicktime and Real Media players on your machine you should be able to watch the clips with few difficulties. These audio and video can help make history come alive for students.

Resource Type: Primary Source Collection; Multimedia Presentation

Figure 12.5: American Rhetoric

****Center for History and New Media: History Matters
http://historymatters.gmu.edu/

A production of the American Social History Project/Center of Media and Learning, City University of New York, and the Center for History and New Media, George Mason University, "History Matters" is a wonderful online resource for history teachers and students. Among the many digital resources are lesson plans, syllabi, links, and exhibits. The Center for History and New Media's resources include a list of "best" Web sites, links to syllabi and lesson plans, essays on history and new media, a link to their excellent "History Matters" Web site for U.S. history, and more. Resources are designed to benefit professional historians, high school teachers, and students of history.
Resource Type: Primary Source Collection; Course Model

*****BBC: History
www.bbc.co.uk/history/

"BBC: History" offers a multitude of sites, activities, games and other resources. Major categories include Ancient History, Archaeology, Church and State, Science and Discovery, Society and Conflict, War and Culture, and Family History (see Figure 12.6). There are also sections entitled Multimedia Room, Historic Figures, Timelines, Programmes, Reading Room, Talk History, For Kids, and History Trails. The BBC Multimedia zone offers games, animations, virtual tours, and galleries. Many games deal with various aspects of British history.
Resource Type: General Reference; Multimedia Presentation

****The History News Network
www.hnn.us/

"History News Network" was created in June 2001 and features articles by historians on both the left and the right who provide historical perspective on current events. HNN exists to provide historians and other experts a national forum in which to educate Americans about important and timely issues, and it is the only Web site on the Internet wholly devoted to this task. HNN is a nonprofit publication run by George Mason University; it is updated daily and averages roughly 1.5 million hits a month.
Resource Type: General Reference

****Digital History
www.digitalhistory.uh.edu/

This impressive site from Steven Mintz at the University of Houston includes an up-to-date U.S. history textbook; annotated primary sources on slavery, and United States, Mexican American, and Native American history; and succinct essays on the history of ethnicity and immigration, film, private life, and science and technology. Visual histories of Lincoln's America and America's Reconstruction contain text by Eric Foner and Olivia Mahoney. The Doing History feature lets users reconstruct the past through the voices of children, gravestones, advertising, and other primary sources. Reference resources include classroom handouts, chronologies, encyclopedia articles, glossaries, and an audiovisual archive including speeches, book talks and e-lectures by historians, and historical maps, music, newspaper articles, and images. The site's Ask the HyperHistorian feature allows users to pose questions to professional historians.
Resource Type: General Reference; Course Model

Figure 12.6: BBC History

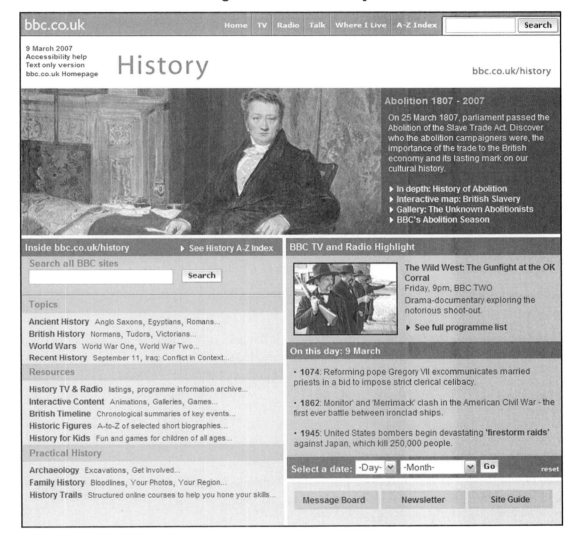

****CNN Education with Student News
www.cnn.com/EDUCATION/

CNN Education provides teachers with instructional materials for integrating current events across the curriculum. A student section keeps students in grades 6–12 aware of the latest news of interest to them. Lesson plans, background material, profiles, links to useful Internet sites, and forums for interaction with other teachers are all included.
Resource Type: General Reference; Lesson or Activity

*****The Internet Public Library
www.ipl.org/div/subject/browse/hum00.00.00/

"The Internet Public Library" is the first public library of and for the Internet community and features online collections and exhibits as well as more traditional library holdings.
Resource Type: General Reference; Primary Source Collection

****PBS Online
www.pbs.org/

A great source for information on a myriad of historical events and personalities. PBS's assorted and diverse Web exhibits supplement their television series and generally include a summary of each episode, interviews (often with sound bites), a timeline, primary sources, a glossary, photos, maps, and links to relevant sites. PBS productions include *American Experience, Frontline,* and *People's Century.* Go to the PBS Teacher Source for lessons and activities arranged by topic.
Resource Type: General Reference; Lesson or Activity

****CNN.com Archives
www.cnn.com/SPECIALS/

"CNN.com Archives" feature special in-depth reports on key current American (and World) events, issues, and personalities. Most special reports supply historical overviews, articles, photographs, timelines or chronologies, video clips, maps, interviews, sources, and more.
Resource Type: General Reference; Primary Source Collection

****H-Net: Humanities and Social Sciences Online
www.h-net.msu.edu/

"H-Net" is an international interdisciplinary collection of scholars who contribute their findings and activities to this research-oriented site (see Figure 12.7). Their free e-mail subscription provides you with the latest information on pertinent collections, exhibits, and grant opportunities; it also allows you to partake in scholarly discussions.
Resource Type: General Reference

****The History Journals Guide
www.history-journals.de/

The Guide is a great Web directory for history journals. Journals are organized according to several criteria and all have at least some online presence.
Resource Type: General Reference

****Project Gutenberg
www.gutenberg.org

"Project Gutenberg" is the oldest producer of free e-books on the Internet and a great source of historical electronic texts as well as audio books and other materials. There are over 19,000 free books in "Project Gutenberg."
Resource Type: Primary Source Collection

****Library and Archival Exhibitions on the Web
www.sil.si.edu/SILPublications/Online-Exhibitions/

The Smithsonian offers this useful gateway to libraries and exhibits on the Web. It features links to online exhibitions that have been created by libraries, archives, and historical societies. It also links to museum online exhibitions with a special focus on library and archival materials.
Resource Type: Primary Source Collection

Figure 12.7: H-Net: Humanities and Social Sciences Online

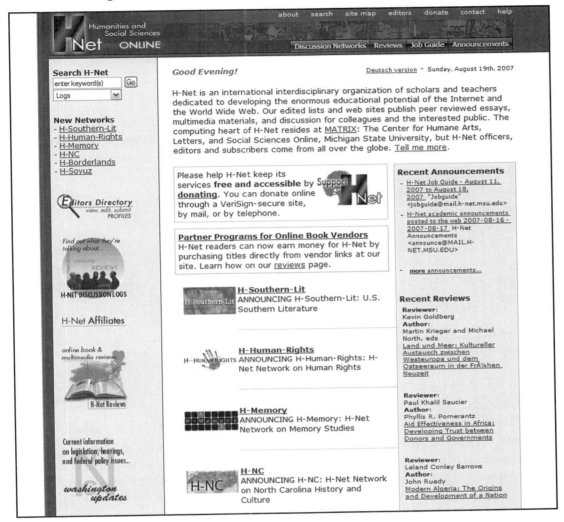

****World Civilizations: An Internet Classroom and Anthology

www.wsu.edu:8080/~dee/WORLD.HTM

"World Civilizations" is an interactive course model that combines excellent web-based materials materials from two World Cultures courses taught at Washington State University. Although designed for freshman university students, "World Civilizations" texts, glossary, and learning modules are also useful for high school level.

Resource Type: Course Model

****Historical Research in Europe

http://digicoll.library.wisc.edu/HistResEur/

University of Wisconsin Digital Content Group has developed this Web site to assist researchers seeking to use European libraries and archives. The database can be searched by keyword or subject headings.

Resource Type: General Reference; Primary Source Collection

****World Wide National Archives

http://home.earthlink.net/~genealogyplanet/links_national_archives.html

"World Wide National Archives" has links to national archives around the world, as well as extensive genealogical resources.
Resource Type: General Reference; Primary Source Collection

****Voice of the Shuttle: History Page

http://vos.ucsb.edu/

Part of an extensive guide to humanities resources that provides numerous links to feature sites, teaching resources, electronic journals, course syllabi, and more. Aimed at university educators.
Resource Type: General Reference

****History Channel

www.historychannel.com/

A companion to the television channel, this commercial site contains a myriad of features and highlights for educators and students alike. Key offerings include study guides and activities, ideas from teachers, special exhibits, speech archives, discussions, and This Day in History. The UK site is located at www.thehistorychannel.co.uk/site/home/ and the student site at www.historystudystop.co.uk/.
Resource Type: General Reference; Primary Source Collection

****The Metropolitan Museum of Art Timeline of Art History

www.metmuseum.org/toah/splash.htm

This interactive timeline is a chronological, geographical, and thematic exploration of the history of art from around the world, as illustrated by the Metropolitan Museum of Art's collection. Each timeline page includes representative art from the Museum's collection, a chart of time periods, a map of the region, an overview, and a list of key events. The timelines—accompanied by world, regional, and subregional maps—provide a linear outline of art history and allow visitors to compare and contrast art from around the globe at any time in history.
Resource Type: Art History; Primary Source Collection

****Art History Resources on the Web

http://witcombe.sbc.edu/ARTHLinks.html

Professor Chris Witcombe of the Art Department at Sweet Briar College has perhaps the best organized gateway to art history sites on the Web. His directory is chock full of useful and regularly updated links and is divided into 21 categories, including Prehistoric Art, Art in Early Europe, Renaissance Art in Italy, and Prints & Photography.
Resource Type: General Reference; Art History

****Art History Research Center

www.harmsen.net/ahrc/

"Art History Research Center" from Concordia University, Canada, is a tool for art historical research. It provides access to newsgroups, mailing lists, library catalogs, article indexes,

online collections, art history and arts Web servers, and links. There is also a short essay entitled "The Internet as a Research Medium for Art Historians."
Resource Type: General Reference; Art History

****The British Museum
www.thebritishmuseum.ac.uk/index.html

The British Museum various online offerings are impressive. Its Web site features interactive multimedia resources, historical reconstructions and 3-D animations and atttracts millions of visitors each year. COMPASS is an online database featuring around 5,000 objects from the British Museum's collections. There are online tours on a variety of subjects, including introductions to the current exhibitions. Childrens' COMPASS offers a special childrens' search, activities and quizes for use in the classroom, noticeboards for children's work, Ask the Expert, and articles written especially for 7- to 11-year-olds. The Ancient Civilizations section highlights impressive achievements of ancient world civilizations and explores cross-cultural themes of human development.
Resource Type: Primary Source Collection; Art History

****EuroDocs: History of the United Kingdom—Primary Documents
http://eudocs.lib.byu.edu/index.php/History_of_the_United_Kingdom:_Primary_Documents

These links, complied by a European Studies biliographer, feature select Western European (mainly primary) historical documents and shed light on key historical events. The sources are organized by country and cover various chronological periods.
Resource Type: Primary Source Collection

****Authentic History: Primary Resources from American Pop Culture
www.authentichistory.com/

Contains an impressive array of pictures, documents, audio, and video from the antebellum period to the 9/11 terrorist attack.
Resource Type: Primary Source Collection

****Conversations with History
http://globetrotter.berkeley.edu/conversations/

In this University of California at Berkeley site, distinguished men and women from all over the world talk about their lives and their work. They reminisce about their participation in great events, and they share their perspectives on the past and reflect on what the future may hold. Guests include diplomats, statesmen, and soldiers; economists and political analysts; scientists and historians; writers and foreign correspondents; and activists and artists.
Resource Type: General Reference

***WebRoots.org Genealogy Foundation
www.webroots.org/

"WebRoots.org" Genealogy and History Library offers free access to United States genealogy and history-related books, diaries, journals, memoirs, letters, manuscripts, and more.
Resource Type: General Reference

****History Now

www.historynow.org/

"History Now" is an impressive new quarterly online journal for history teachers and students that features articles by noted historians as well as lesson plans, links to related Web sites, bibliographies, and many other resources. In each issue, editors bring together historians, master teachers, and archivists to comment on a single historical theme.
Resource Type: General Reference

****Scout Report: Archives

http://scout.cs.wisc.edu/archives/

"Scout Report: Archives" is a searchable and browseable database to years worth of the Scout Report and subject-specific Scout Reports. These impressive reports offer annotations of carefully selected Internet sites. Selections are aimed at university educators.
Resource Type: General Reference

****Perseus Project

www.perseus.tufts.edu/

"Perseus Project" at Tufts University is a rich and multipurpose resource for Greek and Classical resources that contains an extensive library of primary and secondary sources and art objects. Contains a search function.
Resource Type: Primary Source Collection

****Historical Text Archives

http://historicaltextarchive.com/

"Historical Text Archives" is a broad and rich site that offers over 600 articles, 70 books, and over 6,000 links. It also provides documents, historical photos, and its links provide access to external articles, books, documents, photographs, links and even Google searches.
Resource Type: General Reference; Primary Source Collection

****BUBL

www.bubl.ac.uk/

BUBL is a national information service for the higher education community, run by the Centre for Digital Library Research at the University of Strathclyde in the United Kingdom. BUBL offers free access to over 12,000 selected Internet resources. Sites are carefully selected and annotated.
Resource Type: General Reference; Links Collection

****United States Historical Census Data Browser

http://fisher.lib.virginia.edu/census/

"United States Historical Census Data Browser" provides data from census records and other government sources for 1790–1960. Users can view extensive population- and economics-oriented statistical information at state and county levels, arranged according to a variety of categories. Also includes an essay on the history of the census. A great source of historical data.
Resource Type: Primary Source Collection

****TIME Archive: 1923 to the Present
www.nyt.ulib.org/index.cgi

TIME makes available full-text articles from its excellent weekly newsmagazine. "TIME Archive" is a terrific source of both primary and secondary materials.
Resource Type: Primary Source Collection

****Reviews in History
www.history.ac.uk/reviews/

This electronic publication reviews and reappraises significant work in various historical fields and is targeted at post-secondary educators. There are over 500 free reviews at this site, and you can sign up for e-mail alerts. A good reference site for educators and researchers.
Resource Type: General Reference

****Internet Archive: Wayback Machine
www.archive.org/index.php

"Wayback Machine" provides free access to researchers, historians, scholars, and the general public to more than 10 billion pages stored in the Internet Archive's Web archive. Collections include Web, Moving Images, Texts, Audio, and Software. It is a great resource for locating and viewing Web pages as they appeared in years past.
Resource Type: General Reference

****Biography of America
www.learner.org/biographyofamerica/

Companion to the Annenburg/CPB series, "Biography of America" presents American history as a living narrative. For each program you'll find an interactive feature related to the subject or the time period of the program. In addition, you'll find a listing of key events of the period, a map relevant to the period, the transcript of the video program, and a Webography—a set of annotated Web links.
Resource Type: General Reference

****The Research Guide
www.aresearchguide.com/900-919.html

"The Research Guide" is a free, no-frills education site designed for students, teachers, and the general public. It provides an extensive annotated list of history reference sites, organized using the Dewey decimal system.
Resource Type: Links Collection

****Fact Monster
www.factmonster.com/index.html

This is an Online Almanac, Atlas, Dictionary, and Encyclopedia for kids ages 6 to 14. Also includes Homework Center, Games, and Quizzes.
Resource Type: General Reference

Research Guides

NoodleTools
www.noodletools.com/

"NoodleTools" offers an impressive suite of useful free and subscription-based interactive tools designed to aid in online research. "NoodleTools" provides strategies and resources to make online research more effective. An excellent resource for students and educators.
Resource Type: General Reference

Jo Cool or Jo Fool: An Online Game about Savvy Surfing
www.media-awareness.ca/english/games/jocool_jofool/kids.cfm

Includes a checklist for helping you decide if Jo is making a good surfing choice. Has a 20-question quiz at the end, and a 50-page PDF to help teachers use the site. An excellent interactive introduction to plagiarism for middle school and high school students.
Resource Type: Lesson or Activity

A Visit to Copyright Bay
www.stfrancis.edu/cid/copyrightbay/

A fun tutorial that lets visitors navigate Fair Use Harbor, visit Murky Waters, and crash on Infringement Reef. Includes information about AV Materials, Multimedia, and more.
Resource Type: Lesson or Activity

Internet Paper Mills
www.coastal.edu/library/presentations/mills2.html

A librarian has collected links to digital paper mills and plagiarism detection services that helps make educators aware of potential sources of plagiarism.
Resource Type: Links Collection

EasyBib
www.easybib.com/

"EasyBib" provides a free service to teachers and students who want to create proper bibliographic citations.
Resource Type: General Reference

BEST GENERAL HISTORY RESOURCES

****Library of Congress
www.loc.gov/index.html

"Library of Congress" is an outstanding site for American history and general studies. The Library of Congress Learning Page provides a "teacher's eye view" of over 7 million historical documents, photographs, maps, films, and audio recordings. Lesson plans can be searched by theme, topic, discipline, or era. The American Memory collection, a must-see, contains the bulk of digitalized materials: historic maps, images, documents, audio and video. Thomas contains both current and historical national legislative information, while Exhibitions offers dozens of presentations drawn from Library of Congress collections.

Resource Type: General Reference; Primary Source Collection

****PBS Online
www.pbs.org/

PBS is a great source for information on a myriad of historical events and personalities. PBS's assorted and diverse web exhibits supplement specific individual television series and generally include a résumé of each episode, interviews (often with audio excerpts), a timeline, a glossary, photos, and links to relevant sites. Go to the PBS Teacher Source for lessons and activities—arranged by topic and grade level—and sign up for their newsletter. Categories include American History, World History, History on Television, and Biographies. Some lesson plans require viewing PBS video, but many do not. Categories in American History include *American Experience* and *People's Century*.

Resource Type: General Reference; Lesson or Activity

****Center for History and New Media: History Matters
http://historymatters.gmu.edu

"History Matters" is a wonderful online resource for history teachers and students. Among the many digital resources are lesson plans, syllabi, links, and exhibits. Resources include a list of "best" Web sites, links to syllabi and lesson plans, essays on history and new media, a link to the Center for History and New Media, and more. Resources are designed to benefit professional historians, high school teachers, and students of history. "History Matters" is

Figure 12.8: Center for History and New Media: History Matters

CENTER for CH
HISTORY
n M and NEW MEDIA

Search: All of CHNM

building a better yesterday... bit by bit

PROJECTS   TOOLS

Since 1994, the Center for History and New Media at George Mason University has used digital media and computer technology to democratize history—to incorporate multiple voices, reach diverse audiences, and encourage popular participation in presenting and preserving the past. We sponsor more than two dozen digital history projects and offer free tools and resources for historians.

RESOURCES
NEWS   ABOUT

Latest CHNM News

CHNM Podcast — "Digital Campus"

Job Openings - Post-Doc, Digital History Associate, Summer Intern

CHNM launches First Podcast – Mozilla Digital Memory Bank

Our most popular sites . . .   Go

Job Opportunities at CHNM

chnm home | projects | tools | resources | news | guestbook | about

© 1996–2006, Center for History and New Media, George Mason University.

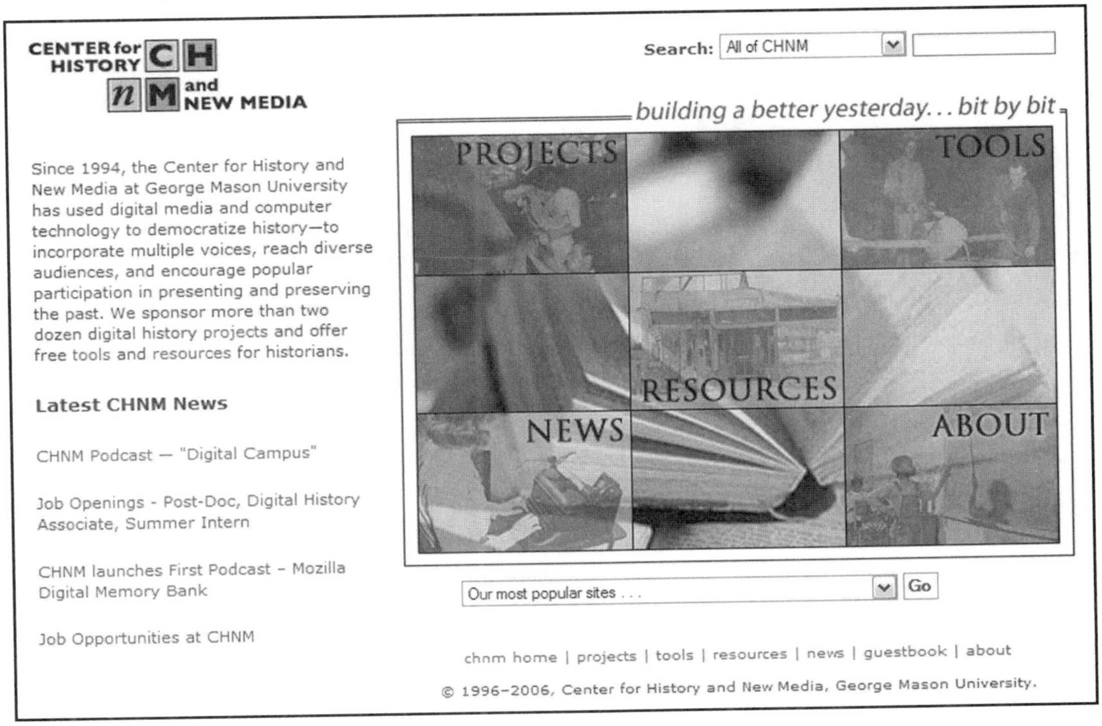

a production of the American Social History Project/Center of Media and Learning at the City University of New York, and the Center for History and New Media at George Mason University.

Resource Type: Course Model

****BBC History
www.bbc.co.uk/history/

"BBC History" offers an impressive array of exhibitions, activities, games, photo galleries and other resources. Major categories include: Ancient History, Archaeology, Church and State, Science and Discovery, Society and Conflict, War and Culture, and Family History. There are also sections entitled Multimedia Room, Historic Figures, Timelines, Programmes, Reading Room, Talk History, For Kids, and History Trails.

Resource Type: General Reference; Multimedia Presentation

****Digital History
www.digitalhistory.uh.edu

This impressive site from Steven Mintz at the University of Houston includes an up-to-date U.S. history textbook; annotated primary sources; and succinct essays on the history of ethnicity and immigration, film, private life, and science and technology. Visual histories of

Insert 12.9: Digital History

Lincoln's America and America's Reconstruction contain text by Eric Foner and Olivia Mahoney. The Doing History feature lets users reconstruct the past through the voices of children, gravestones, advertising, and other primary sources. Reference resources include classroom handouts, chronologies, encyclopedia articles, glossaries, and an audiovisual archive including speeches, book talks and e-lectures by historians, and historical maps, music, newspaper articles, and images. The site's Ask the HyperHistorian feature allows users to pose questions to professional historians.

Resource Type: General Reference; Course Model

****Schools of California Online Resources for Educators (SCORE): History

http://score.rims.k12.ca.us/

The Schools of California Online Resources for Educators (SCORE) project is a terrific resource for teachers and students alike. Here you'll find reviews of education and history-related Web sites, lesson plans, maps, and much more—all arranged by grade level and content area. There are over 5,000 Web sites aligned to California's History/Social Science Curriculum and ten special features.

Resource Type: Lesson or Activity

Figure 12.10: Schools of California Online Resources for Educators (SCORE)

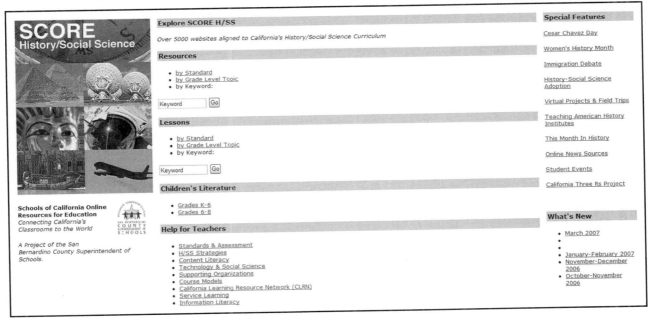

****National Archives and Records Administration

www.nara.gov/

The NARA offers federal archives, exhibits, classroom resources, census records, Hot Topics, and more. The NARA is another great resource for American history research, especially government records and constitutional history. The Constitution of the United States of America, the Declaration of Independence, and the Bill of Rights are all preserved by NARA and available here online as well as many other original documents. Most of the scanned

images of these documents are high resolution, and you can zoom in and examine them in great detail. Visit the Exhibit Center and the Digital Classroom sections for some excellent exhibitions and lesson plans that incorporate NARA holdings. In the Digital Classroom visit Teaching With Documents to find reproducible copies of primary documents, standards-based teaching, and cross-curricular ideas. The Resources section houses the Documents Analysis Worksheets, which help students analyze primary sources. The Our Documents feature contains 100 milestone documents of American history.
Resource Type: General Reference; Primary Source Collection

****The Gilder Lehrman Institute of American History
www.gilderlehrman.org/

The Gilder Lehrman Institute of American History promotes the study and love of American history and targets students, scholars, and the general public. Its Web site provides a portal to American history sites and offers quality educational materials. The Institute provides online exhibitions and an online magazine, modules on major topics in American history, recommended scholarly resources, and more.
Resource Type: General Reference; Course Model

****History News Network
www.hnn.us/

"History News Network" (HNN) was created in June 2001 and features articles, blogs, and podcasts by historians on both the left and the right who provide historical perspective on current events. HNN provides historians and other experts a national forum in which to educate Americans about important and timely issues, and it is the only Web site on the Internet wholly devoted to this task. HNN is a nonprofit publication run by George Mason University.
Resource Type: General Reference

****Historyteacher.net
www.historyteacher.net/

A teacher at the Horace Greeley High School in Chappaqua, New York, has produced a great general site for history teachers that offers AP-level U.S. history materials. It provides many research links and curriculum resources for Global Studies, U.S. AP History, U.S. European History, and American History and Government. Also provides multiple-choice quizzes, Document Based Questions, and more.
Resource Type: Course Model

****History Channel
www.history.com/

A companion to the popular cable television channel, this commercial site contains a myriad of features and highlights for educators and students alike. You can also watch history video, listen to podcasts, browse articles, and visit four special features. Key educational offerings include: study guides and activities, ideas from teachers, special exhibits, speech archives, discussions, and This Day in History.
Resource Type: Multimedia Presentation; Lesson or Activity

World Wide Web Virtual Library: The History Index
http://vlib.iue.it/history/index.html

The Central Catalogue provides a huge number of history links to network sites through its index and maintains a large number of files of pointers for countries, periods, and subjects for which there is not yet a member site. A diverse and broad site with links to a multitude of topical historical areas. The scope of the listed categories is impressive, but some topics have a longer reach than others. Maintained by Lynn Nelson, Department of History, University of Kansas.
Resource Type: Links Collection

****BUBL: History
www.bubl.ac.uk/

BUBL is a national information service for the higher education community, run by the Centre for Digital Library Research at the University of Strathclyde in the United Kingdom. BUBL offers free access to over 12,000 selected Internet resources. Links are extensive and all sites are reviewed.
Resource Type: Links Collection

****History/Social Studies Web Site for K–12 Teachers
http://k-12historysocialstudies.com//boals.html

A retired high school history teacher has produced a well-organized and super-stocked resource of links to history and education-related sites. The categories are so full of links it can feel overwhelming at times. Check out Research and Critical Thinking for teaching ideas.
Resource Type: Links Collection

****Education World
http://db.education-world.com/

This worthwhile commercial site contains lesson plans, special features, and is divided into 20 subcategories, including: Documents, Famous People, Women, Classical/Ancient History, Preservation, and more. They have reviewed over 700 Web sites and have formulated yearly Best Of lists.
Resource Type: Course Model

****Smithsonian Education
www.smithsonianeducation.org/

The site is divided simply into three main categories: Educators, Families, and Students. The Educators section is keyword-searchable and features lesson plans—many pertaining to history. The Students section features an interactive "Secrets of the Smithsonian" that teaches about the special collections at the Smithsonian.
Resource Type: Course Model

RESOURCES FOR GENERAL HISTORY LESSON PLANS AND ACTIVITIES

*****Mr. Donn's Pages: Free Lesson Plans, Activities, and Resources
http://historymatters.gmu.edu/

Teacher Don Donn of the Corkran (Maryland) Middle School provides complete units on various historical topics with daily lesson plans and resources. Units include Ancient History,

World Geography & Maps, World Cultures/Eastern Hemisphere, World Cultures/Western Hemisphere, World History, U.S. History & U.S. Government, Sociology & Psychology, Social Studies & Literature. The numerous lesson plans and resources available at this popular site have been developed by Mr. Donn and other contributors. Lessons are most appropriate for students in grades 5–8.

Resource Type: Lesson or Activity
Grade Level: MS

*****Center for History and New Media: History Matters

http://historymatters.gmu.edu/

CHNM produces historical works in new media, tests their effectiveness in the classroom, and reflects critically on the success of new media in historical practice. CHNM's resources include a list of "best" Web sites, links to syllabi and lesson plans, essays on history and new media, a link to their excellent "History Matters" Web site for U.S. history and more. Resources are designed to benefit professional historians, high school teachers, and students of history. Go to the Digital Blackboard section for lesson ideas that integrate the Internet.

Resource Type: Lesson or Activity
Grade Level: HS, College

*****Learning Page

http://lcweb2.loc.gov/ammem/ndlpedu/

The Library of Congress is an outstanding site for American history and general studies. The Library of Congress Learning Page provides a teacher's-eye-view of over seven million historical documents, photographs, maps, films, and audio recordings. Lesson plans can be searched by theme, topic, discipline, or era. You will find activities, tools, ideas, and features that prove useful for teaching American history.

Resource Type: Lesson or Activity
Grade Level: MS, HS, College

*****PBS Teacher Source

www.pbs.org/teachersource/

PBS is a great source for information on a myriad of historical events and personalities. PBS's assorted and diverse Web exhibits supplement specific individual television series and generally include a summary of each episode, interviews (often with sound bites), a timeline, a glossary, photos, and links to relevant sites. Go to the PBS Teacher Source for lessons and activities—arranged by topic and grade level—and sign up for their newsletter. Categories include American History, World History, History on Television, and Biographies. Some lesson plans require viewing PBS video, but many do not.

Resource Type: Lesson or Activity
Grade Level: LS, MS, HS

*****SCORE—Schools of California Online Resources for Educators

http://score.rims.k12.ca.us/

The Schools of California Online Resources for Educators (SCORE) project is a terrific

resource for teachers and students alike. You'll find lesson plans all rated and arranged by grade level and content area.
Resource Type: Lesson or Activity
Grade Level: LS, MS, HS

*****BBC: History
www.bbc.co.uk/history/

"BBC: History" offers a multitude of sites, activities, games and other resources. Major categories include: Ancient History, Archaeology, Church and State, Science and Discovery, Society and Conflict, War and Culture, and Family History. There are also sections entitled Multimedia Room, Historic Figures, Timelines, Programmes, Reading Room, Talk History, For Kids, and History Trails. The BBC Multimedia zone offers games, animations, virtual tours, and galleries. Many games deal with various aspects of British history.
Resource Type: Lesson or Activity
Grade Level: LS, MS, HS

*****Digital History
www.digitalhistory.uh.edu/

A great site from Steven Mintz that includes: A U.S. history e-textbook; over 400 annotated documents and primary sources on slavery, Mexican American and Native American history, and U.S. political, social, and legal history; short essays on the history of film, ethnicity, private life, and technology; multimedia exhibitions; and reference resources that include a searchable database of 1,500 annotated links, classroom handouts, chronologies, glossaries, an audio archive including speeches and booktalks by historians, and a visual archive with hundreds of historical maps and images. The site's Ask the HyperHistorian feature allows users to pose questions to professional historians.
Resource Type: Lesson or Activity
Grade Level: HS, College

****EDSITEment
http://edsitement.neh.gov/

EDSITEment is a partnership of the National Endowment for the Humanities, the Council of the Great City Schools, MarcoPolo Foundation, and the National Trust for the Humanities. All Web sites linked to EDSITEment have been reviewed for content, design, and educational impact in the classroom. This impressive site features reviewed links to top sites, professionally developed lesson plans, classroom activities, materials to help with daily classroom planning, and search engines. You can search lesson plans by subcategory and grade level; middle school lessons are the most numerous.
Resource Type: Lesson or Activity
Grade Level: MS, HS

****History/Social Studies Web Site for K–12 Teachers
http://k-12historysocialstudies.com/boals.html

A retired high school history teacher has produced a well-organized and super-stocked resource of links to history and education-related sites. Check out K–12 resources for a set of links to roughly 155 sites for lesson plans and links.

Resource Type: Lesson or Activity

Grade Level: LS, MS, HS, College

The Center for Teaching History with Technology
http://thwt.org/

The Center for Teaching History with Technology provides a multitude of free online resources—articles, tips, strategies, and lesson plans—to help K–12 history and social studies teachers incorporate technology effectively into their courses. Visit the center and discover, among other things, the best history activities and games and great examples of inquiry-based World History and United States History lesson plans. Subscribe to the free *Teaching History with Technology* newsletter and receive resources, lesson plans, and tech tips every month. (This site is unrated, since I am its Webmaster.)

Resource Type: Lesson or Activity

Grade Level: MS, HS, College

Figure 12.11: The Center for Teaching History with Technology

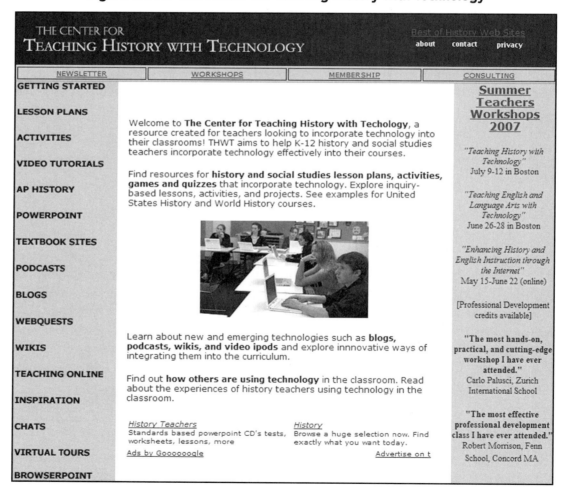

****Blue Web'n for History and Social Studies
www.kn.pacbell.com/wired/bluewebn/contentarea.cfm?cid=8

A Pacific Bell production, the "Blue Web'n" pages are an invaluable source of up-to-date reviews of education-oriented Web sites. New sites are described, rated, and classified by grade level and content. Biweekly e-mail updates are free and are a great source of up-to-date information.
Resource Type: Lesson or Activity
Grade Level: LS, MS, HS

****Social Studies School Service Links
www.socialstudies.com/c/@Zf3U2FJP0utrs/Pages/online.html

Contains lesson plans and teaching strategies, online activities, and tips on teaching current events. Lists are comprehensive and arranged alphabetically. Also sells social studies books, e-books, videos, DVDs, CD-ROMs, and more.
Resource Type: Lesson or Activity
Grade Level: LS, MS, HS

****Lesson Plans and Resources for Social Studies Teachers
www.csun.edu/~hcedu013/

Dr. Marty Levine, Professor Emeritus of Secondary Education, California State University, Northridge (CSUN), has gathered lesson plans and resources from the Internet that social studies teachers should find very useful. Among the categories are Lesson Plans and Teaching Strategies, Online Activities, and Teaching Current Events. The site is detailed and well organized, but not actively maintained and thus there are several broken links.
Resource Type: Lesson or Activity
Grade Level: LS, MS, HS

****Education with Student News
www.cnn.com/EDUCATION/

This CNN "Education" site provides teachers with instructional materials for integrating current events across the curriculum. A student section keeps students in grades 6–12 aware of the latest news of interest to them. Lesson plans, background material, profiles, links to useful Internet sites, and forums for interaction with other teachers are all included.
Resource Type: Lesson or Activity
Grade Level: MS, HS

****The WebQuest Page
http://webquest.sdsu.edu/webquest.html

A WebQuest is a form of project-based and problem-based learning in which the resources are located on the Web. These inquiry-oriented educational sites are produced by educators for use by students and are modeled on a template developed by Professor Bernie Dodge. Some WebQuests are very impressive; others are less so. I would suggest consulting the Portal, which contains an updated matrix of pre-selected Web Quests, and then looking for WebQuests in the "top" category. WebQuest links should be checked to make sure they are active.
Resource Type: Lesson or Activity
Grade Level: LS, MS, HS

****Education World: History Center
www.education-world.com/history/

"Education World" provides practical resources for history educators. You'll find lesson plans, articles about what other teachers are doing, professional development resources and more. "Education World" offers timelines, activities, work sheets, games, homework help, clip art, images, and articles.
Resource Type: Lesson or Activity
Grade Level: LS, MS, HS

****The New York Times Learning Network
www.nytimes.com/learning/

This informative site offers detailed lesson plans and quizzes built around *New York Times* articles. Check out the Lesson Plan Archive and search by keyword, subject, or grade level. Social studies lesson plans are objective and standard-based and are well supported by charts, graphs, and images.
Resource Type: Lesson or Activity
Grade Level: MS, HS

****Discoveryschool.com: Lesson Plan Library
http://school.discovery.com/lessonplans/ushis.html

"Discoveryschool.com: Lesson Plan Library" offers history and government lesson plans for Ancient History, U.S History, and World History. Lesson plans are organized as per Grades K–5, Grades 6–8, Grades 9–12 and provide: Objectives, Materials, Procedures, Adaptations, Discussion Questions, Evaluation, Extensions, Suggested Readings, Links, Vocabulary, Academic Standards, and Credit.
Resource Type: Lesson or Activity
Grade Level: LS, MS, HS

****School History
www.schoolhistory.co.uk/

"School History" is a bountiful online history site that offers huge numbers of freely download-loadable resources, interactive and entertaining history games and quizzes, and interactive online lessons together with comprehensive links to online resources.
Resource Type: Lesson or Activity
Grade Level: LS, MS, HS

****History Lesson Plans and Resources
www.cloudnet.com/~edrbsass/edhist.htm

Edmund J. Sass, Ed.D., developed this page primarily for use by education students at the College of Saint Benedict/St.John's University. He offers an extensive list of history lesson plans as well as lesson plans related to terrorism, tolerance, or the events of September 11.
Resource Type: Lesson or Activity
Grade Level: MS, HS

****HistoryTeacher.net
www.historyteacher.net/

An impressive, award-winning site from a high school teacher at the Horace Greeley High School in Chappaqua, New York. Features many research links and curriculum resources for Global Studies, U.S. AP History, U.S. European History, and American history and government. Also has quizzes, news links, and more.
Resource Type: Lesson or Activity
Grade Level: HS

****The History News Network
www.hnn.us/

"The History News Network" was created in June 2001 and features articles by historians on both the left and the right who provide historical perspective on current events. HNN exists to provide historians and other experts a national forum in which to educate Americans about important and timely issues, and it is the only Web site on the Internet wholly devoted to this task. HNN is a nonprofit publication run by George Mason University, is updated daily, and averages roughly 1.5 million hits a month. Those of you who have visited the U.S. History landing page in *Best of History Web Sites* may have noticed that I link to HNN articles in the U.S. History in the Classroom section.
Resource Type: Lesson or Activity
Grade Level: HS, College

****ThinkQuest Library
www.thinkquest.org/library/index.html

"ThinkQuest Library" is a free educational resource featuring 5,500+ Web sites created by students around the world as part of a competition. Quality of individual sites varies, but some are outstanding and serve as an example to students of what they can accomplish. Go to Libraries to visit sites on Geography and Cultures from students from various countries. Unfortunately some excellent older sites have been taken down.
Resource Type: Lesson or Activity
Grade Level: LS, MS, HS

****History Channel
www.history.com/

A companion to the television channel, this commercial site contains a myriad of features and highlights for educators and students alike. Key offerings include: study guides and activities, ideas from teachers, special exhibits, speech archives, discussions, and This Day in History. Also, try the U.K. site at www.thehistorychannel.co.uk and student site at www.history studystop.co.uk.
Resource Type: Lesson or Activity
Grade Level: MS, HS, College

****Awesome Stories
www.awesomestories.com/index.php

"Awesome Stories" is a free, noncommercial educational Web site for educators (as the basis for lesson plans) and students. Stories link to organized primary and secondary source materials

found principally at U.S. and other worldwide national archives, museums, libraries, universities, news organizations, and government Web sites. The purpose of the site (including its eight separate, stand-alone channels) is to take visitors on a virtual guided tour of relevant on-line source materials. Be sure to check out Click2History.
Resource Type: Lesson or Activity
Grade Level: LS, MS, HS

****National Council for the Social Studies: Social Studies.org
www.ncss.org/

National Council for the Social Studies offers support for social studies educators. Links are categorized by themes of the Curriculum Standards for Social Studies. Teachers share classroom experiences at the site and on the NCSS listserv. The National Council for the Social Studies Data Bank features an annotated list of teaching resources categorized by the ten themes of the Curriculum Standards for Social Studies. Many of these resources involve technology integration, especially Internet use.
Resource Type: Lesson or Activity
Grade Level: LS, MS, HS

****Voice of the Shuttle: History Page
http://vos.ucsb.edu/

Part of an extensive guide to humanities resources that provides numerous links to feature sites, teaching resources, electronic journals, course syllabi, and more. Aimed at university educators.
Resource Type: Lesson or Activity
Grade Level: College

****The Gateway
www.thegateway.org/

Contains thousands of educational resources, including over 3,000 history lesson plans and 2,000-plus history activities. Annotated and organized by grade level.
Resource Type: Lesson or Activity
Grade Level: LS, MS, HS

****US News & World Report
http://usnewsclassroom.com/

Lesson plans are classified according to topic: American Government, Economics, Journalism, Political Science, Sociology, U.S. History, World History.
Resource Type: Lesson or Activity
Grade Level: MS, HS

****C-SPAN in the Classroom
www.c-spanclassroom.org/

Access C-SPAN's complete program archives. "C-SPAN in the Classroom" is a free membership service that offers information and resources to assist educators in their use of primary source, public affairs video from C-SPAN television. You do not have to be a member to use

C-SPAN online resources in your classroom, but membership includes access to teaching ideas, activities and classroom tools.
Resource Type: Lesson or Activity
Grade Level: MS, HS

****Smithsonian Education: Lesson Plans
www.smithsonianeducation.org/educators/lesson_plans/history_culture.html

There are only a dozen or so history lesson plans at the Smithsonian site, but they are engaging, quality teaching resources worth exploring.
Resource Type: Lesson or Activity
Grade Level: MS, HS

****The Educator's Reference Desk: Lesson Plans
www.eduref.org/Virtual/Lessons/

Formerly "AskEric," "The Educator's Reference Desk" is a project of the Information Institute of Syracuse. The Lesson Plan section contains unique social studies and history lesson plans written and submitted by teachers for various grade levels. There are only 15 history lesson plans but dozens of social studies lesson plans.
Resource Type: Lesson or Activity
Grade Level: MS, HS

****The Lesson Plans Page
www.lessonplanspage.com/index.html

"The Lesson Plans Page" is a collection of over 2,500 lesson plans, primarily at the elementary level, that were developed by Kyle Yamnitz, students, and faculty at the University of Missouri.
Resource Type: Lesson or Activity
Grade Level: LS, MS

****Teachers' Virtual School
www.spartacus.schoolnet.co.uk/TVS.htm

The Spartacus "Teachers' Virtual School" History Department provides lessons under Key Stage (2,3,4) and Topic. Teachers are invited to send in details of any online history lessons they have produced for their students.
Resource Type: Lesson or Activity
Grade Level: MS, HS

****Mr. Neal's Virtual Classroom
www.virtualclassroom.net/main/main.htm

A high school social studies teacher has put together an impressive array of multimedia materials for teaching history and social studies. Included are history, geography, economics, and government links; PowerPoint presentations; Internet assignments; and other helpful materials.
Resource Type: Lesson or Activity
Grade Level: MS, HS

****edClass

www.edclass.com

"EdClass" by SchoolKiT is a library of hundreds of classroom-ready learning modules that make use of technology to enhance learning. There are some excellent sample modules to peruse at the site, but you must register to gain access to all the modules.
Resource Type: Lesson or Activity
Grade Level: MS, HS

****Spartacus: History

www.spartacus.schoolnet.co.uk/

Run by a small educational publishing company, this Web site provides free online materials for major history curriculum subjects. Special emphasis on British history.
Resource Type: Lesson or Activity
Grade Level: MS, HS

****Social Studies Lesson Plans

www.col-ed.org/cur/social.html

Much information on government and politics for K–12 students. Has many "mini" activities that do not necessarily involve the Web.
Resource Type: Lesson or Activity
Grade Level: LS, MS, HS

****Digital History: Links to Games About Historical Topics

www.digitalhistory.uh.edu/games/games.cfm

The terrific "Digital History" site has links to several sites that offer quizzes or games.
Resource Type: Lesson or Activity
Grade Level: MS, HS

****Classroom Lesson Plans: Teaching About 9/11

http://hnn.us/articles/954.html

From "History News Network." In addition to the sites listed by HNN, teachers may want to consult "911digitalarchive.org/stories," which is sponsored by the Center for History & New Media at George Mason University and the American Social History Project/Center for Media & Learning at CUNY. This site features a large digital archive of individuals' stories about 9/11.
Resource Type: Lesson or Activity
Grade Level: HS, College

****Out of Many: A History of the American People—Lesson Plans

www.phschool.com/advanced/lesson_plans/hist_faragher_2000/

Focus Lessons for "Out of Many" highlight important ideas and concepts in each chapter as well as the relevant sections in the program's ancillaries. The Focus Lessons, written by an experienced AP teacher, suggest strategies for assessing how well your students understand the important points in each chapter and also provide test-taking tips that will help your students prepare for and take the AP U.S. History test successfully.
Resource Type: Lesson or Activity
Grade Level: HS

****The American Nation: A History of the United States—Lesson Plans

www.phschool.com/advanced/lesson_plans/hist_garraty_2000/

Focus Lessons for "The American Nation" highlight important ideas and concepts in each chapter as well as the relevant sections in the program's ancillaries. The Focus Lessons, written by an experienced curriculum developer, suggest strategies for assessing how well your students understand the important points in each chapter and also provide test-taking tips that will help your students prepare for and take the AP U.S. History test successfully.

Resource Type: Lesson or Activity

Grade Level: MS, HS

****World Civilizations: The Global Experience—Lesson Plans

www.phschool.com/advanced/lesson_plans/hist_faragher_2000/

Focus Lessons for "World Civilizations" highlight important ideas and concepts in each chapter, as well as the relevant sections in the program's ancillaries. The Focus Lessons, written by an experienced AP teacher, suggest strategies for assessing how well your students understand the important points in each chapter, and also provide test-taking tips that will help your students prepare for and take the AP World History test successfully.

Resource Type: Lesson or Activity

Grade Level: HS

***Learn History

www.phschool.com/advanced/lesson_plans/hist_stearns_2001/

"Learn History" is produced by a history teacher at a London high school and features notes, quizzes, exercises and PowerPoint lessons.

Resource Type: Lesson or Activity

Grade Level: MS, HS

***Primary Source Materials and Document-Based Questions

www.kn.pacbell.com/wired/fil/pages/listdocumentpa.html

An Internet hotlist on Document-Based Questions. Many useful links here.

Resource Type: Lesson or Activity

Grade Level: HS

***GCSE History Pages

www.historygcse.org/

Main features of this site include interactive tests and quizzes, revision tips, practice GCSE exam papers with mark-schemes for self-assessment, revision notes, and structured lessons.

Resource Type: Lesson or Activity

Grade Level: HS

***Practice Quizzes and Crossword Puzzles for U.S. History

www.polytechnic.org/faculty/gfeldmeth/USHistory.html

The quizzes and puzzles are part of a general site called American Resources. They are arranged chronologically and thematically; the quiz questions are good, but there are only five per section.

Resource Type: Lesson or Activity

Grade Level: HS

Index

About the Author

Tom Daccord is Academic Technology Advocate for the Humanities (English, History and Classics) at the Noble and Greenough School, and a veteran history teacher. Mr. Daccord is the creator and Webmaster of "Best of History Web Sites," an award-winning portal that receives upwards of 125,000 visitors per month and over two million page views per year. He is also president of the Center for Teaching History with Technology, an organization with over 2,000 subscribers, whose mission is to help K–12 history and social studies teachers incorporate technology effectively into their courses. Mr. Daccord also is the creator and Webmaster of "Teaching English & Language Arts with Technology," a site designed to help English and Language Arts teachers effectively use the latest technology available in their courses. A "laptop teacher" who has instructed in a wireless laptop environment for the last six years, Mr. Daccord has been featured in the *Boston Globe* ("Making Tech Connect," December 29, 2003) for his contributions to teaching with technology. He has presented on educational technology topics at the National Council for the Social Studies Annual Conference, the National Association of Independent Schools Annual Conference, the Laptop Institute, November Learning's Boston Leadership Conference, the Connecticut Association of Independent Schools Technology Conference, and holds various on-site and online educational technology workshops.